No Case To Answer

A retired English detective's essays and
articles on the JFK Assassination: 1993-2005

Ian Griggs

JFK LANCER PRODUCTIONS & PUBLICATIONS

SOUTHLAKE, TEXAS

Published by JFK Lancer Productions & Publications
Southlake, Texas

JFK Lancer books may be purchased for educational use. For information, contact JFK Lancer, 100 Stonewood Court, Southlake, TX 76092.

First Edition
Cover Design by Ken Jacobs
Book Design by Debra Conway

ISBN 0-9774657-0-5

Manufactured in the United States of America

I dedicate this work to three remarkable people, without
whom it could never have reached this stage —
Malcolm Blunt (UK), Russ Shearer, and Betty Windsor (USA),
researchers extraordinaire.

---

*"Like all Holmes's reasoning the thing seemed like simplicity
itself when it was once explained."*

Sir Arthur Conan-Doyle – *The Stockbroker's Clerk*
(published 1893)

Contents

COMMENTS ON NO CASE TO ANSWER

Larry Hancock, author of *Someone Would Have Talked*
August 2005

No Case To Answer is a major advance in dealing with two of the chief "monsters" of the Kennedy assassination. First, its essays address a host of popular research "myths" which continue to perpetuate themselves and waste the time and energy of both novice and experienced readers. Ian Griggs' research enumerates a variety of long-standing myths in regard to events, evidence and people, resolving numerous issues in a clear and concise manner.

That work alone is of great value to the research community. Beyond that, however, Ian's professional experience surfaces and he exposes many of the key issues of evidence as well as methods which should have been addressed decades ago as part of a real criminal investigation of the assassination. In doing so, he highlights key questions which a true criminal enquiry would have had to consider - and which a legal defense for Lee Oswald would certainly have forced as part of any true criminal proceedings.

As a former law enforcement professional, Ian Griggs' work cuts through the morass of issues to highlight points which are worth research – as distinguished from those which have led researchers round in circles for far too long.

Professor Emeritus George Michael Evica, author of *And We Are All Mortal*
September 2005

It is Ian Griggs, the man: his intelligence, experience, humanity and humor; Ian Griggs, his person, his presence, but especially his voice that we hear in this irreplaceable collection of presentations and essays on the death of President John F. Kennedy.

The JFK assassination has attracted a select number of experienced law officers, but none is more important to the truth of the presidential murder than Ian Griggs. His beat work, operational detective experience and fine investigative sense are all demonstrated in his examination of the Oswald line-ups, the non-existent paper sack and his assembling of a duplicate of the alleged assassination weapon, eliminating any possibility that the Mannlicher-Carcano rifle was involved in the JFK assassination.
It is in his extensive witness research and interviews, however, that Ian Griggs demonstrates his relevance, this humaneness and his highly-appreciated wit. Enjoy and learn.

James H. Fetzer, Ph.D., editor, *Assassination Science, Murder In Dealey Plaza,* and *The Great Zapruder Film Hoax*
August 2005

Ian Griggs' studies of the Mannlicher-Carcano and the paper bag make it all too apparent that Oswald was framed using manufactured evidence. It took an English detective to expose the complicity of Dallas police in the death of JFK!

"The authorities are excellent at amassing facts, though they do not always use them to advantage."
Sir Arthur Conan-Doyle – *The Naval Treaty* (published 1893)

THE AUTHOR

Ian Leonard Griggs was born at Hornchurch, Essex on 18th August 1939 – just 16 days prior to the start of World War II. His earliest memories are of Spitfires and Heinkels chasing one another all over the sky. Since RAF Hornchurch, one of Britain's major fighter aerodromes, was less than a quarter of a mile from the Griggs home, such sights were by no means unusual, especially throughout the Battle of Britain.

On 19th September 1944, Herr Hitler decided that it was time for little Ian to be moved, and a V1 flying bomb (*aka* doodlebug or buzz-bomb) fell in an adjacent street, causing four fatalities and badly damaging several houses, including the Griggs residence. As a result of this, Ian and his mother were evacuated to North Wales, where Ian began his education at the local junior school. This was not an outstanding success as the first thing the school did was try to teach the five-year-old Ian to speak Welsh. He was delighted when he and his mother were allowed to return to their home in Hornchurch at the end of the war.

Following a grammar school education, which was largely wasted apart from being in the same 'A-Level' Geology class as jazz/blues/rock musical genius Graham Bond, Ian did two years compulsory military service in the British Army, serving mainly in Kenya and Kuwait.

Then, following a series of dead-end jobs ranging from insurance to surveying to selling roof tiles and then cash registers, he began what was to become a very fulfilling 23-year police career (uniform and CID), retiring in May 1994.

Ian's interest in the assassination of John Fitzgerald Kennedy began on 22nd November 1963 and he has been studying it seriously for the past 35 years. He has become a frequent visitor to Dallas where he has built up a wide range of friends and contacts. He has written and published many articles on the subject, 27 of which are featured in the book before you. He has also presented research papers and acted as a panel moderator at ASK, COPA, Fourth Decade and JFK Lancer conferences in Dallas, Fredonia (New York) and Washington, D.C. He is a founder member of the British research group Dealey Plaza UK, was the group's first Secretary, from 1995 to 2005 and edited its research journal, *The Dealey Plaza Echo*, from 1996 to 2005. Ian is the proud recipient of a JFK Lancer Editor's Award (1995) and in 1998 he received a JFK Lancer New Frontier Award.

Completion of *No Case To Answer* will, he hopes, allow him more time to complete and publish his comprehensive (and as yet untitled) *magnum opus* on the Dallas Police Department of November 1963. Publication target: November 2006.

Interests outside the JFK case include Marilyn Monroe, Janis Joplin, Jack The Ripper, Sherlock Holmes, Tottenham Hotspur Football Club, the Icelandic musician Bjork Gudmundsdottir, the German Occupation of the British Channel Islands (1940/45) and maintaining his extensive collection of police badges and model police cars.

"I confess that I cannot recall any case within my experience which looked at the first glance so simple, and yet which presented such difficulties."

Sir Arthur Conan-Doyle - *The Man with the Twisted Lip*
(published 1889)

ACKNOWLEDGEMENTS

In a work such as this—basically a series of essays and articles rather than a book in the normal sense—it is not easy to list all those people who have assisted me. Some have been close to my research efforts for many years whilst others may have helped with just one aspect, almost unaware of how important their contribution has been.

Obviously foremost, I would mention the name that is top of most researchers' similar lists—that of the late Mary McHughes Ferrell. No matter how unusual or involved my query, Mary always came up with an answer. Almost inevitably, she added additional relevant information. I knew Mary for many years and would always look forward to meeting and greeting her each November at the Dallas conferences.

I feel very privileged to recognize American author/researchers Walt Brown, Milicent Cranor, George Michael Evica, Jim Fetzer, Robert Groden, Larry Hancock, the late Larry Ray Harris, the late Larry Howard, Connie Kritzberg, Harrison Edward Livingstone, Jim Marrs, Dale Myers, John Newman, Vince Palamara, Don Roberdeau, Craig Roberts, Jerry Rose, Gary Shaw, Larry Sneed, Josiah Thompson, Hal Verb, Nancy Weiford and Jack White as friends as well as sources of information and inspiration. To each and every one of these people I offer my sincere thanks.

Other Americans who have played a part in supporting and contributing to my research are from a variety of backgrounds. From the Dallas Police Department, come several retired Officers: motorcycle jockey Bobby Hargis, Sergeant Jim Wallace (Crimes Against Persons Bureau), Homicide Detective Jim Leavelle, Lieutenant Paul Wilkins and Patrolman Robert Hoffman. Sergeant Jeff Westbrook (Columbia, Iowa, PD) supplied much new information on his great uncle, Captain W.R. Westbrook (DPD), and Sergeant Al Carrier (Waterloo, Iowa, PD) gave me valuable technical information. Forensic scientist and bloodstain pattern analyst Sherry Gutierrez, an 'expert' in the true sense of the word, gave great support.

Eyewitnesses the late Shari Angel, the late Chuck Brehm, the late Jean Hill, Ed Hoffman, Bill and Gayle Newman, Beverly Oliver, Aubrey Rike, Malcolm Summers, James Tague, Johnny Calvin Brewer and several others were always happy to help and they often opened up new lines of enquiry. On many occasions, the answer to a question also produced three more questions!

Many American citizens, some of whom have become good friends through our common interest in this tragedy, were always there with local and/ or specialist knowledge. I can never forget the contributions made by Joe Backes, Richard Bartholomew, Roy Bierma, the late Mike Blackwell, Bill Cheslock, Mark Colgan, Jerry Dealey, Bill Drenas, Brian Edwards, Barb Junkkarinen, John Kelin, William Law, Mark Rowe, Steve Thomas, the remarkable Betty Windsor, Andy Winiarczyk and John R. Woods, II.

On my own side of the Big Pond, I must acknowledge indebtedness to Melanie Swift, who has brought her near photographic memory for facts to my aid on many occasions over the past decade or more. You will find her mentioned in several of the pieces herein and her contribution has been far greater than she can imagine.

Several other leading UK researchers have also played leading parts – often without realizing how important they were. I refer here to folks like Francesca Akhtar, Tony Basing, Les Bolland, Justin Bowley, Mark Bridger, Barry Bullock, Paul Byrne, Barbara Carlyon, Rick Caster, Mike Dworetsky, John Gill, Barbara Ireland, Barry Keane, Russell Kent, Chris Mills, Bob Shaw, Matthew Smith and David Watford. They always seemed to be around, with encouragement and support when I needed it.

Elsewhere on the planet, I received immense help about a certain New Zealand newspaper from Mike Lee. I met this pleasant, outgoing Kiwi by chance in Dallas a few years ago. When I urgently needed local information, I turned to Mike and a series of emails between us produced much that was vital to my article. Ray Brown, born in Luton (UK) but living and working in Kobe, Japan, has proved a good friend over the years and has also contributed to my knowledge of how the assassination affected people in Asia.

Closer to home, I have received great support from my son Steve. Although having no more than a passing interest in the assassination, he has always offered what I call technical guidance – particularly when my PC was giving me trouble or I needed help to set up a page or a program.

Almost finally, I have been given great support and attention from my friends Vic and Jen Copsey, the proprietors of Waltham Abbey Stationers. Thanks to these people, I have never run out of paper or other stationery – and they must have made literally thousands of photocopies in connection with my assassination research.

On the 'nuts-and-bolts' side of a book like this, I have no hesitation in offering my deep admiration and heartfelt gratitude to five very special people: Firstly, Debra Conway, who *is* JFK Lancer, a lady I have known since she came into this thing and who has had the faith to publish my work in this form. Next, my two peer reviewers, George Michael Evica and Larry Hancock. Then my English colleague, journalist Chris Robertson who did his best to knock my work into shape. Finally, my long-term friend and fellow researcher, Russell

Kent, who took on the arduous job of indexing the entire text.

As always, I have left two of my most important aides to last. Over the years, Russ Shearer (from Absecon, New Jersey) and Malcolm Blunt (from Cheltenham, Gloucestershire) have supplied me with thousands of documents, photographs, files and reports, most of which they have obtained during their frequent visits to Archives II at Highland Park. Documents of this type are the food and drink upon which researchers rely— and I am no different. These two men, who each exude the qualities of loyalty and enthusiasm which I so admire, have unknowingly perked me up when research seemed to be grinding to a halt or I was frustrated when a promising lead fizzled out to nothing.

My sincere thanks to you all,

Ian Griggs
2005

"It seems to me to have only one drawback, Hokins, and that is that it is intrinsically impossible."

Sir Arthur Conan-Doyle - *Black Peter*
(published 1904)

Holmes disagrees with the plodding Inspector Hopkins'theory that the physically weak John Hopley Neligan could have killed the much larger and heavier Captain Peter Carey by pinning him to the wall with a harpoon. I feel that Holmes'stated opinion here could be applied equally to Lee Harvey Oswald's alleged feat of marksmanship from the sixth floor window!-LIG

AUTHOR'S NOTE

As an ex-English policeman writing about an American criminal offence, I frequently encountered difficulties in resolving the language problems that exist between English-English and American-English. This has occasionally necessitated brief explanatory comments within the text, especially when quoting *verbatim* testimony. I would ask the reader to bear with me when this occurs. It is, of course, a two-way situation and I have also tried to offer the American equivalent of English words and phrases as they occur.

Source notes, where relevant, follow each individual article or essay. Illustrations are confined to three sections following chapters 9, 18, and 26.

I must apologise for a small amount of repetition between some articles. Apart from making additions and amendments in the light of later information, I have endeavoured to stick as closely as possible to the original printed version of each piece.

SEEK - FIND - SHARE.

The author in a reflective mood at the Dealey Plaza UK inaugural weekend seminar at Canterbury, Kent, March 2003 (Photograph by Mike Dworetsky)

PREFACE

HOW IT CAME ABOUT

My initial resolve to present the results of my research into the Kennedy Assassination in this form was born around 1999. At that time, I realized that some of my work had been published in the United States, some had been published in the United Kingdom, some had been published in both countries and some had been published in neither. In addition, of course, some had found its way on to a miscellany of internet websites.

I was very flattered when various fellow researchers requested copies of specific articles I had written, and I did my utmost to assist. This was usually a straightforward task, but occasionally it proved difficult. If the article in question had been published on one side of the Big Pond and the request came from the other, there were inevitable problems.

My particular areas of interest, experience and specialist knowledge in the case are mainly concerned with the Dallas Police Department, the weird and wonderful characters who worked at the Carousel Club, the so-called assassination rifle, the eyewitnesses, media coverage of the event and its aftermath, and the British connections.

I have neither the experience nor the specialist knowledge to examine and discuss the photographic or the medical evidence in any depth and am happy to leave those areas to other people.

The solution was a simple one—publish everything in one self-contained volume and make it available to all. Hence the book before you.

HOW WAS THE ORDER OF THE 27 ARTICLES DECIDED?

Several of the pieces here have undergone expansion, amendment and other changes over the years, but a problem arose when it came to deciding the order in which these 27 articles should be presented here. I must express gratitude to my friend Dr James H. Fetzer, who took my basic manuscript and completely restructured it. This order is very similar to a framework put forward by another good friend, Russell Kent. Russell is also responsible for the monumental task of compiling the name and subject indices for me.

WHAT IS THE SIGNIFICANCE OF THE TITLE?

"No case to answer" is a loosely legal expression used in England but perhaps not in the United States. It basically means that despite thorough investigation, insufficient evidence has been obtained to justify taking the case before a court of law. It has been suggested to me by some American researchers that perhaps the American equivalent would be "No charge to file."

I believe that even after 42 years of argument, counter-argument and allegedly 'new' evidence, just such a situation continues to exist in the Kennedy assassination concerning Lee Harvey Oswald.

WHERE NOW?

I continue to conduct research into my own specialist areas, and I find that new information is still emerging, often from the most unexpected sources. Research, as somebody once observed, is never complete. We can but work hard to keep abreast of it and hope that such endeavours will eventually provide the answers to the questions still confronting us.

"Where a crime is coolly premeditated,
then the means of covering it are coolly premedicated also."

Sir Arthur Conan-Doyle - *The Problem of Thor Bridge*
(published 1922)

No Case To Answer

Prologue:

1. The structure and organisation of the
City of Dallas Police Department in November 1963

Introduction

As a retired police officer in the UK (uniform and CID, 1971-1994) it is only natural that one of my specialist areas of research into the JFK assassination should centre upon the Dallas Police Department. I have studied the DPD for several years, concentrating particularly on that brief period from 22nd to 24th November 1963. Inevitably, I have made occasional comparisons between the DPD of 1963 and its modern counterpart. Similarly, I have sometimes compared the differences in general policing methods, particularly in the investigative field, as carried out on both sides of the Atlantic.

Through my research activities, including many visits to the USA, I have come to know US police officers based in several cities, of different ranks, with many specialist responsibilities and of both sexes.

These contacts, particularly those in Dallas itself, have proved of immense value. I firmly believe that the police service worldwide represents a form of 'club' like Freemasons or Rotarians. Every individual officer can quickly locate a fellow member, no matter where in the world he may find himself.

In this chapter, I have leant heavily on the following:

- Extracts from the Warren Commission 26 Volumes, including the testimony of many DPD officers.
- Documents traced and located in the US National Archives by fellow researchers.
- Documentation found during my visits to DPD Headquarters.
- Carlton Stowers' 1983 book *Partners in Blue: The History of the Dallas Police Department.*
- Personal meetings and correspondence with serving and retired DPD officers.
- Correspondence with fellow researchers and current and retired police officers *via* the internet.

As well as explaining the way each Division of the Dallas Police Department was broken down into its component parts, I have striven to identify senior supervisory officers. I have also included brief notes on some of the better known individuals.

I hope that this information will become a permanent and valuable resource for future researchers seeking basic information on the organizational structure of the City of Dallas Police Department at the time of the Kennedy assassination.

THE NUMERICAL STRENGTH OF THE DEPARTMENT

DPD Inspector of Police James Herbert Sawyer was the subject of a brief WFAA-TV street interview in the shadow of the Texas School Book Depository on the afternoon on Friday 22nd November 1963. He was asked how many police officers there were in Dallas. He replied: "Approximately thirteen hundred." His estimate was very close. In November 1963, the total number of DPD employees was 1,286, comprising 1,066 sworn officers (not including the Police Reserve) plus 220 civilians (known as non-sworn employees). On its establishment in 1881, the DPD had just one Chief of Police and 11 Officers. Today, in 2005, it can boast 3,000 sworn officers and over 550 non-sworn employees.

The first name on any list of DPD personnel in November 1963 was that of Jesse Edward Curry, Chief of Police. He had assumed overall control of the Department on 20th January 1960 and remained at its head until his retirement in March 1966. Perhaps ironically, the last name on the November 1963 personnel list was that of somebody who may or may not have played some part in the Kennedy assassination. He was virtually unknown until 1990 when his son came forward to claim that his late father had shot JFK. I refer, of course, to Roscoe Anthony White. In November 1963, Roscoe White was one of three members of recruit Class No. 79 who were described as 'awaiting school'.

Of the 1,066 police officers, only five were female. None had been promoted from the lowly rank of Policewoman and all five were employed in the Juvenile Bureau. This was a plain-clothes appointment so perhaps it was to save the additional expense of a new clothing contract for female uniforms. This is a far cry from today's DPD where one of my headquarters contacts is a charming lady who holds the position of Deputy Chief in the Crimes Against Persons Bureau. Much of this changed attitude towards female officers emanated from the progressive policies of Frank Dyson (DPD Chief of Police, 1969-1979) who 'inherited' eleven Policewomen when he assumed his post. He had the foresight to realize that they were capable of far more than just dealing with juveniles. He not only assigned them to other tasks but also brought about a steady increase in their numbers. Furthermore, he allowed them on to the promotion ladder for the first time.

In November 1963, the civilian employees, 118 male and 102 female, filled a very wide variety of posts. They included clerks, typists, stenographers, telephone clerks, jailers, porters, cooks, auto pound drivers, etc.

In addition to the 1,066 regular police officers, there was a Police Reserve which appears to have fulfilled much the same role as the Special Constabulary in the UK. It consisted of over 300 unpaid volunteer officers and operated under the command of a full-time regular Captain of Police. For administrative purposes it was deemed part of the Training & Research Section. The Police Reserve is not included in my figures for the DPD numerical strength above.

THE STRUCTURE OF THE DEPARTMENT

HEADQUARTERS AND ADMINISTRATION

Chief of Police Curry maintained a staff of 15 police officers (including himself) as Headquarters personnel based at City Hall. They were supported by eight highly qualified female civilians who were responsible for a wide range of clerical duties.

Curry's second-in-command was Assistant Chief of Police Charles Batchelor, the man who would succeed him as Chief (1966-1969). There were then five Deputy Chiefs of Police, one in command of each of the Criminal Investigation, Patrol, Traffic and Service Divisions, plus one whose responsibilities were concerned with Civil Defence and Disaster Control. Chief Curry's Administrative Assistant and Press Relations Officer was Captain Glen D. King, another member of his staff who became Chief of Police in 1979.

SPECIAL SERVICE BUREAU

This was the first of the specialized departments. It operated under the command of Captain W. P. ('Pat') Gannaway who was supported by six Lieutenants, 34 regular Detectives, 14 Patrolmen who were temporarily assigned to the Bureau and four female civilians (one stenographer and three clerk-typists). The 14 'temporarily-assigned' men were what we in the UK would call Aides to CID or TDCs (Temporary Detective Constables). More of them shortly.

Captain Gannaway (at that time known as 'Mr Narcotics') had been in charge of the notorious 1957 undercover operation and raid that culminated in stripper Candy Barr being arrested for possession of half an ounce of marijuana. For this offence, she was sentenced to 15 years imprisonment, actually serving less than three years before being paroled.

Initially, I had some difficulty in working out what the Special Service Bureau actually did. I established that 18 officers, including Captain Gannaway and one of the female civilians, were mentioned in the Warren Commission's 26 Volumes. Indeed, eight of them testified before the Commission and three of them had their names as titles of Commission Exhibits. Careful study of the appropriate testimony, together with other DPD documents in my possession, finally enabled me to work out the purpose and responsibilities of the Special Service Bureau.

It was basically a covert surveillance and intelligence-gathering unit which, as well as the Criminal Intelligence Squad (CIS), included the Vice Squad and the Narcotics Squad, etc. Its regular officers were plain-clothes detectives. The temporarily-assigned Patrolmen (who also operated in plain clothes) were there for one of two reasons. Some were genuinely 'on trial' or undergoing training prior to being appointed full-time detectives. Others had been drafted in from the uniform branch to undertake basic covert surveillance work in areas where their faces would not be known. A similar system exists in the UK and probably in other countries today.

The Warren Commission testimony of Lieutenant Jack Revill (who became Assistant Chief in 1982) is very revealing in describing the duties and responsibilities of the Special Service Bureau. He stated:

"I am currently in charge of the criminal intelligence section." Later he outlined the overall task of the bureau. "Our primary responsibility is to investigate crimes of an organized nature, subversive activities, racial matters, labor racketeering, and to do anything that the chief might desire. We work for the chief of police. I report to a captain who is in charge of the bureau—Captain Gannaway."

Lieutenant Revill later indicated that he had been assigned to an investigative panel set up to determine how Jack Ruby had gained access to the City Hall basement where he had shot Oswald. This type of enquiry was obviously also the responsibility of the Special Service Bureau.

For a very revealing account of the functions of the CIS, see Philip H. Melanson's article "Dallas Mosaic" published in *The Third Decade*, vol. 1, no. 3, March 1985, pages 12-15. Among other things, Dr. Melanson mentions that "the spooky little unit was physically removed from the rest of the DPD and was headquartered in a building on the state fairgrounds." (Volume IV HSCA 597). The use of the word 'spooky' may or may not be a deliberate clue to something rather sinister.

THE PATROL DIVISION

The Patrol Division, the first of the four Divisions into which the majority of DPD personnel was divided, was by far the largest in terms of manpower. Deputy Chief of Police N. T. Fisher was its overall commander. In November 1963, it had 526 members of whom all but three were police officers. They ranged in rank from Captain (three in total) to Patrolmen (463). The DPD Canine Corps was also part of the Patrol Division. It consisted of just one Sergeant and two Patrolmen/Dog Handlers and had been formed in 1961 with the purchase of three German Shepherds. From the DPD radio log transcripts, it appears that both dog handlers were on duty on 22nd November, initially without their dogs, but later with them.

Like the Traffic and Service Divisions, the Patrol Division was divided into three Platoons. This represented nothing more than a basic revolving eight-hour shift pattern. The First Platoon worked from midnight to 8.00am, the Second Platoon from 8.00am to 4.00pm and the Third Platoon from 4.00pm to midnight. Obviously, this roster meant that the Second Platoon was on duty during the hours of the presidential visit. In view of the additional manpower necessary to ensure the President's safety, some members of the other Platoons were called upon to assist.

Each Platoon was under the command of a Platoon Commander, these being the three Captains mentioned earlier. They were Captain William B. Frazier (First Platoon), Captain Cecil Earl Talbert (Second Platoon) and Captain James M. ('Red') Souter (Third Platoon). Each Platoon was then divided into a Headquarters Station and three Substations, one each for the North-East Area, North-West Area and South-West Area. This substation system had operated since 1956 and was the brainchild of Chief Curry's predecessor, Carl F. Hansson. I have established the exact geographical locations of only one of these areas, but I know that the NW Substation area included Love Field and the NE Substation was just to the north of White Rock Lake. The SW Substation was also known as the Oak Cliff Substation. It was the oldest of the three, having been established around 1908/1909 (exact date not known). In November 1999 I located and visited the former (1963) premises of the SW Substation at 4020 West Illinois Avenue. It has now relocated a block West and the original premises are occupied by a commercial company.

Several members of the Second Platoon of the Patrol Division have become well known through their actions or otherwise during the period 22nd-24th November 1963. Seven that immediately spring to mind are:

- Patrolman J. D. Tippit, the man who came on duty but never completed his shift.
- Patrolmen Billy Lee Bass and Marvin L. Wise, the officers who initially dealt with the so-called three tramps.
- Patrolman Roy S. Vaughn, who failed to notice Jack Ruby enter the City Hall basement via the Main Street ramp. (I decline to comment here on whether or not Mr Ruby did or did not walk down the ramp.)
- Patrolman Maurice N. ('Nick') McDonald, the officer who sustained the scratched cheek during his struggle to arrest Oswald in the Texas Theatre.
- Patrolmen Joe M. Poe and Leonard E. Jez, the first officers to attend the Tippit murder scene.

The 463 officers holding the rank of Patrolman were very much the 'foot soldiers' of the Dallas Police Department, despite the fact that many of them operated behind the wheel of a police car. For the presidential motorcade of 22nd November, they were assigned both static and patrolling duties on foot, plus driving and observer duties in police cruisers, that wonderful unique American expression for patrolling police cars.

THE TRAFFIC DIVISION

This Division, the next largest in size after the Patrol Division, comprised 176 police officers and just three civilians. It operated under the command of Deputy Chief Ray H. Lundy. He took no active part in the events of either 22nd or 24th November but was on duty in his office on the third floor of City Hall on the 22nd. He had, however, played a leading part in the planning of the motorcade route through Dallas.

The Traffic Division was divided into five distinct components. These were Traffic Control, the Accident Prevention Bureau, a group of seven Assignment Men, ten School Safety Officers and the Solo Motorcycle and Special Enforcement Detail. I shall deal with each of these in turn.

TRAFFIC CONTROL

Traffic Control was under the overall command of Captain R. A. Thompson. His deputy was Lieutenant W. F. Southard.

It was by far the largest of the five elements and like the Patrol Division it was composed of three platoons each working an eight-hour shift. Here, however, the shift hours were structured in such a way that there were more officers on duty during the day than at night. The First Platoon worked from 7.00am to 3.00pm with the Second Platoon overlapping as it worked from

10.00am to 6.00pm. The Third Platoon then overlapped again, working from 3.00pm to 11.00pm. It was obviously felt that fewer cars were needed on the streets of the city between the hours of 11.00pm and 7.00am and that any problems at night could be dealt with by the Patrol Division.

Each Platoon consisted of either one or two Sergeants, between 11 and 15 Patrolmen (on foot), between ten and 19 three-wheel motorcycle officers and one female civilian Police Clerk. The disparity in platoon strength was due to the different times of day during which they operated. The foot Patrolmen were deployed at static posts throughout the downtown area, mainly at street intersections. These officers were known within the DPD as 'cornermen'. (See 7H 578) It was not unknown for a cornerman to carry out static duty at the same intersection permanently over a period of years. At the time of the assassination, for example, Patrolman T.M. Hansen, Jr. had worked the 10.00am to 6.00pm shift, Monday to Friday, at the intersection of Main and Akard Streets for 11 years. Patrolman Hansen gained a certain degree of fame as the officer who chased and arrested the man who bit off the top of one of Jack Ruby's fingers during a fight in 1951.

THE ACCIDENT PREVENTION BUREAU

This element was commanded by Captain Perdue William Lawrence. In the absence of Captain Thompson, he assumed operational command of the entire Traffic Division on the day of the assassination. He also drove the very first vehicle in the motorcade – usually referred to a the Advance Car. He had previously worked with Deputy Chief Lunday on the motorcade assignments.

The basic duties of the Bureau appear to have been more investigative than preventative. It consisted of four shift sections organized in an overlapping rota system which covered the 19-hour period 7.00am to 2.00am. One Lieutenant (A. L. Curtis), four Sergeants (J. M. Young, C. F. Williams, B. F. Rodgers and W. R. Russell) and 32 Patrolmen made up the strength of the unit.

Two members of the Accident Prevention Bureau, each normally employed as accident investigators, were Patrolmen J. C. White and J. W. Foster. These two officers have become well known through being deployed on the triple underpass in Dealey Plaza during the motorcade. Another accident investigator, Patrolman Charles T. Walker, found himself inside the Texas Theatre and very closely involved in Lee Harvey Oswald's arrest and subsequent removal to City Hall. (See 7H 34-43)

SPECIAL ASSIGNMENT MEN

These seven individuals present me with something of a problem, and neither their ranks nor their responsibilities are easy to establish. Perhaps they were some sort of back up or reserve. They worked a variety of eight-hour shifts: two of them were on duty from 6.00am to 2.00pm, one from 7.00am to 3.00pm, two more from 8.00am to 4.00pm, one from 3.00pm to 11.00pm and the final one from 6.00pm to 2.00am.

On the day of the President's visit, several of them (in cars) were deployed at the Trade Mart Motor Pool and at static positions on the motorcade route.

Only one of them, however, receives a mention in the 26 Volumes, E. L. Crenshaw being described by another officer as a Detective. This, however, is only in connection with a semi-clerical task a couple of days after the assassination. (See 12H 214)

SCHOOL SAFETY OFFICERS

Ten individuals fulfilled the duties of School Safety Officers, all working the hours 7.30am to 4.30pm. Perhaps they were the Dallas equivalent of our UK lollipop men! They were under the command of Sergeant W. A. Simpson. On the day of the assassination, all ten were given assignments connected with the motorcade.

THE SOLO MOTORCYCLE AND SPECIAL ENFORCEMENT DETAIL

This unit played a major part in the presidential motorcade and the names of several of its members have become familiar to researchers. Obvious people who spring to mind include the following motorcyclists:

- Patrolman Bobby Hargis, who was splattered with blood and brain tissue as he rode slightly behind and to the left of the presidential limousine.
- Patrolman Marrion Baker, who encountered Oswald inside the book depository.
- Patrolman Hollis B. McLain, who is thought by some researchers to be responsible for the 'open microphone'.
- Patrolman E. D. 'Buddy' Brewer, who was one of the lead motorcyclists through Dealey Plaza and on to Stemmons. He rode back to the TSBD, was on the sixth floor when the rifle and the empty shells were found, claimed to have seen the paperbag and later claimed that his "primary job was traffic control".

The detail was comprised of four Sergeants, ten officers on radar duties (in cars) and 22 solo motorcyclists. These officers were divided into two shifts and together they covered the daily period from 6.00am to midnight. On 22nd November 1963, however, I can trace that only three of the four Sergeants were on duty, together with 15 of the 22 motorcyclists. I can find no available record of the radar car drivers' duties for that day.

You are advised to consult Todd Wayne Vaughan's *Presidential Motorcade Schematic Listing* (self-published in limited edition, 1993) for full details of the motorcyclists, their exact positions in the motorcade and their actions following the shooting. Oddly enough, although 18 motorcyclists rode in the motorcade, only five were asked to testify before the Warren Commission (Baker, Brewer, Hargis, Haygood and Martin).

THE SERVICE DIVISION

This was an administrative rather than an operational Division and perhaps for that reason it had the highest percentage of civilian employees of any of the four Divisions. Its total strength of 284 was made up of 97 police officers and 187 civilians. The Division was based mainly at DPD HQ (City Hall), with a few members out at the three Substations. Overall command of the Division rested with Deputy Chief of Police George L. Lumpkin. Each of its separate elements - bureaux, sections, etc. - had its own head.

Several of these units within the Service Division played important parts in connection with the events of 22nd November and the days immediately following.

THE IDENTIFICATION BUREAU

This small bureau was under the supervision of Captain George M. Doughty and was made up of just one operational section - the Fingerprint Section. It was located on the fourth floor of City Hall.

Headed by Lieutenant Karl P. Knight, the Fingerprint Section was staffed by five full-time Detectives, two Acting Detectives and four male civilian clerks. The Section was concerned with the physical fingerprinting of suspects rather than actual crime scene examination. The photographs and fingerprints of Lee Harvey Oswald were taken by members of this Section about an hour after his arraignment in the early hours of Sunday 23rd November (4H 248).

Apart from Lieutenant Knight, only two members of the Section were named in the 26 Volumes. Detective Edwin (or Edward) E. Carlson seemed to be on very good terms with Jack Ruby. An FBI report stated that "Carlson is of the opinion that he, Carlson, knows more about Ruby than any other officer of the Dallas Police Department." (See CE 1180, 22H 294-295). Acting Detective James M. Craft was responsible for taking the well-known portrait photograph of Patrolman Nick McDonald showing the scratches on his left cheek sustained during Oswald's arrest (4H 277).

THE CRIME SCENE SEARCH SECTION

This important element played a major part in the immediate aftermath of the assassination and its head, Lieutenant John Carl Day, became one of the best-known DPD figures. Lieutenant Day had eight Detectives under him, plus an Auto Theft Detective, (Robert Lee Studebaker) who was under training with the Section but was to play a major part in the search of the sixth floor. Although strictly speaking, not a Crime Scene Search Detective, he (Studebaker) is best dealt with here (see below). Several of the regular Crime Scene Detectives were to become very well known through their involvement in various ways. For example:

- Detective Paul L. Bentley, the man with the big cigar seen in the photographs of Lee Harvey Oswald's arrest.
- Detective John B. Hicks, who took Oswald's fingerprints on the evening of his arrest and assisted Det. Barnes with the paraffin test.
- Detective Richard Ward ('Rusty') Livingstone, co-author of the 1993 book *First Day Evidence.*
- Detective Willie E. ('Pete') Barnes, the man who took the photographs at the Tippit crime scene and also administered the paraffin test to Oswald at City Hall.

At the time of the Kennedy assassination, Detective Robert Lee Studebaker was on temporary assignment to the Crime Scene Search Section from the Auto Theft Bureau. One must ask why, after just seven weeks specialist instruction with the Section, a trainee like Studebaker was let loose on one of the most important crime scenes in the history of the United States. His basic task was to assist Captain Day in photographing the scene on the sixth floor. When asked by the Warren Commission what photographic experience he had, Studebaker replied: "Just home photography." His expertise with a camera can be judged by reference to Studebaker Exhibit C (21H 645), a photograph of the semi-hidden rifle. He confirmed that he had taken the photograph by stating: "I know it's mine because my knees are in the picture." (7H 140).

He was also allowed to run around the sixth floor crime scene with a fingerprint dusting kit and he proceeded to cover everything with fingerprint powder. The actions of poor Mr. Studebaker that afternoon, although probably not entirely his own fault, did very little to commend the Dallas Police Department when the muck later hit the fan.

Headquarters Section

By far the largest part of the Service Division, the Headquarters Section consisted of 79 police officers and 183 civilians. They were split up into three Platoons, once again operating a revolving eight-hour shift system (11.00pm to 7.00am, 7.00am to 3.00pm and 3.00pm to 11.00pm). The vast majority of the personnel were based at City Hall where they filled the posts of Radio Dispatcher, Telephone Clerk, Jailer, Jail Guard, Jail Matron, Relief Patrolman, Jail Cook and Porter.

Each Platoon was under the command of a Police Lieutenant and other Lieutenants were in charge of the jail (on the fifth floor at City Hall).

As far as the events of 22nd November 1963 are concerned, one of the most important people was undoubtedly Sergeant Gerald Dalton Henslee. He supervised the Radio Dispatcher's Office and was himself the police dispatcher for Channel 2. His is the voice that can be heard on that channel during the presidential visit. Although his normal period of duty that day should have been from 7.00am until 3.00pm, he did in fact work from 6.30am through to about 5.30pm. I cannot help but mention that prior to joining the DPD, one of his previous jobs had been as a dance instructor with the Arthur Murray Dance Studios (6H 325).

As mentioned above, the jail-based personnel came under the Headquarters Section umbrella. They comprised three Jailers, six Assistant Jailers, three Jail Matrons, 22 Jail Guards, 19 Jail Clerks and one Jail Cook. These posts were filled by civilians. The best known was Jail Clerk Don Ray Ables. Together with two Vice Squad Detectives, he stood with Oswald on three of the identification line-ups at City Hall on 22nd November. He is pictured in Commission Exhibit 745.

Warrant Section and Court Bailiffs

The Service Division included the Warrant Section which was under the command of Sergeant James C. Skains and had 20 uniformed officers performing what were basically clerical duties. He was supported by a female civilian clerk.

The four Court Bailiffs (civilians) were also included in the Service Division.

The Property Bureau

This Bureau, under the command of Police Captain James M. English, supported by two Patrolmen and one General Clerk, was made up of the Property Room Section and the Automobile Pound Section. Thirty-three personnel were employed in the Bureau but none of them warrants a mention anywhere in the Warren Report.

The name of one man, however, will be familiar to those researchers who have studied the lists of property seized during the searches of Oswald's rooming house and the Paine house, plus items of evidential value from the book depository. Herman W. Hill was the Property Room Supervisor and he, almost alone, was responsible for literally thousands of case exhibits. Everything from the Mannlicher-Carcano rifle to Lee Harvey Oswald's socks passed through his hands and his name and signature appear on dozens of police property receipts (see CE 2003: 24H 332-344). If any one DPD employee performed his duties in an exemplary fashion and maybe deserved a medal for his performance, it was this man.

The Automobile Pound Section, under the command of Sergeant Thomas C. Sewell, backed up by one Patrolman, was manned by 22 civilians. These ranged from Pound Supervisors to Wrecker Drivers and it appears that their duties were similar to the tow-away crews we now have in the UK.

THE RECORDS BUREAU/INFORMATION DESK

The final element of the Service Division was known as the Records Bureau. As well as that actual bureau, it included the Information Desk. It comprised 49 male and female civilians who were employed as clerks and stenographers of various grade. They were under the supervision of Captain of Police O. T. Slaughter, who was supported by a Sergeant and two Patrolmen.

THE CRIMINAL INVESTIGATION DIVISION

By the very nature of its purpose and responsibilities, this obviously became one of the busiest and most important elements of the Dallas Police Department on the afternoon of 22nd November 1963 and immediately after. It was composed of five separate Bureaux and was under the overall command of Deputy Chief of Police M. W. Stevenson.

Uniquely, it was also the only Division to have a pool of civilian employees rather than have them attached to individual Bureaux. I will deal with them separately at the end of the CID section

THE HOMICIDE AND ROBBERY BUREAU

The members of this Bureau naturally looked upon themselves as the *elite*. They were instantly recognizable as they were the ones wearing the big white hats. That was the brainchild of Captain John William ('Will') Fritz who was in overall charge of the Bureau, with two principal assistants, Lieutenants James A. Bohart and Ted P. Wells. The highly respected Will Fritz retired in 1970 after 49 years as a law enforcement officer. The rest of the Bureau was made up of 18 Detectives and two temporarily-assigned Patrolmen. Space precludes lengthy accounts of the parts played by each individual Homicide Detective but I feel that mention should be made of the two who appear in the celebrated photographs of the Oswald shooting.

Homicide Detective James R. ('Jim') Leavelle became possibly the most readily recognizable member of the entire DPD through the graphic images on live TV followed by worldwide photographic coverage. He was the detective wearing the very light suit and white Resistol hat who was handcuffed to Oswald when the latter was shot and killed by Jack Ruby. He told me in very positive terms (November 2000) that he remains totally convinced that Oswald was guilty of killing both Kennedy and Tippit. He is adamant that convictions would have been secured on both counts. The other Detective escorting Oswald that day was the late L. C. Graves, who was just about the only H & R Bureau member not to wear a white hat.

During a visit to DPD Headquarters in June 1995, UK researcher Rick Caster and I were shown the original 1963 *Monthly Time Book and Pay-Roll* ledger for Homicide & Robbery. The November section lists every officer from Captain Fritz down, plus two stenographers, Margaret R. Moody and Mary P. Rattan (see below). The exact duty disposition for each individual is clearly shown, together with some revealing side notes. I am convinced that this document has never been seen by any other researcher. I have never managed to work out why it was kept inside a small cupboard within the Crimes Against Persons Bureau administration office. Fortunately, Rick and I were given the opportunity to photocopy this unique record.

THE JUVENILE BUREAU

This was under the command of Captain Frank Martin, supported by three Lieutenants. Its main strength lay in its complement of 25 Detectives, two Patrolmen temporarily-assigned and the only five Policewomen employed in the DPD. Several members of this Bureau were part of the large police presence engaged in the ultimately unsuccessful protection of Oswald in the City Hall basement garage but no member of the Bureau appears to have been actively involved in the tragic events of 22nd November.

The Burglary and Theft Bureau

This was the largest individual unit within the CID, having a total of 53 members. Captain William C. Fannin was in charge and he was assisted by five Lieutenants. There were 41 full-time Detectives and six Patrolmen temporarily-attached. I can trace only one member of this Bureau being directly involved in the events of 22nd/24th November. This was Lieutenant Richard E. Swain, one of the officers who conducted the search of Jack Ruby's car after the shooting of Oswald.

(Note: The DPD Personnel Assignments lists for November 1963 include the name Elbert M. Baker. However, this Detective resigned from the Department on 10th October and his name was included in error.)

The Auto Theft Bureau

This unit was headed by Captain J. C. Nichols, with three Lieutenants, one of whom, Robert E. Hoffman, was the uncle of eyewitness Ed Hoffman. The Bureau also had 24 full-time Detectives. One of them was to gain fame (or should that be notoriety) for the part he played in the happenings on the six floor of the TSBD in the hour of so after the shooting. I refer, of course, to Detective Robert Lee Studebaker, whose *role* I have already described above (Crime Scene Search Section).

The Forgery Bureau

This was the final unit within the Criminal Investigation Division. It was under the control of Captain Orville A. Jones supported by two Lieutenants of Police and it employed 17 Detectives. Several members of the Bureau were deployed at the Trade Mart for the presidential visit.

No Forgery Bureau member appears to have been directly involved in post-assassination investigation. All enquiries concerned with Oswald's handwriting, etc. on various documents were handled by the F.B.I.

Having said that, however, the Forgery Bureau perhaps should have taken control of the investigation into the shooting of Governor Connally. According to Captain Fritz: "The forgery bureau ... handled all shootings where people are not killed." It was this Bureau which had investigated the attempted murder of General Walker (4H 236), although this incident was originally reported to be a 'Burglary by Firearms' offence (CE 2001).

CIVILIAN EMPLOYEES WITHIN THE CRIMINAL INVESTIGATION DIVISION

A pool of 11 female civilian clerical employees was available to be temporarily attached anywhere within the five CID Bureaux when required. As mentioned earlier, two of them, Margaret R. Moody and Mary P. Rattan, appeared on the Homicide & Robbery strength for the month of November. The members of this pool held various Clerk/Stenographer/Typist grades.

As far as the assassination is concerned, the best known were a Stenographer Grade 5 named Mary P. Rattan and a General Clerk Grade 3 called Patsy C. Collins. Each was a certified County of Dallas Notary Public and their names appear on many affidavits made by witnesses, etc. Examples include an affidavit of Captain Fritz recorded by Ms. Rattan (7H 403/404) and an affidavit of Ruth Paine recorded by Ms Collins (9H 433).

When I first became aware of this, I was somewhat perturbed and I sought the advice of researcher J. Gary Shaw, himself a Notary Public in Johnson County, Texas. Gary assured me that there was nothing sinister here and that having Notaries Public employed within the DPD often saved time in having to contact one urgently. This way, there was usually one readily available.

(For the benefit of UK readers, a Notary Public is roughly equivalent to a Commissioner for Oaths in England and Wales and is a person legally authorized to record sworn statements in writing under oath.)

SPECIAL ASSIGNMENT OFFICERS

Four highly trained Detectives were on Special Assignment to the District Attorney's Office and were considered to be part of the CID without being attached to any particular Bureau or office.

THE TRAINING AND RESEARCH SECTION

This consisted of three small departments as follows:

THE PERSONNEL BUREAU

This was a small Bureau located in a suite of offices just down the corridor from the Homicide office and was under the command of the ubiquitous Captain William Ralph Westbrook. He controlled one Sergeant, two Detectives, one Patrolman and three female civilian clerical grades. Captain Westbrook described the work of the bureau as background investigations of applicants and the investigation of personnel complaints.

THE POLICE RESERVE

Captain J. M. Solomon held the position of Co-ordinator of the Police Reserve. Strength and exact functions are explained briefly on page 3. Members of the Reserve were drafted in for duty on the day of the presidential visit and on the day of Oswald's murder.

THE POLICE ACADEMY

Inspector Edward Preston was in charge here and he appears to have been a very busy man as he had only an Assistant Instructor to share his workload. Does that indicate that he did the majority of the instructional work himself? He was allocated a female stenographer but his only other permanent staff appear to be Pistol Range personnel (two).

I have found the 23 members of the current Recruit Class No. 78 listed by name and a further three people were described as 'Recruit Class No. 79 (Awaiting School)'. Presumably they waited until one class had finished and there were sufficient recruits available to form a new one. The three names are listed in alphabetical order and the last one is that of our old friend Roscoe Anthony White. That, however, is another story!

Written 1997.
First published July 1998 on the internet website *DPUK*.
Published November 1998 in *The Dealey Plaza Echo*, vol. 2, no. 3.

Part 1: The Better-Known Witnesses

2. Kennedy assassination witnesses: when pure chance played a part

Introduction

It is widely accepted that the bullet which hit the Elm Street kerb and caused the minor wound to James Tague's left cheek necessitated the invention of the Single Bullet Theory. Without that missed shot, everything would have fitted neatly into place— three shots, three spent cartridges, three hits— case closed. Assistant Counsel Arlen Specter would have had no need to dream up his theory and would never have gained the fame (or should that be notoriety) which has followed him ever since.

What is less widely known, however, is that it had never been James Tague's intention to watch the motorcade that day. It was just pure chance that caused him to be standing where he was at that moment in history.

The element of chance that played such a significant part in Tague's day was also hard at work in the lives of Ed Hoffman, Warren Caster, Johnny Calvin Brewer and the Newman family on Friday 22nd November 1963. There are probably others but I will concentrate on those, mainly because I have had the privilege and pleasure of meeting and interviewing each of them.

As I have mentioned, what happened to James Tague that day was of great importance. Perhaps of the people I will discuss here, his experience was the most far-reaching. In a perverse sort of way, the man responsible for the Single Bullet Theory was James Tague rather than Arlen Specter. I shall leave Tague until last.

Virgil Edward Hoffman

Ed Hoffman remains one of the most important—and most frequently criticized—eyewitnesses to the assassination of President Kennedy. His involvement came about through pure chance and involved a drink of pop, an ice-cube and the sudden realization that he had an unexpected opportunity to see an American President for the first time.

Friday 22nd November 1963 should have been just another ordinary working day in the machine shop at Texas Instruments in North Dallas for Ed Hoffman. That all changed during his mid-morning refreshment break. After finishing his usual paper cup of Dr. Pepper, he was chewing on the ice cubes when he broke one of his teeth. After informing his supervisors, Glynn Bourland and Cecil Harris, he was given permission to leave work to visit his dentist near his Grand Prairie home for treatment. (1)

Ed drove south on U.S. Highway 75 (North Central Expressway) and then on to Ross Avenue. He continued west on Elm Street, through Dealey Plaza and then on to the access ramp leading on to Stemmons Freeway. Here, he suddenly recalled that the presidential motorcade was shortly to pass this way and he decided that it would be worth delaying his dental treatment for a few minutes to see the President. Ed parked his car at the end of the Stemmons ramp and then walked about 100 feet to a vantage point on Stemmons where it passes over the start of the ramp. His idea was to view the motorcade as it passed directly beneath him.

What Ed did not realize at that time, of course, was that this also afforded an unobstructed view across the triple underpass into Dealey Plaza. More significantly, it also gave a perfect view directly into the area of the railroad yards behind the grassy knoll and the picket fence. From his fine vantage point, Ed Hoffman was shortly to witness two men behind that picket fence on the northeast side of the Dealey Plaza grassy knoll. One of them would fire at the presidential limousine with a rifle. Whilst there were many eyewitnesses in the plaza itself, I feel that Ed Hoffman was alone and unique in watching the actual assassination of President Kennedy.

Like James Tague's, Ed's unscheduled involvement in the crime of the century came about purely by chance. I consider that the Dr. Pepper which Ed Hoffman drank that morning was far more significant than any soft drink which may have been enjoyed by an alleged shooter on the sixth floor of a certain large red-brick building in the north-east corner of Dealey Plaza.

JOHNNY CALVIN BREWER

Unlike Tague, Hoffman and the Newmans, Johnny Brewer was not an eyewitness to the actual assassination. He did, however, play a vital part in the arrest of Lee Harvey Oswald. He has a place here because, like the other individuals described, he found himself somewhere that he did not plan to be on that day through no fault of his own.

Brewer was the manager of Hardy's shoe store at 213 West Jefferson Boulevard, Oak Cliff, just a few yards along from the Texas Theatre (which was number 231). You will find his own account of what happened to him that day in Chapter 8, "An Interview with Johnny Calvin Brewer".

Briefly, Johnny Brewer would not have been working at Hardy's that day had it not been for the sudden and unexpected illness of his assistant's young child. Brewer had arranged to have the day off to put his new car through its paces. This was a 1964 model Galaxy CL500 Ford and it was his pride and joy. Brewer's assistant telephoned him at home early that morning and explained that his newborn child was sick and that he was unable to cover for Brewer as had been agreed. Instead of enjoying his new car, Brewer could only admire it from behind his shop counter and, in his own words, "feed nickels to it all day" as it remained at a nearby parking meter.

Whether his assistant would have taken the same action as Brewer when the furtive Oswald appeared in the shop doorway we shall never know.

WARREN CASTER

The situation concerning Warren Caster is the complete opposite to that of the other people whose actions I describe here. They each found themselves thrust *into* the limelight because an element of chance moved them into the forefront of the action on the day of the assassination. Like Ed Hoffman and James Tague, Warren Caster was away from his normal place of work when the gunfire erupted in Dealey Plaza. In Caster's case, however, his normal place of work was the Texas School Book Depository and chance decreed that he would *not* be present when the bullets started to fly. [2]

In November 1963, Warren Caster was the District Manager of the Southwestern Publishing Co., a book publishing company which rented premises within the Texas School Book Depository. Caster's office was situated on the second floor (called the first floor in the U.K.) of the building. It was Room 203 and it looked directly out on to Elm Street.

Warren Caster is the man who, on Wednesday 20th November, two days before the assassination, purchased two rifles (a Remington and a Mauser) from Sanger's department store during his lunch break. The Remington single-shot .22 was to be a Christmas present for William, his elder son, and the 30-03 sporterized Mauser just took his eye and he bought it for himself. He brought them into the TSBD where he encountered Bill Shelley, Roy Truly, Lee Harvey Oswald and others by chance. When they asked him what was in the boxes, he showed them the rifles. After work that day, he took the weapons to his home in the northern part of Dallas in his car.

Unfortunately, some researchers have completely misconstrued Caster's actions here and have intimated that he may have been part of the conspiracy to assassinate the President by introducing the murder weapon into the depository. Having met the man and spent a considerable time in his company, I am satisfied that this is a classic example of people adding two and two and making a thousand and six. The two rifles purchased by Warren Caster are still in the possession of the Caster family, who now live in North Carolina.

Thursday 21st November was just a normal day at the office for Warren Caster but on Friday 22nd, he had a pre-arranged and unavoidable business engagement. This kept him away from the book depository all day. Instead of going to his office as usual, he drove up to North Texas State University at Denton, 35 miles north of Dallas, to keep an appointment with Dr Vernon V. Payne. He was thus out of town when the assassination took place. Caster learnt of the President's death when he and Dr Payne heard the news from some students at the university. It was an added shock to learn later that the site of the tragedy had been Dealey Plaza. Warren Caster immediately left Denton, battled his way through the traffic jams and eventually reached home at 3338 Merrell Road, around two miles northwest of Love Field.

Caster testified before the Warren Commission in Dallas on 14th May 1964. His testimony, taken by Assistant Counsel Joseph A. Ball, occupies just a page and a half in the 26 Volumes. It was concerned solely with his purchase of the two rifles and the fact that he had brought them into the TSBD on that Wednesday afternoon. (3)

Perhaps the most significant aspect of Warren Caster's connection with the events of the day has been given minimal exposure; indeed it is probably completely unknown to most researchers. A good friend of Warren Caster, a gentleman named Roger Williams, had telephoned him on Thursday 21st and had asked if they could meet in Caster's office the following day to watch the presidential motorcade. Caster explained that he had to be in Denton that day (22nd) and would miss the motorcade himself.

He added that it would be pointless to try to watch from his second floor office as the view would be obstructed by trees. The ideal place to watch, Caster told Williams, would be up on the sixth floor where the view was far better. Williams thanked Caster and said that he would go along to the Trade Mart to see the President there instead. (4)

Now just suppose that Warren Caster had *not* had that meeting in Denton scheduled for the 22nd ... !

Three further important but little-known facts emerged from the two-day interview which fellow British researcher Rick Caster and myself conducted with Warren in June 1995.

Firstly, the Special Service Bureau of the Dallas PD carried out an intense search of the entire second floor of the book depository. Was this because they had heard about the two rifles which Warren had brought into the building on the 20th?

Secondly, Warren, his wife Ruthanna and younger son David, returned to the depository the day after the assassination and were surprised to find that they had no trouble entering the building. He recalled that it was rather quiet and as far as he could remember, the sixth floor was not sealed off. For a location which only 24 hours earlier had been one of the most important crime scenes in the history of America, I find this incredible. I also find it odd that as far as I am aware, no researcher has discussed this in print.

Thirdly, as far as Warren Caster could ascertain, neither the Warren Commission nor anybody else ever bothered to confirm his alibi with Dr Payne or anybody else at the university.

THE NEWMAN FAMILY

William Eugene 'Bill' Newman,Jr., a 22-year old electrician, drove his wife Gayle and their two young sons Billy (4 yrs.) and Clayton (2 yrs.) from their Oak Cliff home to Love Field on the morning of the assassination. The object was to see the President and First Lady as they landed and stepped from Air Force One following their short flight from Fort Worth. [5]

Bill and the younger boy, Clayton, managed to get a good view of the Kennedys from a position at the front on the fence line but unfortunately Gayle and Billy found themselves at the back of the crowd. They were able to see practically nothing. Bill realized the problem and managed to get his family out of Love Field very quickly. He remembered from details published in the newspaper that the motorcade would pass through Dealey Plaza so he drove the family there. They managed to beat the motorcade and after parking the car, they found a suitable, unobstructed vantage point on the grass on the northern edge of Elm Street at the front of what later became known as the Grassy Knoll.

For Gayle, there was an added bonus in being able to see the motorcade. Her uncle, from whom the Newmans were renting their house, was DPD motorcycle officer Sergeant Stavis Ellis, one of the five lead motorcyclists in the motorcade. [6]

Both Bill and Gayle still vividly recall the shock of hearing the shots and seeing the result as JFK was shot before their very eyes. Bill told me: "We were the closest individuals to the President as spectators ... when the third shot was fired." Unforgettable images of the Newmans remain in perpetuity thanks to the camera lenses of several of the plaza photographers. Convinced that at least some of the shots were coming from behind them, Bill and Gayle pushed their children to the ground and immediately covered them with their own bodies. Bill beat the ground with his fists in anger and frustration. [7]

Despite being no more than a few feet away from the presidential limousine at the time of the shots, neither Bill nor Gayle Newman was called to testify before the Warren Commission. Bill is convinced that this is because he had said in a Sheriff's Department statement on 22nd November that " ... it seemed that we were in direct path of fire" and "I thought the shot had come from the garden directly behind me." (8) (Read more of Bill Newman's experiences in Chapter 3.)

Had the Newmans set off from home just five or ten minutes earlier that morning, perhaps they would all have had a perfect view of JFK and Jackie at Love Field and never have become among the closest and most important eyewitnesses in Dealey Plaza.

According to the author/historian Richard B. Trask, there could have been an even greater sting in the tail. He states that the Newmans had gone to Love Field "unfortunately forgetting their 8mm movie camera at home." (9) With the willing assistance of my friend and fellow researcher William Law, I checked this out with Gayle Newman. She confirmed: "That's correct. We went off and left it on the dresser that morning." (10) Obviously, any movie footage of the presidential limousine shot from the Newmans' location would have been of inestimable value— particularly in view of the controversy involving the authenticity or otherwise of the Zapruder Film which has arisen in recent years.

JAMES THOMAS TAGUE

In time-honoured fashion, I have left the best until last. Obviously, without James Tague, we would have no Single Bullet Theory. There would simply be no need for it. In my opinion, after the occupants of the limousine and possible marksmen, James Tague was the most important person in Dealey Plaza at 12.30pm on Friday 22nd November 1963. (11)

The 27-year old James Tague witnessed the assassination from a solitary position which he described as "three or four feet" east of the base of the triple underpass on the narrow strip of grass (US 'median strip') which separates Commerce and Main Streets. (12) He was about 120 feet from the presidential limousine when President Kennedy was struck by the fatal headshot.

Why was Tague in such an isolated position? It was hardly by choice. Like Ed Hoffman and the Newman family, it had never been his intention to view the motorcade as it passed through the plaza. He worked as a car salesman for Cedar Springs Dodge and he had arranged to drive into downtown Dallas to meet his girlfriend (later his wife) for lunch. His own words represent a magnificent six-word understatement: "I accidentally came across the motorcade." (13)

In his Warren Commission testimony before Assistant Counsel Wesley J. Liebeler, Tague went on to explain that he was not planning to watch the parade but became involved in a traffic jam at the eastern end of Dealey Plaza.

This came about when all traffic was halted at the Commerce and Houston intersection to allow free passage for the motorcade as it turned right from Main on to Houston. Tague was driving east on Commerce (one-way only) and he stopped literally under the triple underpass. As he described it: "The car was just halfway out from underneath the underpass, and I got out of my car and stopped by the bridge abutment." [14]

Tague indicated his exact position to Mr Liebeler on a detailed aerial map of Dealey Plaza. It was marked as point no. 6 on what later became a commission exhibit. [15] This was confirmed in the testimony of Dallas Deputy Sheriff Buddy Walthers, although Walthers confused point no. 6 with point no. 9, which was opposite the book depository. [16]

Watching the presidential motorcade as it came down Elm Street, Tague heard three shots, the first of which he described as sounding "like a fire-cracker." Three or four minutes later he was joined by Deputy Sheriff Walthers who pointed out that he had blood on his face. Tague replied: "I recall something sting me on the face while I was standing down there." Walthers replied: "Yes; you have blood there on your cheek."

There has been considerable conjecture concerning exactly which shot was responsible for hitting the kerb in front of Tague and causing a fragment of concrete to fly up and hit his cheek. It has become known as 'the missed shot.' Tague himself stated: "I believe that it was the second shot, so I heard the third shot afterwards." [17]

Perhaps the most remarkable aspect of James Tague's involvement was that he was there at all. Once again, his own words sum it up perfectly: "I mean I just stopped, got out of my car, and here came the motorcade. I just happened upon the scene." [18]

NOTES

1. I acknowledge two very important sources which have been responsible for many of the details contained in my Ed Hoffman section here. *Eye Witness* was written jointly by Ed Hoffman and Ron Friedrich and published by JFK Lancer, Grand Prairie, Texas in 1995. *JFK: Breaking the Silence* by Bill Sloan, published by Taylor Publishing Company, Dallas, Texas (1993) devotes its opening chapter to Ed Hoffman's experience.
2. See Rick Caster: "What's in a name?" in *The Kennedy Assassination Chronicles*, vol. 1, issue 3 (September 1995) upon which this section relies heavily.
3. 7H 387-388 (Testimony of Warren Caster). Also interviews with Warren Caster (accompanied by UK researcher Rick Caster) at Albuquerque, New Mexico, 7th/ 8th June 1995.
4. From Albuquerque interviews.

5. William Law/Mark Rowe/Ian Griggs interview with Bill Newman at Mesquite, Texas, 20th November 1997. See transcript in the chapter *An Interview with Bill Newman*.

6. Sloan, as footnote 1 above, page 170. See also Todd Wayne Vaughan: *Presidential Motorcade Schematic Listing*, self-published, 1993, page 4.

7. Richard B. Trask: *Pictures of the Pain*, published by Yeoman Press, Danvers, Massachusetts, 1994, page 39 (Cecil Stoughton #8); page 156 (Richard O. Bothun #4); page 208 (Mrs Wilma Bond #1); page 333 (Harry Cabluck #2); page 376 (Thomas M. Atkins #8); page 401 (Frank Cancellare #2). The Cancellare photograph cited here captures perfectly the bewilderment of the Newman family at that moment.

8. CE 2003 (Dallas Police Department file on investigation of the assassination of the President), page 45 of exhibit (24H 219).

9. Trask, page 400.

10. Exchange of telephone calls and emails between William Law, Mrs Gayle Newman and the author, 3rd February 1999.

11. I was very flattered when James Tague quoted me almost exactly in the back cover blurb of his 2003 book *Truth Withheld: A Survivor's Story*. He said: " ... after the occupants of the car and the assassin(s), James Tague was the most important person in Dealey Plaza Friday November 22nd, 1963.' - Ian Griggs."

12. Tague can be seen clearly (wearing distinctive white shirt) in the first of Frank Cancellare's series of black-and-white still photographs (print in author's collection). There is an excellent blow-up of the right side of that photograph on page 41 of Robert Groden's *The Killing of a President*. The light-coloured car next to Tague is his car. He can also be seen at the extreme left in the Tom Dillard still photograph, no. 1-9 of his sequence, reproduced on page 453 of Trask's *Pictures of the Pain*.

13. 7H 552 (Testimony of James Thomas Tague).

14. 7H 553 (Testimony of James Thomas Tague).

15. CE 354 (Aerial view of Main, Houston and Elm Streets in downtown Dallas.)

16. 7H 546 (Testimony of Eddy Raymond Walthers).

17. 7H 555 (Testimony of James Thomas Tague).

18. ibid.

Written 1997.
First published November/December 1997 on website *Fair Play*, no. 19.
Amended version published March 1999 on website *JFK Link* (Australia), no. 1.
Published March 2000 under title "The Single Bullet Theory was caused by a Traffic Jam" in *The Dealey Plaza Echo*, vol. 4, no. 1.
Research paper at the JFK-Lancer November in Dallas 1999 conference.

3. An interview with Bill Newman

INTRODUCTION

One of the highlights of the 1997 JFK-Lancer Conference in Dallas, Texas was the opportunity for William Law, Mark Rowe and myself to conduct a video-recorded interview of assassination eyewitness William Eugene Newman, Jr. At the time of the assassination, Mr Newman was standing on the north side of Elm Street and can be seen plainly on many films and photographs as he and his wife Gayle threw themselves to the ground to protect their two young children as the shots rang out. Both Bill and Gayle Newman were aged 22 at the time of the assassination.

The chance for Mark and I to be part of this interview came about thanks to William, who had been in regular correspondence with Bill Newman for several months. The interview took place on the afternoon of Thursday 20th November 1997 at the office of the successful electric company which Mr Newman owns and operates at Mesquite, east of Dallas.

THE NATURE OF THE INTERVIEW

What follows is a shortened version of the interview, transcribed directly from the video tape which William Law shot. Nothing considered relevant has been excluded. It is immediately evident that much of this was not in the normal form of a question-and-answer session but rather an opportunity for Mr Newman to recall the events of the day and give his account of what he and his family did, saw and heard. He does not speculate on what may or may not have happened, preferring to relate the facts as they affected him and his family. My own italicised comments in brackets within the text were added later.

Mr Newman also spoke about his experience as an eyewitness at the Clay Shaw trial and gave some good insight into the personality and bearing of Jim Garrison.

BILL NEWMAN'S STORY

WEN: Alright, I'll do my best to tell you what I saw. You know, it's been some time ago and what I have learned over the years is that you're influenced from the time, the day of the assassination, up to this time. Your story tends to be tainted or influenced by what you have learnt or what other people have seen.

On the morning of November 22nd 1963, Gayle and myself and our two sons, Clayton (aged 2) and Billy (aged 4), went out to Love Field to see President Kennedy and Mrs Kennedy come in. We saw the 'plane land and there was a large crowd of people. I can remember, I believe I had Clayton with me—which was the youngest boy—and we kinda ran up to the fence line and we got a good view of the President and First Lady but Gayle and Billy did not. The parade route had been published in the newspaper so we jumped in our car and we drove down near the intersection of Elm and Houston Street. We parked behind J. P. Awalt and Company, one of the buildings there.

We walked a short block or so to the intersection of Houston Street and Elm. There was a crowd of people there, as you are well aware, waiting for the parade to come by and we just walked in behind the crowd of people along the sidewalk towards the triple underpass and where the last two people were, we just fell in beside them. And if I remember correctly, it was an older lady— which is probably my age or younger now *(Bill Newman was 57 years old at the time of this interview - ILG)*—and a younger woman standing there. We were about probably halfway from the intersection of Houston and Elm to the triple underpass, on the north side of the street. We'd been there a very short time, probably no more than five minutes and you could hear the noise of the crowds cheering as the parade came down Main Street. I can remember seeing the President's car turn right on to Houston and go that short block and turn left on to Elm and coming towards us.

"I thought someone had thrown a couple of firecrackers"

WEN: And the President's car was out the distance of one lane from the kerb line and some one hundred and fifty feet from us, some short distance, when the first two shots rang out. And it was a boom-boom. They were very close together and I could remember thinking "Boy, that's a poor thing to do." I thought someone had thrown a couple of firecrackers at the side of the President's car.

At that moment, I didn't realize that it was gunfire and the President had been shot. I can remember his arms go up and I even testified in the Dallas Sheriff's Department later that day that he raised up in the seat. I think if you were to read that statement you'll find that I said he raised up in the seat. There again, seeing the Zapruder film many times, I realize that he didn't raise up—

he just kinda came forward and made a motion and apparently he was hit by one of the first two shots. As the car got closer to us I could see that something was wrong. I could see Governor Connally and I could see his eyes protruding and I could see him holding himself and I could see blood on his shirt.

" ... a bewildered look on his face"

WEN: I can remember that the President looked to me like he was sorta looking into the crowd with a bewildered look on his face. As the car got directly in front of us—and we were on the kerb's edge—and the President was probably not much further than I am from you *(about ten feet - ILG)* the third shot rang out and I can remember seeing the side of President Kennedy's head blow off. *(Here, Mr Newman indicated with his right hand the area of his head immediately above his right ear - ILG.)* There was black matter and then greyish and he fell across Mrs Kennedy, into her lap and she jumped up and hollered: "Oh my God, no. They've shot Jack."

And I turned to Gayle and I said: "That's it—hit the ground." And we turned and pushed our kids down on the grass behind us. It's referred to now as the grassy knoll. We covered our kids—our two children that were two and four years old at the time.

" ... the shots were coming from behind us"

WEN: And what ran through my mind was, with that third shot, that the shots were coming from behind us, directly over the top of our heads. Normally, when I'm talking with a group or someone like yourselves, I leave it at that and the person gets round to saying "Behind where? Behind to your left or behind to your right?"—the left meaning the school book depository and the right meaning the picket fence. From my view it was just "behind" and it was a visual impact it had on me of seeing the head wound and seeing President Kennedy go across the seat. That gave me the impression of the shot being fired from behind and if I refer to it as "shots" I'm really talking about three shots—the first two and then the one I recognized as gunfire.

" ... and the car momentarily stopped"

WEN: And then I can remember that when we were on the ground—I'd like to bring this up if I may—looking back over my shoulder I can remember, I believe it was the passenger in the front seat—there were two men in the front seat—had a telephone or something to his ear and the car momentarily stopped.

Now everywhere that you read about it, you don't read anything about the car stopping. And when I say "stopped" I mean very momentarily, like they hit the brakes and just a few seconds passed and then they floorboarded and accelerated on.

WL: But you don't really see that in the Zapruder film.

WEN: No, you don't. But anyway, that's the impression I'm left with.

WL: Some people have said that the car stopped.

WEN: Yes—and then they shot on. You know, through the overpass, the railroad overpass and that's the last we saw of them.

We stood up and just a few moments later, a man by the name of Jerry Haynes, who was a local person here, 'Mr Peppermint', him and another fellow came up to us and said: "What happened? What did y'all see?" and we said: "Well, we saw the President shot" and he said: "Would you go to WFAA with us?" *(WFAA-TV was a major local television station situated next to the Dallas Morning News building. - LG)* and we said yes we would and we started to cross in the direction of WFAA. If I remember correctly, on Commerce Street, he just stopped a car and said to the man "This man saw the President shot—would you carry us to WFAA?" and he said "Sure" and we jumped in his car and went to WFAA.

We said basically what I've said here. *(Footage of this interview—the first to be given by any eyewitness to the assassination—can be seen on "The Kennedy Tapes", a seven video set of the entire WFAA-TV coverage of the events of 22ⁿᵈ to 24ᵗʰ November 1963. - ILG)*

AT THE DALLAS SHERIFF'S DEPARTMENT

WEN: After that, there was a man there—I guess he was from the Sheriff's Office, Bill Decker's Office, because that's where he carried us. And we went to Bill Decker's office and Gayle and myself both gave an affidavit of what we saw and I think, if I remember correctly, there was 16 of us and they detained us for several hours, three, four, five hours and what they were actually doing was reviewing all these statements to try to see if—they kept us there just to re-question us if necessary and of course they did not re-question myself or Gayle at that time and they turned us loose. (Gayle and Bill Newman's affidavits can be found as CE 2003—pages 43 and 45 of the exhibit respectively—at 24H 218/219 - ILG.)

ILG: About what time did you get out of there?

WEN: It was probably ten o'clock at night or something. It seemed like it was after dark and I couldn't tell you what time of day. You know, in fairness, they looked after us, but they just detained us there. You know, in the event that they saw a conflicting statement—that's pretty much it.

SOME QUESTIONS AND ANSWERS—AND JIM BRADEN

WL: You say you were totally focused on the car, so when the shot hit him in the head, would you say the shot hit him in the side of the head, in the side of the temple? Or couldn't you tell?

WEN: Well I think I testified or made a statement to the extent that it looked to me like the side of his head blew off and his ear blew off. Now I quit saying that now, that his ear blew off, because I've seen autopsy photographs of the President with his ear intact, but you know, there's no way to see a replay of it. I mean it was just like that and whether there was an entrance or an exit wound I can't tell you. I can tell you that the President did go across the car, which gave me the impression that the bullet was coming from my direction, hitting the President, knocking him across the seat.

WL: At Sheriff Decker's office, were you with other people, other witnesses?

WEN: Yes.

WL: Did any of you talk amongst yourselves as to what you'd seen, and share information?

WEN: I don't recall that. We were all kinda stunned, to tell you the truth. The one little story that I can recall—and now, of course, it gets tainted here, because at the time, I hadn't heard the stories on the man, but there was one man there that was in the building next door to the school book depository and he had said he had gone in there to use the telephone and he came back out on the street and the police officers or someone grabbed on to him and the crowd nearly got out of hand. They said "Oh, he's the man that shot the President" and things got a little unruly, so I heard. Well this particular gentleman—I can't tell you his name—he seemed to be very nervous and very upset. He was sitting nearby and I said a few words to him and his comment to me was he was supposed to catch a plane, and he was supposed to be somewhere else and he had to call his office.

MR: That was Braden wasn't it?

ILG: Was this gentleman wearing a hat, can you remember?

WEN: Yes, I think he had a hat. And apparently he was supposed to have had some criminal past.

ILG: Yes, this is a gentleman called Jim Braden.

WEN: Yes, of course. I learnt that 15 or 20 years later. I can remember him. Of the individuals that were in there, he seemed to be the one that was the most upset that he was being detained.

WL: Roy Vaughan said that he is the one who apparently took him in and he had credit cards in his wallet and you didn't see a whole lot of that in '63. So he felt that was real unusual. The part I'm interested in—well, I'm interested in all of it—is Garrison, the Garrison trial. Can you give us some of your impressions of that, your part in it?

Jim Garrison and the Clay Shaw trial

WEN: Well, Gayle and myself did testify in the Garrison trial. I think she went down on Friday and testified and if I remember correctly, I had the flu. We were supposed to be there together and I was still running a fever but I recovered enough that I went down on Monday and testified. Garrison asked me every question beforehand that he asked me on the stand and I understand I was the first individual that he examined on the stand.

What he liked about what I had to say was the fact that the President went across the car seat. And he just asked me where I was at and what I saw and I told him. I can remember in our interview I had said—and he wasn't trying to put words in my mouth—but I had said it was like he had been hit by a baseball bat. I mean he just kinda flew across the seat. He wanted me to emphasize that on the stand and I can remember him saying to me "Now, Mr Newman, is there anything else that you'd like to elaborate on?" I can remember looking at him and saying "No, sir." Then I was cross-examined and the minute I stepped off of the stand I realized what Garrison had wanted me to say. He wanted me to make the baseball bat statement.

I was really impressed with the man. He was nothing like the character Kevin Costner played in the movie. I can say that. In the movie, you had the feeling that Garrison was a person who was kinda outside looking in. Kinda the new boy on the block who was trying to flush the system or something. You know, a kinda naive sort of guy. Jim Garrison impressed me to be someone who was anything but naive. He seemed to me really to know what he was after and seemed to be a very powerful individual to me. That was the one thing in the JFK movie that just kinda jumped out at me. That was not the Jim Garrison I met.

"The Warren Commission—we were not called"

ILG: Could I ask you a couple of questions before we close, Mr Newman? Going back to the Warren Commission, you were not called to testify, were you?

WEN: That's correct. We were not called.

ILG: Were you surprised at that? You were one of the closest witnesses to this thing but they never called you.

WEN: Well, yes, I was somewhat surprised—and somebody told me along the way that the reason we did not testify before the Warren Commission was because we said the shots came from behind us. But I can't tell you why they didn't call us, close as we were. I would say that we were the closest two individuals to the President as spectators. We were the closest two individuals to the President when the third shot was fired.

WL: You see, that's why people like us like to talk to people like you—because we can't understand it either. Nowadays, you'd want people that were the closest, unless you don't want something to come out, maybe.

WEN: When I'm dealing with assassination people I try to stick to what I know and not what I feel or what my opinion is so I pretty well told you what I know. Obviously you knew what I was going to say before you came here today. I would like to say in turn that the vast majority of people I have dealt with because of the assassination I consider to be first class people. I've learnt that the Lincoln assassination is still being studied and I realize that the Kennedy assassination will be looked at for many, many years to come.

WL: Well, Mr Newman, I appreciate your time.

WEN: You're very welcome.

ILG: Thank you very much.

WEN: You bet.

Written 1997
First published March 1998 in *The Dealey Plaza Echo*, vol. 2, no. 1.
Interview video shown at JFK Lancer Conference 2004

4. "Where were you when the President was shot, Beverly?"

INTRODUCTION

One of the most frequently asked questions in connection with the Kennedy assassination concerns the identity of a mysterious young lady who became known as the *Babushka Lady*. She can be seen clearly on the Zapruder film and also on various other movie films and still photographs taken in Dealey Plaza on 22nd November 1963. The Babushka Lady is one of the few eyewitnesses who were not immediately identified. She acquired her rather odd nickname because of the babushka or triangular headscarf tied under the chin which she was wearing that day.

The question which the Babushka Lady provokes has become much more than just "Who is she?" It has become the much more positive "Are the Babushka Lady and Beverly Oliver one and the same person?" Undoubtedly the most important aspect of this lady is the fact that she appears to be filming the motorcade. Her position on the south side of Elm Street, close to eyewitnesses Charles Brehm, Jean Hill and Mary Moorman, means that her film would almost certainly be a near mirror image of the Zapruder film. Perhaps more important than the presidential limousine itself would be what can be seen behind it. The background to the Babushka Lady's film would inevitably include the Texas School Book Depository (perhaps including the so-called sniper's nest window) and the grassy knoll.

The question of the Babushka Lady's identity remained a total mystery following the death of the President. Nobody came forward to claim that they were the mysterious eyewitness and furthermore, nobody could suggest who the lady may have been. There it remained, and perhaps would have continued to remain, were it not for a chance meeting between renowned assassination researcher J. Gary Shaw and a young lady called Beverly McGann. They met shortly after a church service at the First Baptist Church of Joshua, a small Texas town 20 miles south of Fort Worth, in November 1970.

BEVERLY OLIVER'S CLAIM

The aftermath of this meeting is widely known and has been well-documented in many books. Beverly McGann, *nee* Oliver, related to Gary Shaw how she had filmed the motorcade and the assassination from a point on the south side of Elm Street. As anybody who knows Gary would be aware, he did not just accept this stranger's story without question. No; being aware that she had not had the opportunity to see the Zapruder film and the portrayal therein of the Babushka Lady, he took her to Dealey Plaza and asked her to indicate exactly where she had been standing on that fateful day. To Gary's amazement, she did not hesitate but went straight to the point where the Babushka Lady can be seen on the Zapruder film.

CONTROVERSY

The controversy over Beverly Oliver's claim to be the Babushka Lady has raged unabated from that day to this. It remains one of the most vehemently debated aspects of the Kennedy assassination mystery. Whilst there are parts of Beverly's account which I find difficult to understand, I firmly believe that Beverly Oliver and the Babushka Lady are one and the same person. Like many researchers of my acquaintance, on both sides of the Atlantic, I have frequently become involved in heated discussions concerning this question. I am delighted to report that no matter how involved some of these discussions have become, I have not yet ended up exchanging blows with anybody.

I have something of an advantage over many researchers, particularly those outside the United States, in that I have had the pleasure and privilege to meet Beverly Oliver and her husband Charles Massegee on several occasions. I like to think that we trust and respect one another and I am proud to call Beverly Oliver my friend. Perhaps it may be thought that this would tend to colour my opinion that Beverly was the Babushka Lady. I would refute that and stress that by speaking with Beverly regularly over the past few years, I have come to know someone who is, in my opinion, one of the most open and honest people I have ever encountered.

PROOF NEEDED

The ultimate and indisputable proof that Beverly Oliver and the Babushka Lady are identical would be the appearance of the all-important movie film she shot in Dealey Plaza. The circumstances under which Beverly claims it was taken from her by FBI Special Agent Regis Kennedy are too well documented for me to repeat them here. Suffice to say that Beverly still harbours the hope and belief that it will emerge and be returned to her. Wishful thinking perhaps—but Beverly is a strong lady of great faith and she will never give up that hope. There have already emerged several small suggestions that the film really does exist and that it is perhaps secreted away somewhere in the depths of the US National Archives or maybe somewhere more sinister.

So how can we establish for certain whether or not Beverly's claim to be the Babushka Lady is valid? The obvious and irrefutable answer is that we cannot. Beverly knows—and if she is *not* the Babushka Lady, then the real one knows. Other than that, we can only examine the existing evidence—much of which remains uncorroborated—and either agree that Beverly Oliver is the Babushka Lady or agree that she is not. If you do not feel that they are one and the same person, then I challenge you to confront Beverly and call her a liar to her face. This is a classic black-and-white situation and there is no middle ground. To quote, or rather to misquote, a German friend of mine: "The answer is yes or no. You cannot say a girl is slightly pregnant."

In an effort to help the doubter make up his or her mind, allow me to present both sides of the argument as I see them. This is a straightforward process in which we outline the facts which indicate that Beverly was *not* the Babushka Lady and then list those facts which suggest that she *is*.

"Beverly Oliver was not the Babushka Lady—she is a liar!"

(1) The film which Beverly claims to have shot has never been produced to the public or to anybody in the research community. It has still to be located and viewed. Does it exist?

(2) Beverly claims that she shot her film using a Yashica Super-Eight magazine-loading camera which had been given to her by her boyfriend Larry Ronco. There have been strong claims that such a camera was not available to the public in 1963.

(3) Beverly Oliver is unable to produce the camera. When I discussed this with her in 1993, she told me that together with other personal belongings stored in a trunk, it had been stolen several years before.

(4) She was not readily identified or named as an eyewitness on 22nd November 1963 and she did not come forward of her own volition. (Perhaps this fact could equally be used to substantiate her claim that she *was* there!)

(5.) Nobody has come forward to confirm Beverly Oliver's claim that she was in Dealey Plaza that day.

"BEVERLY OLIVER WAS THE BABUSHKA LADY"

(1) Beverly Oliver claims that she was on that spot, filming the motorcade.

(2) The Babushka Lady as portrayed in the Zapruder film bears a remarkable resemblance to Beverly Oliver in terms of age, height, etc. As I have pointed out in an article published in the June 1995 issue of the now-defunct British research journal *Dallas '63*, the Babushka Lady appears to have a some-what ungainly stance. It is a little-known fact that Beverly Oliver has a slightly deformed left foot.

(3) Other films and still photographs also show a Babushka Lady who looks remarkably like Beverly Oliver.

(4) An FBI document dated 25th November 1963 describes what it calls "B-Lady" and adds that this female is "taking pictures from an angle which would have, undoubtedly, included the Texas School Book Depository in the background." Nobody else has ever been identified as being that per-son. Beverly Oliver has a copy of this document in her possession. I also have a copy of it.

(5) Another document, apparently from the National Archives JFK Collection and appearing to be part of an official investigation, closes with the follow-ing intriguing sentence: "Can the Freedom of Information Act shake the Babushka Lady's film from the FBI files?" This would seem to corroborate Beverly's account of the seizure of her film by SA Regis Kennedy. Beverly has a copy of this document in her possession. I also have a copy of it.

(6) Until her chance meeting with researcher J. Gary Shaw, Beverly neither sought nor obtained publicity of any kind; nor did she ever attempt to "cash in" on her claim. Her story was eventually published in autobiographical form with the help of Dallas author Coke Buchanan in 1994 (*Nightmare in Dallas*). Surely, if she were seeking publicity, as has been claimed by some of her detractors, would she really have waited 31 years?

(7) In view of the fate that appears to have befallen certain other people who claim to have seen or experienced something important pertaining to the Kennedy assassination, it is courting danger to make such claims lightly.

(8) With no prior knowledge of the content of the Zapruder film, Beverly took Gary Shaw to the *exact* spot in Dealey Plaza where the Babushka Lady stood and shot her film. I find it doubtful that she had ever read any of the

books on the subject of the assassination to gain this knowledge. She could, of course, have seen individual frames from the Zapruder film as they were reproduced in *Life* magazine, etc. but that had been several years earlier and it is doubtful that she would have been able to locate the exact spot from just that scant data.

(9) Nobody else has ever come forward and claimed to be the Babushka Lady. If her claim is false, then Beverly is risking total humiliation and ridicule if that should ever happen.

(10) Nobody has ever come forward to state that Beverly Oliver was any-where else at the time of the assassination. Like (9) above, such an occur-rence (an alibi in reverse) would completely destroy not only Beverly's claim concerning this event but also her total credibility. Who is going to risk that?

Now you decide

Those, as far as I can present them, are the facts. There are significant points on each side, although the "yes" points do outnumber the "no" points. As I have stated above, it is my personal opinion that Beverly Oliver and the Babushka Lady are the same person. Your view may agree with mine or it may differ. In my opinion, and, I am sure that of most people who have met her, Beverly is an honest, God-fearing lady who has no reason or need to lie about any of this. I think only one living person really knows the truth for certain. Beverly Oliver-Massegee herself—because she was there and she was wear-ing a triangular headscarf and she was filming the President.

Addendum

Shortly after completing this short piece, I submitted it to Beverly Oliver-Massegee for her comments. She echoed my overall sentiments and added the following observation: "No one has had the nerve or 'class' to call me a liar to my face. They only do it behind my back or print it in books they have reason to believe I will never read." I feel that those two sentences sum up my own opinions perfectly.

Written 1996
First published November 1996 in *The Fourth Decade*, vol. 4, no. 1.

5. Putting myself in Ed Hoffman's shoes

INTRODUCTION

Many researchers, in both the United States and in the United Kingdom, are familiar with my published research into the disassembly and reassembly of the Mannlicher-Carcano rifle. My choice of that as a subject of research was perfectly deliberate. I was concerned that I could find no evidence that any previous researcher had ever written and published such an account. I made no claim to be the first researcher to have undertaken the task of taking that rifle apart—but why was there no record of exactly how it is done? I simply set out to do it and then published my findings on both sides of the Atlantic.

This short paper has a very similar background but although I feel it is important to physically re-enact as many aspects of the case as possible, that was not my original intention here. What follows is an account of an hour or so of my life in which I learnt more about Ed Hoffman's terrifying predicament on 22nd November 1963 than I could possibly imagine.

In some ways, it is a horror story.

WHO WAS ED HOFFMAN AND WHY IS HE IMPORTANT?

Virgil Edward Hoffman was employed by Texas Instruments in north Dallas and was a deaf mute. On the day of the assassination, he was at work as usual but during his morning refreshment break he broke a tooth and was given permission to visit his dentist for urgent attention. This drive took him close to Dealey Plaza and recalling that the President was due to pass through, he stopped his car to watch the motorcade. From his elevated vantage point on Stemmons Freeway he had an unrestricted view over not only Dealey Plaza but also the railroad yards behind the picket fence. From this position, Ed saw two men behind the picket fence, one of whom fired a rifle at the motorcade.

Ed was the only person with this unique view and his immediate attempts to report what he had seen were met with impatience and apathy. Nobody could spare the time to try to understand a deaf mute. The President had just been shot. Little did they realize what he was trying to convey. Little did they realize what he had just witnessed.

How it came about

Prior to attending the October 1995 COPA Conference in Washington, D.C., I spoke with fellow UK researchers to ask if there was anything they would like me to bring back; books, videos, etc. The usual "shopping list" was compiled but I was a little surprised by a request from my good friend and fellow Londoner, Rob Shaw.

Rob told me that his wife Sharon was into her second year of tuition and training to become a signer (English Sign Language). She had done very well in her first year and had come top of her class. Totally without Sharon's knowledge, Rob asked me if I could find Gallaudet University in Washington. He explained that it is the world's leading university for the deaf and that it would give Sharon a thrill if I could bring her back a Gallaudet T-shirt and perhaps some other souvenir items. This I agreed to do.

In Washington, D.C.

On arrival in Washington for the conference, I quickly established the location of Gallaudet. I found it to be situated on Florida Avenue, on the south-eastern outskirts of the city. It did not appear to be particularly well-served by Washington's magnificent metro system and it seemed that a cab would be the only way to reach it.

With several fellow British researchers, I played the tourist for a few days and then attended the conference. Our sight-seeing itinerary included the usual places like the White House, the Pentagon, Arlington National Cemetery and Ford's Theatre but not, alas, Gallaudet University.

I was the last of our group to leave Washington. However, I had planned my final day, Tuesday 24th October, meticulously. I did not need to be at Washington National Airport for my flight home *via* New York until mid-afternoon so I had the entire morning to myself. This was my chance to visit Gallaudet. I took a cab from the Omni Shoreham Hotel and within 25 minutes I was at the entrance to the university.

A frightening experience

Walking through the gates I found myself confronted not by one enormous building but by a vast complex of building of various shapes and sizes. I knew that I needed to locate the Visitors' Center but I had no idea where it was. The university grounds were very pleasant in appearance and atmosphere. There was space, there were trees, there were well-cultivated grassy areas and there were students everywhere. They were strolling, they were sitting, they were going about their normal business—and they were all totally silent.

I was completely out of my normal environment. Within just a few yards of a busy main road, I suddenly found myself in an alien situation. Where was the Visitors' Center? How could I find it? Who could I ask? It was a frightening experience.

Within a few seconds I had entered the equivalent of Ed Hoffman's world. For me, however, it was not a case of being a deaf mute in a hearing and speaking world. No; here I was the person with the powers of speech and hearing who was in a world of signing. There were no obvious sounds apart from footsteps on the paths and the occasional closing of a door. I walked along a few of the university roads and paths, looking for the Visitors' Center.

At one point I came across a workman painting a door. Thinking (hoping!) that he may be an outside contractor with the power of speech, I approached him and asked for directions. To my horror, he did not respond. He did, however, realize my problem and we were able to correspond using a notepad I had with me. He was very helpful and pointed out the building I required. I think he was pleased when I was able to sign my thanks in a way I have learnt from Ed Hoffman.

I followed my saviour's directions and soon found the Visitors' Center. Here I made the acquaintance of a charming lady who told me (yes—*told* me) that I needed the University Bookshop for T-shirts and souvenirs. I stressed how relieved I was to have met somebody who could actually speak with me and I am sure she smiled slightly when I told her of my difficulties in the preceding few minutes.

Following her directions, I went to the Bookshop. It was situated in the basement of a large building and it had a wide selection of souvenirs for sale. I selected a suitable T-shirt for Sharon Shaw, together with a few more items, and then proceeded to the cash desk. Once again I found myself in a different world, confronted by a very pleasant young man who did not have the power of speech. He was perfectly accustomed to dealing with people like me, however, and he quickly put me at my ease. My experience of communicating with Ed Hoffman served me well and we were able to make our wishes known to one another.

NOW *YOU* GO AND DO IT!

I made my way out of Gallaudet University a far more humble man than the one who had entered an hour or so earlier. For the first time, I had some real idea of the situation in which Virgil Edward Hoffman had found himself on Friday 22nd November 1963. It is all too easy for the doubters to say that he could have written down what he had seen. It isn't like that at all. You are totally disorientated, confused and helpless. Even being a member of the silent world for all but the first four years of his life would not have been an advantage in Dealey Plaza that afternoon.

If you do not believe me, I urge you to pay a visit to Gallaudet University the next time you are in Washington, D.C. For a few dollars in cab fares and an hour or two of your time, you will learn a great deal about one of the most maligned eyewitnesses in this whole affair. Perhaps you will go there as a sceptic concerning Ed Hoffman's story. I am sure that you will think differently when you leave the university grounds and return to the comfort and reassurance of your own speaking and hearing world.

ADDENDUM

On completion of this paper, I submitted it to the Rev Ron Friedrich, Ed Hoffman's minister and signer. Ron was appreciative of my efforts to convey my feelings on entering Ed's world but he added something I had not realized. During my brief visit to Gallaudet I had encountered only people who were perfectly happy to give me their time. They had tried to help me and had willingly given me their full attention. Ed's difficulties following the assassination were made even harder due to the fact that people were in a state of shock and did not have the patience to give due attention to a deaf mute. (Ed Hoffman, along with Ron Friedrich, wrote, with excellent diagrams, Ed's story, *Eyewitness*, JFK Lancer 1997.)

Written 1996.
Published September/October 1998 on internet website *Fair Play*, no. 24.
Previously unpublished as hard copy.

PART 2: THE LESSER-KNOWN WITNESSES

6. Samuel Paternostro—the witness whose ears may have told him more than his eyes

INTRODUCTION

Samuel Burton Paternostro seems to have become one of the forgotten witnesses to the assassination of President John F. Kennedy. His is not a name that springs readily to mind like those of Howard Brennan, Jean Hill or Abraham Zapruder, when the events of Friday 22nd November 1963 are discussed. I find this strange since Paternostro viewed the event from a perfect and unobstructed elevated vantage point and he appears to have been a totally honest and credible witness. There is even a somewhat vague and uncorroborated report that he saw a rifle pointing out of one of the windows of the Texas School Book Depository at the time of the assassination.

You will search in vain for this gentleman's name in the Warren Commission Report and it appears only twice in the 26 Volumes of Hearings and Exhibits. These appearances, however, seem to be significant and they constitute the basis of this short analysis. Samuel Paternostro's first appearance comes in the form of a very brief Dallas FBI report of an interview with Deputy District Court Clerk Arthur Stevens conducted on 9th January 1964.[1] The second appearance is in another Dallas FBI report, this one dated 20th January 1964, recorded by Special Agent Arthur E. Carter. [2]

WHO WAS SAMUEL BURTON PATERNOSTRO?

Sam Paternostro lived in Cridelle Place, off Harry Hines Boulevard, just north of Love Field. He was an Assistant District Attorney employed by Dallas County and his office was in the Dallas County Records Building on Houston Street, overlooking Dealey Plaza. I have been unable to establish details of his age, length of service, duties, etc., but as an Assistant DA he was obviously no fool.

PATERNOSTRO AS AN ASSASSINATION WITNESS

According to the later of the two FBI reports, that dated 20th January 1964, Sam Paternostro had viewed the presidential motorcade from Criminal District Courtroom No. 2 on the second floor of the Dallas County Criminal Courts Building. He was in the company of Mrs Ruth Thornton, a Deputy District Clerk in Criminal District Court No. 4. This is not in doubt as it is confirmed in a second report, also recorded by SA Carter that day, in which the subject is Mrs Thornton.

The FBI report on Paternostro stated that he "believed that a police officer. E. R. Gaddy was possibly present." In her own FBI interview of 20th January 1964, however, Mr. Thornton, failed to confirm this. The FBI report of that interview [3] stated that "she said the only person she recalled that was present while she was watching the shooting of the President was Sam Paternostro."

Mrs Thornton also described how she moved her position within the building to follow the progress of the motorcade as it turned from Main Street on to Houston Street. "She said she was looking out of a window on the Main Street side of the building and then walked over to a window on the Houston Street side, as the Presidential car drove toward the triple overpass." Although neither he nor Mrs Thornton mentions it, I feel it is logical to assume that Paternostro would have done likewise.

Dallas Police Department records indicate that during November 1963, Detective Elmo R. Gaddy was on special assignment to the District Attorney's Office [4] so it is possible that Paternostro knew him. I am happy to accept that Paternostro made a genuine and innocent mistake here.

SA Carter's FBI report on Sam Paternostro consists of five paragraphs, the first two of which deal with his recollections of the assassination. The first paragraph closes thus:

> "... he and Mrs. Thornton were watching the Presidential car and they heard a report or shot which he believed came from the Texas School Book Depository (TSBD) building or the Criminal Courts Building or the triple underpass."

It is obvious that this belief of Paternostro should have been examined under sensible follow-up questioning from SA Carter. That, however, does not appear to have happened and it was left in that precarious and inexplicable position. Surely Paternostro must have had a better appreciation of where that first shot had emanated. A quick glance at a basic plan of the layout and buildings of Dealey Plaza is enough to indicate that he cannot seriously name those three locations as being equally likely sources of that first shot. One of the three was actually the building in which he was positioned at the time. It is significant that he never mentioned echoes or other reverberations. We must not lose sight of the fact that Paternostro was describing only the *first* shot here.

Unfortunately, Paternostro's companion, Mrs Thornton, was not asked her opinion of the source of that shot, or of any later shots. Five other people who witnessed the assassination from the second floor of the same building were also spared this question although they, too, were the subjects of FBI interviews and reports in January 1964. [5]

Paternostro estimated that there was a time gap of four or five seconds between the first shot he heard and the second and third reports. He ventured no opinion on the source or sources of those subsequent shots. He described how he had observed the President grab his head after the first shot and then fall against Mrs Kennedy and into the rear of the vehicle after the following shots.

The report went on to state that Sam Paternostro said that he did not observe any person or persons in the window of the Texas School Book Depository building. It also said that "he doubted that he could have seen anyone in the window where the alleged assassin was reported to have fired the shots from." This is interesting since from the second floor of his building he should have had a far better view into that TSBD window than Howard Leslie Brennan, who was at street level. Brennan of course, claimed to have seen so much. Paternostro's remark gains even more significance when we later consider what was to follow in the second FBI report.

THE IMPORTANT QUESTION THE FBI FAILED TO ASK

The third paragraph of that first FBI report stated that Paternostro knew nothing more about the assassination, that he had discussed the fact that he had viewed the parade with Arthur Stevens (Deputy District Court Clerk), and importantly, that he had not been interviewed by FBI agents.

The final two paragraphs are a little confusing and are worth quoting *verbatim*:

"Mr. Paternostro advised he has never known Lee Harvey Oswald or Jack Ruby personally. He does know Ruby when he sees him and has spoken to him personally but has no knowledge concerning Ruby's background.

He said he knew of no association between Lee Harvey Oswald and Jack Ruby."

It was almost standard FBI practice to close all eyewitness interviews by asking if the witness knew Oswald or Ruby. Here, the witness does mention a minor link with Ruby but SA Carter, conducting the interview, apparently failed to recognize it. It is both surprising and frustrating in this instance that the report contains nothing to explain just when and why Paternostro had spoken to Ruby personally.

THE SECOND FBI REPORT—AND AN UNEXPLAINED CLAIM

Apart from Paternostro's vague multiple choice opinion of the source of the first shot, and his strange remark about his acquaintance with Jack Ruby, he does not really appear to have offered anything particularly significant to the investigation. That is hardly the case when we consider the contents of the second FBI report mentioned in the Introduction to this paper. [6]

It is a record of an interview of the aforementioned Arthur Stevens by Special Agent George T. Binney, conducted in Dallas on 9th January 1964. Note that this was 11 days *prior to* SA Carter's report upon which I have relied above.

SA Binney's report consists of just one sentence:

"On January 9, 1964, Arthur Stevens, Deputy District Court Clerk, Dallas County District Court, 505 Main Street, advised SA George T. Binney that he had received information that the Assistant District Attorney of Dallas, Texas, Sam Paternostro, had seen a rifle protruding from a window in the Texas School Book Depository building on November 22, 1963, at the time President Kennedy was assassinated."

Three immediate questions present themselves:

(1) Why was this not mentioned in the second FBI report in which Sam Paternostro specifically denied knowing for certain where the shots had originated?

(2) What was the source of the information concerning Paternostro's sighting of this rifle?

(3) If Paternostro had really seen a rifle under these circumstances why is this not mentioned anywhere other than in this obscure and insignificant little report which is hidden away, almost unnoticed, in the depths of Volume 24 of the 26 Volumes?

CONCLUSION

As stated in the Introduction, I have no reason to doubt Samuel Paternostro's veracity or reliability. However, he does appear to have been uncertain of several important aspects in all this. I find his reported opinion of the source of the first shot almost unbelievable. The uncorroborated report of him seeing a rifle in the window of the TSBD appears to be highly suspicious. It is also odd that neither the position of the window nor its floor is indicated.

I find myself repeatedly asking why this man was not questioned more thoroughly by the FBI. Furthermore, like the other eyewitnesses in the County Courts Building, [7] he was never asked to testify before the Warren Commission. As already stated he had a perfect and unobstructed view of the assassination. Is the fact that he would not say positively that he heard shots from the Texas School Book Depository the reason for these strange omissions on the part of the official investigators?

Despite an extensive search for more information on this alleged sighting of a rifle by Sam Paternostro, I am unable to find anything to either confirm or deny it.

The more I think about it, the more I am suspicious of the third-hand and unattributed report that Paternostro had seen a rifle in a window of the book depository. Like so much in this case, it just does not hang together as it should.

Notes

1. CE 1998 (FBI report of interview conducted on January 9, 1964 of Arthur Stevens at Dallas, Tex.)
2. CE 2106 (FBI report dated January 20, 1964, of interview of Samuel Burton Paternostro at Dallas, Tex.)
3. CE 2107 (FBI report dated January 20, 1964, of interview of Mrs. W. L. "Jack" Thornton (Ruth Thornton) at Dallas, Tex.)
4. Details of the duty of Detective Gaddy can be found in Batchelor Exhibit No. 5002, page 28 of exhibit (12H 145)
5. CE 2098 (Deputy District Court Clerk Mrs Lillian Mooneyham)
   CE 2099 (Deputy District Court Clerk Robert Reid)
   CE 2100 (Deputy District Court Clerk Mrs Rose Clark)
   CE 2101 (Deputy District Court Clerk Mrs Jeannette E. Hooker)
   CE2103 (Deputy District Court Clerk Cecil Ault)
6. As (1) above.
7. Mrs Ruth Thornton and the five people mentioned in (5) above.

Written 1996.

First published March 1997 on the internet website *JFK - Voice of Reason*, issue 1. Later published November 1999 in *The Dealey Plaza Echo* vol. 6, no. 1.

7. Which side would have called
Ronald B. Fischer and Robert E. Edwards?

INTRODUCTION

As a result of the televised coverage of the O. J. Simpson trial (1994/ 95), many of us became familiar with the appearance and testimony of a rather strange character called Brian 'Kato' Kaelin. This aspiring actor ('aspiring' for several years) had been a close friend of both victim Nicole Brown Simpson and accused Oranthal James Simpson. It was debatable which side, the prosecution or the defence, would call Kaelin to appear for them during the criminal trial. In the event, he was called by the prosecution. His evidence, however, seemed to be of equal value to the defence.

I feel that Ronald B. Fischer and Robert Edwin Edwards would have proved similarly valuable to both prosecution and defence if Lee Harvey Oswald had lived long enough to be allowed his day in court.

Fischer and Edwards were eyewitnesses to the assassination of President John Kennedy in Dealey Plaza, Dallas on 22nd November 1963 and were thus of considerable importance. However we need to examine exactly what they saw, or what they said they saw, in order to judge what their individual value may have been in a court trial, for whichever side they may have appeared.

WHO WAS RONALD B. FISCHER?

Ronald B. Fischer was 25 years old when the assassination took place. He lived with his wife and two children in the Dallas suburb of Mesquite and had been employed by the Dallas County Auditor's Office as an auditor for five years. His office was situated in the Dallas County Records Building, overlooking Dealey Plaza. A well-educated man, he had completed his high school education and then taken courses towards an accounting degree at Arlington State College. This man was no fool.

Dealey Plaza

On the day of the presidential visit, Fischer and a friend, fellow Auditor's Office worker Robert Edwin Edwards, had lunch at 11.45am. A few minutes later, with the permission of their supervisor, Mr Lynn, they left the building and went down to street level to watch the presidential motorcade when it passed by. At around 12.05pm or 12.10pm, they took up positions just outside the combined Records and Courthouse building on Main Street. They then realized that they would have a better view of the motorcade a little further along Houston Street and at 12.20pm they found a more suitable vantage point on the kerb on the southwest corner of Houston Street and Elm Street. This would have put them just a few feet to the right of Howard Brennan.

A few seconds before the first car in the motorcade turned on to Houston Street, Edwards drew Fischer's attention to a man in the window of the east corner of the south side of the sixth floor of the Texas School Book Depository.

The man in the window

According to Fischer's Warren Commission testimony, the man "held my attention ... because he appeared uncomfortable ... and ... he didn't look like he was watching for the parade. He looked like he was looking toward the Trinity River and the triple underpass ... toward the end of Elm Street."

Fischer then provided a thorough description of what this man was wearing:

> "I could see from about the middle of his chest past the top of his head ... He seemed to be sitting a little forward ... he had on an open-neck shirt, but it could have been a sport shirt or a T-shirt. It was light in color; probably white, I couldn't tell whether it had long sleeves or whether it was a short-sleeved shirt, but it was open-neck and light in color."

He then went on to describe the man's personal appearance:

> "He had a slender face and neck ... and he had a light complexion ... he was a white man. And he looked to be 22 or 24 years old ... His hair seemed to be neither light nor dark ... well, it was brown ... but as to whether it was light or dark, I can't say. He couldn't have had very long hair because his hair didn't seem to take up much space—of what I could see of his head. His hair must have been short and not long."

Remarkably detailed as this description was, and remember this was over five months after the event, Fischer went even further when Warren Commission Assistant Counsel David W. Belin asked him whether he had seen the man full-face or in profile. Fischer said: "I saw it at an angle but at the same time I believe I could see the tip of his right cheek as he looked to my left."

On Monday 25th November 1963, a mere three days after the assassination, Fischer had been visited at his home by Dallas Homicide Detectives Walter Potts and Fay Turner, who showed him a photograph of the deceased Lee Harvey Oswald. According to Detective Potts' subsequent report: "He would not say definitely it was the man he saw, but he stated it looked like him." (Potts Exhibit B).

Fischer conceded that he had not seen the man's hands and so was unaware whether he was holding anything. He saw nobody with the man, but observed: "There were boxes and cases stacked all the way from the bottom to the top and from the left to the right behind him."

Fischer's attention had next been attracted to the presidential limousine and he watched it pass in front of him. After it had made the wide turn from Houston Street on to Elm Street, he was watching the following cars when he heard a shot. Like many other witnesses, he likened this first shot to a firecracker. He then described two further shots and made a strange remark in his testimony: "At first, I thought there were four, but as I think about it more, there must have been just three." Is this an example of a witness being subconsciously influenced later by outside factors and unintentionally introducing his own doubt to what he has actually seen?

CORROBORATION BY ROBERT EDWIN EDWARDS

Edwards was employed by the Dallas Court Auditor's Office on a temporary basis. He was actually in his final year as a student at Northeastern State College, Oklahoma. He was working as a utility clerk in the same office as Fischer. In his Warren Commission testimony, he confirmed Fischer's account of them standing together on the corner of Houston and Elm, facing the book depository, and he described seeing "one individual who was up there in the corner of the sixth floor which was crowded with boxes."

His description of this man was almost identical to that given by Fischer. He described a white man, neither tall nor short, wearing a light-coloured, short-sleeved open-neck shirt, average build (possibly thin), light brown hair. Like Fischer, Edwards had seen the man from the waist up but had not observed his hands and could not say whether he was holding anything.

As Mr Belin carefully led Edwards through his testimony, the witness produced what has become one of the most incredible answers to any question in the entire investigation. It is also one of the most frequently quoted. This has to be seen in print to be believed:

BELIN: "How many shots did you hear, if you remember?"

EDWARDS: "Well, I heard one more than was fired, I believe."

It is not often appreciated that probably no more than half an hour separated this amazing answer from Fischer's "At first I thought there were four ..." reply as described above. (Both Fischer and Edwards were examined by Mr Belin in Dallas on 1st April 1964, Edwards beginning at 11.00am, Fischer following at 11.20am.)

To his credit, Mr Belin refused to allow this totally unexpected answer to throw him off balance and he referred to Edwards' affidavit in an attempt to retrieve the situation. This, however, served only to weaken his position because in his affidavit, made on the afternoon of the assassination, Edwards had also claimed to have heard four shots. Furthermore, he had said that he saw the man on the *fifth* floor of the book depository.

DIRECTION OF THE SHOTS

Despite the obvious difficulty with Robert Edwards' confused statement concerning the number of shots he heard, the foregoing evidence and testimony of both Fischer and Edwards would doubtless have been of value to the prosecution in any *People v. Oswald* trial. However, let us look a little deeper and a little longer at what else these two men had to say. Perhaps what follows may have been enough to dissuade the prosecution from calling either of them. Perhaps it would have tempted the defence to use them instead—despite the description of the man in the window which fitted Lee Harvey Oswald like a glove (no O. J. Simpson trial reference intended!).

Both Fischer and Edwards described hearing shots; three (but originally four) in Fischer's case and four in Edwards' case.

In his Warren Commission testimony, Ronald Fischer was asked by Mr Belin: "Where did the shots appear to be coming from?" Fischer replied: "They appeared to be coming from just west of the School Book Depository Building. There were some railroad tracks and there were some railroad cars back in there." Mr Belin continued: And they appeared to be coming from these railroad cars?" to which Fischer replied: "Well, that area somewhere."

Fischer then went on to describe how he and Edwards had run down Elm Street, past a family lying on the ground, obviously the Newmans, and then "up to the top of the hill where all the Secret Service men had run, thinking that that's where the bullets had come from since they seemed to be searching the area over there."

With those answers and opinions, Ronald B. Fischer suddenly ceases to be a star prosecution witness able to positively identify Lee Harvey Oswald as the lone gunman in the sixth floor window. Instead, he becomes a potentially damaging witness who will tell the court that the shots did not come from the Texas School Book Depository at all.

In the case of Robert Edwards, as if enough damage had not been caused by his "one more shot than was fired" comment, he replied "I have no idea" when asked by Mr Belin where he thought the shots had originated. Mr Belin pointed out to him that in his affidavit of 22nd November 1963 he had stated that the shots had come from "the building there"—meaning the TSBD. Edwards reply to that was straight to the point:

"No; I didn't say that."

Needless to say, those words *do* appear in Edwards' affidavit. Perhaps we should now question why. It almost goes without saying that Mr Belin did not follow up that line of questioning.

Like his friend and colleague Ronald B. Fischer, Robert Edwin Edwards could hardly be described as a reliable prosecution witness and it is a near certainty that he too would never have been called to testify in court against Oswald.

CONCLUSIONS TO BE DRAWN

It seems irrefutable that both men saw a figure in one of the book depository windows, probably on the sixth floor. Their descriptions of this man match one another and are also very close to describing Oswald. There, however, any value that Fischer and Edwards may have had to the prosecution comes to an end.

On the defence side, neither man could (or would) swear to the shots being fired from that window. Indeed, in Fischer's case, he would say that the shots came from the grassy knoll/triple underpass direction.

Neither man would have made a suitable or safe witness for either the prosecution or the defence. In *The People v. Lee Harvey Oswald*, his fictionalized study of the trial that never was, Walt Brown includes both Fischer and Edwards in a list of 'witnesses who were subpoenaed but never called.' I wonder if Dr Brown has taken an easy option here. I am certain that had either or both of these eyewitnesses appeared at Lee Harvey Oswald's trial, we would have been treated to a similar spectacle to that presented by the charismatic Mr

Kaelin in the O. J. Simpson trial. It would have been fascinating to watch, but possibly damaging to both sides.

Postscript to Ronald Fischer's affidavit/testimony

At the end of Fischer's affidavit, a very strange remark appears which I do not believe has ever been properly investigated. He said:

> "I do remember one particular thing that happened just at the time I saw the man up there. There was a girl walked in the Texas School Book Depository Building, a rather tall girl, and looked to me like she might be an employee of that building. She was walking in while everybody else had been coming out."

That, as they say, is another story. Perhaps someone, somewhere, can throw some light on it and perhaps put a name to this female and suggest what she was doing.

Sources

Since almost all the above information is readily available to researchers I have not included specific footnotes.

Fischer's Warren Commission testimony is at 6H 191-200. His affidavit appears as Fischer Exhibit No. 1 at 19H 650.

Edwards' Warren Commission testimony is at 6H 200-205 and his affidavit appears as Edwards Exhibit A at 19H 746.

Written 1995.
First published December 1995 in *Kennedy Assassination Chronicles*, vol. 1, issue 4.

8. An interview with Johnny Calvin Brewer

HOW IT CAME ABOUT

On Monday 25th November 1996, as a result of my friend the late Mike Blackwell acting as the middleman, I had the opportunity to meet and interview Johnny Calvin Brewer. Like most researchers, I knew Brewer as the shoe store manager who had seen Lee Harvey Oswald acting suspiciously on West Jefferson Boulevard, Oak Cliff, and then ducking into the Texas Theatre a matter of minutes after the shooting of Patrolman J. D. Tippit.

The 45-minute interview was held at Johnny Brewer's house in a pleasant part of Austin, Texas. American researchers Mike Blackwell, Richard Bartholomew and Mark Rowe were also present. Brewer had no objection to the interview being recorded on audio-tape and it soon became obvious that he had anticipated some of the areas of the case in which I was particularly interested.

What follows is a greatly shortened transcript of the interview. I have concentrated here only on the part Brewer played in the build-up to the arrest of Oswald. In addition to that, he also revealed that he had lived in the same apartment block complex as Carousel Club stripper Kathy Kay. He had known her and her two young daughters, Susan and Sheri. [1]

THE INTERVIEW

ILG: Right, John, if you would just begin please by telling me how old you were when the assassination of President Kennedy took place.

JCB: Twenty-two. September 17th 1941 I was born.

ILG: Now you worked at Hardy's shoe store at 213 West Jefferson. What was your position there?

JCB: Madashnager.

ILG: So you were in overall control of that shop?

JCB: Right.

ILG: How long had you been there—doing that job?

JCB: Probably since August of '62.

ILG: To your knowledge, was Lee Harvey Oswald ever one of your customers?

JCB: Yes, he was.

ILG: So that obviously means that you'd seen him in the shop?

JCB: At the time that I saw him at the theatre, I knew I had seen this guy before—and possibly that's why he got my attention. Not the main reason he got my attention. I did not place him until, I don't know, it may have been a month before. I could even tell you the shoe that he bought. It was a two-eyelet, crepe-soled shoe, model 8110, size eight and a half. [2]

ILG: Robert Groden has said—and I don't know the source for this—that Oswald once entered your shop, tried on almost every shoe in the place and left without buying anything. Is there any truth in that?

JCB: No. He bought. He was very fastidious and meticulous—or just a jerk. I'm not quite sure which.

ILG: And there was just this one occasion?

JCB: Just on the one occasion. Like I say, I didn't have a clue who he was—just a sale. Certain customers stand out in your mind and you try to avoid them next time you see them coming. He was a pain in the butt.

ILG: So there was something about him?

JCB: Oh sure—yeah.

ILG: Did he pay cash money—a normal sale?

JCB: A normal transaction, yes.

ILG: How long before the assassination was that, John? Can you remember?

JCB: That I cannot remember. I do not know. It was probably only a matter of weeks—but again it could have been months. I'm not sure. I don't know. I can only place him as a customer who bought this model 8110 black, two-eyelet, crepe-soled shoe for five dollars and seventy cents. [3]

ILG: Okay, let's get on to the day itself, 22nd November 1963. You were at work in the shop that day. How did you initially hear about the shooting of Kennedy?

JCB: I was listening to a radio broadcast on a portable radio I had.

ILG: I know this is a crazy question but is there any way of recalling which programme, which station, you were listening to?

JCB: A Dallas station. I have a feeling it may have been KLIF. That would be one of the stations I would ordinarily be listening to, but I honestly don't know. It was just the normal run of the motorcade and all of a sudden you hear all the commotion and then you hear something about shots being fired and then, you know.

ILG: So it was actually being broadcast live. I see. What about Tippit's murder?

JCB: I also—now that was just a few blocks away. But I'd heard there was a shooting in the Oak Cliff area. Now they didn't say anything about who it was. I don't recall that it was said that there was a policeman down, or what, but I do recall hearing something about a shooting in the Oak Cliff area. And just very shortly after that, the sirens of the cars all converging on Zangs and Jefferson or just going towards it.

ILG: So you're interested, obviously, because it's close to your location.

JCB: Oh yeah, yeah. But never connecting what happened here to downtown.

ILG: Now, this is difficult. Can you remember when you heard about the Tippit killing—the shooting of the policeman?

JCB: I never really thought about it.

ILG: But at the time, there was no connection between Kennedy and Tippit?

JCB: Not that I knew.

ILG: Fine. Was there, if you can recall, any description of the suspect in either of these killings given out on the radio?

JCB: In the shooting, I'm pretty sure it was the shooting, a description of the shooter. You know, it was—I don't recall if they said white or black. But I do recall a male, five feet nine, medium size build. There was no description of a shirt or jacket.

ILG: I understand. Now I know the layout of the shop—the way the door was recessed and the display panels on the sides. Now your counter—your location—would that be facing the door or on the side?

JCB: As you face the door, if you were outside facing into my store, I would have been on the left just as you open the door. There were two swing doors, I recall. On the left, there was a counter that was running parallel to the showcase windows. And then there was a centre aisle with the chairs. And the whatnots and the hose and socks and whatnot were behind the polished mahogany counter. It was running parallel with the left-hand windows as you're facing in.

ILG: So you would be there, listening to the radio and you have got a view of the door and the street through it.

JCB: Oh yeah. There's the door right there. I have a full view of the front.

ILG: Now we're obviously leading up to your view of this man acting strangely. When this happened, John, were you in the shop by yourself?

JCB: There were two other men in there. They were from IBM—they were in the neighbourhood. I had known them ever since I came there. [4]

ILG: Customers?

JCB: No, they weren't customers. They'd just come in and kill time and lounge around.

ILG: Right. Were there any other salesmen in the shop apart from yourself?

JCB: No, there were not. In fact I had planned to be off that day—except that my assistant called me in. His newborn was ill. I had just taken delivery of a brand new '64 Galaxy CL500 Ford and I had no intention of being at work that day. And it was parked out in front of the store and I was feeding nickels to it all day long, just waiting to get off. And they just stood around and talked, the IBM men.

ILG: Now your attention is alerted to this character who is acting furtively in your doorway as the police cars are going by. Am I correct in that?

JCB: Of course my attention is drawn out because of the sirens of the police cars going by. And knowing of the shooting in the area. And I was actually on my way to come out from behind the counter and go outside, to watch out and see what was going on when this fellow entered from my left as I'm standing there.

ILG: Ah—now that's important because I've never seen anywhere, in any book, which direction he's come from.

JCB: He's come from the Zangs Boulevard direction, which is the intersection. He walked into the recessed area and stood—and we were looking at each other. And actually, I was a little annoyed because I thought it was someone coming in as I was fixing to go out. And then when the police had gone by he looked over his shoulder and then walked out on to the sidewalk again, looked, and then walked quickly but calmly—and I stood there, it couldn't have been more than five seconds.

ILG: And he's walking in which direction now?

JCB: Towards the theatre.

ILG: In your testimony, you said he looked funny. Those were the actual words you used. Can you expand on that at all? Looked funny in what way?

JCB: Well he obviously wasn't looking for shoes.

ILG: When you left the shop to see what this chap was doing, did you mention anything to the other two fellows who were in the shop?

JCB: Oh yes, I think I said something. And I walked out on to the sidewalk. Are you familiar with the furniture store?

ILG: Yes. Thomsen's. I know where that was. [5]

JCB: And he was right in that area when I picked up again and saw him.

ILG: Now you were suspicious of him because of his appearance and the fact that he'd been in the recess of your shop for what appeared to be reasons of concealment. Is that correct?

JCB: Well, and also, why wasn't he interested in all the police cars going by as everyone else was? Everyone was out on the street looking. Like right now, if a police car came by, we'd all be out there looking. That's the way it is. So that kinda struck me as odd.

ILG: So that's why you stepped out of the store and looked—and he's walking down and he's by Thomsen's and he's still walking.

JCB: Uh huh.

ILG: Okay. Now I understand he then entered the Texas Theatre.

JCB: Right. I saw him go in. [6]

ILG: Okay. From your vantage point could you see that he went in without buying a ticket?

JCB: Well, you could see the cashier's booth which was out on the sidewalk. I didn't really know for sure whether he bought a ticket or not. I saw him walk in and that's when I went back and—I can't remember either of their names—but one of them closed up for me while I was gone. When I came back, the store was locked. I said I'm going to check.

ILG: You got a feeling all was not right?

JCB: Right. So they stayed there and I walked up, all the time thinking what am I doing here? And I saw Julie ... [7]

ILG: Now you knew Julia Postal, didn't you? What did you say to her?

JCB: I said 'Julie, did you sell a ticket ...?' and I gave her a description of the guy. She said no, she hadn't. She'd been out on the street watching. And I said 'Julie, I'm gonna go inside and see if I can see him—there's something funny.'

ILG: You went in and saw someone, didn't you?

JCB: Yes, as I walked inside. Butch Burroughs, he was the concessionaire and ticket taker and whatever else, and I asked Butch if he had seen anybody in the theatre and he said no, but he had been down behind the counter, stocking concessions and whatever. He had not seen anybody. And I said 'Butch, come with me' and we went up into the balcony. And using the screen as a backlight we could see that there were no heads up there.

ILG: So the balcony was totally empty?

JCB: Yes.

ILG: Okay, in your affidavit on December 6th —two weeks later—you said that you and Butch checked the exits to see if any of them had been opened. Now can you describe to me exactly what you did, and why. [(8)]

JCB: Well first of all, I walked all the way down the left aisle and just kinda looked for somebody who looked like him but I still didn't see anybody so I walked behind the curtain—there was a curtain there—to the left of the stage and it was a fire exit and if anybody leaves by a fire exit, it has to be reset.

ILG: You push a bar to open it, don't you?

JCB: Right. It has to be reset. But it was still locked. Nobody had gone out. So I walked back up to the other side and walked out and I said to Julie "Call the police" and I said "Butch, you stay here out front and if anybody matching his description leaves, then stop them. I'm gonna go back to the back and the exit out on to the alley."

ILG: Were they the only entry and exit points, John? The front entrance and this one fire escape door by the stage. They're the only ways out of the place?

JCB: Yes, out of the building.

ILG: So Butch stayed at the front entrance and you were at the back, down by the stage. Is that right?

JCB: I don't know exactly where Butch was. I just told him to stay outside and I would go to the back.

ILG: So you'd asked Julie to contact the police and tell them what?

JCB: Just that there was a suspicious person in there. I still had no reason to have somebody call the police. I'm not sure what the hell I was doing here to start with.

ILG: I've read her testimony and she explains that she rang the police station. She initially spoke to a woman and that lady put her on to a man and she told him there was a suspicious man there and would they come down. Now I understand that you let a lot of them in through that back door.

JCB: Right.

ILG: Now what happened? Did they bang on the door and say "Police" or were you waiting by the door?

JCB: First of all, before they got to the door, I thought it's dark and I don't see anything. Well they turned the house lights on but the movie's still running. When the house lights came on I looked up at the balcony and I seen the police in already. Plain clothes and uniformed officers. They'd come in the front. And at about that time, I see Oswald. Didn't know who he was at the time. He got up and walked towards the aisle on his right.

ILG: He'd been sitting downstairs?

JCB: Yes, towards the centre.

ILG: And did you recognize him as the man who'd been in the front of your store?

JCB: Right. He got up and he took a couple of steps like he was going to exit and then he sat down again—probably not the same chair he'd occupied. One next to it or the next one. And about that time—and this happened real fast—I hear them knocking on the door. When I opened the door, they grabbed me and pulled me out into the alley and I explained to them that I had seen this man acting suspiciously.

ILG: Can I butt in on one thing here, John? How tall were you then?

JCB: Six three. [9]

ILG: Six three—and we're talking about Oswald who was five nine. So there's not really a possibility that they're mixing you up. I mean you didn't fit the description of the fellow they were looking for, did you? Not at six three.

JCB: No.

ILG: So they grab you, put a gun on you and what did you do? You tell them what?

JCB: Basically, that I'm on your side. The person that you're here for is out there. I knew Officer McDonald. I'd known him for several months.

ILG: These people now, are they all in uniform or are some in plain clothes?

JCB: Some are both.

ILG: So they're a mixture of uniform and plain clothes?

JCB: Right. There were policemen on the fire exit and that. They were all over the place.

ILG: Now, the fellows who actually came in through that door where you were, that was both uniform and plain clothes?

JCB: Well it was uniform men who got up on the stage with me because you get up on the stage from there. Two of them. The first was McDonald. And there were others there but they were all standing back. Nobody was really converging.

ILG: But you actually pointed the man out, didn't you? Can you remember what you said?

JCB: I said 'That's the man—in the brown, in the checkered shirt' or whatever.

ILG: So they converged on him. I think McDonald was the first to get to him, wasn't he?

JCB: McDonald jumped off the stage and another policeman jumped off the stage and I don't know who followed him but they were tapping the patrons on the shoulder—some down the front—and telling them to get up and move. So they were actually clearing it. All the while, Oswald's looking at them and they're getting closer and closer to him.

ILG: Were the house lights up?

JCB: They were on.

ILG: Was the film running or stopped?

JCB: I think by now it was stopped.

ILG: And then there was a bit of a scramble, a bit of a scrap, wasn't there?

JCB: Well, McDonald walked over to Oswald and tapped him and told him to get up. And then, you know, there's a lot of blur and I think I heard Oswald say "It's over now" or something like that. Anyway, he got up and he's trying to hit McDonald and he's knocked him back.

ILG: Was that a fist, a punch?

JCB: Right. And a good one too. McDonald was not a small man. And about that time, he reaches under his shirt and pulls out a pistol. And McDonald is getting back up and lunging for him and Oswald's got the gun. McDonald says he pulled the trigger but I feel I saw the hammer—um, McDonald, I believe, says that the hammer hit the fleshy part of his hand between the firing pin and the hammer. I know he had the gun out there.

ILG: He's trying to shoot McDonald?

JCB: In the head. And then after that he got real excited. There was Oswald and the police falling over the chairs and whatnot and by this time, also, out come more policemen with their guns out and I got down. And as they wrestled the gun from him, I'm looking up. There were several fists thrown in Oswald's direction and he was handcuffed and led out. And they led him out the aisle towards me and we were just a couple of feet apart and he was actually looking at me when he said "I'm not resisting arrest."

ILG: You heard him say that?

JCB: Right.

ILG: Did he say that to you?

JCB: No. He said that in general but he was actually looking at me. I don't know if he kinda recognized me from the shoe store.

ILG: And they took him out through the front entrance on to West Jefferson?

JCB: Yes, and as I was going to leave I was stopped by two FBI or plain clothes and they took my name and address. [10]

ILG: Once that was all finished, John, once they'd arrested Oswald, handcuffed him and taken him outside and spoken to you briefly, what did you do?

JCB: Well he was gone by the time I walked out. The police were all gone— and I walked back to my store.

NOTES

1. These details were of value to me in my separate study of Kathy Kay.

2. These shoes are included in the list of property seized during the search of Oswald's rooming house at 1026 North Beckley on 23rd November 1963. See CE 2003 (page 285 of exhibit) at 24H 343. They are described as 1 Pair man's black low quarter shoes "John Hardy Brand". They are pictured as CE 147 (16H 514) and also appear in the photograph at top right of page 167 of Robert Groden's *The Search for Lee Harvey Oswald*, published by Penguin Studio Books, New York (1995). They are the central of the three pairs of footwear shown. On 10th March 1997, at my request, Mike Blackwell showed a copy of CE 147 to Johnny Calvin Brewer who immediately confirmed that it depicted the shoes he had sold to Oswald.

3. It could perhaps be considered suspicious that Brewer is able to recall this sale in such detail. I am satisfied, however, that there is nothing untoward here. If he were deliberately trying to embellish his account, he would surely not be this vague concerning the date on which it occurred.

4. These two men have not been identified.

5. The Thomsen Furniture Mart occupied the building adjacent to the Texas Theatre. See page 150 of Robert Groden's *The Search for Lee Harvey Oswald*.

6. The proximity of Hardy's shoe store to the Texas Theatre can be judged by the fact that they were numbered 213 and 231 respectively. It must be stressed, however, that during the making of the film *JFK*, Oliver Stone was denied permission to recreate Hardy's at no. 231. In reality, what is shown to be "Hardy's" in *JFK* was four stores closer to the theatre than the true no. 231. (The caption to the picture on page 145 of *The Search for Lee Harvey Oswald* is inaccurate. That photograph actually shows the *JFK* version of Hardy's shoe store rather than the real one.)

7. It was noticeable that Brewer continually referred to Mrs Postal as Julie rather than Julia.

8. Brewer's affidavit is at CE 2003 (Dallas Police Department file on investigation of the assassination of the President), page 14 of exhibit (24H 203).

9. There have been sketchy and uncorroborated claims that a man was seized by the police in the alley outside the rear door of the theatre. I am satisfied that if this did indeed happen (which I doubt), that man was not Brewer. He was much taller and heavier than the suspect whose description had been circulated and could not have been mistaken for him.

10. Since the FBI had nobody talking names in the theatre, it must have been the DPD, presumably detectives since Brewer says they were in plain clothes. Unfortunately, no such list is now known to exist so it appears that either the list was not actually completed—or it has subsequently been lost.

Written 1997.
First published July 1997 in *The Dealey Plaza Echo*, vol. 1, no. 3.

9. The British Female Connection

INTRODUCTION

Whilst the assassination of President Kennedy was apparently a purely *American* affair, it obviously had a profound and lasting effect on the rest of the world. There was not a country on the planet that was not affected in some way. This applied equally to the countries of the 'free' world and to those under Communist or totalitarian influence. As one of the United States' foremost allies, the United Kingdom shared the shock and revulsion of the event more keenly than most.

It is not widely known, however, that various British citizens played important parts in several aspects of the assassination, its aftermath and subsequent investigation. Purely by coincidence, the majority of these people were female. Perhaps that is significant since the UK has been a virtual matriarchy for more than half a century. Our Queen has reigned since 1952 and Margaret Thatcher was our political leader for several years (1979-1990).

There was also a worrying time during the late-90s when it seemed that the country had been taken over by the Spice Girls!

My purpose here is to identify a few of the most significant of those ladies who were embroiled in some way in the Kennedy assassination and to explain briefly the part which each of them played.

I begin with a vital Parkland witness (Nurse Diana Bowron). My second subject is a minor member of the British nobility who was a prominent journalist (Lady Jean Campbell). I then discuss one of Lee Harvey Oswald's fellow passengers on the bus to Mexico City (Mrs Meryl McFarland) and I conclude with a brief look at a British sculptress whose work is a feature of today's Dallas (Dame Elisabeth Frink). (Please see Chapter 20. "Search for a Stripper" for details of the British-born Carousel Club stripper Kathy Kay.)

NURSE DIANA HAMILTON BOWRON

Diana Bowron was a nurse at the emergency room at Parkland Memorial Hospital. She had been born in Yorkshire, was 22 years old and had been in Dallas for just three and a half months at the time of the assassination. She had completed three years and three months nurses' training at Hope Hospital in Salford, England in February 1963. After answering an advertisement in a nursing journal, she had moved to the United States from her home in Buxton, Derbyshire to take up a one-year contract at Parkland in August 1963. [1]

AN INCOMING PATIENT

At the time of the assassination, Nurse Bowron was on duty in the minor medicine and surgery part of the emergency section at Parkland. She responded to an intercom call for nurses to attend at the emergency entrance to deal with an incoming patient. At the time, there was no indication of this patient's identity.

Nurse Bowron hurried to the emergency entrance with a stretcher trolley. A second stretcher trolley was also rushed to the same location. In a report which appeared in the British national press, she said: "I realised who the man in the car was as soon as I saw Jackie Kennedy." [2] She then explained that they had to remove Governor Connally from the car before they could get to the President.

INTO THE TRAUMA ROOM

In her Warren Commission testimony, Nurse Bowron described the President's appearance: "He was moribund—he was lying across Mrs. Kennedy's knee and there seemed to be blood everywhere. When I went around to the other side of the car I saw the condition of his head ... it was very bad, you know ... I just saw one large hole."

She went on to describe how the President was removed from the car: "I helped to lift his head and Mrs. Kennedy pushed me away and lifted his head herself onto the cart and so I went around back to the cart and walked off with it. We ran on with it to the trauma room and she ran beside us." [3]

During the frantic attempts to save President Kennedy's life, Nurse Bowron continued to be heavily involved. Together with Nurse Margaret M. Henchcliffe, she helped to cut away his clothing and to administer intravenous injections. Whilst doing a cutdown on his left arm, Nurse Bowron removed his gold watch as it was in the way. She slipped it into her pocket and forgot about it until the President's body was being removed. She suddenly recalled it and handed it to hospital administrator O. P. Wright.

Together with others in Trauma Room One, Nurse Bowron assisted in giving blood transfusions and she also handed instruments to the doctors who performed the tracheotomy operation. At one stage, she left the room for about five minutes to fetch more blood—this being the only time she was not with Kennedy's body from the time he was removed from the Lincoln to the time he was placed into the coffin.

After President Kennedy had been pronounced dead, Nurse Bowron helped to wash the body and she also assisted in lifting it into the bronze casket which had been brought into the room. [4]

DIRECT CONTACT WITH NURSE BOWRON

In 1992, British researcher Paul Henwood successfully traced Diana Bowron on behalf of Harrison Edward Livingstone. At her specific request, both men agreed never to divulge her present (married) name or her whereabouts, an arrangement that I know has been scrupulously maintained by them both.

In early 1993, Livingstone conducted a series of telephone conversations with Diana Bowron and she also gave written answers to specific questions he sent to her. She indicated that she was certain that the throat wound (which she had first seen before Kennedy was removed from the car) was an entry wound. She also wrote on an autopsy photograph of the President's back: "THIS IS NOT THE BACK I SAW" in capital letters. [5] This comment was prompted by her opinion that the entry wound she had observed was actually lower than that shown in the photograph.

In his 1993 book *Killing The Truth*, Livingstone devotes an entire chapter to Nurse Bowron, describing her as "the nurse who was with the body of President Kennedy almost every moment from the time he was rushed to the hospital, to the time his body was wheeled away." [6]

Yes, she was that important a witness!

LADY JEAN CAMPBELL

When news of the assassination of President Kennedy broke, it was a story of such enormity that journalists from many countries immediately flew to the United States and descended upon the city of Dallas. No self-respecting newspaper, irrespective of its country of origin or political leanings, could afford to lag behind in the race to cover what was obviously one of the major news stories of the century.

One of London's three evening newspapers of the time, *The Evening Standard*, was fortunate in that it had one of its leading news journalists already in the United States where she was its US Political Correspondent, based in New York City. This was Lady Jean Campbell—although she did not use her title in her byline. A granddaughter of Lord Beaverbrook, she was almost certainly the only member of the British nobility to dash to Texas to cover the assassination story. She had also been the third of Norman Mailer's six wives, being married to him from 1962 to early 1963, and had borne him a daughter. [7]

Nor surprisingly, Lady Campbell had difficulty finding accommodation in Dallas when she rushed there from New York. All available hotel space had quickly been snapped up by the hundreds of press people who had converged on the city and got there before her. It is fortunate that she found somewhere suitable in Irving or perhaps her unique part in this case would never have occurred.

Each day, she would drive into Dallas from Irving, her route taking her along East Irving Boulevard. Purely by chance, she noticed that a shop that she passed each day (no. 149) had a prominent sign with the words GUN SHOP in red letters above the door. Knowing that Lee Harvey Oswald had been in the habit of visiting his wife and two daughters in Irving, Lady Campbell surmised that he had also passed this shop. Was it possible, she mused, that he could perhaps have visited it? As she said somewhat dramatically in one of her *Evening Standard* pieces: "I knew that he was as fascinated by guns as some women are by diamonds."

Acting purely on that journalist's hunch, Lady Campbell paid a visit to the shop. The exact date of this visit is difficult to ascertain but she later advised FBI agents that it was "approximately November 27th, 1963" and she added that she was accompanied by Jerry Allen Herald, a photographer employed by the French *Paris-Match* magazine in New York. [8] Although he had arrived in Dallas just over four hours after the assassination, it seems that like Lady Campbell he had failed to find accommodation in Dallas and had also based himself at Irving.

Lady Campbell spoke with the shop's proprietor, Mrs Edith Whitworth, and her close friend, Mrs Gertrude Hunter. To the journalist's surprise, she found that despite the GUN SHOP sign, the establishment sold second-hand furniture rather than firearms. She nevertheless pursued her original line of enquiry and asked Mrs Whitworth if she knew Lee Harvey Oswald. Mrs Whitworth then proceeded to describe her interesting encounter with what was apparently the entire Oswald family (Lee, Marina and their two daughters) a few weeks previously.

She told Lady Campbell that between 2.30pm and 3.00pm on either Wednesday 6th or Thursday 7th November, Oswald had entered the shop together with "his wife, their two or three month old infant and an older daughter about two years of age." Oswald asked if it was a gun shop and enquired where he could get a plunger for a gun. Mrs Whitworth explained to him that it was now a furniture shop and directed him to the Irvington Sports Shop. Mrs Hunter had been present during this incident and she corroborated Mrs Whitworth's account.

After looking around for a few minutes, the Oswalds had left the shop and got into a 1956 or 1957 two-tone blue Ford, Chrysler or Plymouth. Oswald then turned the car around and drove off in the direction of the sports shop. [9]

Lady Campbell later interviewed Mrs Ruth Paine in connection with this alleged sighting of the Oswald family. She said that it was confusing because Mrs Paine "vowed up and down" that Mrs Oswald never went anywhere, either by car or on foot. Mrs Paine was adamant that Mrs Oswald had not been out of the house with her children on either the 6th or 7th of November. [(10)]

Whilst I consider it very fortuitous that this account of the alleged Oswald family visit to the former gun shop should emerge in this fashion, it is by no means certain whether it was the "real" Oswald or an impostor. If it were a deliberate and carefully orchestrated set-up, then it was carried out in exemplary fashion—especially as it also involved an impostor Marina and two impostor children of exactly the same age as the Oswald children. It also represents a valuable example of Lee Harvey Oswald driving a car. [(11)]

In retrospect, it would appear that Lady Jean Campbell's hunch and her subsequent findings perhaps caused more confusion than assistance.

MRS MERYL MCFARLAND

I appreciate that there is a body of opinion which claims that Oswald never made his much-publicised visit to Mexico City in September 1963. For the purposes of this chapter, however, I will ask you to assume that he did.

According to eyewitnesses, Lee Harvey Oswald boarded a Mexico City-bound *Transportes del Norte* bus at Laredo, on the Texas/Mexico border on 25th September 1963. His fellow passengers were a mixed bunch and included two young Australian women, (Pamela Mumford and Patricia Winston), a mysterious Englishman called Albert Osborne, aka John Howard Bowen, who shared a double seat with Oswald [(12)] and an English couple (Dr John Bryan McFarland and his wife Meryl). According to Miss Mumford's Warren Commission testimony, the McFarlands "were travelling down to the Yucatan to study the Indians and their way of life."

Dr and Mrs McFarland were from Liverpool and on 28th May 1964, they attended at the United States Consulate in that city where they made a joint affidavit before Wilfred V. Duke, Consul of the United States. [(13)]

This affidavit is a strange document. It is in a strict Q & A format and there is nothing to indicate which of the McFarlands is answering which question. In reply to Consul Duke's questions, they explained that they had engaged in conversation with Oswald on the bus and he had mentioned that he was "the secretary of the New Orleans branch of the Fair Play for Cuba Organisation, and that he was on his way to Cuba to see Castro if he could." They stated that he had also conversed with the two Australian girls and with "an elderly gentleman who sat in the seat next to him for a time."

In 1995, Liverpool-based researcher David Williams successfully traced

Dr and Mrs McFarland and spoke with them in Liverpool. Dr McFarland was happy to discuss the Mexico City bus incident but his wife was very reluctant to do so. She expressed displeasure and unease when her husband did so. She appeared frightened and gave the impression that she would prefer to forget the whole thing. Unfortunately, Dr McFarland was unable to add anything of significance to what had appeared in their 1964 affidavit.

There is a strange link here with the unsolved 1888 Jack The Ripper murders in London. A recently developed Ripper theory (1993) names a rich Liverpool cotton merchant, James Maybrick, as a possible Ripper suspect. Ironically, Maybrick and his family lived in the same house in the late 1880s as the McFarlands occupied in the early 1960s. [14] The McFarlands no longer live at that address.

DAME ELISABETH JEAN FRINK

This is a name which will, I am sure, be completely unknown to most students of the Kennedy assassination. This lady has, however, left an indelible mark on Dallas.

Those of you who have visited the city of Dallas are aware that there is no Kennedy Square, no Kennedy Boulevard and no Kennedy Tower. All we have in downtown Dallas is the stark and ugly cenotaph known as the Kennedy Memorial. It is located on Main Street, between South Houston Street and South Market Street, directly behind the Old Dallas County Courthouse ('Old Red').

I have to admit here and now that for several years, I was under the mistaken impression that the Kennedy Memorial was the work of the British sculptress Dame Elisabeth Frink. I knew that it had been designed by Philip Johnson, one of the United States' leading sculptors and a friend of the Kennedys but I thought that Dame Elisabeth was responsible for its actual construction in 1970. My error here originated from Dame Elisabeth's obituary in that normally most trustworthy of British newspapers, *The Daily Telegraph*. It was stated therein that she had been responsible for "the Kennedy Memorial in Dallas, Texas" (verbatim quote, including the capital letter M).

Thanks to a friendly and productive exchange of several emails with Sixth Floor Museum Curator Gary Mack in mid-2000, I came to realise that Dame Elisabeth had no connection whatsoever with the downtown Kennedy Memorial. Gary went out of his way to assist me and during my annual November visit to Dallas that year, I spent a very pleasant and instructive hour in his office where he showed me various documents pertaining to the sculpture for which Dame Elisabeth Frink *was* responsible in Dallas. [15]

Hers was an earlier and far more poignant memorial to the slain President. It is situated at what was to have been the scene of JFK's proposed luncheon speech, the Dallas Trade Mart. It takes the form of an eagle and is cast in bronze. I was already aware that one of Dame Elisabeth's most famous works is the eagle lectern in Coventry Cathedral (1962) and I was amazed to learn that she had produced a companion casting of it to commemorate JFK two years later.

The eagle can be found on the west side of the Trade Mart, a few feet from the main front door. It is on a plinth approximately five feet high and is depicted in a challenging standing position with head thrust forward and wings outstretched. Its wingspan is over three feet. At ground level, as part of the extended plinth, there are three horizontal inscriptions.

(a) The main one consists of lines from the English poet William Blake (1757-1827): *"When thou seest an eagle, thou seest a portion of genius. Lift up thy head."*

(b) The second indicates the origin of the eagle: *"Placed in memorial by the friends of President John Fitzgerald Kennedy who awaited his arrival at the Dallas Trade Mart November 22, 1963."*

(c) The third, suitably small and unobtrusive, but a source of immense pride to those of us from across the Atlantic, reads simply: *"The Eagle by Elisabeth Frink of England 1964."*

Appropriately, the dedication service on 12th October 1964 included an address delivered by The Right Reverend Cuthbert Bardsley, the Bishop of Coventry. He unveiled the eagle and dedicated it to the glory of God with these words:

"In the name of God we dedicate this eagle to the glory of God to be a link between two great cities, and to the memory of John Kennedy, a great leader of men.

As the eagle flies over mountains so may the spirit of reconciliation fly over oceans, bringing peace and mutual understanding between many nations.

As Cathedral and commerce are joined together by this same emblem, so may church and state ever work together for the welfare of mankind and the peace of the world.

As the eagle soars into the air so may we believe that the soul of John Kennedy has soared into life and into eternity.

May this eagle point the way to peace, purpose and prosperity for all men everywhere." [16]

Dame Elisabeth Frink was born on 14th November 1930 at Thurlow, Suffolk, England but was of Dutch and German origin. She was the most notable British sculptress of her generation and her work is widely acclaimed throughout the world. Many of her works appear to have been influenced by her family's grim experiences in Europe during World War II. Her most characteristic images of men, animals and birds suggest pent-up power, aggression and violence. A Roman Catholic agnostic, she married three times and bore one son. She was appointed a CBE in 1969 and a DBE in 1981. She died in 1993, aged 62. [17]

NOTES

1. Basic biographical information from 6H 135 (Testimony of Diana Hamilton Bowron) and from Bowron Exhibits 2, 3 and 4 (Copies of articles which appeared in the British newspapers *The Observer*, the *Daily Mail* and the *Daily Mirror* in the days immediately following the assassination). It is noted that there is no Bowron Exhibit 1 mentioned or located in the 26 Volumes. Since there cannot be a '2' without a '1' the obvious questions must be asked – what was Bowron Exhibit 1 and where is it now?
2. Bowron Exhibit 3 (Extract from the *Daily Mail*).
3. 6H 136 (Testimony of Diana Hamilton Bowron).
4. As footnote 1 above.
5. Harrison Edward Livingstone: *Killing The Truth*, published by Carroll & Graf, New York, 1993: first photograph in the photographic section, opposite page 368.
6. ibid, chapter 6 (pages 179-199) "Diana Bowron".
7. Biographical information from *Who's Who*, UK, 1996 edition.
8. CE 1335 and CE1337 (New York and New Orleans FBI reports of interviews with Lady Jean Campbell and Jerry Allen Herald on 7th and 18th July 1964 respectively).
9. 11H 253-292 (Individual and joint testimony of Mrs Gertrude Hunter, Mrs Edith Whitworth and Mrs Marina Oswald) and *The Evening Standard* (London), 29th November 1963 edition. Also FBI Memorandum from C. D. DeLoach to Mr. Mohr, dated 6th December 1963 (copy in author's possession).
10. FBI Memorandum as in footnote 9 above, page 2.

11. See Chapter 12."Oswald: A Driving Force?".

12. See Chapter 25. "Forty Years of Press Coverage of the JFK Assassination".

13. 11H 214-215 (Affidavit of John Bryan McFarland and Meryl McFarland)

14. Shirley Harrison: *The Diary of Jack The Ripper*, published by Smith Gryphon Ltd., UK, 1993, page xvii. The house is at 7 Riversdale Road, Aigburth, Liverpool. Now, as in the Maybrick days, it is called Battlecrease House and is a large and imposing residence. As mentioned in the text, it is no longer the home of Dr and Mrs McFarland.

15. Meeting with Gary Mack, 21st November 2000, in company of researchers Mark Rowe and Russ Shearer.

16. From documents supplied to me by Gary Mack.

17. Biographical notes from *Debrett's Distinguished People of Today* (UK, 1988 edition) and Dame Elisabeth's obituary in *The Daily Telegraph*, UK.

Written 1996.

Published June and July 1997 on website *JFK - Voice of Reason* (UK), issues 3 - 4.

Unpublished in hard copy.

*Chief of Police Jesse E. Curry
(John R. Woods, II collection)*

*Captain J.W. Fritz, head of
Homicide & Robbery
(John R. Woods, II collection)*

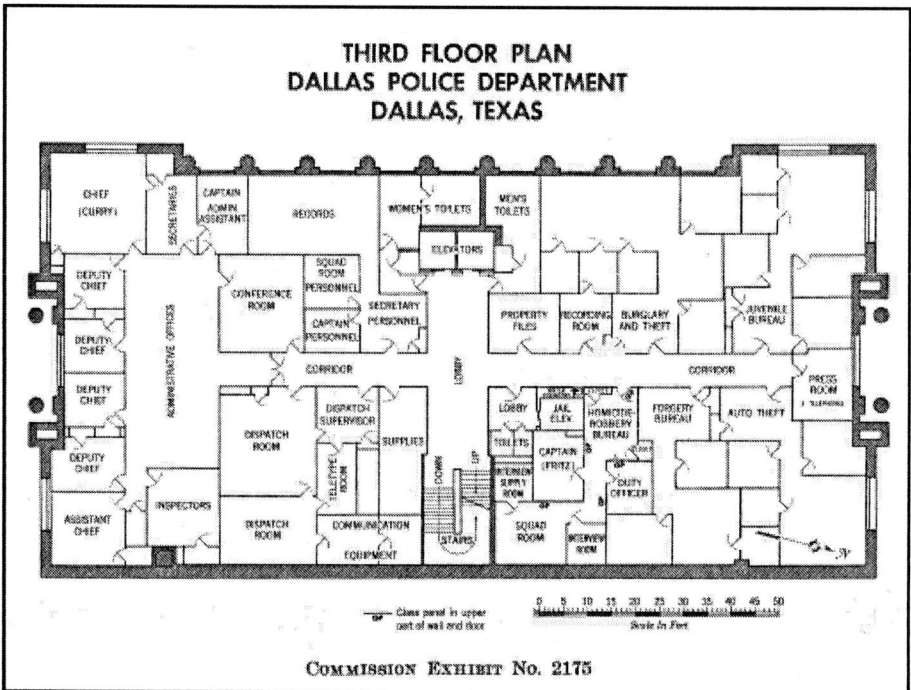

THIRD FLOOR PLAN
DALLAS POLICE DEPARTMENT
DALLAS, TEXAS

COMMISSION EXHIBIT No. 2175

James Tague signs Volume I of the author's 26 Volumes, Plano, TX, November 1993 (Photograph by Larry N. Howard)

Beverly Oliver with her husband Charles Massagee, Dallas, TX, November 1993 (Photograph by Chris Mills)

Ed Hoffman with his friend and interpreter, Ron Friedrich. (Photograph courtesy JFK Lancer)

1.
DL 100-10461
AEC:mvs

On January 9, 1964, ARTHUR STEVENS, Deputy District
Court Clerk, Dallas County District Court, 505 Main Street,
advised SA GEORGE T. BINNEY that he had received information
that the Assistant District Attorney of Dallas, Texas, SAM
PATERNOSTRO, had seen a rifle protruding from a window in
the Texas School Book Depository building on November 22,
1963 at the time President KENNEDY was assasinated.

CE 1998: FBI report of interview conducted on January 9, 1964, of Arthur Stevens at Dallas, TX (CD 385, p. 10) in its entirety.

Texas Theater and Hardy's Shoe Store (now Alicia's) photographed November 1996.

The author with Johnny Calvin Brewer after the interview at Brewer's home in Austin, TX in November 1996. (Photograph by Mark Rowe)

Shoes purchased by Oswald from Hardy's Shoe Store described as "1 Pair man's black low quarter shoes" "John Hardy Brand" appear on official DPD property report.

Hearings Before the President's Commission

on the

Assassination of President Kennedy

TESTIMONY OF JOHNNY CALVIN BREWER

The testimony of Johnny Calvin Brewer was taken at 3:15 p.m., on April 2, 1964, in the office of the U.S. attorney, 301 Post Office Building, Bryan and Ervay Streets, Dallas, Tex., by Mr. David W. Belin, assistant counsel of the President's Commission.

Mr. BELIN. Will you stand and raise your right hand. Do you solemnly swear that the testimony you are about to give will be the truth, the whole truth, and nothing but the truth, so help you God?

Mr. BREWER. I do.

Mr. BELIN. Would you please state your name for the record?

Mr. BREWER. Johnny Calvin Brewer.

Mr. BELIN. How old are you, Mr. Brewer?

Mr. BREWER. Twenty-two.

Mr. BELIN. Where do you live?

Mr. BREWER. 512 North Lancaster, apartment 102.

Mr. BELIN. What city and state?

Mr. BREWER. Dallas, Tex.

Mr. BELIN. Were you born in Texas?

Mr. BREWER. Born in Miami, Okla.

Mr. BELIN. In Oklahoma?

Mr. BREWER. Yes.

Mr. BELIN. When did you move to Texas?

Mr. BREWER. About 2 years after I was born. My father was foreman on a construction company and we moved to Texas.

Mr. BELIN. Where did you go to school in Texas, please, sir?

Mr. BREWER. I went first year in Lockhart. The second year we moved to Houston, for a year, and moved back to Lockhart, and I went there 10 years in Lockhart.

Mr. BELIN. You graduated from high school?

Mr. BREWER. Yes.

Mr. BELIN. Did you go to school after you graduated from high school?

Mr. BREWER. I went to Southwest Texas State Teachers College in San Marcos a year, and a year in Nixon Clay Business College in Austin.

Mr. BELIN. Then what did you do?

Mr. BREWER. I got married and quit school and went to work for Hardy's Shoe Store. I—that was in September, and I got married in December. And I have been with them ever since.

Mr. BELIN. When did you go to work for Hardy's Shoe Store?

Mr. BREWER. In September of 1961.

Mr. BELIN. Do they assign you to any particular store?

Mr. BREWER. I worked at the Capital Plaza Shopping Center in Austin for about 10 months, and then they transferred me to Dallas and gave me a store down on Jefferson.

Mr. BELIN. In Austin were you just a shoe salesman?

Mr. BREWER. I was assistant manager.

Ian — Great talking to you. John Brewer 11-25-96

1

Brewer signed his printed testimony at 7H 1.

PART III: FRAMING OSWALD

10. The Oswald line-ups and the
riddle of Howard Leslie Brennan

INTRODUCTION

As I think all serious researchers are aware, Lee Harvey Oswald seemed to be officially declared 'guilty' within a very short time of his arrest. Indeed, some may say that this situation existed *before* his arrest. When I say 'officially' I mean in the eyes of the Dallas Police Department, the Dallas County Sheriff's Office, the Dallas District Attorney's Office and the FBI. Since it was so obviously an 'open-and-shut' case and the murderer of Kennedy and Tippit was safely in custody, there was nothing more to do but complete a few reports, wrap up the files and all go out for a celebratory drink to mark a job well done. [1] I think the expression "case closed" saw the light of day in Dallas 30 years before Gerald Posner used it as the title of his pro-Warren Commission book in 1993.

Maybe this was also the reason that the separate identity parades which Oswald attended had been conducted in such a haphazard, unfair and downright sloppy manner. They could have been filmed and shown to future police recruit classes as how *not* to do it.

THE (UN)RELIABILITY OF EYEWITNESS TESTIMONY

Illogical as it may seem, the *least* reliable form of identification is that of the eyewitness. This may be seen as an obvious anomaly since it is natural to assume that this would be the most accurate and straightforward means of verifying a person's presence at a certain place at a certain time. How often do we hear the phrase "I saw it with my own eyes" as a means of stressing that something is true? The human perception and memory are, however, nowhere near as accurate as we mistakenly believe.

As a retired police officer with considerable experience as an operational detective, I can say that it is widely felt amongst police that eyewitness testimony is suspect. Please allow me to quote examples from some classic cases and some significant literature.

In early 1962 in England, James Hanratty's legal representatives, Emmanuel Kleinman and Michael Sherrard, were fighting desperately in their appeal against their client's conviction for what had become known as the A6 murder. They even wrote to British Home Secretary, 'Rab' Butler. Much of the prosecution case relied heavily on eyewitness evidence and they stressed to the Home Secretary: "There is no class of evidence more likely to fall victim to the frailties of human judgment than that relating to identity." Such evidence, they added, was made more difficult to evaluate "by reason of its coming from honest, unprejudiced witnesses". They concluded that the 'honest but mistaken' witness was a central problem for the criminal justice process. [2]

In Brian Lane's *The Encyclopedia of Forensic Science*, in the section on 'Identification' the author wrote:

> "It might logically be expected that a person who has just witnessed an incident is the perfect source of identification. In reality this proves to be far from the truth—quite often, sometimes with alarming consequences, an eye-witness proves counter-productive to the investigation. This is because, excluding the professional observers such as police officers, we tend to imagine our powers of recall and description to be better than they really are, and those powers are likely to be confused by any number of physical and psychological factors. For instance, alarm or fright at being so close to a serious crime or accident can momentarily 'paralyse' the mind as it might the body." The author later stated: "There is growing concern to support the accusation that the (eyewitness) identification of the offender is the largest single cause of miscarriages of justice."[3]

Dr Elizabeth F. Loftus, Adjunct Professor of Law at the University of Washington, Seattle, is considered a leading authority on eyewitness testimony and its problems. Her 1979 book *Eyewitness Testimony*, described many examples of incorrect eyewitness testimony, including details of cases in which she was successfully involved. [4]

Dr Cyril Wecht, whose name is very familiar to Kennedy assassination researchers, devoted a chapter to the Robert Kennedy murder in his book *Cause of Death*. He wrote of RFK's wounds: "The forensic evidence, which is irrefutable, directly contradicted all the eyewitnesses. Forensic evidence does not lie." [5]

In James Fetzer's 1998 book *Assassination Science*, Dr David W. Mantik contributed an important chapter on the authenticity or otherwise of the Zapruder film. He pointed out that there are different types of eyewitness evidence. In the section 'Can these Eyewitnesses be Trusted?' he stated that "there is no question but that eyewitnesses are notoriously unreliable for identifying the faces of strangers briefly glimpsed." He went on to qualify this by saying that "when many dozens of witnesses recall an event—such as the slowing of the limousine at a critical moment—(it) strongly suggests that they are recalling the event correctly." [6]

On a personal level, I have no qualms about relying on my own professional experience over many years in dealing with eyewitnesses giving descriptions of people they have seen. I even recall an occurrence in 1974 when, despite seeing his assailant clearly, my witness, a victim of street robbery, got the man's colour wrong.

WAS THERE REALLY A HOWARD BRENNAN LINE UP?

It should have been a relatively straightforward task to track down the records of the Oswald line ups. That, however, was not the case. Apart from discrepancies in some of the official records and documentation, I encountered some confusing claims in assassination literature. For example, I read in Ray and Mary La Fontaine's book *Oswald Talked* that "(John) Elrod says today that he was put on a chain with Oswald (and) appeared in lineups ..." That is patently untrue, but then as far as I am concerned, so is even the title of that book. [7]

The Warren Report carefully detailed a list of the (unnamed) eyewitnesses who claimed that they had seen Lee Harvey Oswald at the Tippit scene. They were covered in the following very straightforward and convincing terms:

> "At least 12 persons saw the man with the revolver in the vicinity of the Tippit crime scene at or immediately after the shooting. By the evening of November 22, five of them had identified Lee Harvey Oswald in police lineups as the man they saw. A sixth did so the next day. Three others subsequently identified Oswald from a photograph. Two witnesses testified that Oswald resembled the gunman they had seen. One witness felt he was too distant from the gunman to make a positive identification. [8]

The above paragraph, extracted word-for-word from the Warren Report, appears very convincing to the unwary. It gives us nine positive identifications from 12 eyewitnesses in the close proximity of the murder of Officer J. D. Tippit. Only one of the 12 was reported as completely failing to recognize Oswald. The six witnesses who had *"identified Lee Harvey Oswald in police lineups"* attended four separate parades, three on the Friday and the final one on Saturday. They were Mrs Helen Markham, Ted Callaway, Sam Guinyard, cab driver William Whaley and the Davis sisters-in-law Barbara and Virginia.

In addition to those 12 at or close to the Tippit murder scene, three more claimed to have either seen or had direct contact with Oswald in connection with the assassination of the President around three quarters of an hour previously. These were the bus driver Cecil McWatters, [9] the cab driver William W. Scoggins [10] and the man whose uncertain actions prompted my initial curiosity and brought about this paper, Howard Leslie Brennan. [11] These three men also looked at Oswald in identity line-ups—or so some reports suggest.

From the above, we have learnt that according to the Warren Report, the suspected double killer was paraded before nine eyewitnesses in separate identity parades. These were said to have been convened in that period of around 45¹/2 hours between his arrest in the Texas Theatre and his unfortunate demise in the police station basement. I feel that this perhaps merits a place in the *Guinness Book of Records*.

As I slowly and meticulously studied all these parades and witnesses, I found that I was gradually becoming more and more uncomfortable with them. Something was not adding up. It took a little while to recognize what was wrong. Eventually, it came to me. Where was corroboration or confirmation that the Howard Leslie Brennan line-up had really taken place? The other four line-ups had been fully and carefully described in the official account, but the Brennan identity parade seemed to have slipped away down a crack somewhere. I was beginning to form a suspicion that the line-up involving Brennan never actually took place. Either that or something even more alarming had happened .....

Let us now look at it all carefully, logically and thoroughly from the beginning.

WHO WAS HOWARD LESLIE BRENNAN AND WHY WAS HE SO IMPORTANT?

Howard Leslie Brennan, a 45-year old married man, had worked as a steamfitter for 20 years and on the day of the assassination, he was employed by Wallace & Beard, a local construction company. He was working as part of a seven-man gang in the Katy Railroad Yards, adjacent to the Texas School Book Depository, a job he had been on for the previous three months and which was expected to continue for a further six months. He lived with his wife Louise at 6814 Woodard in the Dallas suburb of Urbandale. [12]

The importance of Howard Leslie Brennan was that he claimed to have seen a man with a rifle up at the sixth floor window of the Texas School Book Depository immediately before and at the time of the assassination. He described the man's colour, height, weight, clothing and actions in considerable detail. Brennan observed him from a vantage point on the white brick retaining wall at the northern end of the reflecting pool directly across Elm Street from the TSBD where he sat to watch the motorcade pass by.

Brennan related what he had seen, including a description of the man in the window, to a police officer (unidentified) and it is thought that this is how a description which fitted Lee Harvey Oswald was circulated so quickly. There are, however, serious doubts among some researchers that this really was the source of that description.

Brennan's description of what he saw and heard, as given to the Warren Commission, however, is confusing in the extreme: "

> Well, as the parade came by, I watched it from a distance of Elm and Main Street, as it came on to Houston and turned the corner at Houston and Elm, and going down the incline to the railroad underpass. And after the President had passed my position, I really couldn't say how many feet or how far, a short distance I would say, I heard this crack that I positively thought was a backfire." He went on to say: "Well, then something, just right after this explosion, made me think that it was a firecracker being thrown from the Texas Book Store. And I glanced up. And this man that I saw previous was aiming for his last shot." [13]

It seems to me that what Brennan originally perceived as a backfire, became a firecracker report and then a rifle shot. His description of the rifle is also unsatisfactory. He stated that he could observe that it was "some type of high-powered rifle" but twice added that he did not know whether or not it had a scope. [14]

There is little doubt that what Howard Brennan claimed to have seen as he awaited and then watched the presidential motorcade on 22nd November 1963 would have made him a star prosecution witness had Lee Harvey Oswald ever been brought to trial for the assassination of the President.

How the Oswald line-ups were organised

Under *English* Law, with which I am obviously far more conversant, the rules and procedures for the conduct of identity parades (line-ups) have always been very strictly laid down and adhered to. In England in 1963, as now, it was required for the parade to consist of at least *eight* persons plus the suspect. They were to be "of similar age, height, general appearance and position in life" as the suspect. Unfortunately for Lee Harvey Oswald, the situation in Dallas, Texas, in November 1963, was considerably different.

The Oswald line-ups were conducted in what was known colloquially as the "showup room" (sometimes also called the "assembly room" or the "lineup room") in the basement of DPD Headquarters. I believe I am one of very few researchers who has had the opportunity to visit this part of the old City Hall. [15] It ceased to fulfil that function several years ago and when I was there in November 1996, it was being used as an office with refreshment facilities. The raised wooden platform on which the line-up members were paraded was still in its original position on the left as you enter the room. The set of horizontal lines painted in white on the wall behind it, indicating each person's height, had long since been painted out. So too had the individual numbers, 1 to 6, below which each member of the line-up stood in order to be identified by the eyewitness. [16]

When asked during his Warren Commission testimony to describe the room, Chief Curry said: "It is a police assemblyroom [sic] where we hold our regular rollcalls. They have a stage whereby prisoners are brought up on this stage ... the room, I would say, is perhaps 50 feet long and 20 feet wide" [17] It was the scene of the well-known press conference at 12.30am on the morning of 23rd November. This was the occasion when Oswald was paraded before the press and Jack Ruby gained admittance and corrected DA Henry Wade when he misquoted the name of the Fair Play For Cuba Committee as Free Cuba Movement. [18] Standing there on that platform 33 years later, it was easy to relive the scene in November 1963. It was a scary experience.

The procedure for each of the Oswald line-ups was identical and he was included with just three other individuals. [19] Those three would line up first and Oswald was then invited to take whatever position he chose. All four men were then handcuffed together and they stood under strong lighting facing a one-way nylon screen. They could not see through it but the eyewitness, who could either stand, or sit on a chair on the other side of it, could see them. The members of the parade were allocated the numbers 1 to 4, these numbers being displayed over their heads.

When the eyewitness was in position, the normal procedure was for each man in turn to take a step forward and state his name and place of work. The eyewitness then studied the four men full-face and, if he requested, also in profile. The witness had been instructed that if he recognized the suspect, he should indicate that person's number to one of the officers conducting the line up. [20]

I have never heard it asked where the people in these line ups were obtained and how they were selected. I think it important that this is addressed. To answer it, we can do no better than go directly to the Warren Commission testimony of DPD Homicide Detective Elmer L. Boyd. [21] In the following dialogue, he is being questioned by Assistant Counsel Joseph A. Ball, who put that very point to him. It must be appreciated that Boyd's reply is based on the normal circumstances when the suspect is being held in the cells on the fifth floor. In Oswald's case, he was usually in Captain Fritz' office on the third floor, immediately prior to be taken downstairs for each line up.

BALL: "What is the usual thing—when you are going to have a showup and you are in charge of investigation, who picks the people who appear in the showup?"

BOYD: "Well, most of the time we call down to the jail office and have them send us down—if he's already in jail, we just have them send up there and get him and just how many we want in the showup and we will tell them to give us this particular one—or three or four men—whatever the case may be."

BALL: "Who picks them?"

BOYD: "The jailers upstairs."

BALL: "Do you tell them to get them all the same color?" (Huh? - ILG)

BOYD: "Yes, sir; we always tell them to get them all the same color. I never have had too much trouble getting them all the same color." *(Double huh! - ILG)*

BALL: "What about the size and weight?"

BOYD: "Now, we always tell them to get them as near the same size and age and weight as they can. Sometimes they do and sometimes they don't."

There is obviously no need to labour this point. It seems that there were no set rules and regulations laid down for the procedure when assembling a line up. It appears almost to have been made up as it went along. Even the number of people on a line-up seemed to depend on the whim of the officer in charge. [22] It did not seem particularly important that the size, age and weight of the line up members were similar to those of the suspect. As Detective Boyd said: *"Sometimes they do and sometimes they don't."* Let us give credit where credit is due however. At least they tried to get people the same *colour* as the suspect—and as far as I can find, there were no females on any of the Oswald line- ups!

In each of the four line-ups I propose to examine and discuss here, Lee Oswald was accompanied by three other people—but not always the same three. Some of them appeared on more than one line-up. Altogether, eight individuals were involved in those four line-ups with Oswald. [23]

The following are brief descriptions of Oswald and the eight people who appeared with him on those four line-ups. [24] Please bear in mind Detective Boyd's comment that they tried "to get them as near the same size and age and weight" as the suspect.

Lee Harvey Oswald, the suspect in the assassination of President Kennedy and the murder of Patrolman J. D. Tippit. Age 24, 5' 9" tall, weight 131 pounds, brown hair, grey eyes, wearing a brown shirt and dark trousers. (He changed to a white T-shirt for the parade on Sunday 23rd.) He had a black eye and cuts to his forehead and lip. According to Detective Boyd, Oswald's clothes were "a little rougher in character" than the others and the others were "better dressed than Oswald". It is on record that during an FBI interview on 23rd, Oswald raised an objection that he had been denied a request to dress more similarly to others on at least one of the line ups. [25]

William E. ('Bill' or 'Billy') Perry, an Acting Detective with the DPD Vice Squad. Late 20s, 5' 11". 150 pounds, brown hair, blue eyes, medium fair complexion. Wearing brown sports coat, no tie. Commission Exhibit 1054 shows two photographs of Perry with the next two gentlemen I describe.

Richard L. Clark, a DPD Vice Squad Detective. Late 20s, 5' 11", weighed about 177 pounds, blond hair, blue eyes, fair complexion, Wearing red vest (waistcoat), white short-sleeved shirt, brown trousers with belt. This man was very blond, two inches taller than Oswald and 46 pounds heavier!

Don R. Ables, a civilian Jail Guard employed by the Dallas PD at City Hall. Ables was in his mid-20s, 5' 9" tall, weighed around 165 pounds, and had dark hair, brown eyes and a ruddy complexion. On each of the three line-ups he attended, he wore a white shirt, a grey knitted sweater and dark trousers. [26] (There is an individual photograph of Ables at Commission Exhibit 745.)

Richard Walter Borchgardt, a remand prisoner being held on suspicion of firearms, burglary and theft offences. He was 23 years old, 5' 9" tall, 161 pounds and had brown hair, blue eyes and a fair complexion.

Ellis Carl Brazel, another prisoner, on remand for motoring offences. He was 21 years old, 5' 10" tall, 169 pounds and had blond hair, green eyes and a ruddy complexion.

John Thurman Horne, also on remand for motoring offences. He was 18 years old. Other details not known.

David Edmund Knapp, another prisoner, on remand on suspicion of burglary and theft. He was also 18 years old. No other details.

Daniel Gutierrez Lujan, another prisoner, arrested on 21st November on suspicion of narcotics offences but released on 24th with no charge. He was 26 years old, 5' 8" tall, weighed 170 pounds and had black hair, brown eyes and an olive complexion. He confirmed that he was of Mexican descent. He was wearing a blue shirt and a brown jacket. [27] This man was an inch shorter than Oswald but nearly 40 pounds heavier!

A table included in the photo section may illustrate these points more clearly. [28] I will now take you through those four line-ups and as I do, I am certain that you will agree with me that the deck was very much stacked against the suspect. I will spend some time setting the scene for the first line-up, but those that followed were conducted in an identical manner.

THE FIRST LINE UP—MRS. HELEN LOUISE MARKHAM, THE 'UTTER SCREWBALL'

The first line up was convened less than three and a half hours after the murder of Patrolman J. D. Tippit. Its purpose was to give 47-year-old Dallas waitress Mrs Helen Louise Markham the opportunity to pick out the man she claimed to have seen shoot the officer to death. Since no other person stated that they had witnessed the actual shooting, Mrs Markham's identification of Oswald as the killer was vital in the development of the case against him.

I will point out here that there are problems establishing the exact times of all these line ups. For the sake of consistency, I will use the time given in the official DPD investigation file [29] for each line up. According to that record, the Markham line up was held at 4.35pm on Friday 22nd November 1963.

As he was to do on all three line-ups on the day of the assassination, Oswald selected the number 2 position in the four-man line. He was hand-cuffed to the man on either side of him. His companions were Acting Detective Perry (number 1), Detective Clark (number 3) and Jail Clark Ables (number 4).

When Mrs Markham had been brought in and was in position on the other side of the one-way nylon screen, each man was asked to step forward and state his name and place of employment. Perhaps significantly, only Oswald was truthful here. The three DPD employees (by their own admission in their later sworn testimony), each gave fictitious answers. Oswald was the only one of the four with facial injuries; he had been named and shown on TV that afternoon and it had also been broadcast that his place of employment was believed to be the source of the shots which had struck down the President. In view of these facts, it cannot be claimed that everything (or, indeed, *anything!*) was being arranged with scrupulous fairness to the suspect.

As for the witness, Mrs. Markham was hardly in a fit state to undertake the responsible task of identifying (or *not* identifying, as the case may be) the killer of Officer Tippit. Homicide Detective L. C. Graves, one of those officers organizing the line up, said that she was "quite hysterical" and "crying and upset" and "she was saying—what most hysterical women say—wringing her hands and talking about the shooting" [30] and there was even talk of her being sent to hospital.

In his testimony, Captain Fritz stated: "We were trying to get that showup as soon as we could because she was beginning to faint and getting sick. In fact, I had to leave the office and carry some ammonia across the hall, they were about to send her to the hospital or something and we needed that identification real quickly, and she got to feeling all right after using this ammonia." [31]

I doubt that the wheels of justice would have been slowed down too much if this lady had been given a few hours to compose herself. I cannot understand why Captain Fritz was in such a frantic rush to "get that showup as soon as we could ."

According to the Warren Report, Mrs Markham "identified Oswald as the man who shot the policeman." [32] The Report also stated that "in testimony before the Commission, Mrs. Markham confirmed her positive identification of Lee Harvey Oswald as the man she saw kill Officer Tippit," [33]

Sylvia Meagher, in her book *Accessories After The Fact*, argued that the testimony of this alleged eyewitness to the shooting of Tippit by Oswald, "lacks any semblance of credibility". She also pointed out the little-known fact that at the Tippit murder scene, Mrs Markham "was in hysterics and somehow managed to leave her shoes on top of Tippit's car." [34] Several members of the Warren Commission staff have subsequently voiced their opinions of Mrs Markham's value as a witness. Assistant Counsel Liebeler has described her testimony as "contradictory and worthless" [35] whilst Assistant Counsel Joseph Ball described her as "an utter screwball." [36]

If a humble ex-British cop can rip so many holes in the actions and mental attitude of this so-called star witness, imagine what a smart defending attorney would have done in court.

Norman Redlich, another Warren Commission staff member, is quoted as saying: "The Commission wants to believe Mrs Markham and that's all there is to it." [37] I think this remark is very important, since Mrs Markham was the only witness who ever claimed to have actually *seen* Tippit being shot. Like it or not, the investigators were stuck with her. If she had announced that the Earth was flat, they would have been hard-pressed not to accept her statement as the truth.

What the Warren Report failed to reveal about the testimony of its star Tippit witness was that she required considerable prompting concerning her positive identification of Oswald. In her testimony, she initially stated *six* times that she had recognized nobody in the line up. Tiring of this, Assistant Counsel Ball unashamedly produced one of the most amazing leading questions ever asked: "Was there a number two man in there?" After a few similar questions, he managed to get her to say: "I asked—I looked at him. When I saw this man I wasn't sure, but I had cold chills run all over me ... when I saw the man. But I wasn't sure ... and I said number two. So when I said that, well, I just kind of fell over." [38]

As already stated, I do not intend to deal with the other line-ups in as much detail as this one. I will, however, reveal a few discrepancies and some glaring examples of unfairness, inconsideration and downright bias against the suspect.

THE SECOND LINE-UP—A TRIO OF CONFUSED PEOPLE

Oswald attended a second line-up at 6.30pm that same evening. [39] It was held in the same showup room and featured exactly the same four people as had been shown to Mrs Markham. They took up the same positions as before, with Oswald again choosing to stand between Perry and Clark in the number 2 position.

On this occasion, the line-up was viewed simultaneously by three witnesses. These were Ted Callaway, Sam Guinyard and Cecil McWatters. It strikes me as strange that *three* witnesses should attend the same parade but there was even more to it than that. They were not even witnesses to the same crime!

The Warren Report tells us that both Callaway and Guinyard "picked Oswald as the man who had run south on Patton with a gun in his hand" immediately following the shooting of Tippit. [40]

Cecil McWatters was the driver of the bus in which Oswald was alleged to have attempted to make his getaway after killing the President. According to the Warren Report, McWatters "picked Oswald from the lineup as the man who had boarded the bus at the 'lower end of town on Elm around Houston'" [41] On the same page of the Report, however, it is stated that McWatters later "said he had been in error and that a teenager named Roy Milton Jones was the passenger he had in mind." The closing sentence of this rather ungainly and confusing paragraph seems very appropriate in the circumstances: "However, McWatters' recollection alone was too vague to be a basis for placing Oswald on the bus."

Whilst the Warren Report states that each of these three witnesses identified Oswald, there are serious doubts in each instance. Callaway's powers of observation had been so sharp at the scene that he had asked another witness which way the gunman had fled. [42] Guinyard's overall powers of observation also have to be questioned since twice in his testimony he told Mr. Ball that the four men in the line up "wasn't all about the same color." They were, in fact, four white men, namely Oswald, Perry, Clark and Ables. [43]

As for McWatters, as described above, it is obvious from his testimony that he was totally confused about exactly who he was trying to identify. As Joe Backes has explained in a 1998 article in the internet magazine *Fair Play* [44] it does indeed appear that McWatters was under the impression that he was identifying Roy Milton Jones, a teenager who was another passenger on his bus and who was totally unconnected with Lee Harvey Oswald. As I pointed out above, even the Warren Report went back on its earlier positive statement and concluded: "However, McWatters' recollection alone was too vague to be a basis for placing Oswald on the bus." [45]

I think it accurate to say that the so-called 'positive identifications' of Oswald by each of these three witnesses, Callaway, Guinyard and McWatters, would have been described in an English court as 'unsafe' and rejected out of hand.

The Third Line Up—The Sisters-in-Law

Barbara Jeanette Davis and her 16-year old sister-in-law, Virginia Ruth Davis (Mrs Charlie Virginia Davis), were living in separate apartments on the ground floor (first floor in USA) at 400 East 10th Street on 22nd November 1963. That is the house right on the corner of 10th and Patton. Virginia was the wife of Barbara's husband's brother. Neither of them claimed to have seen the actual shooting of Tippit. They were together in Barbara's apartment when they were alerted by the sound of shots. Together they ran to the front door and looked out. They saw a man running from the approximate area of the crime. Later that afternoon, they each retrieved one of the four spent cartridge cases which he had emptied from a revolver.

Together, they attended an identity line-up at City Hall at 7.55pm on the 22nd. [46] The line-up again had Oswald in the number 2 position but this time his companions were two of the remand prisoners, Richard Borchgardt and Ellis Brazel, at positions 1 and 3 respectively. Presumably, the two Vice Squad detectives had gone off duty. Jail Clerk Don Ables was again in the number 4 position. The procedure was identical to the previous two line-ups.

The Warren Report deals with the result of this line-up in a very cold and matter-of-fact way. It states that the ladies "viewed a group of four men in a lineup and each one picked Oswald as the man who crossed their lawn while emptying his pistol." [47] A few lines later, we read that the two women "were sitting alongside one another when they made their positive identification of Oswald. Each woman whispered Oswald's number to the detective. Each testified that she was the first to make the identification." I find it difficult to imagine two witnesses sitting side by side at an identity parade and casually indicating their opinions by whispering to a detective. To me that almost defies belief. It also appears that they were in competition with one another to see who could make the identification first.

It seems that there were two line-ups in operation here. We had the Oswald line-up behind the screen whilst in front, we had a row of three chairs on which, from left to right, sat Virginia Davis, Barbara Davis and an unnamed DPD detective. [48] The only officers named as being "with witnesses" here were Detective Dhority and Acting Detective Brown. [49] As the Warren Report said, each of the witnesses whispered Oswald's number to the detective, whom I presume was either Dhority or Brown.

When they were later asked if they had watched any television that afternoon, both ladies claimed that they had not. Virginia Davis, however, also added: "Our television was blurred anyway, so we couldn't hardly tell." [50] Now do you not agree with me that such a remark is significant? At one stage, I thought it odd that these two near-eyewitnesses to a policeman's murder would not have subsequently turned on their television, but that remark convinces me that they *did*! Well, wouldn't *you*? It's human nature.

Perhaps significantly, in connection with her powers of observation, Virginia also stated at one point that there were five men on the line up. [51]

The final line-up—the two taxi drivers

The final line-up was assembled in the same City Hall showup room at 2.15pm the following day, Saturday 23rd November 1963. [52] Again, it was an example of two witnesses attending together. This line-up, however, is even stranger than the one involving the Davis sisters-in-law. At least those two ladies claimed to have seen and experienced roughly the same thing.

The two men on this fourth line-up were William Wayne Whaley and William W. Scoggins. Whaley was alleged to have carried Oswald in his cab from the bus station in downtown Dallas to Oak Cliff. Scoggins claimed to have seen both Tippit and his killer on 10th Street a few minutes before the shooting.

As we had seen on a previous line-up, these two men were not even witnesses in the same case! The only thing they had in common, apart from their first name, was the fact that they were both cab drivers. In the absence of any other explanation, I can only assume that to be the reason they attended the same line up.

The line-up consisted of Oswald with three different remand prisoners: the teenagers John Horne and David Knapp and the Hispanic Daniel Lujan. This time, Oswald forsook his previous number 2 position and occupied the number 3 position, with Knapp on his right and Lujan on his left.

It was now over 24 hours since the deaths of Kennedy and Tippit and the arrest of Oswald. The world's media—radio, TV and the press—had covered very little else in that period. Oswald's name, his photograph, his description, his place of work, his personal history, including his defection to the Soviet Union, had been thrust unceasingly at the public through every branch of the media. So, of course, had his undoubted guilt of both murders. Lee Harvey Oswald was now probably as famous as the late President himself! As if that were not enough to indicate him as the suspect, his actions and attitude on this fourth line-up certainly gave away a few clues. By now, he was doubtless growing increasingly tired of this succession of strangers who were being wheeled in to peer at him through the nylon screen as if he were a circus freak.

Consider this, from Whaley's testimony: "

> But you could have picked him out without identifying him by just listening to him because he was bawling out the policemen, telling them it wasn't right to put him in line with these teenagers and all of that ... he showed no respect for the policemen, he told them what he thought of them. They knew what they were doing and they were trying to railroad him and he wanted his lawyer ... I said anyone who wasn't sure could have picked out the right one just for that."

Whaley thought that Oswald was in a line "with five others ... just young kids they might have got them in jail." [53] In view of all this, is it any surprise that both Scoggins and Whaley picked out Oswald? He might just a well have had the word "KILLER" tattooed across his forehead!

The 'other' line up—Howard Leslie Brennan

As I said in my opening remarks, I originally believed that the four line-ups I have described here were the only ones which took place. However, the Warren Report states that Howard Leslie Brennan also attended a line-up at City Hall at which he "identified Oswald as the person in the lineup who bore the closest resemblance to the man in the window but he said he was unable to make a positive identification." This line-up is reported to have taken place at an undisclosed time "during the evening of November 22." [54]

As far as I can find, the only examples of corroboration of this claim that Brennan attended a line-up are in his own Warren Commission testimony, in his posthumously-published 1987 book *Eyewitness To History* [55] and in the confused and confusing testimony of Secret Service Agent Forrest V. Sorrels. [56] When I was getting close to completing this paper, however, I learnt of another published source that claimed Brennan had attended the same line-up as the Davis sisters-in-law. [57] I will discuss this later under the heading "A strange claim".

In Brennan's testimony, he said that he was picked up by Secret Service Agent Patterson (on Friday 22nd) "at 6 o'clock, at my home, and taken to the Dallas Police Station." [58] Confusingly, he then went on to say that there was "a possibility seven more or less one" in the line-up. [59] Since the line-up positions were permanently numbered from 1 to 6, it was physically impossible for there to be more than six people on the same line-up. [60] When asked by Mr. Belin: "Were they all white, or were there some Negroes in there?" Brennan produced the incredible reply: "I do not remember." [61] I have tried in vain to find the reason for that question. Brennan was never asked and did not volunteer the time of the line-up.

In his book, [62] Brennan quoted a different time for his journey to City Hall and described how he received a telephone call at home *"about 7:15pm."* He said that he was asked by FBI Agent Robert C. Lish to "come down to make an identification." He was then driven to City Hall by "One of the FBI [sic] agents who had been watching the house." This man has been identified as Dallas-based Secret Service Agent William H. Patterson. [63] It is unfortunate that there is no explanation of this odd occurrence and why the Secret Service had apparently mounted a surveillance operation on Brennan's home.

In both his Warren Commission testimony (24th March 1964) and in his book (published 1987, four years after his death), Brennan described his experience at the line-up. He said that he had entered the room and immediately recognized Oswald as the number 2 man in "perhaps as many as seven." [64] However, he steadfastly refused to identify him. He explained that he felt personally threatened by the whole situation and as it was obvious to him that the police had got their man, he felt that his positive identification would not make any difference. According to the account in his book, he was driven back to his home, arriving "about 9:00 in the evening." [65] As mentioned earlier, Brennan lived at 6814 Woodard Street, Urbandale, a section of East Dallas about six miles by road from City Hall.

Forrest Verne Sorrels' Warren Commission testimony explained it was his idea to get Brennan to a line-up that evening and that he had arranged for SA Patterson to bring Brennan to City Hall. He said that Brennan was reluctant to identify Oswald and had said: "I am sorry, but I can't do it ... I just can't be positive. I'm sorry." [66] Like Brennan, Sorrels seemed uncertain of the number of men on the line up, telling the Commission: "As I recall it, there were five. In other words, all told there were five or six—I don't remember. I believe there were five." [67]

A STRANGE CLAIM

As mentioned a few paragraphs earlier, I received some late information from a fellow researcher of a published claim that Howard Brennan had been present at the same line- up as the Davis women. The origin of this claim was the 1969 Judy Bonner book *Investigation of a Homicide.* [68]

On page 13, Ms Bonner wrote: "7:40pm—Third "show up". Howard Brennan identifies Oswald as man he saw in sixth floor window of Texas School Book Depository when shots were fired at motorcade. Jeanette and Virginia Davis identify him as man they saw fleeing from scene of Tippit's shooting." On page 156, she wrote: "At the third show-up, Howard Brennan picked Oswald..."

Perhaps significantly, Ms Bonner failed to offer anything even remotely resembling a source note for this unique piece of information. Brennan attended the same line up as the Davis women? Who says so? The Dallas PD? No. The Warren Commission? Again, no. Even Brennan failed to mention this in either his testimony or in his subsequent book. I can find *nothing* to substantiate Ms Bonner's claim. Quite the opposite, in fact. Nothing in the accounts or testimony of the Davis women indicates that they shared that line-up with Howard Leslie Brennan or anybody else. Ms Bonner stated that Brennan identified Oswald, but we know that he did no such thing. Ms Bonner's book is very DPD-orientated, perhaps to be expected since she was a local newspaper crime reporter with contacts in the police department. She later moved to London and worked on the *Daily Mirror*.

In an effort to check every possible angle on this point, I contacted fellow researcher Dale K. Myers, author of the 1998 book *With Malice: Lee Harvey Oswald and the Murder of Officer J. D. Tippit.* [69] I had become acquainted with Dale at the 1998 JFK-Lancer Research Conference in Dallas when I moderated a panel on which he appeared with David Lifton. I was aware that when he was researching his book, Dale had been in contact with the Davis sisters-in-law. I was delighted when he agreed to put the point to them on my behalf.

On 8th February 1999, he spoke with the elder of the two ladies, Barbara Jeanette Davis, on the telephone. [70] As he then said to me: "she has a tough time recalling this event." However, she was as helpful as she could be and when Dale asked if any other witnesses were also viewing the line-up she replied that it was "just me and my sister-in-law" and "some guys from the law enforcement." When Dale specifically asked about someone wearing glasses, she could not recall him. Although Brennan's glasses "were prescriptioned, I believe, a possibility less than a year before the incident" [71], he said that he only used them "to see fine print and more especially the Bible and blueprint."

Dale advised me to be careful in putting too much stock in Barbara's recollection alone. She repeatedly mentioned only two officers (presumably Detectives Brown and Dhority) but on one occasion, she mentioned a third. I feel certain, however, that had this third man been Brennan, she would have known that he was there as another eyewitness.

I think Judy Bonner's unique, interesting but uncorroborated remarks here can safely be accepted as unreliable—and that is precisely how I intend to regard them.

No mention of a Brennan line-up

I find it significant that Leslie Howard Brennan's attendance at a Lee Harvey Oswald identity line-up is not mentioned in any of the following places where one would surely expect to find it described in detail:

(a) Commission Exhibit 2003 (Dallas Police Department file on investigation of the assassination of the President), page 293 of the exhibit. This is the Warren Commission's official and comprehensive listing of all the identity parades involving Lee Harvey Oswald. It is entitled "SHOWUPS OF OSWALD". It details the four line-ups I have described and includes the names of all persons present, together with their function. The 12 members of the Dallas Police Department who supervised these parades are all named, as are the eight eyewitnesses who viewed the parades, and Oswald's eight line-up companions. There is not one single mention of Brennan.

> (Two pages of handwritten notes relating to the Oswald line ups are reproduced on pages 458-459 of Dale Myers' book on the Tippit murder. Myers gives their source as Box 1, Folder 10, Item 3, pages 1 and 2 at the Dallas Municipal Archives and Records Center. These notes are identical in every respect to those described as "SHOWUPS OF OSWALD" and were obviously the source of the information contained therein. I cannot overstress the fact that only four line-ups are covered. There is no mention whatsoever of a separate Howard Brennan line up or of Brennan being present on any of the four documented line-ups.)

(b) The name Brennan does not appear in the testimony or affidavits of any of the DPD officers who supervised the line-ups. [72] Captain Fritz described the four line-ups in detail in his testimony [73] but nowhere does he volunteer anything about one involving Brennan. When specifically asked by Warren Commission staff member John J. McCloy if he was present "at the showup at which Brennan was the witness" Fritz produced one of the most confusing answers even the Warren Commission ever heard:

"I don't think I was present but I will tell you what, I helped Mr. Sorrels find the time that that man—we didn't show that he was shown at all on our records, but Mr. Sorrels called me and said he did show him and he wanted me to give him the time of the showup. I asked him to find out from his officers who were with Mr. Brennan the names of the people that we had there, and he gave me those two Davis sisters, and he said, when he told me that, of course, I could tell what showup it was and then I gave him the time."

John J. McCloy, doubtless as confused by this as you and I are now, sought basic clarification and asked: "But you were not present to the best of your recollection when Brennan was in the showup?" Fritz replied: "I don't believe I was there, I doubt it." Mr McCloy obviously felt it prudent not to pursue the matter and immediately went on to ask Captain Fritz questions about an unrelated subject (the Neely Street house). [74]

(c) The name Brennan does not appear in the testimony of any of Oswald's fellow line-up members. [75]

(d) The name Brennan does not appear in the testimony of any of the other eyewitnesses who attended the line-ups. (See my remarks concerning the Davis sisters-in-law above.)

(e) The name Brennan *does*, however, appear in the Warren Report where it is stated that he "identified Oswald as the person in the line up who bore the closest resemblance to the man in the window but he said that he was unable to make a positive identification." [76]

TWO POSSIBLE SOLUTIONS TO THE PUZZLE

Is there any logical reason that a line-up which was held with Howard Leslie Brennan as the witness would not be mentioned by any of the participants?

The obvious conclusion is that such a line- up never took place.

There is, however, the other more sinister possibility which I touched upon earlier. Supposing that the Brennan line-up *did* take place but he completely failed to pick out Oswald, perhaps by choice, because he was concerned for the safety of his family. This is exactly what he claimed in his testimony. [77] If the powers that be were unable to get Brennan to identify Oswald at all in the line-up, would it not be in their interests to expunge all reference to that line-up? I appreciate that this is a somewhat Orwellian conception and smacks of *Nineteen-Eighty-Four* but it would not be unique in this case.

Howard Leslie Brennan had very quickly been elevated almost to celebrity status but if, when it mattered most, he failed to deliver the goods, what else could the authorities have done except adopt a head-in-the-sand attitude, deny that he even attended a line up, and hope that the problem would go away? Perhaps it did go away—until now.

Brennan's co-authored book, *Eyewitness To History*, over which the investigators and report writers had no direct influence, did not appear until 24 years later, four years after Brennan's death. What about the Warren Report, you may ask? Why does that document state that Brennan attended an Oswald identity parade if the plan was to delete all reference to it? Well, as I detailed earlier, after stating that Brennan *did* attend a line-up, the Report stated that he *did not*. This is an outstanding example of the Warren Commission confusing even itself as it sought to confuse the future readers of its Report.

I leave you to ponder the answer here. Whatever that may be, I contend that it was yet another ingredient in the well-organized plan to railroad the unfortunate Lee Harvey Oswald, a plan that continued (and continues!) even after his untimely but convenient demise.

A CLOSING THOUGHT

On page 169 of the Warren Report, we read: "The Commission is satisfied that the lineups were conducted fairly."

Firstly, why was it necessary to make this statement unless the Warren Commission feared there would be adverse criticism of the way the line-ups were conducted?

Secondly, as the Chief Justice of the United States Supreme Court, the man whose name the Commission bears, Earl Warren, was the highest ranking official in the United States judiciary. In view of what I have written about the manner in which those line-ups were run, can any reader of this paper continue to have any faith in the United States' legal system as it existed in 1963/64? If Earl Warren and his cohorts were *"satisfied that the lineups were conducted fairly"* then it should have been obvious to all that they were looking at the evidence with their eyes tightly closed.

NOTES

1. Just two days after the assassination, the American press was quoting Homicide & Robbery Chief Will Fritz as saying: "We're convinced beyond

any doubt that he killed the President. I think the case is cinched" beneath headlines proclaiming POLICE SAY PRISONER IS THE ASSASSIN *(New York Times*, 24th November 1963).

2. Bob Woffinden: *Hanratty - The Final Verdict*, published by Pan Books, London, 1999, page 304.

3. Brian Lane: *The Encyclopedia of Forensic Science*, published by Headline Book Publishing plc, London, 1992, pages 387 and 388. The first of these passages is very important in connection with the actions, recollections and memory of the Tippit murder eyewitness, Mrs. Helen Louise Markham. (See also footnote 34 below)

4. Elizabeth F. Loftus: *Eyewitness Testimony*, published by Harvard University Press, USA, second edition, 1996.

5. Cyril Wecht, M.D., J.D: *Cause of Death*, published by Dutton Books, USA,1993, page 85.

6. Editor James H. Fetzer, Ph.D.: *Assassination Science*, published by Catfeet Press, Chicago, 1998, pages 278-279.

7. Ray and Mary La Fontaine: *Oswald Talked: the New Evidence in the JFK Assassination*, published by Pelican Publishing Company, Inc., USA, 1996, page 41.

8. Warren Report, page 166.

9. Warren Report, page 159.

10. Warren Report, page 166.

11. Warren Report, page 145.

12. Brennan's personal details gleaned from his Warren Commission testimony at 3H 141 and his book *Eyewitness To History*, co-authored with J. Edward Cherryholmes, published by Texian Pres, Waco, Texas, 1987, pages 1-2.

13. 3H 143-144 (Testimony of Howard Leslie Brennan).

14. 3H 144 (Testimony of Howard Leslie Brennan).

15. 22nd November 1996. With the complete relocation of DPD Headquarters from the old City Hall to the brand-new, custom-built Jack Evans Police Headquarters on South Lamar Street in January 2003, it is now impossible to visit the site of the Oswald line ups.

16. The horizontal 'height' lines, plus one of the six numbers below which the line up members stood, are clearly visible in photographs in Jesse Curry's *Personal JFK Assassination File*, self-published,1969, pages 76-77. (The position of the number 6 in the centre-right photograph on page 77 shows that there could be a maximum of only six people, including the suspect, in a line-up.) There is an even better photograph, taken at the 12.30am press conference, on the first page of photographs in Larry Sneed's 1998 book *No More Silence*, published by Three Forks Press, Dallas. This shows much of the wall with the horizontal 'height' lines and the position numbers 4, 5 and 6. (See also footnote 18 below.)

17. 4H 166 (Testimony of Jesse Edward Curry).

18. Brief footage of this press conference is included around 46 minutes into the 105 minutes long, 1992 G. G. Communications (US) version of Nigel Turner's *The Men Who Killed Kennedy*. Part of the stage and the horizontal 'height' lines on the wall are clearly visible. (Full transcript of this press conference appears as CE 2169.)

19. Details of the organization and set-up of the line ups involving Lee Harvey Oswald can be found in the Warren Commission testimony of Homicide Detectives Elmer L. Boyd (7H 119-137), Charles N. Dhority (7H 149-158), Richard M. Sims (7H 158-186), Walter E. Potts (7H 195-202), L. C. Graves (7H 251-260), James R. Leavelle (7H 260-270) and Acting Homicide Detective Charles W. Brown (7H 246-251).

20. For some reason which is lost on me, the number of police officers conducting each line up (and accompanying each eyewitness) varied greatly. For example, at the first line up, five officers were named as being *"with the witness"* (Mrs Markham). These were Chief Curry, Captain Fritz, Detectives Graves and Leavelle and Acting Detective Brown.

For the line up on the Sunday afternoon, however, two eyewitnesses (Scoggins and Whaley) were attended only by Detective Leavelle.

21. 7H 131 (Testimony of Elmer L. Boyd).

22. 7H 253 (Testimony of L. C. Graves). He virtually reiterated what Boyd had said: "When we want to show a person up, we call the jail supervisor and tell him what we want and who we want in the showup, and to put two or three or four other people with him, the approximate age, size and so forth."

23. CE 2003 (Dallas Police Department file on investigation of the assassination of the President), page 293 of exhibit (24H 347).

24. Compiled from the Warren Commission testimony of the detectives named in footnote 20 above.

25. FBI report dated 25th November 1963 of Oswald interview on 23rd in which the final paragraph reads as follows: "OSWALD complained of a lineup wherein he had not been granted a request to put on a jacket similar to those worn by some of the other individuals in the lineup."

26. 7H 240 (Testimony of Don R. Ables).

27. 7H 245-246 (Testimony of Daniel Gutierrez Lujan).

28. See chart in Photo Section Two

29. As footnote 23 above.

30. 7H 252 (Testimony of L. C. Graves).

31. 4H 212 (Testimony of J. W. Fritz).

32. Warren Report, page 167.

33. *ibid.*

34. Sylvia Meagher: *Accessories After The Fact*, published by Vintage Books, New York, 1976, page 256. Mrs Meagher gives CE 1974 as her source. The

actual citation is on page 96 of the exhibit (23H 879) and is an excerpt from the DPD radio log as follows:

26 (Patrolman G. W. HAMMER)   "See if you can raise somebody over there at TIPPIT's car"

221 (Patrolman H. W. SUMMERS) "221 (SUMMERS) just left there, what do you want to know?"

26 (Patrolman G. W. HAMMER)   "Go back and get this witness's shoes she left on the hood of the car and we'll be in Homicide Bureau."

221 (Patrolman H. W. SUMMERS) "Captain Doughty has got them."

26 (Patrolman G. W. HAMMER)   "10-4."

The thought of the sole eyewitness to Tippit's murder placing her shoes on the hood (bonnet in UK) of the victim's car may raise a smile. Her strange action is, however, very important when considering the accuracy and credibility of her later recollection and description of the event. See footnote 3 above, particularly the first of the two cited passages which I quote in the third paragraph of the section "The (un)reliability of eyewitness testimony".
35. Edward Jay Epstein's interviews of Assistant Counsel Wesley J. Liebeler at Newfane, Vermont, 20th June – 1st July 1965.
36. Assistant Counsel Joseph A. Ball, speaking at a public debate at Beverly Hills, California, 4th December 1964.
37. Assistant Counsel Norman Redlich, during Epstein's Vermont interviews at footnote 35 above.
38. 3H 310-311 (Testimony of Mrs Helen Markham).
39. As with the Markham line up, I rely on footnote 23 above to establish the time of this line up.
40. Warren Report, page 169.
41. Warren Report, page 159.
42. 6H 452 (Testimony of Domingo Benavides). Benavides was another witness at the Tippit murder site but was never called to attend any of the line-ups. He stated: "And so Ted (Callaway) then got in the taxicab and the taxicab came to a halt and he asked me which way he (the gunman) went."
43. 7H 399 (Testimony of Sam Guinyard).
44. *Fair Play* internet website, no. 24 (September/October 1998).
45. As footnote 41 above.
46. As footnote 23 above.
47. Warren Report, page 168.

48. 3H 350 (Testimony of Mrs Barbara Jeanette Davis); 6H 462 (Testimony of Mrs Charlie Virginia Davis).

49. As footnote 23 above.

50. 6H 462 (Testimony of Mrs Charlie Virginia Davis).

51. ibid.

52. As footnote 23 above.

53. 2H 261 (Testimony of William Wayne Whaley).

54. Warren Report, page 145.

55. Howard L. Brennan with J. Edward Cherryholmes: *Eyewitness To History*, published by Texian Press, Waco, Texas, 1987.

56. 7H 332-360 (Testimony of Forrest V. Sorrels). In discussions with me, researcher Larry Hancock put forward a suggestion that both the DPD and the Secret Service seemed to show an intense interest in Brennan. As was often the case, however, they did not appear to be sharing information or working together. Could this be the reason for the confusion over Brennan's attendance at City Hall on the evening of Friday 22nd? At this time, the Dallas Police Department was in charge of the investigation, including the organization and handling of the ID line-ups and the Secret Service should have played no official part in the proceedings. Such disputes of jurisdiction had, however, been unable to prevent the body of the deceased President being flown out of Dallas earlier in the day.

57. Judy Whitson Bonner: *Investigation of a Homicide: The Murder of John F. Kennedy*, published by Droke House Publishers, Anderson, South Carolina, 1969.

58. 3H 145 (Testimony of Howard Leslie Brennan).

59. 3H 147 (Testimony of Howard Leslie Brennan).

60. See footnote 16 above.

61. 3H 147 (Testimony of Howard Leslie Brennan).

62. Brennan with Cherryholmes, page 24.

63. Kathlee Fitzgerald: *Who's Who in the Secret Service*, self- published, 1996, page 168.

64. Brennan with Cherryholmes, page 25. As I have already pointed out, the maximum possible number of persons who could be present was six.

65. *ibid*, page 27.

66. 7H 355 (Testimony of Forrest V. Sorrels).

67. 7H 354 (Testimony of Forrest V. Sorrels).

68. See footnote 54 above, pages 13 and 156.

69. Dale K. Myers: *With Malice: Lee Harvey Oswald and the Murder of Officer J. D. Tippit*, published by Oak Cliff Press, Milford, Michigan, 1998.

70. Transcript of the relevant parts of this telephone conversation, Myers/ Virginia Davis, are contained in Myers' email to the author dated 9th March 1999.

71. 3H 147 (Testimony of Howard Leslie Brennan).

72. Chief Jesse Curry, Homicide Detectives Sims, Boyd, Graves, Leavelle, Dhority, Moore and Potts and Acting Detective Brown. Detectives Hall and Senkel were not called to testify before the Warren Commission.

73. 4H 215, 217, 227 (Testimony of Captain J. Will Fritz).

74. 4H 237 (Testimony of Captain J. Will Fritz). At one point in his testimony, Captain Fritz described the line-up of 2.15pm, Saturday 23rd specifically as "Showup No. 4" (4H 227). This effectively excludes the alleged Brennan line up altogether.

75. Detectives Clark and Perry, Jail Clerk Ables and remand prisoner Lujan (7H 243-246). None of the other remand prisoners involved were called to testify.

76. Warren Report, page 145.

77. 3H 148 (Testimony of Howard Leslie Brennan).

Written 1993 – and regularly updated
First published November 1993 in *Dallas '63*, vol. 1, no. 1.
Later published (as *Eyewitnesses to the Kennedy and Tippit Murders)*, November 1993 in *The Fourth Decade*, vol. 1, no. 2.
Spring 1999 in *Assassination Chronicles*, vol. 5, no. 1.
May/June 1999 in internet website *Fair Play*, no. 28.
July 1999 in *The Dealey Plaza Echo*, vol. 3, no. 2.

11. A repudiation of the claim that Lee Harvey Oswald shared a Dallas jail cell with John Franklin Elrod

INTRODUCTION

As a long-time Kennedy assassination researcher with a career in practical law enforcement (UK) behind me, I am aware that police and investigative procedures sometimes vary on different sides of the Atlantic. In most cases, the methods and procedures adopted are those that best achieve the objectives sought in the prevailing circumstances. I have presented research papers and written articles which demonstrate some of these differences. Despite quite often drastic variations in procedure, however, police forces in both the UK and the USA seem satisfied with the way *they* do it and are happy with the results achieved. I have, however, occasionally come across startling examples of procedure which seem completely inadequate and downright wrong. What follows here was spawned by a report of just such an example.

MORE 'NEW EVIDENCE' OFFERED

In 1996, the research community welcomed yet another book that promised new information and a vital key to the assassination of President John Fitzgerald Kennedy. I refer, of course, to *Oswald Talked*, written by the husband-and-wife team of Ray and Mary La Fontaine. [1] The book saddled itself with the pretentious and not entirely original sub-title *The New Evidence in the JFK Assassination*. Perhaps that should have sounded the alarm bells.

I bought and read the book. Its title perfectly summed up the La Fontaines' claim that during his brief incarceration between fortuitous arrest in the Texas Theatre and convenient murder in the City Hall basement, Lee Harvey Oswald shared a cell with one John Franklin Elrod, a complete stranger. This buddy-buddy cellmate situation somehow prompted Oswald to open up his heart to his new friend. That, of course, was something that the Dallas PD, the FBI and even the US Postal Service had failed to persuade him to do during many hours of subtle questioning by their highly-trained professional interrogators.

According to the La Fontaines' book, Oswald told Elrod that he had attended a meeting in an unspecified motel room at which four other men had been present. One of these other men had been Jack Ruby and the purpose of the meeting was to advance a certain sum of money and make arrangements in connection with a gun-running exercise. [2] If true, this account would place Oswald in the same room as Ruby, discussing a criminal undertaking involving firearms, just a few days before the Kennedy assassination. Also, conveniently, one of the other men present was claimed to be another fellow prisoner in Dallas, but there was no claim that he shared the Oswald/Elrod cell.

It was immediately apparent that neither the date nor the exact *venue* of this meeting was given. Indeed, those important facts appear nowhere in the book and no reason is ever given for their absence. It is intimated that the meeting was held to deal with the sale and movement of certain firearms stolen from the Texas National Guard armory at Terrell (20 miles east of Dallas) during the night of Wednesday 13th/Thursday 14th November. Some of the stolen weapons surfaced at the conclusion of a badly handled DPD car chase which culminated in a Ford Thunderbird crashing in Dallas on the evening of Monday 18th. It would be logical to assume that the reported motel room meeting took place between those dates. Its location, however, remains open to conjecture. If the authors of *Oswald Talked* ever sought these details, then surely they should have informed their readership of their results.

Early in *Oswald Talked*, it was explained that Mary La Fontaine had liaised closely with the respected California researcher Bill Adams and had discovered the DPD Arrest Report in respect of Elrod. [3] This was hailed as a major breakthrough and was to become the basis for the book. When I read about this, however, I experienced a strange feeling of *deja vu*. Somehow, this information did not seem new to me. I felt that I had either read about it or heard about it several years previously. Eventually I tracked down the reference that I recalled. It is in Joachim Joesten's pre-Warren Report book *Oswald: Assassin or Fall Guy*. [4] If you can locate a copy of this scarce book, you can read all about the strange arrest of the unnamed Elrod. [5]

Joachim Joesten ended that chapter of his book with an optimistic but misguided expression of hope: "These are the unresolved puzzles which, it is hoped, the Warren Commission will clarify when it interrogates the Dallas police." [6] Dream on, Joachim, dream on .....

THE RUSS BURR ARTICLE

The La Fontaines described how Oswald and Elrod shared a cell as if that were the normal procedure when an alleged murderer is arrested and remanded in custody. As researcher Russ Burr pointed out in his fine article "Did Oswald Talk?" in *The Kennedy Assassination Chronicles*, however, that simply did not happen. [7]

Two of the most heinous crimes it was possible to commit in the United

States in November 1963, or indeed today, are the assassination of the President or the murder of a policeman. In *Oswald Talked*, we are given to understand that Lee Harvey Oswald had been arrested for committing one or possibly both of those offences. Surely it does not take an Einsteinian intellect to work out that the *last* thing to happen would be for such a prisoner to be placed in a cell with somebody else. The simple implications of such an act are just horrendous. Consider the following:

- As a suspected assassin/murderer/both, Oswald might continue his killing spree and also kill his cellmate.

- As either a patriotic JFK-loving American, or maybe one of those non-violent criminals who deplores cop-killing, the cellmate might attack and kill Oswald.

- No police force or department could allow either of those acts of violence to occur in one of its cells.

These were my first thoughts when I read the opening chapter of *Oswald Talked*. I was amazed, therefore, that there was no immediate uproar within the research community. Some criticism, yes, but nowhere near as much as I would have expected. It seemed a classic case of *The Emperor's New Clothes*, with nobody willing to raise their voice too much at the absurd suggestion that Oswald shared a jail cell with another person in Dallas. Perhaps, I thought, they really *do* lock up assassins and murderers in the same cell as lesser criminals in America and nobody finds it as unacceptable as I do.

I was unhappy with the La Fontaines' documentary "proof" of Oswald's cell number and location. This seemed to rely on nothing better than some incomplete telephone record sheets and various statements from jail personnel and policemen which appeared to have been very carefully sifted. I was also unhappy that the two telephone record sheets shown in *Oswald Talked* [8] seemed to assume some sort of unimpeachable status. In my opinion, they require closer scrutiny—particularly the second of the two. I would also consider it imperative that they be married up to the "jail record cards used to record prisoner's phone calls" as described by Assistant Jailer Arthur E. Eaves in an affidavit dated 14th August 1964. [9] These have the additional value of bearing the times of the calls, something which was absent on the sheets.

I am sure that like me, the La Fontaines went to the trouble of checking out the names of all those jail and police officers whose names appeared on the telephone record sheets. Although the second sheet shown in *Oswald Talked* purports to cover part of the Third Platoon (3.00pm to 11.00pm) on 22nd November 1963, only two of the six people named were Third Platoon personnel.

These were Jail Guard Carroll Honeyman and Patrolman Johnny C. Reid. The signature on the Oswald entry, the final one on the sheet, is that of Patrolman Buel T. Beddingfield, a member of the Second Platoon of the Patrol Division at Headquarters but on 23rd November, carrying out the duties of Assistant Jailer. In an affidavit of 17th August 1964, he stated: "I was assigned in front of the cell occupied by Lee Harvey Oswald to keep a close watch on him." [10] No mention here of a cellmate.

THE RECOLLECTIONS OF CHIEF JESSE CURRY

Rather than rely on apparently incomplete telephone records that demand a certain amount of conjecture to interpret, I prefer to go along with more solid documentation. In this connection, I would refer to Police Chief Jesse Curry's *JFK Assassination File*. [11] If anybody really knew the details of Oswald's incarceration in the City Hall cellblock, then it was surely this man.
On page 74, we read the following:

"The Platoon Lieutenant was instructed that no reporters or photographers would be allowed within the City Jail proper. The suspect, Lee Harvey Oswald, was to be kept in a maximum security cell in F block on the fifth floor. All other prisoners were removed from adjacent cells, and a police guard was kept directly outside the cell opposite the door."

Then, on page 80, describing events in the early hours (around 1.45am) of 23rd November, immediately following Oswald's arraignment when he was charged with the murder of President Kennedy, we read:

"Oswald was returned to his cell by the two officers who had taken him downstairs for the arraignment. The doors on the cell in F block clicked shut for the night and Oswald was left alone with only his own thoughts to haunt him. A police guard remained on duty only a few yards away. No one was allowed to see him or bother him throughout the remainder of the night so that he would have some time to rest."

Staying with Chief Curry, let us move on to his Warren Commission testimony and consider the following exchange:

RANKIN: "Will you describe the place where he was kept while he was there in the jail?"

CURRY: "Well, it is in one of our maximum security cells, much the same as any other jail. But he was isolated away from the other prisoners, and there was two jail guards set immediately outside his cell."

RANKIN: "Did you isolate him or was that in accordance with your instructions?"

CURRY: "No; this is customary with a prisoner of this type and Chief Lumpkin in charge of the service division had issued these orders." [12]

SIGNIFICANT WORDS FROM CAPTAIN WILL FRITZ

During his Warren Commission testimony on 22nd April 1964, Captain Fritz, head of the Homicide & Robbery Bureau, explained to Assistant Counsel Ball how the identification line-ups (also called 'showups') had been organised. For the first two line-ups, on the afternoon of the day of the assassination, Oswald's companions in the line had been two Vice Squad detectives and a civilian jail clerk. It was normal procedure for such *roles* to be taken by current remand prisoners of similar general appearance to the suspect. [13]

When Mr Ball commented on this (two cops and a DPD employee in the line with Oswald), Captain Fritz said:

"I borrowed these officers, I was a little bit afraid some prisoner might hurt him, there was a lot of excitement and a lot of feeling right about that time so we didn't have an officer in my office the right size to show with him so I asked two of the special service officers if they would help me and they said they would be glad to ... and we used a man who works in the jail office, a civilian employee as a third man." [14]

Captain Fritz later explained to Mr Ball how Oswald had been paraded before the press in the basement assembly/showup room around midnight. He said:

"I was a little bit afraid something might happen to him in front of that stage, someone in the crowd might hurt him but he (Chief Curry) said no, he wanted him out there in the front, and I told him I would like to put him on the stage so that the officers could jerk him inside the jail office if anything happened ..." [15]

Later, Mr Ball asked: " ... what precautions did you take for his safety in custody?" to which Captain Fritz replied:

"In custody. We took all kinds of precautions to keep him, anyone from hurting him. We had an officer go with the jailer and back and we did everything we thought we could do. As I told you a while ago, we even put officers at the end of the stage with him so they could get quickly to him if anybody tried to hurt or molest him."

Fritz added that he was not responsible for the jail but he concluded: "I am sure though they used more than average precautions up there." [16]

Captain Fritz was obviously conscious of the potential physical danger to Oswald should he be allowed too close to other prisoners, or even to the gentlemen of the press. Is it likely that Captain Fritz, or any other responsible member of the DPD, would later allow the prime suspect to be locked in a cell with a total stranger?

I think not.

CONFIRMATION FROM JIM LEAVELLE

Returning to Russ Barr's article, he quotes from interviews he conducted with former DPD Homicide Detective James R. Leavelle and says: "But Leavelle also said that Oswald was always isolated while he was in jail. ALWAYS." Leavelle also confirmed that Oswald was placed "in a seclusion area that contained three cells and he was placed in the middle." I understand that Oswald was in cell F2 and that cells F1 and F3 were empty. Ironically, after being arrested, searched and documented after shooting Oswald to death, Jack Ruby was also placed into cell F2.

CONCLUSION

In closing, I would offer my unqualified support for Russ Barr's conclusions in this matter. However, I do find it strange that at the time I wrote this piece (early 1999), very few researchers had come forward to challenge the hypothesis put forward by the La Fontaines, particularly along the lines I have indicated above.

I fully appreciate the extreme irony that, despite all the intricate precautions taken for the safety of Lee Harvey Oswald, he should still be successfully attacked by Jack Ruby under the very noses of the Dallas Police Department. That event, however, was certainly not the result of having him 'doubled up' in a jail cell with another prisoner. That simply did not happen.

NOTES

1. Ray and Mary La Fontaine: *Oswald Talked: The New Evidence in the JFK Assassination*, published by Pelican Publishing Company Inc., Gretna, Louisiana, 1998.
2. La Fontaine, page 16.
3. The Elrod Arrest Report is reproduced on page 28 of *Oswald Talked*.
4. Joachim Joesten: *Oswald: Assassin or Fall Guy*, published by Marzani & Munsell Publishers Inc. New York, 1964.
5. Joesten, pages 72-73.
6. Joesten, page 74.
7. *The Kennedy Assassination Chronicles*, vol. 4, no. 2, Summer 1998, pages 34-37.
8. La Fontaine, pages 394-395.
9. CE 1999 (affidavits of Arthur E. Eaves dated August 14, 1964, and Buel T. Beddingfield dated August 17, 1964, executed at Dallas, Tex.) at 24H 34.
10. *ibid* at 24H 35.
11. Jesse Curry: *JFL Assassination File*, published by American Poster and Printing Company, Inc., Dallas, 1969.
12. 4H 153 (Testimony of Jesse Edward Curry).
13. In *Oswald Talked* (page 41), the La Fontaines wrote: "Elrod says today that he was put on a chain with Oswald , (and) appeared in lineups ..." Nothing is offered in the way of proof or corroboration of this statement and I am perfectly comfortable in saying that it is completely untrue. Elrod was not "put on a chain with Oswald" and he did *not* appear in any of the Oswald line-ups.
14. 4H 212 (Testimony of J. W. Fritz).
15. 4H 219 (Testimony of J. W. Fritz).
16. 4H 232 (Testimony of J. W. Fritz).

Written 1999.
First published Spring 1999 in *Kennedy Assassination Chronicles*, vol. 5, issue 1.
Published November 2002 in *The Dealey Plaza Echo*, vol. 6, no. 3.

12. Oswald — a driving force?

INTRODUCTION

Many researchers have addressed the question of whether Lee Harvey Oswald could drive. Most appear to have reached the conclusion that he could not. There is conflicting evidence that a driver's licence was ever issued in the name of either Lee Harvey Oswald or Alek James Hidell. There is, however, far more to it than that.

Throughout the testimony, statements and affidavits of witnesses, plus police and FBI documentation and various other sources, there are numerous suggestions that Oswald was capable of driving a car. These suggestions, some of which are very positive, were either totally ignored or given no more than a perfunctory glance by those investigating the assassination and Oswald's background.

I do not propose to delve deeply into each individual piece of evidence suggesting that Oswald could drive. Rather, I will merely outline a few examples, together with relevant sources and maybe a few comments of my own. I then leave it up to the reader to decide on the credibility of each example and, finally, on the overall validity of the sum of these examples. I would be a fool to claim that I have unearthed every example of evidence that Oswald could drive a car. I have, however, listed those I feel to be the most significant.

Purely for convenience, I have listed these examples in the order in which they *should* logically have occurred: obtaining a driver's permit, learning to drive, taking a test, etc. As will soon become apparent, however, this was *not* the sequence in which these events (or alleged events) did occur.

I also leave it up to the reader to decide whether these examples apply to the 'real' Oswald or to one or more 'lookalikes'.

"WE SHOULD GET A CAR LEE"

The earliest reference I can find to the potential purchase of a motor vehicle by the Oswalds comes on the third page of a Dallas FBI teletype, presumably sent to J. Edgar Hoover's office. Unfortunately, I do not have a date for this document but it appears to marry up with similar communications of early December 1963. It was originally RESTRICTED but was released under the JFK Act. [1]

It dealt with an interview of Marina Oswald and included the following paragraph:

> "Marina stated she had insisted on several occasions that Oswald buy a car but he objected that he did not have sufficient money to buy it, and further, the car would require repairs. She knows of no occasion when he saw anyone about the purchase of an automobile or mentioned to her that he had seen someone or intended seeing someone about the purchase of an automobile."

The wording of the opening sentence fascinates me. There are two things in it that suggest to me that Marina is referring to a specific car. The comment that 'he did not have sufficient money to buy *it*' surely indicates a particular vehicle. If that is not the case, then the word '*it*' would have been replaced by the word '*one*.'

Furthermore the reference to the car requiring repairs surely indicates a specific vehicle. On 24th October 1963, Michael Paine had paid $200 for a 1955 or 1956 blue and white Oldsmobile sedan which he apparently offered to Lee Harvey Oswald. [2] The second sentence of the FBI teletype extract above is very positive in saying that Lee never went along with Marina's request. However .....

TRYING TO OBTAIN A 'LEARNER'S DRIVING PERMIT'

On the morning of Saturday 9th November 1963, Ruth Hyde Paine drove to Oak Cliff with Lee and Marina Oswald, their two daughters and her own two children as passengers. There are several available accounts of this important event but I will restrict myself to just one. This appears in an affidavit executed by Mrs Paine on 24th June 1964. It contains the following statement:

> "On the occasion of Saturday, November 9, 1963, about which I testified before the Commission, when I took Marina and Lee Oswald in my station wagon to the Automobile Drivers Bureau in the Oak Cliff section of Dallas, Texas to enable Lee Oswald to make application for an automobile driver's learner permit, each of my two children and both of the Oswald children, June and Rachel, accompanied us.
>
> Upon our arrival at the Automobile Drivers License Bureau, which was located in a shopping center area in Oak Cliff we discovered that the Automobile Drivers License Bureau was closed ..." [3]

This incident, which I have no reason to believe did not occur, is surely an indication of Oswald's serious intention of learning to drive. There is, in fact, a report that he returned to the Automobile Drivers License Bureau the following Saturday (16th) when "he had arrived before closing time but still too late to get in because there was a long line ahead of him the place having been closed both the previous Saturday for election day and the following Monday, the 11th, Veterans Day" [4]

LEARNING TO DRIVE

The earliest intimation I can find concerning Lee Harvey Oswald being given any sort of driving tuition comes from a letter written in Russian by Ruth Paine and sent to Marina Oswald, living at this time with Lee in New Orleans. It is dated 24th August 1963 at a time when Ruth was staying at the residence of Arthur Young (her husband's step-father) in Paoli, Pennsylvania.[5]

The English translation of the relevant paragraph reads as follows:

"Lee told me that he learned a little from his uncle how to drive a car. It would be very useful for him to know how to drive. It is hard to find time for this when he works every day." [6]

During her lengthy testimony before the Warren Commission, Mrs Paine was questioned by Assistant Counsel Arthur E. Jenner, Jr. about that particular paragraph. He told her that "the Commission is very interested in the subject matter of Mr. Oswald, of Lee Oswald being able to drive a car." [7] Now why were they so concerned with that?

There exists solid and apparently irrefutable evidence that Oswald was receiving driving instruction from Ruth Paine—presumably in Ruth's own car, a 1955 light green Chevrolet station wagon. This car was one of three vehicles owned by the Paines. [8]

A letter written by Ruth to her mother on 14th October 1963 included the following passage:

"If Lee can just find work it will help so much. Meantime, I started giving him driving lessons last Sunday (yesterday). If he can drive this will open up more job possibilities and more locations." [9]

There was corroboration of this in the testimony of Michael Paine as the following brief exchange with Assistant Counsel Wesley J. Liebeler indicated:

LIEBELER: "Did your wife ever tell you that she had seen Oswald driving a car or she was trying to teach him how to drive a car?"

PAINE: "Yes; she did."

LIEBELER: "Did she indicate what proficiency he had at operating an automobile?"

PAINE: "She thought he was, she observed how much one has to learn in order to drive a car. He had a difficulty in some manner, perhaps it was in judging when to turn the wheel when parking. And I think she said he over controlled it, turned too far." [10]

In her own testimony, Mrs Paine answered a string of questions about Oswald's driving efficiency [11] and she had this to say about the course of lessons upon which she seems to have embarked with him:

"I offered to give him—give Lee lessons on Sunday afternoons and we managed to do it a few Sunday afternoons, I think three altogether and there were a couple of weekends when we didn't get the lesson in, something intervened ... I think the last lesson was November 10, being the last Sunday." [12]

Taking a driving test?

The following is taken from the Warren Commission testimony of Buell Wesley Frazier at Washington, DC, 11th March 1964:

BALL: "From that time until November 22, did he ride home with you every weekend?"

FRAZIER: "No, sir; he did every weekend except one."

BALL: "And why did—did he tell you why he wasn't going to ride home that weekend?"

FRAZIER: "Yes, he did. He said he was working on his driving license and he was going to take a driving test."

BALL: "Did you ever ask him afterward if he had taken his driver's test?"

FRAZIER: "No, sir; I never did. I assumed that he had taken it and passed it whatpart of the test he was taking." [13]

A little later in this testimony, there is the following:

BALL: "Did you ever talk to him on whether or not he could drive a car, knew how to drive a car?"

FRAZIER: "Well, I say, I believe the first afternoon, the first time we was going home and we were talking about that and he said he was working onhis driving license then and then naturally like I told you several weeks later, then he told me he was going to take his driving test and I assumed he could drive a car as being as old as he was because most everybody in State of Texas by the time you are my age if you can't drive a car something is wrong with you." [14]

TRYING TO OBTAIN AUTOMOBILE INSURANCE

A single-page Dallas FBI report deals with an apparent enquiry by Lee Harvey Oswald concerning automobile insurance. [15]

The report, written on 2nd December 1963, states that an Edward A. Brand had telephoned the office earlier that day and had reported a visit made to his insurance office by an individual identifying himself as O.H. Lee "approximately two weeks before President John F. Kennedy was assassinated." Brand's insurance business, known as the Tower Insurance Agency, was situated at 1045 North Zangs Boulevard—"directly across the street" from Oswald's rooming house at 1026 North Beckley Avenue.

Brand stated that Mr Lee was enquiring regarding automobile liability insurance. However he (Brand) was unable to quote any exact insurance rates as the gentleman said that he did not own a car, but intended to buy one in the near future. Brand suggested that Mr Lee return after purchasing his car.

Let me quote directly from the report:

"Brand also was of the opinion that the only identification he saw of Lee's was a Texas drivers license, but did not notice if the initials were O. H., but believed the last name was Lee on this drivers license.

"Brand concluded by saying he did not immediately recognize Lee Harvey Oswald's photograph in the Dallas newspapers, or on television, until after reading Oswald had in the past used the name Lee at which time he did recognize Oswald's photograph as being the individual who contacted him regarding insurance under the name of O. H. Lee."

Considering the purchase of a car?

One of the cornerstones of the theory that there was a concerted and determined effort to create a number of 'false' Oswalds prior to the assassination involved a well-documented incident centred on the Downtown Lincoln-Mercury agency at 118 East Commerce Street, Dallas. This remains the best-known example of Lee Oswald—or a deliberately-created lookalike—driving a motor vehicle.

Albert Guy Bogard was the unfortunate car salesman at the centre of this incident. In his Warren Commission testimony, [16] Bogard was certain that the incident had taken place in the early afternoon of Saturday 9th November and he described it thus:

> "I think it was around 1:30 or 2 o'clock ... A gentleman walked in the door and walked up and introduced himself to me, and tells me he wants to look at a car. I show him a car on the showroom floor, and take him for a ride out Stemmons Expressway and back, and he was driving at 60 to 70 miles an hour and came back to the showroom. And I made some figures, and he told me that he wasn't ready to buy, that he would be in a couple or 3 weeks, that he had some money coming in. And when he finally started to leave I got his name and wrote it on the back of one of my business cards, and never heard from the man any more.
> "And the day that the President was shot, when I heard that—they had the radio on in the showroom, and when I heard the name, that he had shot a policeman over in Oak Cliff, I pulled out some business cards that I had wrote his name on the back on and said, 'He won't be a prospect any more because he is going to jail,' and ripped the card up."

Bogard, having lost a potential sale, threw the card away. It was never recovered but he confirmed that the name he had written on it was "Lee Oswald"—the name given by his possible customer. Bogard further explained that the car in question had been a red Mercury Comet Caliente, a two-door hardtop, with a $3,000 price tag.

In addition to mentioning the speed at which his prospect had driven, he also made the following significant comment: "He might have drove a little reckless, but other than that, he knew how to drive." [17] Bogard's story was corroborated by his sales manager, Frank Pizzo, and two salesmen, Oran Brown and Gene Wilson, who were present at the time of Oswald's visit. [18]

As stated above, this incident occurred on the afternoon of Saturday 9th November 1963. It was during the morning of that day that Ruth Paine had driven Oswald to Oak Cliff on his unsuccessful attempt to obtain an Automobile Drivers Learner Permit. She was adamant that Oswald had spent the afternoon of that day at her house in Irving. As she said in her affidavit of 24ᵗʰ June 1964:

"... all of us entered my home where we remained throughout the balance of that day and evening." [19]

Furthermore, an internal FBI memorandum dated 14ᵗʰ January 1964 authorised the Dallas office to conduct a polygraph examination of Bogard. This was in part due to the fact that "Mrs. Ruth Paine places Oswald in her home on 11/9/63 (election day) and states that in her opinion it would not have been possible for Oswald to have travelled to the automobile agency on 11/9/63 as he was not out of her sight for a sufficient portion of that day to have made the trip. Accordingly, it appears that Bogard's story is untrue," [20]

When Albert Bogard took his FBI polygraph test in Dallas on 24ᵗʰ February 1964 "the responses recorded were those normally expected of a person telling the truth." [21] Unfortunately, however, that was not the result required so "the Commission has placed no reliance on these results." [22] If that sounds familiar cast your mind back to what was said when the paraffin test applied to Oswald's left cheek failed to indicate that he had fired a rifle. It was almost identical. It seems the game rules are: make the test—if the results are favourable that's great—if the results are not favourable, ignore them!

REPORTED SIGHTINGS OF OSWALD DRIVING

There are several well-documented reports of Lee Harvey Oswald driving a car. I will mention just three. One important alleged sighting puts Oswald in the town of Alice, Texas on 3ʳᵈ October 1963 but since this incident has been examined in depth by my friend and fellow researcher Chris Courtwright, of Carbondale, Kansas, I will not cover it here.

THE FURNITURE STORE VISIT

This incident is one of the best-known and most-frequently quoted in connection with the 'multiple Oswalds' theory. It also introduces very strong and corroborated evidence that Lee Harvey Oswald drove a car—if, indeed, it really *was* Oswald. Funnily enough the incident came to light virtually by accident. This happened through the curiosity of a prominent British journalist, Lady Jean Campbell, the US Political Correspondent of the London *Evening Standard*. Lady Campbell was normally based in New York City [23] but like many other journalists she was assigned to Dallas immediately following the assassination. As well as being a minor member of the British nobility, she was also one of Norman Mailer's ex-wives and had borne him a daughter during their year-long union. She was highly-regarded within her profession.

The following account is based on various FBI documents [24] and on Lady Campbell's published piece in her newspaper. [25]

> The rush by journalists to reach Dallas to cover the assassination story meant that all spare hotel space in the city was immediately snapped up. When she arrived from New York City Lady Campbell could find no accommodation nearer than Irving. She hired a car and drove into downtown Dallas each day usually allowing *Paris-Match* photographer Jerry Herald to share the ride.

> On her daily drive from Irving to Dallas, Lady Campbell noticed that a shop she passed at 149 East Irving Boulevard, Irving displayed a sign with the words GUN SHOP in red letters above the door. Female intuition allied to a journalist's hunch suggested that maybe Oswald had visited the shop ("I knew that he was as fascinated by guns as some women are by diamonds" she wrote in her paper).

> Lady Campbell visited the shop and spoke with the proprietor, Mrs Edith Whitworth, and her friend Mrs Gertrude Hunter, who was in the shop at the time. To her surprise, Lady Campbell found that despite the sign over the door the shop sold second-hand furniture rather than firearms.

> In answer to Lady Campbell's query about Oswald, Mrs Whitworth told her that he had indeed visited her shop between 2.30pm and 3.00pm on Thursday 7th November, together with "his wife their two or three week old infant and an older daughter about two years of age." Oswald had enquired whether he could get a plunger for a gun but was informed that the shop sold only furniture. Mrs Whitworth referred him to the Irving Sports Shop. The Oswalds looked around for a few minutes before leaving.

> Lady Campbell stated that Mrs Hunter told her "that when the Oswalds left the store, Marina placed the older child into a 1956 or 1957 two-tone Ford or Chevrolet and then entered the vehicle herself with her infant daughter. Oswald entered the vehicle, sat behind the steering wheel and turned the vehicle around and proceeded in the direction of the Irving Sports Shop."

> According to Lady Campbell: "Mrs. Hunter related Oswald, in doing this was proceeding the wrong way in a one-way street and had to turn the vehicle around again."

The Warren Commission seemed uncertain exactly how to handle and examine the evidence of Mrs. Whitworth and Mrs. Hunter. In the end, Assistant Counsel Wesley Liebeler deposed each lady separately on the same day, Wednesday 22nd. July 1964. He dealt with Mrs Whitworth at 5.00pm and Mrs Hunter at 5.50pm. These two short sessions preceded the three-ring circus which developed two days later when both ladies, plus Marina Oswald (and her two children), appeared again. This time, Mr Liebeler was not alone. William A. McKenzie and Henry Baer, counsel for Mrs. Oswald; Peter Paul Gregory, interpreter; and Forrest Sorrels and John Joe Howlett, special agents of the US Secret Service, were also in the room.

This session opened at 11.00am and whilst no time is given for its completion, its transcription occupied 26 pages, (11H 275-301), so it was lengthy. Any researcher in need of a little relaxation and light relief is urged to peruse the little exchanges between Marina and the two ladies.

My object here is not to analyse the Hunter and Whitworth eyewitness testimony other than to stress that they described Oswald driving a two-tone blue-and-white Ford, Chevrolet or Plymouth car. [26]

THE BARBER OF IRVING

Clifton M. Shasteen was the proprietor of Clifton's Barbershop at 1321 South Storey, Irving. He testified before the Warren Commission that Oswald had his hair cut several times at the shop and that he had personally cut Oswald's hair "three or four times." He had no doubt about this customer's identity and recalled a conversation they once had about a pair of unusual yellow shoes that Oswald was wearing. Shasteen said that Oswald told him he had got them "down in Old Mexico." [27]

Shasteen's certainty about this man's identity is given great credence by the fact that he (Shasteen) knew Ruth Paine by sight and had seen them together.

Midway through his testimony, Shasteen was asked by Assistant Counsel Albert E. Jenner, Jr., whether Oswald had ever driven an automobile up to the shop. Shasteen replied: "He drove that there 1955, I think it's a 1955, I'm sure it's a 1955 Chevrolet station wagon. It's either blue and white or green and white—it's two-toned—I know that." [28] There is little doubt that Shasteen is describing Ruth Paine's car, with Oswald driving it.

At the beginning of Shasteen's testimony, Mr Jenner came out with a sample of verbal nonsense which was hardly designed to put the Irving Barber at his ease: "I understand that in the course of your looking at television on the 22nd of November 1963, there occurred to you upon seeing some of the people shown on the screen that you had rendered some tonsorial services to Lee

Harvey Oswald?" Why did he not just ask Shasteen if he had ever given Oswald a haircut?

REPORT OF OSWALD DRIVING JACK RUBY'S CAR

I consider this to be one of the oddest, most-important and most-neglected alleged examples of Lee Harvey Oswald driving a car. It also represents one of the best (or perhaps worst!) examples in the whole case of the Dallas Police Department dragging its heels to such an extent that it lost a potential valuable witness through rank inefficiency. An internal DPD report dated 11th December 1963 contained the following:

> (A confidential) "source states that she was told by another person that a mechanic from a garage in the downtown area who regularly services Jack Ruby's automobile, had stated that subject (Lee Harvey Oswald) had driven Ruby's car several times prior to the assassination of President Kennedy." [29]

An unattributed footnote rejected the content of this report and stated that "subject did not know how to drive an automobile."

Perhaps because of that footnote, no action was taken for almost three months. Another DPD internal report (dated 3rd April 1964) repeated the content of the first, adding that the mechanic had mentioned that Oswald "had been driving Jack Ruby's automobile for approximately two months and that he (the mechanic) knew this because Oswald had brought Ruby's car to his garage for repairs." [30]

The report named the mechanic as William J. Chesher and stated that the previous day, 2nd April 1964, Detectives Biggio (the author of the report) and Stringfellow had attempted to contact him (presumably for the first time) but "the officers were informed that subject (Chesher) had died on March 31 1964 of a heart attack." They had literally missed him by two days—and they were not going to get a second chance to interview him!

Chesher's untimely death was sufficiently suspicious to earn him a place in Craig Roberts and John Armstrong's excellent book on the subject. [31]

AN ADMISSION FROM THE FBI

An URGENT teletype memorandum from SAC, Dallas to SAC, San Antonio dated 30th November 1963 opens with a brief item of information on Oswald's return to Dallas from Mexico. It then continues with what is undoubtedly a reply to a previously asked query concerning Oswald's ability to drive. At the risk of becoming involved in semantics I am intrigued by the final two words of the second sentence below:

> *"To date investigation has not reflected that Oswald has ever been in possession of automobile. He does not have driver's license and is not believed to know how to drive very well."* [32]

"Very well"? I can find only one interpretation of that. The writer is indicating that Oswald *does* know how to drive a car but he is not very proficient. There is no other way to read it.

CONCLUSION

Whilst I am not prepared to say categorically whether or not Lee Harvey Oswald had the ability to drive a car, I feel that the weight of evidence suggests that he could.

NOTES

1. Copy of document in author's possession.
2. See Carol Hewett, Esq.: *Ruth and Michael Paines' Mystery Vehicle*, published in the *Conference Abstracts of the Second Annual National Conference of COPA, 1995*. See also 2H 413 (Testimony of Michael R. Paine).
3. 11H 153-154 (Affidavit of Ruth Hyde Paine).
4. 2H 516 (Testimony of Ruth Hyde Paine).
5. See Steve Jones: *Ruth Paine: My Summer Vacation*, published in the *Conference Abstracts of the Second Annual National Conference of COPA, 1995*.
6. CE 424 (Translation of Commission Exhibit No. 423) first page of exhibit (17H 148). Curiously the paragraph I have quoted was underlined by hand in the typewritten English translation, but not in the Russian handwritten original which is shown as CE 423.
7. 2H 502 (Testimony of Ruth Hyde Paine).
8. According to the Warren Commission testimony of Michael R. Paine, he owned a 1956 Oldsmobile and a Citroen while his wife owned a station wagon (2H 413). Carol Hewett, Esq. (see 2 above) states that Mrs Paine's station wagon was a 1955 light green Chevy. Researcher Chris Courtwright has directed my attention to a DPD memo dated 23rd December 1963 in which it is stated

that Ruth drove a 1955 Chevrolet station wagon, two-tone green with Texas licence NK 4041.

9. CE 425 (Letter from Ruth Paine to her mother, dated October 14, 1963), second page of exhibit (17H 151).

10. 2H 413 (Testimony of Michael R. Paine).

11. 2H 513-516 (Testimony of Ruth Hyde Paine).

12. 2H 514 (Testimony of Ruth Hyde Paine).

13. 2H 217 (Testimony of Buell Wesley Frazier).

14. 2H 218 (Testimony of Buell Wesley Frazier).

15. Internal Dallas FBI report by SA James R. Graham, Jr.—copy in author's possession.

16. 10H 352-356 (Testimony of Albert Guy Bogard).

17. 10H 354 (Testimony of Albert Guy Bogard).

18. 10H 342-344 (Testimony of Frank Pizzo)—note: neither Brown nor Wilson was asked to testify before the Warren Commission.

19. 11H 154 (Affidavit of Ruth Hyde Paine).

20. Copy of this document in author's possession.

21. CE 3031 (FBI report dated February 25, 1964 of polygraph interview of Albert Guy Bogard at Dallas, Tex.)

22. Warren Report footnote no. 696 on page 840.

23. Lady Campbell was interviewed by the FBI at her office at Room 1002, Carnegie Hall, 57th Street and 7th Avenue, New York City on 6th July 1964.

24. Washington FBI HQ memorandum dated 6th December 1963, written by C. D. DeLoach; New York FBI Office report dated 7th July 1964; Dallas FBI Office report dated 29th July 1964; Houston FBI Office report dated 14th August 1964—copies of all these documents in author's possession.

25. *London Evening Standard*, Friday 29th November 1963, back page (continuation of front page story entitled "The back room boy vanishes").

26. 11H 253-262 (Testimony of Mrs Gertrude Hunter) and 11H 262-275 (Mrs Edith Whitworth).

27. 10H 311 (Testimony of Clifton M. Shasteen).

28. 10H 317 (Testimony of Clifton M. Shasteen).

29. DPD internal report from Detective W. S. Biggio Criminal Intelligence Section, to Captain W. P. Gannaway Special Service Bureau, 11th December 1963—copy of document in author's possession.

30. DPD internal report as above but dated 3rd April 1964—copy in author's possession.

31. Craig Roberts and John Armstrong: *JFK: The Dead Witnesses*, published by CPL, Tulsa, Oklahoma, 1995: page 9.

32. Copy of this document in author's possession.

Written 1996.

First published January/February 1997 on internet website *Fair Play*, no. 14.

Later published April 1997 in *JFK/Deep Politics Monthly*, vol. 2, no. 3.

13. Lee Harvey Oswald in Helsinki, Finland: October 1959

Amongst guests and visitors to the Hotel Torni, Helsinki, since it opened in 1931 have been: an American President (Herbert Hoover), a Finnish President (General Mannerheim), a Soviet Premier (Aleksei Kosygin), Finland's leading composer (Jean Sibelius) and novelist (Mika Waltari), members of the Swedish nobility (Prince Bertil and Count Folke Bernadotte), a Nobel Prize winner for literature (Frans Eemil Sillanpaa) ... and an American alleged assassin and lone nut (Lee Harvey Oswald)

INTRODUCTION

I have long advocated the merits of going back to primary sources whenever possible. I may have upset one or two fellow researchers with my criticism of those who do not follow my philosophy here. This piece is the result of going back to an original source in a *physical* rather than a literary sense.

To retrace Lee Harvey Oswald's October 1959 footsteps to Helsinki may be looked upon by some people as a wasted effort. Maybe that is the reason that I can find no example of any researcher undertaking it previously. My own opportunity came in 2000 when I was making plans to attend the Voices of Europe choral concert at Johanneksen Kirkko, Helsinki. This was part of the European Cities of Culture project.

I felt that it would be foolish indeed to spend time in Helsinki and not make enquiries into Lee Harvey Oswald's mysterious 1959 visit to the Finnish capital *en route* to defect to the Soviet Union. It is well-documented that he spent one night at the Hotel Torni, followed by four nights at the Hotel Klaus Kurki before travelling on to Moscow.

PREPARATIONS

After ascertaining that the Hotel Torni was still operating, I booked a room there for the nights of Wednesday 30th and Thursday 31st August 2000. I liaised briefly with fellow researcher Barb Junkkarinen. Barb's husband Juha was born in Finland and I had got to know him when I spent time as the Junkkarinens' house guest in Portland, Oregon in December 1999. Both Juha and Barb were very helpful and gave me much invaluable information about the city and its people.

A few weeks before I was due to fly to Finland, I wrote to the manager of the Hotel Torni, introduced myself and enquired whether the 1959 hotel registers and records were still available for study. I was very disappointed to learn that the hotel had changed ownership in the early '70s and the whereabouts of those records could not be established. However, the manager was sympathetic to my request for information and suggested that we meet when I arrived at the hotel.

THE HOTEL TORNI

On checking into the hotel on the afternoon of Wednesday 30th August 2000, I asked the young lady at reception if I could see Mr Peuralahti, the hotel manager. After recovering from her initial amusement, the receptionist informed me that the hotel manager was *Mrs* Peuralahti.

Mrs Kaisu Peuralahti and myself then enjoyed a very friendly and fruitful hour in the hotel's splendid American Bar. She had been very busy on my behalf. Mrs Peuralahti presented me with a book entitled *Torni: 50 vuotta hotellin ja gastronomian vaiheta*, written by Jussi Talvi and published in 1981. Obviously it was written in Finnish. However a brief English translation of some of the more relevant passages had also been prepared under the title *Hotelli Torni: A Short History of the Hotel Torni*. This was to prove very useful indeed.

The Hotel Torni occupies a prestigious position in the centre of Helsinki. It is lined by streets on three sides and has the postal address Yrjönkatu 26. In American terms, it could be described as occupying a complete city block. The city's main thoroughfare, Mannerheimintie, is less than 100 yards away. The original building was erected in 1903. The addition of its characteristic tower converted the building into one of Scandinavia's first high-rise structures and when it became a hotel in March 1931, it was with the proud boast that it was *"the first skyscraper hotel in Finland"*. The hotel's name, Torni, is the Finnish word for "tower". The top of the tower incorporates the Ateljee Bar (which hosts monthly art exhibitions) and an observation platform which remains the highest vantage point in Helsinki. It is claimed that on a clear day, the coast of Estonia is visible some 60 miles away across the Bay of Finland.

The original hotel had 100 rooms. Following subsequent extensions and a major refurbishment during the mid-1990s, that number has now increased by over a half.

The original lift, which holds just six people, is still the only one in the hotel. This tiny lift caused a problem during the 1977 visit of Soviet Prime Minister Kosygin. Helsinki's mayor, Teuvo Aura, accompanied Mr Kosygin as they ascended but their interpreters had to wait below. Apparently the "conversation" at the top of the building was conducted in mime until the interpreters could join them. Several of the original marble staircases are still in place, and it is a pleasure to use them, pausing on the landings to admire the stained glass windows.

SOME OF THE HOTEL'S BETTER-KNOWN GUESTS

As listed above, the Torni has attracted major political guests together with others from the world of the arts and at least one Royal family. During the first years of its existence, the Hotel Torni was undoubtedly the city's leading hotel. The Torni kitchen rapidly established a fine reputation and the hotel even published its own newspaper.

The obvious question to arise from all this is a simple one: how did an allegedly penniless drifter like Lee Harvey Oswald come to stay at the Hotel Torni in October 1959, at a time when the hotel was the height of elegance? The 1950s had seen the hotel regain its reputation as a gastronomic leader following problems during the war. Superior food and excellent service were of paramount importance. Perhaps the answer to the mystery of Oswald's presence lies in some of the Hotel Torni's less well-known historical connections and background.

WORLD WAR II AND AFTER

The following is a direct quote from the English notes on the hotel's history: "The beginning of World War II affected the Torni in many ways ... Many foreigners, particularly the British, saw great possibilities in the Torni as an espionage headquarters."

I have been unable to expand on this statement but presume that Finland would have attracted diplomatic attention from both the Allies and the Axis powers. I wonder if photographs of the hotel from the wartime years would reveal the top of its tower bristling with radio antennae. Finland was not directly involved in World War II and was never occupied by German forces. The country was, however, engaged in hostilities with the Soviet Union, (the so-called Winter War of 1939/40), followed by several years of Soviet occupation.

To quote further from the same source: "After the end of the war in 1944, the entire hotel was taken over by Soviet authorities. They maintained control of it until 1947. Upon their departure, the property was found to be terribly run-down." On the wall directly outside the hotel's main entrance there is a brass plaque which states, in Finnish and in English: "The Control Commission of the Allied Powers (Soviet Union) resided in this hotel during 1944-1947."

Following the departure of the Soviets, the hotel required and underwent major refurbishment but by the early 1950s it had regained its pre-war reputation and was surpassing even its earlier glories. It had more rooms, smart bars and superior restaurants and it resumed publication of its newspaper.

OSWALD'S 1959 VISIT

So what have we here? The tallest building in one of Europe's most beautiful capitals, situated in the centre of the city, which was probably used as a World War II spy centre by the Allies (and maybe also, by definition, the Axis powers). It had then been under Soviet occupation and control for three years before rising like a phoenix from its ashes to regain its reputation as the smartest place in town. Can it be relevant that the Soviet Consulate, like the other embassies and consulates, is within walking distance? Is there now a pattern emerging to suggest why, of all the hotels in Helsinki, this is the one to which the fleeing Oswald was directed in October 1959?

THE HOTEL KLAUS KURKI

After just one night (10th/11th October) at the Torni, Oswald booked out and moved to the Hotel Klaus Kurki. He remained there for five days and four nights before checking out late on Thursday 15th, boarding a train, and crossing the Finnish/Soviet border at Vainikkala *en route* for Moscow (CE 2676).

Like the Torni, the Hotel Klaus Kurki was, and is, a high-class hotel in the centre of Helsinki. Its address in Bulevardi, one of the "best" streets in town, indicates its nature and its status. If the Torni was the number one hotel in town, then the Klaus Kurki, described as a "boulevard hotel", was probably number two. The two hotels are no more than 300 yards apart and are both plainly visible from the junction of Yrjönkatu and Bulevardi. They are now members of the Sokos Hotel Group.

THE HOTEL TORNI TODAY

The Torni was sold in the early 1970s and in accordance with Finnish Civil Law, all documents relating to it remained in the possession of the previous owners. Unfortunately, they are no longer in business so all records and registers, including that with the historic Oswald entry, are lost for ever. Efforts to locate them have proved fruitless.

A second major refurbishment programme was completed in 1997. The hotel now has 154 rooms, an American Cocktail Bar, a Rooftop Bar, five conference rooms, four saunas, an outside terrace bar, a well-appointed restaurant and an Irish pub! Some of the flights of stairs have been replaced but several of the original marble staircases remain. There was not sufficient space to replace or enlarge the original lift and it is still restricted to a maximum of six (preferably very slim!) passengers. To me, it has the charm and comfort of a broom cupboard and it seems strangely out of place amid the affluence of this splendid hotel.

FIFTY YEARS OF THE HOTEL TORNI

In 1981, to commemorate its 50th anniversary, a book on the Hotel Torni was published. Written by local author Jussi Talvi, it concentrates on the wonderful gastronomic reputation which the hotel has enjoyed from its opening. It does, however, find room for a very short mention of Oswald's visit which translates as: "Famous persons would appear at the Torni to be met with looks of surprise, but no one knew Lee Harvey Oswald when he stayed briefly."

CONCLUSION

That, then, is a brief account of my findings during an all-to-short visit to Helsinki. Like others I still seek the so-called "smoking gun" in this case and as expected, I did not find it in Finland's capital city. I hope, however, that I have demonstrated that Lee Harvey Oswald's stay at the city's two best hotels raises even more suspicions than we held before. Perhaps the plan was for him to stay one night at the Hotel Torni, meet a contact, collect his travel papers, Soviet entry visa, etc., and be on his way. Perhaps there was an unexpected delay which necessitated his move to the Hotel Klaus Kurki and a longer stay in Finland than expected.

Perhaps, perhaps, perhaps ... perhaps we shall never know.

THANK YOU

Many people, researchers and non-researchers alike, have assisted me in various ways with this project and I must express my particular gratitude to the following:

Mrs Kaisu Peuralahti, the present manager of the Hotel Torni, who supplied valuable background information on the hotel and its history—and was kind enough to present me with a copy of the Hotel Torni book, its English translation notes and other documentation. Prior to my arrival in Helsinki, she also went to considerable trouble to make enquiries at the Hotel Klaus Kurki on my behalf.

Barb and Juha Junkkarinen, assassination researchers from Forest Grove, Oregon, who patiently indulged my endless queries and translated many Finnish passages for me.

Chris Mills, from Nottingham, England, for his earlier work on Oswald's Finland flight which acted as a spur to me.

Lauri Salmi, a good internet friend from Riihimaki, Finland, who was responsible for getting me my concert ticket and thus provided the reason for me to go to Helsinki in the first place.

SOURCES

Warren Commission 26 Volumes: CE 2676 and 2677 (CIA reports which, from the way in which they are worded, strongly suggest that no CIA personnel actually took the time or trouble to visit Helsinki!)
Edward Jay Epstein: *Legend: The Secret World of Lee Harvey Oswald*, published by Hutchinson, UK (1978)
Anthony Summers: *Conspiracy*, published by Victor Gollancz, UK (1980)
Jussi Talvi: *Torni: 50 vuotta hotellin ja gastronomian vaiheita*, published by Otava, Finland (1981)
Unattributed notes: *The History of Sokos Hotel Torni, Helsinki*. English translation of passages taken from the above Torni book.

Written 2000.
Research paper at the JFK-Lancer November in Dallas conference, 2000
First published March 2001 in *The Dealey Plaza Echo*, vol. 5, no. 1

14. "Just another day at the office"

The actions of Captain W. R. Westbrook
on the day the President came to town

INTRODUCTION

In any police force, be it the Dallas Police Department of November 1963 or any other, then or now, each individual officer, no matter his rank, is assigned certain duties and responsibilities. He will normally carry these out at a given location or locations during his period of duty. These obvious and essential functionary duties must be adhered to irrespective of any but the most urgent outside events or influences. The overall discipline and well-being of the force relies on every officer fulfilling his or her individual part in the overall scheme of things.

The report of an attack upon President John F. Kennedy in Dealey Plaza, Dallas on Friday 22nd November 1963 was obviously just the type of occurrence to throw normal routines and procedures into disarray. Nevertheless it should not have been expected that individual officers would act independently of specific orders. In the situation which developed immediately following the shots at 12.30pm, it was even more important than usual that officers of all ranks, other than those directly involved, such as the motorcycle officers escorting the motorcade, should await specific orders from their supervisors.

Although some researchers may disagree, I feel that the vast majority of DPD officers acted correctly during that hectic two-hour period after the shots. They followed their specific routines, they acted upon the orders they received, they carried out those mundane yet essential tasks such as crowd and traffic control, and they located and took details from many eyewitnesses. When given the relevant information and orders, they acted promptly in effecting the arrest of the suspected assassin.

Inevitably, there were a few exceptions, some of them important. For example:

a. Traffic control at Elm and Houston was relaxed almost immediately after the shooting.

b. The possible crime scene behind the picket fence was not preserved.
c. There were no crime scene investigation reports of bullet strikes south of Elm Street.
d. No precise and accurate list of TSBD employees was ever made.
e. No list was made of the cars in the parking lot behind the picket fence.

CAPTAIN WESTBROOK'S DUTIES AND RESPONSIBILITIES

Captain William Ralph Westbrook [1] was born at Benton, Arkansas and was just two weeks short of his 46th birthday on the day of the assassination. He had joined the Dallas Police Department on 13th June 1941, was promoted to Sergeant after about four years and had gained the rank of Captain in 1952. His was purely an administrative task which did not even require him to wear his police uniform if he preferred not to. He held the position of Officer in Charge of the Personnel Bureau. This was part of the Training & Research Section and was located on the third floor of Police Headquarters at City Hall.[2]

Under his direct command, Captain Westbrook had Sergeant Henry H. Stringer, Patrolman J. L. Carver and Detectives William M. McGee and Joe Fields. His normal bureau complement was completed by three female "non-sworn employees"—civilian support staff. These were Marjorie Bright (Personnel Clerk, Grade 6), Nancy Drake (General Clerk, Grade 4) and Roma D. Worley (Stenographer, Grade 4). [3]

Sergeant Gerald Lynn Hill, a member of the Patrol Division, was on temporary assignment to the Personnel Bureau on the day of the assassination. As he explained to author/researcher Larry A. Sneed, he was involved in doing background checks on potential recruits and was working that day with Captain Westbrook. [4]

Perhaps the importance of the bureau's work can be judged by Marjorie Bright's grade. There was only one clerical civilian on the entire DPD staff with a higher grade. This was Eunice Sorrells, Grade 8, Chief Curry's secretary. [5]

The only other components of the Training & Research Section were the Police Academy and the Police Reserve. The Section was independent of the four main Divisions of the Department, namely Patrol, Traffic, Service and CID. In view of this, it is not readily obvious who Captain Westbrook's immediate superior would have been. From my own knowledge and experience of the basic structure of various police forces, I would surmise that he would have reported directly to Charles Batchelor, Assistant Chief of Police.

In his Warren Commission testimony, Captain Westbrook described his job thus: "At the present time I am personnel officer. We conduct all background investigations of applicants, civilian and police, and then we make—

we investigate personnel complaints—not all of them but the major ones." [6] Sergeant Gerald Hill described it to Larry Sneed in far more basic terms as "a combination of Personnel and Internal Affairs." [7]

When asked whether he was obliged to wear uniform, Captain Westbrook replied: "Well, it is optional. I don't wear one." [8] DPD Radio Unit Call Sign 550 was assigned to "Personnel Captain" [9] so there must have been times when Captain Westbrook was required to leave the building. Perhaps such occasions were connected with his applicant vetting or personnel complaint duties.

From that brief outline of Captain Westbrook's position and duties within the DPD, I think we can safely describe him as a police officer who was basically doing a civilian job. It involved personnel management, the vetting of staff, and dealing with personnel complaints—whatever that entails. It was surely never envisaged that his job would one day involve him rushing around the streets of Dallas and Oak Cliff in a variety of police vehicles, arming himself with a shotgun to search premises, and finally supervising the arrest of the man alleged to have assassinated the 35th President of the United States.

That, however, is exactly what Friday 22nd November 1963 was to bring.

AN OUTLINE OF CAPTAIN WESTBROOK'S ACTIONS

Having now introduced you briefly to Captain Westbrook and his function within the Dallas Police Department, it is time to examine his actions on the day that President Kennedy was shot.

Since Captain Westbrook was on what he described as "just my own routine duties" and was working his normal day shift hours from 8.15am to 5.15pm, not in uniform, [10] he should really have had nothing whatsoever to do with the presidential visit to the city. Furthermore, he should have had nothing to do with events following the shooting. In reality, however, he became part of more aspects of the immediate search for the assassin and the arrest of the suspect than possibly any other individual officer:

- He assisted in the search of the Texas School Book Depository

- He rushed to the Tippit murder scene

- He was involved in the finding of what was claimed to be the fleeing Oswald's discarded jacket

- He joined in the false alarm when it was thought that the escaping assassin had taken refuge in the Oak Cliff public library

- He was the highest-ranking police officer at Oswald's arrest in the Texas Theatre and he took charge of the operation. When the Warren Commission published its 26 Volumes of Hearings, he even appeared in one of the Oswald arrest photographs. [11]

These actions are fully described in Captain Westbrook's Warren Commission testimony which was taken in Dallas during the morning of Monday 6th April 1964 by Assistant Counsel Joseph A. Ball. [12] That source is one of many I have used to compile the following sequence of events.

CAPTAIN WESTBROOK'S DAY

Captain Westbrook arrived at his office on the third floor of City Hall at 8.15am on Friday 22nd November 1963. As usual, he was dressed in civilian clothes rather than police uniform. For him, there was no scheduled involvement in the presidential visit. It was due to be an ordinary day spent in the Personnel Bureau dealing with purely routine administrative matters. One must wonder whether he felt a little neglected at not being part of the big day. Perhaps he even thought that his closest connection with the event would be when he left his office to stand in the street and watch the motorcade as it passed the building and turned right on to Main Street. [13]

According to his testimony, the first that Captain Westbrook knew of the President being shot was when "one of the dispatchers came into the office and told us." He named this dispatcher as "Mrs. Kinney." [14] Sergeant Gerald Hill, who was also present in the office, described this person as "a lady by the name of Kemmey." [15] There was no female employee of either name on the strength of the DPD but there was a telephone clerk named Mrs. Beulah Kimmey on duty on the 7.00am to 3.00pm shift and I am confident that this is the lady in question. [16]

Almost at once, somebody else, whose name Captain Westbrook could not recall, came into the office and said that "they needed some more men at this Texas Depository Building." He immediately sent all four of his normal police subordinates, Sergeant Stringer, Patrolman Carver and Detectives McGee and Fields, plus Sergeant Hill, to that location. For some reason, he described Carver as a Sergeant but contemporary records show him to be a Patrolman. Perhaps he had acting rank. [17]

To explain what happened next, I can do no better than quote Captain Westbrook's Warren Commission testimony *verbatim*. I feel that the way in which he described his thoughts and mental frustrations may be the key to his subsequent actions.

He said:

" ... and then I walked down the hall spreading the word and telling the other people that they needed some men down there, and practically everybody left immediately. I sat around a while—not really knowing what to do because of the—almost all of the commanding officers and supervisors were out of the city hall and finally I couldn't stand it any longer, so I started to the Texas Depository Building, and believe it or not, I walked. There wasn't a car available, so I walked from the city hall to the depository Building ..." [18]

Initially, of course, Captain Westbrook has acted in an exemplary manner. As well as responding to the urgent call for assistance by sending his own men to the scene, he took the initiative and mobilized other officers on the third floor of the building. After this, he suddenly found himself alone and isolated, and apparently destined to take no part in what seemed likely to become the biggest day in DPD history since the bodies of Bonnie Parker and Clyde Barrow had been returned to their home town in May 1934. [19] Had he known just how deeply he was to become involved, I wonder whether he would have taken that walk down to Dealey Plaza.

AT THE TEXAS SCHOOL BOOK DEPOSITORY—AND BEYOND

Upon reaching the book depository, Captain Westbrook contacted Sergeant Stringer, who was standing outside the building. He then entered and began to assist in the search of the building, He had got no further than the first floor, however, when he heard somebody, presumably a policeman, shout that an officer had been shot and killed in Oak Cliff. [20]
Captain Westbrook's testimony describes what happened next:

"Well, then of course, I ran to my radio because I am the personnel officer and that then became, of course, my greatest interest at the time, and so, Sergeant Stringer and I and some patrolman—I don't recall his name—then drove to the immediate vicinity of where Officer Tippit had been shot and killed. [21] Of course, the body was already gone, the squad car was still there, and on one occasion as we were approaching this squad car, a call came over the radio that a suspicious person had been seen running into the public library at Marsalis and Jefferson, so we immediately went to that location and it was a false— it was just one of the actually—it was one of the employees of the library who had heard the news somewhere on the radio and he was running to tell the other group about Kennedy. So, we returned to the scene and here I met Bob Barrett, the FBI agent, and Sergeant Stringer and Barrett and I were together, and then an eyewitness to the shooting of the officer from across the street, a lady, came to the car, and she was telling us how this happened." [22]

Captain Westbrook has really got the bit between his teeth at this point. He has commandeered a patrol car and its driver, and with neither orders nor authority, has rushed from the TSBD to the Tippit murder scene at Oak Cliff. He has then dashed over to the Oak Cliff Branch Library where he was obviously anxious to be in on the arrest of the suspect. This is better than being stuck in an office confronted by a pile of paperwork!

This brief diversion at the library is mentioned in many books on the subject, but a fascinating remark by Captain Westbrook in his testimony seems to have been either missed or ignored. During questioning by Mr. Ball on the subject of firearms, Captain Westbrook indicated that he was armed when he was at the library but that he did not have a gun at the later arrest of Oswald. [23] This point was not pursued by Mr. Ball. Later in his testimony, however, whilst discussing the finding of a zipper jacket at a nearby parking lot, and without any prompting or for any apparent reason, Captain Westbrook said: " ... and at this time I had a shotgun—I had borrowed a shotgun from a patrolman." [24] Nothing more.

Once the library raid had proved to be a red herring, Captain Westbrook continued towards the Tippit murder site at 10th and Patton. On the way, according to the Warren Report, he became involved in yet another important event—the finding of the zipper jacket which was later claimed to have been discarded by Oswald as he fled the Tippit murder scene. [25] Obviously, it must be asked why the finding of this jacket was not introduced in chronological order. The answer to that has continued to elude researchers to this day. It was not mentioned in Captain Westbrook's testimony until much later.

It was, in fact, approaching the end of his testimony when Mr. Ball asked him a classic leading question: "Did you ever find some clothing?" [26] Captain Westbrook appeared somewhat evasive and seems to have been very much on his guard as he replied: "That was before, Mr. Ball." He went on to say that he had not found the jacket personally but that it had been pointed out to him by "some officer" and that he, Westbrook, had picked it up. Yet again, we have an example of Captain Westbrook's incredible lack of recall when it came to people's names.

According to the Warren Report: "Westbrook walked through the parking lot behind the service station and found a light-colored jacket under the rear of one of the cars." [27] This sentence is supported by two footnotes directing the reader towards Captain Westbrook's testimony but nowhere there does he ever state that he found the jacket. Mr. Ball showed Captain Westbrook three photographs of views of the parking lot where the jacket had been found [28] and Captain Westbrook identified them. His answers in response to Mr. Ball's questions concerning the photographs and what they depict were, to say the least, unconvincing. [29]

Mr. Ball then showed Captain Westbrook the jacket itself. [30] This was not preceded by any preparatory questions as to its colour, style or size. Instead, Mr. Ball simply produced it and said: "I show you Commission Exhibit 162, do you recognize that?" Captain Westbrook, doubtless with great relief, replied: "That is exactly the jacket we found." [31] Nowhere in this testimony is there any mention of its colour. For that, we have to go to the Contents page at the beginning of Volume 16 of the 26 Volumes of Hearings where CE 162 is described simply as "Gray zipper jacket."

From the available evidence, I am unable to state with any degree of certainty exactly who found the jacket, or precisely when. Sylvia Meagher [32] and Joachim Joesten [33] are among leading early researchers who have studied this at length but still nobody has produced the definitive answer. Be that as it may, however, there is no disputing the fact that the ubiquitous Captain Westbrook was, as usual, there or thereabouts.

A billfold (wallet), later claimed to have been Oswald's, was found at the Tippit murder scene and there is evidence that both Captain Westbrook and FBI Special Agent Robert Barrett handled it. Captain Westbrook makes no mention of it in his testimony, an omission I find very strange indeed, whilst SA Barrett was never called to testify.

AN ENCOUNTER WITH MRS. MARKHAM

As already mentioned, Captain Westbrook had been approached by a female eyewitness to the Tippit shooting at the scene itself. This was none other than Mrs. Helen Louise Markham. Here, Captain Westbrook appears to have displayed remarkable initiative, perhaps calling upon his 'personnel complaints' experience and knowledge of human behaviour. In his own words: "I got someone else there to be sure and get her name for the report." [34] It seems he was a good enough judge of character to see that although she claimed to be an eyewitness, she would probably prove a little troublesome.

OFF TO THE CINEMA

Captain Westbrook's day was still not over. Just as Mrs. Markham was beginning to blurt out her story, a patrolman (identity unknown) called out: "It's just come over the radio that they've got a suspicious person in the Texas Theater." [35] To learn what happened next, let us return to Captain Westbrook's Warren Commission testimony:

"Then Sergeant Stringer, I and Agent Barrett got in another squad car, and I don't know who was driving this one, but then when we arrived and were approaching the theater, I directed the patrolman to turn down into the alley instead of going to the front because I figured there would be a lot of cars at the front. There were two or three at the back." [36]

FBI Special Agent Barrett then accompanied Captain Westbrook through the side door into the theatre where they encountered a man described by Captain Westbrook as "an employee of the theater" but whose name he could not recall. According to other testimony, it appears that this was actually Johnny Calvin Brewer, the manager of Hardy's shoe store. [37] Captain Westbrook and SA Barrett went to opposite sides of the stage and the 'employee' then "pointed to a man that was sitting about the middle—the middle row of seats pretty close to the back and he said, 'That is the man you are looking for.'" [38] At this point, Captain Westbrook was on the right hand side of the stage facing the auditorium.

This part of Captain Westbrook's testimony produced an unexpected and unintended piece of nonsense which would perhaps have been more suitable as part of a Monty Python sketch. If only as light relief, it is repeated here exactly as it appears in the testimony:

BALL: "Which side were you on?"

WESTBROOK: "I was facing the audience—I would be on the right side."

BALL: "Facing the audience—that would be on the right side?"

WESTBROOK: "I was on the right side."

BALL: "And if you were facing the screen you would have been on the left?"

WESTBROOK: "I would have been on the left."

BALL: "The man that was pointed out to you was sitting next to the aisle, if you were facing the screen?"

At this point, Captain Westbrook resisted the obvious reply that there would hardly have been any point in someone indicating the man if he (Westbrook) had his back to the audience. [39]

Captain Westbrook next described Oswald's arrest by Patrolman M. N. McDonald and added that he recognized McDonald as they had worked together as radio patrolmen. This was an important remark as Captain Westbrook pointed out that "the stage was still dim." In total contrast to his series of odd questions regarding Captain Westbrook's position on the stage, Mr. Ball then put a very significant question: "Were the lights on in the theater?" Captain Westbrook replied: "Very dim ones; the picture was still running, but the lights were on very dim." [40] This comment is in direct contrast to the recollections of several other witnesses, both police and civilian. [41]

Captain Westbrook ran from the stage, again accompanied by SA Barrett, and seemed to take something of a leading part in the remainder of the arrest drama. He ascertained that an officer had taken possession of Oswald's revolver and later recalled that he heard Oswald say something about 'police brutality.' He also unintentionally introduced a little piece of humour into his testimony:

BALL: "Were the handcuffs on him at the time you arrived?"

WESTBROOK: "They were putting the handcuffs on him—they had one handcuff on one hand and they were trying to find the other one and they were having difficulty in locating it because there were so many hands there."

BALL: "How many officers were there?"

WESTBROOK: "In fact—that was one of the only humorous things about the whole thing—somebody did get ahold of the wrong arm and they were twisting it behind Oswald's back and somebody yelled—I remember that, 'My God, you got mine.' I think it was just an arm that come up out of the crowd and somebody grabbed." [42]

Unprompted by Mr. Ball, Captain Westbrook then added that he ordered officers in the theatre "to be sure and take the names of everybody in the theater at the time." This would obviously be of great importance later in the investigation. However, that order was either ignored or the list was compiled and then lost. I know of nobody who has ever seen such a list. Only two of those Texas Theater patrons appear to have been identified: George Jefferson

Applin, Jr. and John Gibson. Applin testified that he gave his name and details to an officer [43] but Gibson told the Commission that no police officer took his name and address. Furthermore, he did not recall them taking details from any other cinema patron that afternoon. [44]

The arrest complete, Captain Westbrook hurried the prisoner out of the theatre, shouting loudly at the officers: "Get him out of here. Get him in the squad car and head straight to the city hall and notify them you are on the way." [45] This was done and that radio call, logged at 1.52pm, was sent under Radio Call Sign 550-2 (Sergeant Gerald Hill): "Suspect on shooting of Police Officer is apprehended and enroute to the station." [46] It will be noted that there is no mention of the arrested man being suspected of the President's killing at this stage.

RADIO CALL SIGNS

There appears to have been considerable confusion concerning the radio call signs in use by the Dallas Police Department that day. As already stated, call sign 550 was allocated permanently to Captain Westbrook in his capacity as the Personnel Captain. Sergeant Gerald Hill, as Captain Westbrook's number two (albeit temporarily) was assigned the call sign 550-2.

There are several examples in the official radio log of these being confused. [47]

TWO IMPORTANT PHOTOGRAPHS

It is a little known fact that photographs were taken inside the Texas Theater in the course of Oswald's arrest. The cameraman was a *Life* magazine freelancer, James MacCammon, and like Captain Westbrook, he managed to be at the centre of the action many times that day. His photographs include Dealey Plaza, the exterior of the TSBD and the Tippit murder scene as well as Oswald's arrest. One of MacCammon's internal Texas Theater photographs appears in the Warren Commission's 26 Volumes of Hearings. As explained by Sergeant Hill in his testimony, it shows six people: Sergeant Hill himself, Lee Harvey Oswald, Detective Paul Bentley, Officer C. T. Walker (DPD), one man unidentified by Sergeant Hill, plus, of course, Captain William Ralph Westbrook. [48] This photograph appears to be the second of the three which Jim MacCammon took inside the theatre. [49] For some reason which is unclear to me, the name of James MacCammon does not appear to be widely known. Indeed in Richard Trask's excellent photographic study, it fails to get a mention. [50]

His day's work now apparently complete, what did Captain Westbrook do next? In his own words: "I went back to the city hall and resumed my desk." [51] Is this man cool—or is this man *cool*?

However, Captain Westbrook was not finished. When Patrolman McDonald arrived at City Hall, Captain Westbrook noticed the scratch on his face which he has sustained during his struggle with Oswald. In the Captain's words: "I had him go to the Bureau to have his picture made." [52] This is the well-known and widely published portrait, taken at 2.00pm that day. [53]

THE FINAL TWIST

Surely that was it. No. There was to be one final twist to the story of Captain Westbrook's day. Almost as an afterthought, just a couple of minutes from completing Captain Westbrook's testimony, Mr. Ball asked him: "Were you in the personnel office at the time that a gun was brought in?" Captain Westbrook replied: "Yes, sir; it was brought to my office when it shouldn't have been." [54] This prompts an obvious question: why, of all the offices in the many departments of City Hall was that weapon, which turned out to be the revolver seized during Oswald's arrest, [55] brought to Captain Westbrook's office and placed on Detective McGee's desk, together with its ammunition? [56]

I eventually succeeded in resolving this small mystery, but only at the expense of creating a new one. In his testimony, Sergeant Gerald Hill, who had retained possession of Oswald's revolver from the time it was handed to him by Detective Bob Carroll inside the Texas Theater, stated: "The gun remained in my possession ... until ... Detective T. L. Baker of the homicide bureau ... came to the personnel office and requested that they be given to him, and I ... turned them over to him at this point." [57]

So that is how Oswald's revolver came to be in Captain Westbrook's office. Apparently, Sergeant Hill, together with Detectives Paul Bentley and Bob Carroll and Patrolmen C. T. Walker and K. E. Lyons, had "adjourned to the personnel office, which was further down the hall from homicide and I sat down and started to try to organize the first report of the arrest." [58] It is logical to suppose that those five officers, unable to find the space and quiet to put their report together in the Homicide Bureau, would have sought somewhere away from all the frantic activity. It just seems a remarkable coincidence that of all the offices in the building; they should choose Captain Westbrook's. Surely it was just a coincidence.

Conclusion

So that was Captain Westbrook's day. As I stressed earlier, he should have done nothing more active than remain at his desk, carrying out normal administrative tasks and armed with nothing more lethal than a pen. In reality, he did nothing of the sort.

It would be natural to expect that Captain Westbrook's vast and varied involvement with the events of the day would make him one of the most frequently mentioned and quoted characters in the final Warren Report. His name, however, appears on only one page, and then only in connection with the finding of the mysterious zipper jacket. Check it for yourself. The name of Captain W. R. Westbrook appears just four times on that page, [59] on the Contents page—and nowhere else in the rest of the 888 pages of the published Warren Report.

For me, that represents the final and perhaps the greatest mystery.

Notes

1. Details of Captain Westbrook's correct first and middle name supplied by his great nephew, Jeff Westbrook, during email correspondence in early 2004. I am greatly indebted to Jeff, a Sergeant in the Columbia, Missouri, PD. He supplied me with other background details and proved to be a valuable and willing source of information.
2. CE 2175 (Floor plan of third floor, Dallas Police Department, Dallas, Tex.) This is at 24H 848 and is also on page 197 of the Warren Report.
3. Batchelor Exhibit No. 5002 *(Dallas Police Personnel Assignments, November 1963)*, page 31 of exhibit (19H 148).
4. Larry A. Sneed: *No More Silence*, Three Forks Press, Dallas, 1998, page 292.
5. As (3) above but page 2 of exhibit (19H 119).
6. 7H 110 (Testimony of Captain W. R. Westbrook)
7. Sneed: page 292.
8. 7H 110 (Testimony of Captain W. R. Westbrook).
9. CE 705 (Radio log of channel 1 of the Dallas Police Department for November 22, 1963) (17H 493).
10. 7H 110 (Testimony of Captain W. R. Westbrook).
11. Hill (Gerald) Exhibit A (Photograph of Lee Harvey Oswald being subdued in the Texas Theatre) (20H 156). Captain Westbrook is the bareheaded man in the foreground on the left.
12. 7H 109-118 (Testimony of Captain W. R. Westbrook).
13. 7H 44 (Testimony of Sergeant Gerald Lynn Hill).

14. 7H 110 (Testimony of Captain W. R. Westbrook).

15. 7H 44 (Testimony of Sergeant Gerald Lynn Hill).

16. As (3) above but page 20 of exhibit (19H 137).

17. 7H 110 (Testimony of Captain W. R. Westbrook). See also (3) above but page 31 of exhibit (19H 148).

18. 7H 110 (Testimony of Captain W. R. Westbrook).

19. Carlton Stowers: *Partners in Blue: The History of the Dallas Police Department*, Taylor Publishing Company, USA, 1983, page 72.

20. This information can only have originated from a police radio transmission. It may even have come directly from citizen T. E. Bowley's call on Tippit's squad car radio (transmission serial nos. 898-918 on DPD Radio Log [Channel 1] timed at 1.18pm). See Arch Kimbrough's transcript of the DPD radio tapes (1970). Details of certain of these transmissions also appear in the Warren Commission Hearings: Sawyer Exhibit A, at 21H 388-400.

21. 7H 79 (Testimony of Sergeant Calvin Bud Owens). Owens appears to have been the driver ("some patrolman") of this police car.

22. 7H 111 (Testimony of Captain W. R. Westbrook).

23. 7H 113 (Testimony of Captain W. R. Westbrook).

24. 7H 116 (Testimony of Captain W. R. Westbrook).

25. Warren Commission Report, page 175.

26. 7H 115 (Testimony of Captain W. R. Westbrook).

27. As (25) above.

28. Westbrook Exhibits B, C and D, at 21H 725, 726 (Photographs of the area where the zipper jacket was found).

29. 7H 117-118 (Testimony of Captain W. R. Westbrook).

30. CE 162 (Gray zipper jacket).

31. 7H 118 (Testimony of Captain W. R. Westbrook).

32. Sylvia Meagher: *Accessories after the Fact*, Vintage Books, New York, 1976, pages 274-280.

33. Joachim Joesten: *Oswald: The Truth*, Peter Dawnay Ltd., London, 1967, pages 217, 233, 237.

34. 7H 111 (Testimony of Captain W. R. Westbrook).

35. ibid. See also Arch Kimbrough's transcript of the DPD tapes (1970). Transmission serial no. 1377 on Channel 1, timed at 1.45pm (from Dispatcher): "We have information that a suspect just went in the Texas Theater on West Jefferson."

36. 7H 111 (Testimony of Captain W. R. Westbrook).

37. 7H 93 (Testimony of Patrolman Ray Hawkins).

38. 7H 111 (Testimony of Captain W. R. Westbrook).

39. 7H 111-112 (Testimony of Captain W. R. Westbrook).

40. 7H 112 (Testimony of Captain W. R. Westbrook).

41. 7H 5 (Testimony of Johnny Calvin Brewer), 7H 19 (Testimony of Detective

Bob K. Carroll), but see also 7H 31 (Testimony of Patrolman Thomas Alexander Hutson) who said: "The lights were on in the theater, but it was dark."
42. 7H 112 (Testimony of Captain W. R. Westbrook).
43. 7H 90 (Testimony of George Jefferson Applin, Jr.)
44. 7H 73 (Testimony of John Gibson).
45. 7H 113 (Testimony of Captain W. R. Westbrook).
46. CE 705 (Radio log of channel 1 of the Dallas Police Department for November 22, 1963) (17H 420).
47. ibid but 17H 390-485.
48. As (11) above. See also 7H 50 (Testimony of Sergeant Gerald Lynn Hill) for identification of the people shown.
49. John R. Woods II: *JFK Assassination Photographs: A Comprehensive Listing*, self-published, 1993, page 203.
50. Richard B. Trask: Pictures of the Pain, Yeoman Press, Danvers, Massachusetts, 1994.
51. 7H 115 (Testimony of Captain W. R. Westbrook).
52. 7H 114 (Testimony of Captain W. R. Westbrook).
53. CE 744 (Photograph of Officer M. N. McDonald of the Dallas Police Department, taken on November 22, 1963, at 2pm). Photograph was taken by A/Detective James M. Craft (temporarily assigned to the Identification Bureau) under the supervision of Lieutenant John Carl Day (4H 277—Testimony of Lieutenant Day).
54. 7H 118 (Testimony of Captain W. R. Westbrook).
55. CE 143 *(.38 calibre revolver, serial No. V510210).*
56. 7H 118 (Testimony of Captain W. R. Westbrook).
57. 7H 56 (Testimony of Sergeant Gerald Lynn Hill).
58. 7H 59 (Testimony of Sergeant Gerald Lynn Hill). See also CE 2175 (Floor plan of third floor, Dallas Police Department, Dallas, Tex.) This is at 24H 848 and is also on page 197 of the Warren Report.
59. Warren Commission Report, page 175. Ironically, three of the four mentions of Captain Westbrook on that page contain blatant inaccuracies in indicating that he was personally responsible for finding the zipper jacket.

Written 1994
Presented October 1995 at the COPA Annual Conference, Washington, D.C.
First published January 1996 in *The Fourth Decade*, vol. 3, no. 2.

15. The four faces of Harry D. Holmes

INTRODUCTION

Dallas Postal Inspector Harry D. Holmes was, in my opinion, one of the most fascinating characters connected with the investigation of the Kennedy assassination. Most people in the case fall into one of the accepted categories: assassination eyewitness, expert witness or police witness. Mr Holmes, however, could be said to drop into all three of those categories—plus another one.

In his book *And We Are All Mortal*, George Michael Evica described Holmes as "one of the many all-purpose Commission witnesses to testify in a number of areas." [1]   That sums him up perfectly.

In strict chronological order, the four faces of Harry D. Holmes were as follows:

1. As part of his duties as a Postal Inspector in Dallas, Holmes was in certain respects an FBI informant. One of his main functions was to keep the Bureau and the Secret Service appraised of all changes in the allocation of post office boxes in the Dallas area. [2]

2. Holmes was also an eyewitness to the assassination. He watched the Dealey Plaza shooting through binoculars from a window in his office on the fifth floor of the Post Office Terminal Annex building on the southern side of the plaza. [3]

3. Holmes became an 'expert witness' in his capacity as a Postal Inspector. As such, he testified before the Warren Commission, giving very precise details of the working of:

   • The post office box system
   • The tracing of the paperwork connected with the mail order purchases of Lee Harvey Oswald's rifle and revolver. [4]

4. Holmes was present during the final interrogation of Lee Harvey Oswald at City Hall immediately before the alleged assassin was taken downstairs to the basement and shot dead by Jack Ruby. Holmes was an active participant in the proceedings and also took copious notes. [5]

Just who was Harry D. Holmes?

Harry D. Holmes was born the son of a goatherd in Indian Territory, Oklahoma on 2nd July 1905. Since Oklahoma was not admitted to the United States (as the 46th state) until 16th November 1907, I am not certain whether Holmes could be classified as a true American. He died after a struggle against heart disease and cancer on 14th October 1989 in Dallas, Texas. He was survived by his widow, Helen Grace Holmes, daughter Helen Joyce and twin sons Richard and Robert. His connection with the case was deemed to be of sufficient importance to be mentioned in detail in his obituary in both Dallas newspapers. [6]

Holmes' early background gave no indication of his future connections with the Kennedy assassination. He told Warren Commission Assistant Counsel David Belin: "I graduated from high school in Kansas City, and went through 2 years to William Jewell College at Liberty, Mo., and went almost through my third year in Kansas City. Went to dental college in Kansas City." [7]

It is clear that Holmes never followed his apparent dental vocation since he joined the Postal Service in Kansas City as a mailhandler at the age of 18. He was working as a post office clerk when the United States entered the Second World War. In April 1942, he went into the Postal Inspection Service as a postal inspector. He remained continuously in that branch, transferring to Dallas on 1st July 1948 and was still holding that position on 22nd November 1963. [8] I am tempted to wonder if that initial transfer into the Postal Inspection Service introduced him to military postal censorship and could have provided his first steps into other fields of postal surveillance.

When he retired from the United States Postal Service at the age of 61, Holmes had been assigned to the Obscenity Section and he claimed that he made over 500 arrests. [9]

During the initial groundwork for the British TV 'live' presentation The Trial of Lee Harvey Oswald (shown on both sides of the Atlantic in November 1986), Holmes was invited to participate but he declined the offer. I understand from another witness who did appear that the deal included an all-expenses paid visit to London for two weeks. [10] Perhaps Harry D. Holmes turned it down due to his advancing years. He was then in his early-eighties.

The FBI informant

The claim that Harry D. Holmes was an informant for the FBI has been published in several books, notably Sylvia Meagher's *Accessories After The Fact* and George Michael Evica's *And We Are All Mortal*. [11] In each case, the author mentioned that Holmes was allocated Dallas informant number T-7.

Although the late Mrs Meagher has a footnote directing the reader to Commission Exhibit 1152, no official document is known or quoted in which Holmes is positively identified at T-7. Close perusal of CE 1152 reveals a plethora of information and other clues which unfortunately do no more than suggest that 'Confidential Informant, Dallas T-7' was Postal Inspector Holmes. [12]

I have since learnt, moreover, that he was just one of several postal officials operating under T-numbers in Dallas at that time. T-7 could, in fact, have been one of his colleagues with access to similar information and thus in possession of similar knowledge. [13] If that is the case, then I feel that number T-7 could have been assigned to one of Holmes' colleagues, possibly Postal Inspector Armstrong, at this time. [14]

In his Warren Commission testimony, Holmes inadvertently began to reveal some of his informant activities (Secret Service as well as FBI) until Assistant Counsel David Belin cut him short in the usual way. Consider the following:

> BELIN: "All right, what was the next thing you did in connection with the investigation of the assassination?"

> HOLMES: "Well, throughout the entire period I was feeding change of addresses as bits of information to the FBI and the Secret Service, and sort of a coordinating deal on it, but then about Sunday morning about 9:20__"

> BELIN: "Pardon me a second (Discussion off record) Anything else now, Mr. Holmes?"

> HOLMES: "I might cover the record of his rental of the post office box in New Orleans. Do you want me to go into that?" [15]

For neither the first time, nor the last, a Warren Commission investigator chose to play the 'Discussion off record' card at just the right time to avoid the introduction of something which could prove embarrassing or awkward. I cannot resist being fascinated by what Holmes was beginning to say concerning "about Sunday morning about 9:20 -"

As I shall detail later, it was only ten minutes after that time that the final Oswald interrogation session began—with Harry D. Holmes taking an active part.

EYEWITNESS TO THE ASSASSINATION

Harry D. Holmes was probably unique amongst the hundreds of people who saw the assassination. He was the only one who told the Warren Commission that he watched it through a pair of binoculars. For no apparent reason, David Belin asked him a very odd question: "Were you looking with the aid of any optical instrument?" to which Holmes replied: "I had a pair of 7½ x 50 binoculars." [16]

Holmes had earlier set the scene when he said that he was in his office "on the fifth floor of the terminal annex building, located at the corner of Houston and Commerce Streets." [17]

I am obliged to Gerald Posner who has provided the following excellent description of the layout of the Post Office Terminal Annex building in his book *Case Closed*: "The first and second floors were parcel post, the third mail processing, the fourth letter mail, and the fifth was both the cafeteria and the postal inspectors' offices. The building's view across Dealey Plaza is unobstructed." [18]

Unfortunately, nothing appears to have been published to indicate the exact window on the fifth floor from which Holmes witnessed the assassination. I believe, however, that through a lapse in concentration during his testimony, Holmes inadvertently provided that information although, for some unknown reason, it was never requested. David Belin questioned Holmes closely concerning the exact location of the Terminal Annex building in Dealey Plaza and Holmes answered him plainly and fully. When Belin asked: "On which corner is your building?" Holmes, either mishearing or misunderstanding the question, replied: "It is on the northeast corner." [19]

As anyone who has visited the scene knows, it is plain that the building concerned is not on the northeast corner of the plaza—it is in the southeast corner. I believe that Holmes' answer accidentally gave the location of his office within the building. If my interpretation is accurate, then something which has eluded researchers for a third of a century has now been resolved. Looking across Dealey Plaza from the grassy knoll to the Terminal Annex building, I am satisfied that the furthest left large, square top floor was Holmes' vantage point from inside his office.

If one intends to watch the motorcade from that office window, using a pair of binoculars, it is logical to open the window. Study of the movie film shot by Robert Hughes clearly shows this window to be open immediately following the shots sequence. [20] This, I feel, is the clincher.

Holmes testified that "there was several of us looking out of the window ..." [21] but I am unaware that any of these people was ever identified or interviewed by the investigative agencies. Gerald Posner, however, claims to have interviewed six of them and states that "three of them watched the assassination with a pair of binoculars." [22] Since Harry D. Holmes stated that "I had my binoculars on this car, on the Presidential car all the time" [23] it seems likely that there was at least one more pair of binoculars being used up on that fifth floor. I believe that Postal Inspectors were issued with binoculars as part of their official accoutrements, so that would account for it.

Posner states that one particular employee, Francine Burrows, had watched the motorcade from ground level and he names three other eyewitnesses as Tom Weaver, John Crawson and Bernie Schram. He claims to have interviewed all four in March 1992 but apart from saying that each claimed to have heard three shots, nothing of particular significance is revealed. [24]

During Holmes' testimony he produced a mysterious and oft-quoted phrase. When asked by Assistant Counsel Belin if he had seen anyone run across the railroad track, Holmes replied: "No. I saw nothing suspicious and I am a trained suspicioner." [25]

THE EXPERT WITNESS

Quite apart from being an informant for both the FBI and the Secret Service, and also, by his own admission "a trained suspicioner", Harry D. Holmes' position within the US Postal Service brought him to the fore of the investigation right from the start. Even before being contacted officially, he appears to have got himself involved. In his Warren Commission testimony he told Mr. Belin: "I never quit. I didn't get to bed for two days" and "I was doing all I could to help other agencies." [26]

According to his testimony, Holmes' involvement was underway very rapidly. He told Mr Belin: "One of the box clerks downstairs came up after an hour or so when the radio reports came in about the apprehension of Lee Oswald following the shooting of Officer Tippit, and said, 'I think you ought to know, Mr Holmes, that we rented a box downstairs to a Lee Oswald recently, and it is box so-and-so.' That was my first tip that he had a box downstairs in the terminal annex. That box is No. 6225." [27]

Of course, Box No. 6225 at the Terminal Annex is not to be confused with Oswald's previous rented box, no. 2915, at the Dallas Main Post Office.

Holmes' Warren Commission testimony went on to describe in detail Lee Harvey Oswald's application for a box at the Terminal Annex building just 22 days prior to the assassination. He also stated that the clerk responsible for the application form "could not recall what the man (the applicant) looked like" and "he could not identify him (Oswald) as actually being the man that rented the box, because I have talked to him about it." [28]

He then went on to explain that after learning that Box 6225 was rented in the name of Oswald, "we kept a 24-hour, round-the-clock surveillance from about well into Sunday, I think, 3 days." [29] From the way he described it, this action appears to have been on Holmes' own initiative.

On the morning of the day following the assassination, Holmes learnt from one of his fellow Postal Inspectors (unfortunately unnamed) that an FBI agent had enquired "how they could obtain an original post office money order" and "I went on up to my office, but somewhere I got the information that the FBI had knowledge that a gun of this particular Italian make and caliber had been purchased from Klein's Sporting Goods in Chicago, that it had been purchased, and the FBI furnished me with the information that a money order of some description in the amount of $21.95 had been used as reimbursement for the gun ... and that the purchase date was March 20, 1963." [30] (Postal Inspector McGee of Chicago later telephoned Holmes to correct the above details. In fact the money order was in the sum of $21.45 and Klein's had received it on 13th March.)

Unfortunately, no times are given for either Holmes' brief conversation with his colleague or for his contact with the FBI, but he does mention that he "had some men begin to search the Dallas money order records." He continued: "I didn't have any luck, so along about 11 o'clock in the morning, Saturday, I had my boys call the postal inspector."

Now aware that the rifle had been purchased by mail order, presumably as the result of a magazine advertisement, Holmes sent his secretary out to purchase what he described as "outdoor-type magazines such as Field and Stream, with the thought that I might locate this gun to identify it, and I did." [31]

As we now know, the magazine that Holmes' secretary obtained for him was both a different title and a different date to that allegedly used by Oswald to order the rifle. Holmes actually obtained the November 1963 issue of *Field and Stream* whereas the Oswald rifle had been ordered from a full-page Klein's advertisement in the February 1963 issue of *The American Rifleman*.

THE FINAL INTERROGATION OF LEE HARVEY OSWALD

There are many strange aspects to Harry D. Holmes' various parts in this case but perhaps the strangest and most difficult to understand is his attendance and participation in Lee Harvey Oswald's final interview. In his Warren Commission testimony, Holmes referred to it thus: "I presume my next part in connection with this was when I joined the interrogation period of Oswald on Sunday morning of November 24 at about 9:30 a.m." [32]

He went on to say that he had driven to church with his wife but that after dropping her there he suddenly decided to return to the police station (City Hall) where he simply walked in and saw Captain Fritz. He claimed that Fritz said: "We are getting ready to have a last interrogation with Oswald before we transfer him to the county jail. Would you like to join us." Holmes replied: "I would." [33] Just like that.

Now what exactly was all that about? Why did the Chief of Homicide invite an off-duty Dallas Postal Inspector to attend such an important session? Remember, they had been grilling Oswald relentlessly since his arrest and had just about managed to establish his identity. What did Fritz think that Holmes could achieve that his highly-trained officers had failed to do? I appreciate that the Inspectors of the United States Postal Service carried a lot of weight and responsibility in 1963 (as they continue to do today) but I still find this Fritz/Holmes double-act hard to understand. This, more than anything else discussed here, convinces me that there was a great deal more to Harry D. Holmes than we can imagine.

The other people present were local Agent in Charge Forrest V. Sorrels and Inspector Thomas J. Kelley, both of the Secret Service and, depending on whose testimony you believe, either three or four Homicide detectives. It was Holmes' stated opinion that their function was solely to guard Oswald. The interview took place in Captain Fritz' office, room 317 at City Hall.

In subsequent years it seems to have been readily accepted that no record was kept of this interview or of any of the previous Oswald interviews. During Assistant Counsel Ball's Warren Commission examination of Captain Fritz, the following disturbing exchange took place:

BALL: "Did you have a tape recorder?"

FRITZ: "No, sir; I don't have a tape recorder. We need one, if we had one at this time we could have handled these conversations far better."

BALL: "The Dallas Police Department doesn't have one?"

FRITZ: "No, sir; I have requested one several times but so far they haven't gotten me one." [34]

With the 1997 disclosure that Captain Fritz had taken very sketchy but nonetheless contemporaneous notes of these interviews, we now know that a written record was made of at least some of Oswald's questioning. Perusal of Fritz' notes reveals that at the final session, he merely recorded the date, time and the names of those present. [35] I think he felt it unnecessary to do more than that—because he had noticed that Harry D. Holmes was himself taking notes. There would have been no point in two officers taking notes of the same interview.

The notes taken by Holmes were undoubtedly very detailed and comprehensive. Now, why he took it upon himself to do this is as much a mystery as why he was present in the first place. It is not known whether he was acting of his own volition or had been asked to take notes during what was to prove Oswald's final interview. I personally believe it was the former. However, in his Warren Commission testimony, Holmes does indicate that the FBI later "asked me if I would object to giving them a statement as to what went on in that room ..." I wonder if it is possible that Holmes, conscious of his duty to keep the FBI up to date with certain matters, took his notes on the off chance that the Bureau would later want to know what went on during that interview.

You will find the result of Holmes interview notes not once but twice in the 26 Volumes. Each time they appear in the form of a report, dated 17th December 1963. [36] As if that were not enough, Holmes' notes are also reproduced under the title Report of U.S. Postal Inspector H. D. Holmes as part of one of the appendices to the Warren Report. [37] It should be pointed out that these three published reports are identical.

Holmes did not just sit there quietly recording notes, however. He also took an active part in the interview, asking many questions of Oswald, particularly regarding his use of post office boxes. The interrogation, which according to Holmes' notes/report opened at 9.15am, seemed to go on longer than Captain Fritz had anticipated. In his testimony, the Homicide & Robbery Bureau chief stated that he had intended closing it at 10.00am. [38] As we know, it went on for an hour later than that.

Holmes later stated in his 29th June 1989 interview with Postal Inspectors Herrara and McDermott that Chief Curry "was beating on the door." [39] Obviously, had the session ended at 10 o'clock or shortly afterwards and Oswald's transfer then been put into motion, we would not have found the ubiquitous Mr Ruby waiting downstairs in the basement clutching his little gun in anticipation. Or would we .... ?

CONCLUSION

There is a great deal more to Dallas Postal Inspector Harry D. Holmes than I have the time and space to outline here. Other researchers continue to examine his background and particularly his early life in the Post Office.

I will leave you with one tiny example of the influence that this man had. How many witnesses who testified before the Warren Commission were officially permitted to keep any of their exhibits? Harry D. Holmes was twice allowed to do just that

He introduced one of those well-known "Wanted for Treason" posters and stated that this particular one had been found in a Dallas postal collection box on the morning of the assassination. When Mr. Belin stated that he intended to mark it as an exhibit, Holmes protested: "I want to save that." [40] It was then agreed that he could retain the original and that the court reporter would make copies for the official record. What we now know as 'Holmes Exhibit No. 5', therefore, is no more than a photocopy of the original. He had earlier asked to retain what Mr Belin described as "the advertisement you cut out" and this was also copied by the court reporter so that Holmes could keep the original. The copy is now 'Holmes Exhibit No. 2'. Ironically, however, this is the Klein's advertisement from *Field and Stream*, November 1963, which has no connection at all with the advertisement used to order the Mannlicher-Carcano rifle (CE 139).

NOTES

1. George Michael Evica: *And We Are All Mortal*, published by the University of Hartford, Connecticut, 1978, page 7.
2. 7H 296 (Testimony of Harry D. Holmes).
3. 7H 290/291 (Testimony of Harry D. Holmes).
4. 7H 292-295, 526-530 (Testimony of Harry D. Holmes).
5. 7H 296-298 (Testimony of Harry D. Holmes). See also CE 2064 (FBI report concerning memorandum furnished by Postal Inspector H. D. Holmes, Dallas, Tex., of an interview he took part in with Lee Harvey Oswald on November 24, 1963).
6. *Dallas Morning News* and *Dallas Times Herald*, both of 16th October 1989.
7. 7H 290 (Testimony of Harry D. Holmes).
8. ibid.
9. Interview of Harry D. Holmes at his home (Garland, Texas) by Dallas Postal Inspectors H. Herrera and D. P. McDermott on 29th June 1989, three and a half months before his death. Details of interview published in an official *Inspection Services Bulletin* in 1991.
10. Author's tape-recorded interview of Johnny Calvin Brewer at Austin, Texas on 25th November 1996.
11. Sylvia Meagher: *Accessories After The Fact*, published by Vintage Books, New York, 1976, page 228 and Evica (footnote 1 above), page 51.
12. CE 1152 (FBI report dated January 7, 1964, concerning Lee Harvey Oswald's rental of Post Office Box 6225, Dallas, Tex.)
13. Information from researcher John Armstrong during conversation at JFK-Lancer Conference, Dallas, November 1997.
14. Postal Inspectors Holmes and Armstrong apparently shared the same fifth floor office in the Terminal Annex Building. Armstrong greeted Holmes with the words "They got Oswald" when Holmes entered the office on his return from City Hall about five minutes after the end of the final Oswald interview.
15. 7H 296 (Testimony of Harry D. Holmes).
16. 7H 291 (Testimony of Harry D. Holmes).
17. 7H 290 (Testimony of Harry D. Holmes).

18. Gerald Posner: *Case Closed*, published by Random House, New York, 1993, page 262.

19. 7H 290 (Testimony of Harry D. Holmes).

20. The Hughes film is shown and discussed in Robert Groden's video film *The Assassination Films*: New Frontier Productions, Boothwyn, Pennsylvania, 1995.

21. 7H 291 (Testimony of Harry D. Holmes).

22. Posner (footnote 18 above), page 262.

23. 7H 291 (Testimony of Harry D. Holmes).

24. Posner (footnote 18 above), page 262.

25 - 33. 7H 292-297 (Testimony of Harry D. Holmes).

34. 4H 232 (Testimony of J. W. Fritz).

35. ARRB Press release, 20th November 1997, together with photocopies of Fritz' notes.

36. CE 2064 (FBI report concerning memorandum furnished by Postal Inspector H. D. Holmes, Dallas, Tex., of an interview he took part in with Lee Harvey Oswald on November 24, 1963)

37. Warren Report, Appendix XI (pages 633-636).

38. 4H 233 (Testimony of J. W. Fritz).

39. As footnote 9 above.

40. 7H 307-308 (Testimony of Harry D. Holmes).

Written 1996.
Presented November 1997 at the Lancer Conference, Dallas.
Published May 1998 on internet website JFK-Lancer.
Published July 1998 in *The Fourth Decade,* vol. 5, no. 5.

16. Firearms, photographs and Lee Harvey Oswald

INTRODUCTION

The so-called 'backyard photographs' [1] give us the most celebrated pictures of Lee Harvey Oswald bearing arms. Like many researchers, I have serious doubts about the authenticity and history of those photographs. Here, however, I intend to regard them as 'Oswald' photographs. However it happened, whether by normal photographic means or as a result of something more sinister, there can be no denying that those images do indeed show a rifle, a revolver and the face of Lee Harvey Oswald.

What is less widely known, perhaps, is the existence of several other photographs in which Oswald is shown with firearms of various types. Four of these are perfectly straightforward. Another photograph, however, which is described at length in the Warren Commission testimony of Mrs. Marguerite Oswald but which no researcher has ever seen, presents almost as many problems as those allegedly taken in the backyard of 214 Neely Street, Oak Cliff, Dallas, possibly on Sunday 31st March 1963. [2] It is almost certainly the fifth 'backyard photograph' in the series.

THE 'BACKYARD PHOTOGRAPHS'

I obviously have to deal with the 'backyard photographs' here, but I do not intend to dwell overlong on them. That has been done by many researchers with far greater knowledge and expertise on the subject than I will ever possess. Suffice to say that there were either one [3] or two [4] negatives and two developed prints found by Detectives Rose and McCabe during their search with other police officers of the garage of Michael and Ruth Paine's house at 2515 West Fifth Street, Irving on Saturday 23rd November 1963.

In the words of Detective Guy Rose:

"Yes; I found two negatives first that showed Lee Oswald holding a rifle in his hand, wearing a pistol at his hip, and right with those negatives I found a developed picture—I don't know what you call it but anyway a picture that had been developed from the negative of him holding this rifle, and Detective McCabe was standing there and he found the other picture—of Oswald holding the rifle." [5]

Unfortunately, Irving Police Department Detective John A. McCabe, who has been named as finding one of the most vital pieces of evidence in the investigation, was not considered of sufficient importance to be mentioned in the Warren Report. Furthermore, his name does not appear on any of the property receipts for items seized during that search. [6] The Paine house was in Irving, where the Dallas Police Department had no jurisdiction, so it was obligatory that someone from either the Dallas County Sheriff's Department or the Irving Police Department be present with the DPD officers. McCabe does get a few lines in an FBI report dated 26th March 1964, when he describes his part in that search, but for some inexplicable reason, did not mention finding the photograph. [7]

That same FBI report also describes how, on 23rd March 1964, McCabe had provided a full account of his discovery, during the 23rd November 1963 search of the Paine residence, of the Imperial Reflex camera (CE 750) which was later claimed to have been used to take the 'backyard photographs'. He had, however, neither seized nor mentioned it during or immediately after the search "since he did not consider it to be of evidentiary value." As we now know, that camera was to remain in a box in the Paine garage until 8th December when Robert Oswald took possession of the residue of his late brother's property and found it. He later realized that it could be relevant and handed it to the Dallas Office of the FBI on 24th February 1964. [8]

That FBI report then goes on to describe how the camera was shown to Marina Oswald on 25th February 1964. She "identified it as the camera belonging to Lee Harvey Oswald with which she had taken the picture (note singular) of Oswald holding the rifle and newspaper and wearing the pistol." [9] This tends to suggest that as late as three months after the assassination, Marina Oswald still maintained that she had taken only *one* so-called 'backyard photograph.'

Two more 'backyard photographs'

Two further 'backyard photographs' gained notoriety when they were discovered separately in later years. The first came to light when George de Mohrenschildt returned from Haiti in early 1967 and found the third 'backyard photograph' in a piece of luggage which he had left in storage during his absence. [10] On the back of it there were two handwritten inscriptions: "To my friend George from Lee Oswald—5/IV/63" and in Russian Cyrillic script: "Hunter of Fascists ha-ha-ha!!!"

Some researchers believe that the first of these inscriptions is in Oswald's handwriting. The style in which the date is written, however, has long caused general concern. British researcher Anthony Summers wrote: *"A researcher's check of the dozens of letters and documents written by Oswald has not provided one example of a date written like the one on the back of the photograph,"* [11]

In the course of assisting me to research this article however, my friend and fellow researcher Melanie Swift did discover just such an example. A postcard written by Lee Harvey Oswald (in Minsk) to brother Robert (in Fort Worth) bears the date 10/V/62. [12] In it, the message refers to Lee's daughter June as being *"almost three months old now"* and since she was born on 15th February 1962, that date (10/V/62) is obviously 10th May 1962. This provides a precedent for Lee writing a date in this 'European' format with a Roman numeral following the day of the month and indicating the month itself. It also reveals that the inscription on the de Mohrenschildt 'backyard photograph' was written on 5th April 1962, a date incidentally just five days prior to the attempt on the life of Major General Edwin A. Walker. [13] (Subsequent to the completion and publication of this paper, I have discovered two further examples of Oswald writing a date in the 'European' style. These both occur on the same document—a one-page note written to the Director of the Minsk Radio Factory in which Oswald tenders his resignation. The date is twice written as "18/V/62". An English translation confirms this as "5-18-62". See CE 1314.)

The origin of the second (Russian) inscription remains unknown. It has been suggested that Marina Oswald may have been the writer. [14]

The photograph itself shows Oswald in a similar pose to that in CE 133A but with both arms held higher. Photographic analyst Jack White has claimed that the de Mohrenschildt photograph appears to have been taken with a far more sophisticated camera than the others. He claims that it shows greater detail. [15]

Yet another 'backyard photograph' emerged in 1976 during the Schweiker-Hart assassination investigation. This one was found in the possession of Mrs Geneva Ruth Dees, the widow of former Dallas Police Officer 1884 Roscoe Anthony White. [16] The picture was reportedly found among a collection of 40 photographs retained by White as souvenirs. [17] There has been a belief that during his brief DPD career (two years to the day: 7th October 1963 to 7th October 1965) [18] White had spent some time as a photographic technician? [19] The former Crime Lab detective, 'Rusty' Livingstone strenuously denies this, however.

Oswald in the United States Marine Corps (a)

In his book *The Killing of a President*, Robert J. Groden includes what he describes as "the only known legitimate photograph of Oswald holding a rifle." [20] This photograph, take during US Marine Corps training, shows a row of men apparently firing their rifles in the same direction (to the right) from a semi-kneeling position. At first I wondered if these men had been deliberately posed like this. Had each of them taken his turn to be the 'front man' to give each the opportunity to be the cameraman's principal subject?

Supposedly, however, it was pure chance—and yet another bizarre coincidence—that the man closest to the camera happens to be US Marines recruit 1653230 Lee Harvey Oswald. The photograph is virtually of Oswald alone with his colleagues extending in a straight line away from the camera into the background.

Even under his jauntily-angled forage cap, we can recognize the young Oswald. He was undoubtedly only 17 years old at the time and this photograph was taken during his boot camp training. Oswald had enlisted into the service on 24th October 1956, just six days after his 17th birthday. From 26th October 1956 to 18th January 1957 he was with the 2nd Recruit Training Battalion, Marine Corps Recruit Depot, San Diego, California. He continued and completed his training between 20th January and 26th February 1957 as a member of "A" Company, 1st Battalion, 2nd Infantry Training Regiment, Marine Corps Base, Camp Pendleton, California. [21]

It was normal practice for Marine Corps recruits to undergo three weeks intensive weapons instruction during the course of their Marine training. [22] This practice usually took up the seventh, eighth and ninth weeks with the first two days devoted entirely to dry firing. This aspect of training was to ensure that the recruit was totally familiar with his rifle before being entrusted with any live ammunition. I have no reason to suspect that Oswald's training schedule was anything but normal and it is thus possible to 'date' this photograph as being taken on either the 10th or 11th December 1956 during dry firing training. [23]

Oswald in the United States Marine Corps (b)

The next photograph only just qualifies for inclusion here, but it *does* show Oswald with what is undoubtedly a rifle. The photograph shows a group of about ten Marines relaxing somewhere apparently in the Far East. They are on a beach with palm trees in the background. As in the preceding USMC photograph Private First Class (Pfc) Oswald is the central figure. He is sitting cross-legged wearing Marines fatigues. He is facing left and like his companions is wearing a forage cap. In the foreground at Oswald's feet, are his helmet and rifle. Edward Jay Epstein has identified Oswald's fellow Marines as Godfrey Jerome Daniels, George A. Wilkins, Jr. Zack Stout, Bobby J. Warren and James R. Persons. He states that neither the Warren Commission nor the FBI ever questioned any of these men. [24]

Several books have featured this photograph [25] and one has indicated in its caption that the group is waiting to board *USS Terrell County*. [26] If that is true, then I maintain that the photograph was taken in the Yokosuka area of Japan on 20th November 1957 [27] the only occasion on which Pfc Oswald sailed on that ship. [28] I have since learnt that Epstein endorses this opinion. [29]

Much additional attention has been give to this photograph by researchers interested in Roscoe Anthony White. It has been claimed by his son Ricky that Roscoe appears in the background standing on the left side. [30] Pfc (later Corporal) 1666106 Roscoe White was once in the same unit as Oswald [31] but military records indicate that Roscoe was in Okinawa on the date I believe this photograph was taken. [32]

ON LEAVE FROM THE MARINES

I now come to the first of two photographs appearing in Gerald Posner's book *Case Closed*. It shows Oswald with a severe Marines-style haircut, dressed in casual clothes, standing alone in a field, clutching what appears to be some sort of rifle. [33] He is holding the weapon by his left side in a very relaxed manner. The caption reads: "A rare photo of Lee hunting while on his first leave from the Marines in February 1958, when he visited his family in Fort Worth, Texas." The photograph appears courtesy of Robert L. Oswald, Lee's elder brother. It had in fact, appeared originally in Robert Oswald's book Lee under the caption: "Lee and I went squirrel hunting with Vada's brother on the Mercers' farm in February, 1958, when Lee was at home on leave from the Marines. That's my .22 rifle." [34]

I am mystified by Mr Posner's statement that this photograph was taken during Oswald's first leave in February 1958. Oswald joined up in October 1956. Surely he did not have to wait 16 months for his first leave.

I feel there is nothing sinister about this photograph. It depicts what appears to be a happy individual relaxing away from the rigors of a career with the US Marine Corps. [35]

OSWALD THE SCHOOLBOY

The second photograph of interest in *Case Closed* was also taken from Robert Oswald's book and once again, Mr Posner has made a significant change to its caption. In *Lee* the caption reads: "Lee always wanted to try on my school hat when I came home on vacation from Chamberlain-Hunt Military Academy. He is wearing it in this picture taken in 1948, in the living room of our house in Benbrook. The cap pistol is his."

When Mr Posner uses the picture, however, he captions it thus: "In this seldom seen photo eight-year old Lee plays with his cap pistol while wearing brother Robert's military academy hat. At school, he had already developed a reputation as a bully." [36]

The photograph does indeed show the young Oswald wearing a military cap and pointing a cap pistol. Funnily enough and probably to Mr Posner's disappointment, he is not pointing the gun at the photographer but at some imaginary target way off to the left and completely out of view of the camera. Note how in his altered caption Mr Posner has subtly made the cap pistol Lee Oswald's main interest rather than his brother's military cap. Furthermore, he cannot resist the totally irrelevant remark about developing a bully's reputation at school. I feel that this photograph, with its two captions, reveals more about Posner's motivation than about Oswald's.

I question Mr Posner's motive in including this photograph in his book. *Case Closed* contains only 36 photographs amongst its 607 pages and it seems strange that the author includes this one to the exclusion of others which would, in my opinion, have been of far greater value. There could, for example, have been more than just two which were taken during the shooting sequence in Dealey Plaza (Altgens 1-6 and the Moorman 3 polaroid).

WAS THERE A FIFTH 'BACKYARD PHOTOGRAPH?

I now return to what are loosely-termed the 'backyard photographs' to examine the photograph which originally inspired this paper.

Mrs Marguerite Oswald, the mother of the accused assassin, testified before the Warren Commission at Washington, D.C. on Monday 10th, Tuesday 11th and Wednesday 12th February 1964. On the morning of the first day, she made the following amazing statement concerning events at the Paine house on Friday 22nd November 1963, presumably in the evening:

"Now, gentlemen, this is some very important facts. My daughter-in-law spoke to Mrs. Paine in Russian. 'Mamma,' she says. So she takes me into the bedroom and closes the door. She said, 'Mamma, I show you.' She opened the closet, and in the closet was a lot of books and papers. And she came out with a picture—a picture of Lee, with a gun. It said 'To my daughter June'—written in English. I said, 'Oh, Marina, police.' I didn't think anything of the picture." (It has been suggested to me by researcher George Michael Evica that the word 'police' could have been misheard by the stenographer and that the word here should be 'please'.)

After rambling on in a similar vein for a minute or so, Mrs Oswald continued:

"But I say to my daughter, 'To my daughter, June,' anybody can own a rifle, to go hunting. You yourself probably have a rifle. So I am not connecting this with the assassination—'To my daughter, June.' Because I would immediately say, and I remember—I think my son is an agent all the time—no one is going to be foolish enough if they mean to assassinate the President, or even murder someone to take a picture of themselves with that rifle, and leave it there for evidence."

At this stage, according to Mrs Oswald, Marina tried to persuade her to take the picture but she refused.

"I said, 'No, Marina. Put back in the book.' So she put the picture back in the book. Which book it was, I do not know."

So the next day, when we were at the courthouse—this is on Saturday— she—we were sitting down, waiting to see Lee. She puts her shoe down, she says, 'Mamma, picture.' She had the picture folded up in her shoe. Now, I did not see that it was the picture, but I know that it was, because she told me it was, and I could see it was folded up. It wasn't open for me to see." [37]

At this point there was nothing to indicate whether or not this was one of the series of photographs apparently taken in the Neely Street backyard. A few minutes later, however, J. Lee Rankin, General Counsel to the Warren Commission, showed Mrs Oswald an enlargement of one of the two known (at that time) 'backyard photographs' allegedly found during the search of the Paine garage, together with a composite of those two photographs. [38]

Mrs Oswald said: "No, sir, that is not the picture. He was holding the rifle up, and it said, 'To my daughter, June, with love.' He was holding the rifle up.'

The question and answer sequence then continued:

RANKIN: "By holding it up, you mean—"

OSWALD: "Like this." (apparently demonstrating)

RANKIN: "Crosswise, with both hands on the rifle?"

OSWALD: "With both hands on the rifle."

RANKIN: "Above his head?"

OSWALD: "That is right." [39]

After further questions and answers on other matters, Mrs Oswald described how the photograph was destroyed during the evening of Saturday 23rd November. This took place in a suite at the Executive Inn (now the Love Field Inn) [40], where Mrs Oswald, Marina and the two Oswald children were being held in protective custody.

Mrs Oswald's monologue appears to have been directed solely towards Mr Rankin despite six other Commission members, including Chief Justice Warren, also being present:

> "While there, Marina—there is an ashtray on the dressing table. And Marina comes with bits of paper, and puts them in the ashtray and strikes a match to it. And this is the picture of the gun that Marina tore up into bits of paper, and struck a match to it. Now, that didn't burn completely, because it was heavy—not cardboard—what is the name for it—a photographic picture. So the match didn't take it completely.
>
> "The last time I had seen the picture was in Marina's shoe when she was trying to tell me that the picture was in her shoe. I state here now that Marina meant for me to have the picture, from the very beginning, in Mrs. Paine's home. She said—I testified before—'Mamma, you keep picture.'
>
> "And then she showed it to me in the courthouse. And when I refused it, then she decided to get rid of the picture. She tore up the picture and struck a match to it. Then she took it and flushed it down the toilet." [41]

It is simple to assume automatically that this photograph was another part of the series taken in the backyard of the Oswalds' Neely Street address in early 1963. That Mr Rankin showed the other two known 'backyard photographs' to Mrs Oswald tends by association to reinforce this belief. However, that was never actually said and was not even suggested by his questions. As

Sylvia Meagher observed, the weapon being held above his head by Oswald could have been the shotgun he had owned in Russia, and the photograph could well have been taken in that country. [42]

I was unwilling to leave this matter unresolved, and in October 1994 I had the opportunity to put this point directly to Mrs Marina Oswald Porter. Without hesitation she confirmed that the photograph was indeed a 'backyard photograph.' As she stressed, had it been an innocent picture taken in Russia, why would she have gone to such lengths to destroy it? It would not have mattered. There the matter stands.

CONCLUSION

There is not a formal conclusion to a paper of this type. I did not set out to prove or disprove any contentious point. However, if I have provoked the reader into prodding the surface and searching a little deeper to seek the truth, then I have achieved my objective. Over 40 years have passed since the assassination, and thousands of researchers have studied the case, some of them literally devoting their lives to it. Hundreds of books, articles and videos have been produced. Despite all this attention, however, there still remains much to be learnt. How did that dated postcard from Lee to his brother remain unnoticed and unrecognized until Melanie Swift realized its significance? What similar gems remain to be found and deciphered?

NOTES

1. CE 133A and 133B (Photographs of Lee Harvey Oswald holding a rifle)
2. Warren Report, pages 127/128.
3. ibid, page 127.
4. 7H 231 (Testimony of Guy F. Rose).
5. ibid.
6. CE 2003 (Dallas Police Department file on investigation of the assassination of the President), pages 263-272 of exhibit (24H 332-337).
7. CE 2557 (FBI report dated March 26 1964, of investigation of ownership of Imperial Reflex camera), page 2 of exhibit (25H 792).
8. ibid, page 3 of exhibit (25H 793).
9. ibid, bottom paragraph.
10. Jim Marrs: *Crossfire: The Plot that killed Kennedy,* published by Carroll & Graf, New York, 1989, pages 287/288; Anthony Summers: *Conspiracy,* published by Victor Gollancz, London, 1980, pages 240/241.
11. Summers, page 241.

12. CE 321 *(Post card from Lee Harvey Oswald to Robert Oswald dated April 4, 1962)*. It is worth noting here that the Warren Commission authors seem totally confused by the date on this exhibit. The date on the postcard is shown as "10/V/62." By no stretch of the imagination could that ever be interpreted as *"April 4, 1962."*

13. Warren Report, page 183.

14. Written note from Walt Brown to author, November 1994.

15. Jack White, in *Fake* video film (JFK Video Group, 1990).

16. Robert J. Groden: *The Killing of a President*, Viking Studio Books, New York, 1993, page 170.

17. J. Gary Shaw and Larry Ray Harris: *Cover-Up*, published by Thomas Publications Inc., Austin, Texas, 1992, page 208.

18. SECRET internal DPD memorandum from Corporal/Investigator Jack L. Beavers to Captain W. R. Rollins (DPD Intelligence Division) dated 28th January 1988 in connection with a request for assistance from the Midland County DA's Office. Copy of this document in author's possession.

19. As (16) above.

20. Groden, page 165.

21. CE 1961 *(Information relating to Lee Harvey Oswald's service in the Marine Corps furnished to the Commission by the Assistant General Counsel (Manpower), Department of Defense)*, page 3 of exhibit (23H 796).

22. 11H 302 (Testimony of Major Eugene D. Anderson, USMC).

23. Author's discussion with Craig Roberts (ex-USMC), Olathe, Kansas, 19th October 1964.

24. Edward Jay Epstein: *Legend: The Secret World of Lee Harvey Oswald*, published by Arrow Books, London, 1978, page 284.

25. Epstein: first page of photographs; Matthew Smith: *JFK- The Second Plot*, published by Mainstream, Edinburgh, 1992, page 195; Henry Hurt: *Reasonable Doubt*, published by Sidgwick & Jackson, London, 1986, 12th page of photographs.

26. Epstein as above.

27. As (21) above but page 4 of exhibit (23H 796).

28. ibid.

29. Epstein, page 73.

30. Ricky Don White press conference at the JFK Assassination Information Center, Dallas, Texas, 6th August 1990.

31. DPD memorandum, see (18) above.

32. USMC Sea and Air Embarkation Slips 1957/58 in respect of Roscoe White. Copies in author's possession.

33. Gerald Posner: *Case Closed*, published by Random House, New York, 1993, fifth illustration.

34. Robert L. Oswald: *Lee*, published by Coward-McCann, Inc., New York,

1967, fifth page of illustrations.

35. Following the initial publication of this paper in the March 1995 issue of *The Kennedy Assassination Chronicles*, I received a letter from researcher Arthur Swanson challenging my claim that this photograph was not "sinister." Mr Swanson pointed out that according to USMC pay records (CE 3099 at 26H 716), Lee Oswald was in the Far East in February 1958 and could not have been hunting in the USA. This is indeed true and we must therefore question the accuracy of Robert Oswald's claim that this photograph was taken when he says it was, February 1958. Is it possible that this is yet another example of a Lee Harvey Oswald lookalike – or was Robert simply mistaken as to the date. Perhaps it was Lee's first leave after all.

36. Posner: second illustration.

37. 1H 146 (Testimony of Mrs Marguerite Oswald).

38. 1H 147/148 (Testimony of Mrs Marguerite Oswald).

39. 1H 148 (Testimony of Mrs Marguerite Oswald).

40. Terry J. Moore: *Sites for JFKers*, published in *The Dealey Plaza Echo*, vol. 7, no. 3, November 2003.

41. 1H 152 (Testimony of Mrs Marguerite Oswald).

42. Sylvia Meagher: *Accessories after the Fact*, published by Vintage Books, New York, 1976, page 201 (footnote).

43. Author's discussion with Mr. Marina Oswald Porter, Olathe, Kansas, 16th October 1994.

Written 1994-1995.
First published March 1995 in The *Kennedy Assassination Chronicles*, vol. 1, issue 1.

17. The Mannlicher-Carcano: disassembly and reassembly

INTRODUCTION

At the end of a 1994 presentation on the subject of the rifle allegedly used in the assassination of President Kennedy [1] I was pleased to answer questions from an enthusiastic and knowledgeable audience. One question concerned a screwdriver or breakdown tool for the Mannlicher-Carcano rifle, the alleged assassination weapon. [2] I confirmed that there was no evidence to suggest that either of those implements had been found on the sixth floor of the Texas School Book Depository or in Lee Harvey Oswald's possession. I was then asked whether it could have been possible for the Mannlicher to have been disassembled and later reassembled using a small coin. It is known that Oswald had cash amounting to $13.87 on him when he was arrested. This sum included three dime coins. [3]

Much of my presentation was centred on the fact that I distrust the Warren Commission's account of the finding and subsequent handling of the Mannlicher-Carcano. [4] Furthermore, I seriously question the very existence of the paper sack in which the weapon is alleged to have been carried by Oswald from Irving to the TSBD on the morning of the assassination. The official version would have us believe that Oswald carried the disassembled rifle to work in a "heavy brown bag"—the paper sack CE 142 and/or 626—on the back seat of Buell Wesley Frazier's car that morning. [5] The word 'disassembled' is one which very few, if any, researchers have taken the trouble to examine in depth. What exactly does the word mean in the present context?

'DISASSEMBLED'

This is a word which seems to have been accepted without question. The Mannlicher-Carcano, CE 139, reportedly measures 40.2 inches in length in its assembled condition. When broken down or disassembled, its longest component, the wooden stock, is 34.8 inches long. [6] In his Warren Commission testimony, FBI weapons expert Robert A. Frazier explains this but he goes no further. We are left to assume that disassembly of the weapon is a quick, simple and straightforward process at the end of which we have the rifle in two pieces: the wooden stock and the remainder of it consisting of the metal part. In reality, this is far from the truth.

At this point, I must also question the object of taking the time and trouble to completely disassemble and then reassemble the weapon in order to make a saving of less than six inches in its length.

Twelve separate components—plus a sling

Perhaps it is appropriate at this stage to explain exactly what is involved when you disassemble this weapon. Despite the automatic assumption that you have a 'wooden part' and a 'metal part', there is far more to it than that. When *fully* disassembled, which it *has* to be to isolate the wooden stock, the rifle is broken down into no fewer than 12 separate components. Yes, twelve! Now that is something which the Warren Commission omitted to reveal. Even then, there is a further item to consider, although it is not strictly speaking part of the rifle. This is the sling (which was fitted to the alleged assassination weapon when it was found).

If we then go along with the Warren Commission's main conclusion that Oswald was the lone assassin, we have to add an ammunition clip and four unexpended rounds of ammunition. I can just visualize Oswald climbing into Frazier's car carrying a paper sack in which all those assorted ingredients of the rifle are jangling about.

The Warren Report claims that Oswald had disassembled the Mannlicher to enable it to fit into the paper sack. [7] It then uses CE 1304 to imply that the rifle would be in just *two* parts at this point.

The lower of the two photographs which comprise CE 1304 purports to show the Mannlicher-Carcano in its disassembled state. It does indeed show the weapon broken down into two parts, one wooden and one metal, as described above. Like much of the Warren Commission's so-called evidence, however, all is not what it seems at first glance.

The CE 1304 lower photograph shows a rifle which has been completely disassembled and then reassembled but without the main metal part (comprising the barrel, bolt, firing mechanism, trigger, chamber, etc.) being included in the reassembly. Close examination of the photograph reveals that all five retaining screws are in their correct positions, but they are certainly not retaining the main metal component, since it is not there. The photograph bears no caption and on the Contents page to Volume XXII in which it appears, it is described simply as "Photographs of wrapping-paper bag and of component parts of rifle." (The upper of the two photographs shows a long paper bag.)

The photograph is a complete waste of time and space, and it has evidential value of precisely nil. It is totally misleading. I have thought long and hard but cannot find any justification for it other than to deliberately mislead and confuse. It is nothing but a con, a lie, a fraud and a deliberate deception, and I defy anyone to prove otherwise.

THE RE-ENACTMENT

During a visit to Dallas in June 1994, I again had the opportunity to handle and examine a Mannlicher-Carcano identical to that allegedly found on the sixth floor of the TSBD on 22nd November 1963. This is the same weapon that I had studied in November 1993 when it had formed a central part of the late Larry Howard's JFK Assassination Information Center display.

This time, I photographed, measured and studied that rifle even more closely. Most important, I took it to pieces and then put it together again well over a dozen times. Not having the correct breakdown tool for this type of weapon, I experimented with two makeshift alternatives; a screwdriver and a dime coin. As already mentioned, the small change in Oswald's possession when he was arrested, included three dime coins. [8] It was therefore a possibility that one of these coins could have been used as an alternative means of loosening and tightening the five screws on the weapon.

In his testimony before the Warren Commission, Cortlandt Cunningham, a Special Agent in the FBI Firearms Laboratory (Firearms Identity Unit) indicated that he had been able to reassemble the Mannlicher-Carcano (CE 139) in a few seconds over two minutes using a screwdriver and in six minutes with a dime. [9]

THE TWELVE SEPARATE COMPONENTS THAT MAKE UP THE RIFLE

I make no claim to be a weapons expert and so I cannot quote all the correct technical names for the various parts of the disassembled Mannlicher. I shall, therefore describe them in basic layman's terms. I do not include the sling here as one was not available when I conducted my reassembly experiments.

As already explained, the longest individual part is the wooden stock. There is a second wooden component, a short piece about 7 1/2 inches long, known as the top stock, which sits atop the wooden stock, just forward of and below the front end of the fitted scope. This serves no functional purpose in the actual operation of the rifle but is necessary to keep other parts in position.

The main metal component consists of the barrel and the firing mechanism. The latter includes the chamber, firing pin, bolt and trigger. For the purposes of this exercise the telescopic sight, permanently screwed to the top of this metal section, can be described as being part of it. It is not necessary to remove the scope when disassembling the rifle. It is inevitable, however, that during disassembly/reassembly, the precise alignment of the scope must be affected. This may be only minimal but nevertheless, it must have an effect.

There are two metal collars that hold the main metal part into a recessed section on top of the larger of the two wooden parts (the stock). The first of these two collars is at the forward end of the wooden stock just 5^1/2 inches from the tip of the barrel. The second collar is situated a further 5^1/2 inches behind it. The combined magazine well/trigger guard fits into place directly beneath the trigger mechanism.

All the above parts are held in place by five retaining screws. Two *almost* identical screws secure the forward collar which holds together the front end of the wooden stock and the barrel. They vary only in their length. The forward of the two is ^{1}/16 of an inch shorter than its near twin and they are not interchangeable. Another slightly but obviously longer screw similarly holds the rear collar firm and this in turn keeps the top stock in place. This screw also fits into the forward sling swivel to hold it in position on the left side of the rifle.

The magazine well/trigger guard sits in a recessed position and is secured by two larger and heavier screws, the forward one being considerably larger that the one at the rear.

In 2003 I found myself in disagreement with another researcher who claimed that it was not necessary to remove the magazine well/trigger guard when disassembling the rifle. As its recessed position is reasonably snug, this may well be true but those two screws still have to be removed to disengage internal parts of the rifle from the wooden stock. Once they are removed, the magazine well/trigger guard may or may not fall away. It is obviously safer to remove it rather than risk it falling away and being lost.

Those then are the 12 separate components, (not including the sling), into which the 6.5mm Mannlicher Carcano is broken down. The weapon cannot be disassembled whilst loaded.

THE PRACTICAL EXPERIMENT

As mentioned earlier, I spent several hours familiarizing myself with the weapon and the method by which it is taken apart and then put together again. Assuming that Lee Harvey Oswald did indeed carry the disassembled rifle into the book depository, (a view to which I personally do *not* subscribe), then it would have been no simple task for him to reassemble the weapon given the conditions prevailing at the time.

Put yourself in his position for a few moments. You have a limited time for the task and there is the obvious risk that somebody could come across you at any time. You are presumably in a confined space—perhaps in the so-called sniper's nest. [10] More significant, of course, is the knowledge of your purpose in putting that rifle together. You are about to bring a fellow human being's life to a violent and abrupt end. Not just a random human being, but the single most powerful man on the planet. If that factor alone does not make your fingers sticky with sweat and your heart feel like it is trying to burst out of your chest, then nothing will. You will find yourself in a greatly increased state of emotion, anxiety and downright fear.

The conditions under which I assembled the weapon were very much more relaxed. I was in a roomy, well-lit, air-conditioned environment with no external pressures whatsoever. I knew that if I accidentally dropped one of the screws or mistakenly tried to fit one of them in the wrong place, it did not matter. I could simply start all over again. I ensured in advance that the screwdriver I intended to use was a suitable fit for all five screws.

I sat on a low revolving chair with all the rifle components lined up in the correct order on a table beside me. I began with the wooden stock in a horizontal position across my lap. I knew that at some stages, I would have to change its position to vertical and I ensured that I had sufficient room to do this.

The rifle found on the sixth floor of the Texas School Book Depository was fitted with a makeshift sling but I did not have one. However for Oswald to have acted exactly as the Warren Commission concluded I think he would have had the sling fixed only to the rear sling anchor on the left side of the butt stock when the rifle was in its disassembled state. It could *not* have been fixed to the forward sling swivel as well.

Stage one was probably the trickiest of all. The rearmost of the two collars has to be fitted loosely around the barrel section of the main metal part and then the other collar is pushed into position in front of it. The entire metal part then has to be manipulated into position along the recessed section at the top of the wooden stock. This requires considerable dexterity since there is only one position in which it will sit cleanly in the correct place. *(If this is difficult to understand, then please believe it was much more difficult to write—and even more difficult to do! - ILG)*

The two collars are now pushed along the barrel until they engage in their correct positions. The front collar is particularly tight and is not easy to site accurately. The first three screws, two in the front collar and one in the other, are positioned and tightened at this stage, beginning at the front and working backwards.

The first is the most difficult since it needs great care and a steady hand to ensure that it also engages a small hole in the metal at the base of the barrel. Having had considerable practice, and being under no pressure, I found that this had become fairly straightforward. Under 'Oswald' conditions however, I can well imagine some moments of great anxiety and near panic. The second screw in the front collar is no problem, provided the first one has been fitted correctly.

Before fixing the second collar, the wooden top stock is placed along the top of the recessed barrel in its correct position. According to FBI weapons expert Cortlandt Cunningham: "Once in a while with regard to the top portion—namely the retaining screw and the top stock—you have trouble getting them engaged on this particular model." [11]

The "trouble" SA Cunningham mentions here comes in the form of the sling swivel. This has to be engaged by the screw which retains that second collar in position. A tiny v-shaped nick in the collar has to fit into a corresponding projection in the base of the sling swivel screw. The sling, which has been fixed to the rigid anchor on the left side of the butt stock throughout all this, is now ready to be fixed to the forward sling swivel.

Finally, the combined magazine well/trigger guard is held in place below the trigger mechanism and is secured by the final two screws. These are of similar gauge but the front one is longer by half. It is essential that the correct screw is in the correct position. After tightening these two screws, reassembly is complete. The weapon is ready for use.

CONCLUSION

I felt very privileged at being able to conduct a practical experiment of this nature. It is one thing to study books and documents, and perhaps unearth some important new facts, but to physically duplicate the actual actions allegedly undertaken by the supposed assassin was a source of great satisfaction and considerable pride. I would be naive indeed to suppose that I am the first researcher to do this—but I am certainly unaware of any previous written account of such an action.

So what did I learn from all this? Well, firstly, it is no simple task to reassemble this rifle. Certainly not as simple as those glib words in the Warren Report or that deliberately misleading CE 1304 photograph would suggest.

Secondly, whilst it was reasonably easy to tighten the screws with a screwdriver, it was certainly no simple task using a dime. The coin is thin enough to fit into the recessed head of the screws but due to its tiny diameter, about two thirds of an inch, there is hardly any leverage and this makes it very difficult to exert sufficient pressure to tighten the screws sufficiently. A similar problem is encountered when trying to disassemble the weapon, particularly with the front screw on the magazine well/trigger guard.

Thirdly, as already mentioned, I was under no pressure whatsoever, whereas Oswald would have been confronted by almost unimaginable mental and physical problems and would be suffering everything from near panic to sweat running down into his eyes.

Finally, I had practised many times before undertaking my 'real attempt' at putting that gun together. I knew precisely where each part was and in what order it should be fitted. I knew exactly when I had to change the position of the rifle from horizontal (across my lap) to vertical (between my knees). There is no evidence to suggest that Oswald had either the time or the opportunity to carry out 'dry runs' or rehearsals.

How long did it take me to reassemble the Mannlicher-Carcano? Well, my best time was two minutes and four seconds using a screwdriver. I have to confess that I admitted defeat using a dime coin. Having begun several times and fallen hopelessly behind the clock, I have to look on SA Cunningham's time of six minutes with a certain degree of scepticism. Trying to put that rifle together using just a dime resulted in me sustaining two blood-blisters on my fingers and a small cut on the joint of my right thumb.

In September 1995 I was successful in purchasing my own deactivated Mannlicher-Carcano and I have disassembled and reassembled it possibly a hundred times. [12] Many of these times have been before an audience of students or fellow researchers.

MY FINAL THOUGHTS

I remain convinced that Lee Harvey Oswald had neither the time, the place nor the correct conditions to have put that rifle together at any time during the $4^{1}/2$ hours between his arrival at the Texas School Book Depository at about 8.00am [13] and the time at which he allegedly used it to kill the 35th. President of the United States at 12.30pm. [14]

NOTES

1. Meeting of *Dallas '63*, Liverpool, England, Monday 9th May 1994.
2. Question by John Rudd, *Dallas '63* Secretary.
3. CE 1148 and 1149 (Two FBI reports, both dated December 10, 1963, describing property of Lee Harvey Oswald, and the DPD property room invoice of money in the possession of Lee Harvey Oswald on his arrest)
4. Warren Report, page 79.
5. Warren Report, page 131.
6. 3H 395 (Testimony of Robert A. Frazier). These measurements have been physically checked and confirmed by the author using several rifles identical to that which is the subject of this paper.
7. Warren Report, pages 134 and 135.

8. As (3) above.

9. 2H 252 (Testimony of Cortlandt Cunningham).

10. Warren Report, page 135. See also *The Fourth Decade*, vol. 1, no. 5, July 1994, page 5: "The Sniper's Nest That Never Was" by Allan R. J. Eaglesham quoting from *The New York Times*, 23rd November 1963.

11. As (9) above.

12. Serial no. S1003, manufactured at Terni. Purchased from Trident Arms, Nottingham. Telescopic sight, identical to that on the Oswald rifle, purchased from Martin B. Retting, Inc., Culver City, California (with assistance of Craig Roberts). Scope fitted by Roding Armoury, Abridge, Essex.

13. 2H 214 (Testimony of Buell Wesley Frazier).

14. Warren Report, page 3.

Written 1994 and regularly updated.

First published August 1994 in the *Dallas '63* journal, vol. 1, no. 3

Practical demonstration given before 100+ students of American History, 6th December 2001 at Canterbury Christ Church University College, Kent

Presentation/Demonstration 20th March 2004 at 2nd DPUK Weekend Seminar at Canterbury, Kent.

18. The Paper Bag That Never Was

INTRODUCTION

One of the most questionable of all Warren Commission exhibits has to be CE 1302. This is a photograph which, according to its caption, purports to show "Approximate location of wrapping-paper bag ... near window in southeast corner." The Contents page to Volume 22 of the Warren Commission's 26 Volumes of Hearings and Exhibits, in which this appears on page 479, describes this exhibit as "Photograph of southeast corner of sixth floor of Texas School Book Depository Building showing approximate location of wrapping-paper bag and location of palmprint on carton."

From those positive and uncomplicated descriptions, we would expect to see a photograph showing a bag made out of wrapping-paper. In reality, the photograph shows no paper bag—just a dotted line rectangle which has been printed on to the photograph and which bears the legend: "Approximate location of wrapping-paper bag."

In accordance with normal police practice, other items of potential evidential value at the sixth floor crime scene were photographed where they lay—for example, the rifle, the spent cartridges and the book carton with the palm print on it. Why then, was the paper bag not afforded this attention? May I be as bold as to suggest that this most vital item of 'evidence' did not actually exist at the time? It is my earnest belief that the paper bag was made up (in both senses) some time later.

In this paper, I will examine:

(a) The reasons for the bag becoming such a vital piece of evidence against Oswald,
(b) The circumstances under which it was allegedly found,
(c) My unsuccessful attempts to establish who found it and
(d) The method by which Oswald is alleged to have brought it into the building.

I will also address the infamous 'curtain rods' story, discuss where the bag is claimed to have been made, and question why those investigating the case felt it necessary to give it two different exhibit numbers and then construct a 'replica' bag.

THE IMPORTANCE OF THE PAPER BAG TO THE WARREN COMMISSION

In several instances, police, Sheriff's Department and book depository employees unwittingly confirmed that something very strange had taken place concerning this vital piece of evidence.

> BALL: "Did you ever see a paper sack in the items that were taken from the Texas School Book Depository building?"
> HICKS: "No sir; I did not." (7H 289)

> BELIN: "Was there any long sack laying in the floor there that you remember seeing, or not?"
> CRAIG: "No; I don't remember seeing any." (6H 268)

> BALL: "Does the sack show in any of the pictures you took?"
> STUDEBAKER: "No; it doesn't show in any of the pictures." (7H 144)

> "The Dallas police did an extremely capable job of documenting with photographs the crime scene that had just been discovered." (Extract from *First Day Evidence* by Gary Savage, published by The Shoppe Press, Monroe, Louisiana 1993 - pp 145/146)

> BALL: "Did you see Oswald come to work that morning?"
> DOUGHERTY: "Yes—when he first come into the door."
> BALL: "Did he have anything in his hands or arms?"
> DOUGHERTY: "Well, not that I could see of."
> BALL: "In other words, you would say positively he had nothing in his hands?"
> DOUGHERTY: "I would say that—yes, sir." (6H 376/377)

> "Lt. DAY recalls that on evening of 11/22/63 about 11.30pm. one of Captain FRITZ's officers requested that he show this thick brown sack to a man named FRAZIER. Lt. DAY said that FRAZIER was unable to identify this sack and told him that a sack he observed in the possession of OSWALD early that morning was definitely a thin, flimsy sack like one purchased in a dime store." (FBI memo, 29th November 1963)

The final verdict of the Warren Commission (and I use the word 'verdict' deliberately) was: "The shots which killed President Kennedy and wounded Governor Connally were fired by Lee Harvey Oswald." [1] An essential part of the Commission's conclusion revolves around Oswald bringing his Mannlicher-Carcano rifle into the Texas School Book Depository unnoticed on the morning of the assassination.

The sworn testimony of two people, Buell Wesley Frazier [2] and his married sister Mrs Linnie Mae Randle, [3] was enough to satisfy the Commission that Oswald had concealed and carried the rifle in a long paper bag (or sack) which he had brought to work that morning when he was a passenger in Frazier's car. No other means of bringing the rifle to the book depository was ever suggested or explored by either the Warren Commission or by anybody else in the official investigative field. Had the matter ever come to court, that paper bag would have been as essential an item of real evidence as anything else in the entire case.

The paper bag had to be put forward and maintained as a means of both transportation and concealment. Without it the prosecution would have been hard-pressed to suggest how Oswald could have brought the rifle from its hiding place in the Paine garage at Irving to the sixth floor of the Texas School Book Depository in Dallas. The evidential value of the paper bag was equal to that of the rifle itself. Perhaps it was of even greater value. I feel that we can go as far as to say that without the paper bag, there could be no rifle—certainly no rifle in the possession of Lee Harvey Oswald. Where would that have left the prosecution case against him?

Dallas Police Lieutenant J. C. Day
AND THE FINDING OF THE BAG ON THE SIXTH FLOOR

The fact that there is no photograph of the paper bag *in situ* immediately raises suspicion as to whether it was found where the Warren Commission said it was found. On the face of it, this should not prove an insurmountable problem. It is surely a simple task to refer to the testimony of the police officer who first saw it. Here, however we encounter a major problem. There is no way of establishing exactly who that may have been. According to the Warren Report: "At the time the bag was found, Lieutenant Day of the Dallas police wrote on it, 'Found next to the sixth floor window gun fired from. May have been used to carry gun. Lt. J. C. Day'" [4]

There is nothing in that brief statement to indicate when the bag was found or, more importantly, by whom. As is so often the case, however, there is far more information to be gained from a study of the 26 Volumes of Hearings and Exhibits than from the incomplete and often ambiguous conclusions of the final Warren Report.

Lieutenant John Carl Day, head of the Dallas Police Department Crime Scene Search Section, testified before the Warren Commission at the Commission's offices in Washington, D.C. on 22nd April 1964. The vast majority of his examination was conducted by Assistant Counsel David W. Belin but there were also occasional questions from Commissioner John J. McCloy.[5]

When Mr Belin begin to question Lieutenant Day about the paper bag, it was soon apparent that there was considerable confusion as to which paper bag was being discussed. At first, Lieutenant Day appeared to be referring to a lunch bag—presumably the one that had been found to contain the remnants of a fried chicken meal. Mr Belin then asked him: "What other kind of sack was found?" Lieutenant Day's reply was a strange one: "A homemade sack, brown paper with 3-inch tape found right in the corner, the southeast corner of the building near where the slugs were found." [6]

As a former operational detective with formal training and experience in investigative and interviewing techniques, I find this very much an unnatural and 'prepared' response. It gives far more information than the question has asked. This type of answer is neither common nor natural. The word 'slugs' is an obvious error and was quickly corrected by Mr McCloy who intervened to seek confirmation that Lieutenant Day meant 'hulls' (empty or spent cartridges).

Mr Belin showed Lieutenant Day a photograph of the interior of the southeast corner of the sixth floor of the Texas School Book Depository—that area which later became known as the 'sniper's nest.' [7] Mr. Belin said: "I will ask you to state if this picture was taken before or after anything was removed from the area." Lieutenant Day dutifully replied: "The sack had been removed." No explanation was offered. None was sought. Unaccountably, the point was never pursued.

WHO FOUND THE PAPER BAG?

The simple truth is that we do not know who found the paper bag. Furthermore, only one person has said that he saw the paper bag where the dotted outline on CE 1302 indicates it was. That person was Detective Robert Lee Studebaker. He was the man who, at the request of firstly an unidentified FBI Agent [8] and then of Warren Commission Assistant Counsel Joseph A. Ball, actually drew that dotted outline. [9] I will return to Detective Studebaker later.

Let us examine the testimony of some of the other law enforcement officers (Dallas Police Department and Dallas County Sheriff's Department) who should have been in a position to see the bag *in situ*.

DALLAS COUNTY DEPUTY SHERIFF LUKE MOONEY

The Warren Report describes a very important find as follows:

"Around 1 p.m. Deputy Sheriff Luke Mooney noticed a pile of cartons in front of the window in the southeast corner of the sixth floor. Searching that area he found at approximately 1:12 p.m. three empty cartridge cases on the floor near the window. When he was notified of Mooney's discovery, Capt. J. W. Fritz, chief of the homicide bureau of the Dallas Police Department, issued instructions that nothing be moved or touched until technicians from the police crime laboratory could take photographs and check for fingerprints. Mooney stood guard to see that nothing was disturbed. A few minutes later, Lt. J. C. Day of the Dallas Police Department arrived and took photographs of the cartridge cases before anything had been moved." [10]

Those few sentences inevitably raise a series of relevant questions, each of which seems to have two possible answers:

1. Why is there no mention of Mooney finding or seeing the paper bag during his search of that area? Two immediate possibilities spring to mind: either Mooney failed to notice it because he was standing on it—*or perhaps it was not there.*

2. Captain Fritz ordered that nothing be disturbed, but when that scene was photographed why does the paper bag not appear in any photograph? Again there are two possible answers: either the photographer (who may or may not have been Lieutenant Day himself) failed to realize its relevance and moved it himself (an unlikely possibility)—*or perhaps it was not there.*

3. Is it possible that one of the police officers present either ignored or misunderstood Captain Fritz' orders and *did* remove the bag? The two possibilities are that either someone committed one of the most serious errors ever in the history of crime scene preservation—*or perhaps it was not there.*

DALLAS COUNTY DEPUTY SHERIFF ROGER DEAN CRAIG

When Deputy Sheriff Craig gave his testimony before Assistant Counsel David W. Belin in Dallas in the early afternoon of 1st April 1964, there was some initial confusion as to which bag (sack) was being discussed. This was not a unique situation. We have already seen evidence of it in Lieutenant Day's testimony. The testimony of several witnesses was subject to similar problems. Remember, there were supposed to be a large paper bag (said to have contained a deadly rifle) and a smaller paper bag (said to have contained the remains of a dead chicken).

Mr Belin established that Craig had gone to the southeast corner of the sixth floor immediately after the finding of the spent cartridges. Craig confirmed that he had noticed: "the kind of paper bag you carry your lunch in" on top of a box. Mr Belin then asked: "Was there any long sack laying in the floor there that you remember seeing or not?" Craig's reply was instant and straightforward: "No; I don't remember seeing any." [11]

Perhaps because Craig's answer to that had been so positive, Mr Belin did not press the point and he never returned to the question of the longer bag during the remainder of Craig's questioning.

DALLAS POLICE SERGEANT GERALD LYNN HILL

Sergeant Hill testified before Mr Belin in Dallas on the afternoon of 8th April 1964. Like Deputy Sheriff Craig, he described seeing "a chicken leg bone and a paper sack which appeared to have been about the size normally used for a lunch sack" on top of a stack of boxes in the southeast corner of the sixth floor. [12] He did not mention any other sack or bag in the area and the subject was not reintroduced until much later in his testimony. Sergeant Hill then came out with the following strange, disjointed and almost unintelligible comments in reference to a previous conversation with Mr Belin:

"You were asking Officer Hicks if either one recalled seeing a sack, supposedly one that had been made by the suspect, in which he could have possibly carried the weapon into the Depository, and I at that time told you about the small sack that appeared to be a lunchsack, and that that was the only sack that I saw, and that I left the Book Depository prior to the finding of the gun. Or the section, if it was found up there on the sixth floor, if it was there, I didn't see it." [13]

DALLAS POLICE DETECTIVE JOHN B. HICKS

Since his name had been mentioned by Sergeant Hill, it is logical to examine what Detective Hicks, a member of Lieutenant Day's Crime Scene Search Section, had to say about the finding and existence of the long paper bag. Detective Hicks worked in the Crime Laboratory and he testified before Assistant Counsel Joseph A. Ball in Dallas on 7th April 1964.

Towards the end of his testimony, during an examination of his actions and functions within the Crime Lab, the following exchange took place:

BALL: "Did you ever see a paper sack in the items that were taken from the Texas School Book Depository building?"
HICKS: "Paper bag?"

BALL: "Paper bag."
HICKS: "No, sir; I did not. It seems like there was some chicken bones or maybe a lunch; no, I believe that someone had gathered it up."

BALL: "Well, this was another type of bag made out of brown paper; did you ever see it?"
HICKS: "No sir; I don't believe I did. I don't recall it,"

BALL: "I believe that's all, Mr. Hicks." [14]

DALLAS POLICE DETECTIVE RICHARD M. SIMS

Detective Sims was a member of the Homicide & Robbery Bureau. His Warren Commission testimony, taken by Assistant Counsel Joseph A. Ball in Dallas on 6th April 1964, contains much valuable peripheral information concerning the search of the sixth floor of the book depository.

In my Introduction to this chapter I stressed the significance of the fact that no photograph exists to show exactly where (or whether!) the large paper bag was found. Whilst discussing Deputy Sheriff Mooney's part in the finding of various items of evidence, I quoted the Warren Report as saying that Lieutenant Day had photographed the scene. Detective Sims' answers to Mr Ball's questions, however, offered some more revealing information regarding who actually took the crime scene photographs in the southeast corner of the sixth floor of the building.

The exchange was as follows:

BALL: "Did you see the picture taken of the hulls?"
SIMS: "Yes, sir."

BALL: "You saw Day take the pictures, did you?"
SIMS: "Yes, sir."

BALL: "He was the cameraman, was he?"
SIMS: "Well, there was another one there too. Actually, it was Detective Studebaker that works for him."

BALL: "Studebaker and Day?"
SIMS: "I believe it was Studebaker." [15]

A minute or so later, the following exchange of questions and answers took place:

BALL: "Did you ever see a paper bag?"
SIMS: "Well we saw some wrappings—a brown wrapping there."

BALL: "Where did you see it?"
SIMS: "It was there by the hulls."

BALL: "Was it right there by the hulls?"
SIMS: "As well as I remember—of course, I didn't pay much attention at that time, but it was, I believe, by the east side of where the boxes were piled up—that would be a guess—I believe that's where it was."

BALL: "On the east side of where the boxes were—that would be the east?"
SIMS: "Yes, sir; it was right near the stack of boxes there. I know there was some loose paper there."

BALL: "Was Johnson there?"
SIMS: "Yes, sir; when the wrapper was found Captain Fritz stationed Johnson and Montgomery to observe the scene there where the hulls were found."

BALL: "To stay there?"
SIMS: "Yes sir."

BALL: "That was Marvin Johnson and L. D. Montgomery who stayed by the hulls?"
SIMS: "Yes, sir; they did. And I was going back and forth, from the wrapper to the hulls." [16]

Detective Sims then went on to describe how the hulls, (empty cartridge cases), and the rifle had been photographed, preserved and taken into police possession. However there was no further mention of what he had called a 'wrapper'—indeed it was never mentioned again in the rest of his testimony, which was not completed until the following day.

The late Sylvia Meagher, that most-respected of researchers, commented that Detective Sims' action in "going back and forth, from the wrapper to the hulls" was a clever trick on his part "as they were separated by a distance of perhaps two feet." [17]

Detective Sims' testimony does however provide the names of two further police officers who may be able to help us—Marvin Johnson and L. D. Montgomery.

DALLAS POLICE DETECTIVE MARVIN JOHNSON

A fellow officer of Detective Sims in the Homicide & Robbery Bureau, Detective Johnson gave testimony before Assistant Counsel David W. Belin in Dallas on the afternoon of 6th April 1964. On the surface, his testimony appeared to go a long way towards confirming the existence of the long paper bag. As we shall see, however, it was greatly at variance with that of Detective Montgomery, his partner, who was with him at the time. In fact, very little of Detective Johnson's evidence was supported by anything.

After being questioned at length about the small paper bag, the remnants of fried chicken and a pop bottle, Detective Johnson stated: "We found this brown paper sack or case. It was made out of heavy wrapping paper. Actually it looked similar to the paper that those books was wrapped in. It was just a long narrow paper bag." He added that his partner (Detective Mongomery) picked it up from the floor and unfolded it. He stated that it was in the corner of the building and had been left in a double-folded condition. [18]

Mr Belin showed him a photograph on which Detective Studebaker had drawn an outline of where he claimed the bag had been located. [19] Detective Johnson responded: "It looks like somebody penned that in to show the sack was laying there. That would show it unfolded."

Detective Johnson was never asked his opinion of the dimensions of this paper bag. When asked by Mr Belin if there was anything else he could remember about the bag, he volunteered a very intriguing remark: "No; other than like I said, my partner picked it up and we unfolded it and it appeared to be about the same shape as a rifle case would be. In other words, we made the remark that that is what he probably brought it in. That is why, the reason we saved it." [20]

Considering the near-clairvoyant gifts he demonstrated with those remarks, it is difficult to imagine why Marvin Johnson, in his ten years police service in Dallas, had risen no further up the promotion ladder than basic Detective.

DALLAS POLICE DETECTIVE LESLIE DELL MONTGOMERY

Detective Montgomery testified twice before the Warren Commission but only his second appearance concerns us here. On that occasion, his testimony was taken by Assistant Counsel Joseph A. Ball at Dallas on 6th April 1964, immediately after Detective Johnson. His testimony represents an outstanding example of confusion between the two bags. At one stage, as Detective Montgomery studied a photograph of the southeast corner of the sixth floor, the dialogue went like this:

MONTGOMERY: "Right over here is where we found that long piece of paper that looked like a sack, that the rifle had been in."

BALL: "Does that have a number—that area—where you found that long piece of paper?"
MONTGOMERY: "It's No. 2 right here."

BALL: "You found the sack in the area marked 2 in Exhibit J to the Studebaker deposition. Did you pick the sack up?"
MONTGOMERY: "Which sack are we talking about now?"

BALL: "The paper sack?"
MONTGOMERY: "The small one or the larger one?"

BALL: "The larger one you mentioned that was in position 2."
MONTGOMERY: "Yes."

BALL: "You picked it up?"
MONTGOMERY: "Wait a minute—no; I didn't pick it up. I believe Mr. Studebaker did. We left it laying right there so they could check it for prints."[21]

There the exchange ended. It does, however, reveal much. Detective Montgomery, as an experienced homicide detective, should have been accustomed to cross-examination in court and would have undergone training in that area. Here, however, he appeared to become totally confused. It has to be said that there were distinct indications that he had been coached as to what he was expected to say. Having said that, however, I also recognize what appear to be signs of stress and uncertainty under some less than vigorous questioning from the 62-year old Joe Ball.

Detective Montgomery totally failed to corroborate Detective Johnson's claim that he (Montgomery) had picked up the long paper bag and unfolded it. He stated that they did not touch it, but perhaps Detective Studebaker did. The mention of fingerprints is significant. It was later claimed that Oswald's fingerprints had been found on the bag—but there was no mention of any others.

A very interesting photograph showing Detectives Johnson and Montgomery removing a long paper bag and a Dr Pepper pop bottle from the book depository has been published.[22] Detective Johnson does not appear to be exercising much care as regards the preservation of any evidential value the bottle may have. In the case of Detective Montgomery, one has to say that two things are blatantly obvious about the bag he is carrying. Firstly, it appears to be over four feet in length and secondly it is being held in a vertical position by means of something rigid inside it. That could be just about anything from a broom handle to a Mauser rifle! Whatever it is, there is no doubt that it is very effectively contaminating/destroying any trace evidence inside the bag. I cannot accept that this is the same paper bag which was described by Buell Wesley Frazier and his sister as being around two feet or 27 inches long.

Continuing to follow the trail from one named officer to another, we must now return to Detective Studebaker, the man whom Detective Montgomery claimed had picked up the paper bag.

DALLAS POLICE DETECTIVE ROBERT LEE STUDEBAKER

As already mentioned, Detective Studebaker was a man with a vital *role* in the matter under discussion here. He may or may not have been the person who first came across the paper bag and he may or may not have picked it up. What is indisputable, however, is the fact that he did *not* photograph it.

According to Dallas Police Department records for November 1963, Detective Studebaker was a member of the Auto Theft Bureau, part of the Criminal Investigation Division. [23] From his Warren Commission testimony before Assistant Counsel Joseph A. Ball in Dallas on 6th April 1964, it becomes evident that on the day of the assassination he was attached to the Crime Scene Search Section of the Identification Bureau. In view of some amazing testimony on his part, it appears that he was not only a newcomer to that Section—but was also little more than a trainee.

That being the case, it is almost inconceivable that part of the responsibility for photographing the so-called 'sniper's nest' should become his. Unfortunately, however, that is exactly what happened. As becomes apparent in the following exchange, Detective Studebaker's photographic qualifications were sadly lacking.

BALL: "But you have photography in your crime lab work?"
STUDEBAKER: "Yes."

BALL: "For how long?"
STUDEBAKER: "Was about two months."

BALL: "How long have you done photography altogether?"
STUDEBAKER: "In my lifetime?"

BALL: "No, as one of the assistants in the crime lab, what period of years?"
STUDEBAKER: "Two months. I went to the crime lab in October, the 1st of October."

BALL: "You did—have you done any photography before that?"
STUDEBAKER: "Just home photography." [24]

Together with Lieutenant Day, and sharing the only camera they had brought with them [25], Detective Studebaker photographed the three hulls and he then took photographs of the rifle *in situ* before it was moved. One of these is the infamous picture [26] in which Detective Studebaker demonstrated his remarkable photographic skills by getting his own knees in the photograph. In his own words, when asked who took that photograph: "I know it's mine because my knees are in the picture." [27]

Detective Studebaker failed to photograph any large paper bag despite the fact that it cannot have been more than a few feet away from the hulls—or *perhaps it was not there*. The bag became the subject of the following exchange:

BALL: "Now, did you at any time see any paper sack around there?"
STUDEBAKER: "Yes, sir."

BALL: "Where?"
STUDEBAKER: "Storage room there—in the southeast corner of the building—folded."

BALL: "In the southeast corner of the building?"
STUDEBAKER:"It was a paper—I don't know what it was."

BALL: "And it was folded you say?"
STUDEBAKER: "Yes." [28]

Mr Ball showed Detective Studebaker a photograph of the so-called 'sniper's nest' area in the southeast corner of the sixth floor. No paper bag could be seen on the photograph but a dotted line rectangle had been added to the photograph. [29] When asked by Mr Ball if he had drawn that diagram, Detective Studebaker replied: "I drew a diagram in there for the FBI, somebody from the FBI called me down—I can't think of his name, but he wanted an approximate location of where the paper was found." [30]

Detective Studebaker confirmed that the dotted line indicated the approximate position of the 'paper wrapping' and when asked how long it was, the following exchange ensued:

BALL: "How long was it approximately?"
STUDEBAKER: "I don't know—I picked it up and dusted it and they
took it down there and sent it to Washington and that's the last I have
seen of it, and I don't know."

BALL: "Did you take a picture of it before you picked it up?"
STUDEBAKER: "No."

BALL: "Does that sack show in any of the pictures you took?"
STUDEBAKER: "No it doesn't show in any of the pictures." [31]

A short while later, Mr Ball returned to the question of the unphotographed paper bag and offered Detective Studebaker a photograph identical to the first one but without the added dotted-line rectangle. He then asked: "Can you draw in there showing us where the paper sack was found?" and Detective Studebaker complied. [32]

The last minute or so of Detective Studebaker's testimony was again concerned with the size of the paper bag. The exchange was as follows:

BALL: "Now how big was this paper that you saw—you saw the wrapper— tell me about how big that paper bag was—how long was it?"
STUDEBAKER: "It was about, I would say, 3 and a half to 4 feet long."

BALL: "The paper bag?"
STUDEBAKER: "Yes."

BALL: "And how wide was it?"
STUDEBAKER: "Approximately 8 inches." [33]

At that point, probably to the relief of both men, Detective Studebaker's testimony ended.

(Author's note: I am reminded here of the police investigation into the 1943 murder of Sir Harry Oakes in the Bahamas. In an incredibly badly handled crime scene, a single fingerprint, belonging to the prime suspect, was found on a Chinese screen close to the body. It was dusted, lifted and preserved but because the examiner, who was both the Chief of the Miami Homicide Bureau and allegedly a fingerprint expert, had 'left his fingerprint camera behind' in Florida, it was never photographed *in situ*. The doubt expressed over this fingerprint's authenticity was one of the principal factors in the failure of the prosecution case.)

SUMMARY OF THE TESTIMONY PERTAINING TO THE FINDING OF THE PAPER BAG

In the period immediately following the shooting in Dealey Plaza one of the principal functions of the Dallas Police Department and the Dallas County Sheriff's Department was to seek, find and preserve anything of evidential value. In the case of items such as the rifle and the spent cartridge cases found on the sixth floor of the TSBD, they appear to have carried out these duties admirably. As is obvious from the testimony of the various law enforcement officers involved, however, that was not the case with another vital piece of evidence—the large paper bag.

Despite considering the position in the most favourable manner possible, the testimony quoted above gives me no confidence in the claim that such a bag was found at the sixth floor crime scene. As I have repeated several times in the foregoing paragraphs, it is my earnest belief that the paper bag never existed—certainly not until later, when it became essential that some means of conveying a concealed rifle into the building had to be established.

We must now consider another important aspect of the affair and study the testimony of the only two people who claimed to have seen Lee Harvey Oswald with the paper bag in his possession—Buell Wesley Frazier and his married sister, Mrs Linnie Mae Randle.

BUELL WESLEY FRAZIER

On the morning of the assassination of President Kennedy, Lee Harvey Oswald was driven the 15 miles to the Texas School Book Depository by fellow-worker Buell Wesley Frazier. Frazier lived at no. 2439 West Fifth Street, Irving, just three houses down from no. 2515 where Oswald's wife Marina and their two daughters were lodging with Mrs. Ruth Paine. Frazier was a relative newcomer to the area, having moved to Dallas from Huntsville, Texas in early September and taking up employment at the Texas School Book Depository on 13th September. Like Oswald he was an order filler at the depository. Although Oswald had cheap lodgings in Oak Cliff, a southern suburb of Dallas, he spent the night of 21st/22nd November with his family at the Paine house.

The 19-year-old Frazier appeared twice before the Warren Commission and his initial testimony was obviously considered to be of great importance. It was taken not in Dallas but at the Commission's offices in Washington, D.C. Furthermore, instead of being questioned by just one of the Assistant Counsel, he was honoured by receiving the full works.

Frazier was recalled by the Commission four and a half months after his first examination. On that occasion, however, he was questioned in Dallas and was asked less than a dozen questions by Assistant Counsel Wesley J. Liebeler. Since those questions were concerned with the journey to work on the morning of the assassination, they are relevant here and I will deal with them in due course.

FRAZIER'S INITIAL TESTIMONY BEFORE THE WARREN COMMISSION (WASHINGTON, D.C.)

Frazier's initial testimony was taken on 11th March 1964 at Washington, D.C. in the presence of Chief Justice Earl Warren (Chairman); two full members of the Commission (Senator John Sherman and Representative Gerald R. Ford); General Counsel J. Lee Rankin; five Assistant Counsel (Joseph A. Ball, David W. Belin, Albert E. Jenner, Jr., Wesley J. Liebeler and Norman Redlich) and two observers (Charles Murray and Lewis E. Powell Jr.). [34]

One can but speculate on the unfortunate Frazier's state of mind when, alone and many miles from home, he found himself confronted by this august gathering.

I think it is worth stressing here the exact preparations which were made prior to Frazier's entrance. The following comes verbatim from the Warren Commission 26 Volumes.

THE CHAIRMAN: "The Commission will be in order."

MR. BALL: "I would like to assign Commission Exhibit No. 364 to a paper sack which the FBI has identified as their C-109 Exhibit. That will be the Commission's Exhibit No. 364 for identification at this time."

THE CHAIRMAN: "All right."

(The paper sack referred to was marked Commission's Exhibit No. 364 for identification.)

MR. BALL: "Also for the record I would like to announce that prior to— this morning, Mr. Cortlandt Cunningham and Charles Killion of the Federal Bureau of Investigation laboratory, the Ballistics Division, Firearms Division, I guess it is, broke down, that is unscrewed Commission Exhibit No. 139, an Italian rifle, and that rifle has been placed in, after being disassembled, has been placed in Commission's No. 364 for identification, that paper sack."

THE CHAIRMAN: "All right."

MR. BALL: "We have also here before the Commission, Commission No. 142 which is a paper sack which is identified as the FBI's Exhibit No.10. I think that has its number, exhibit number on it.

"I have been informed that was 142. My notes show that the brown paper sack is 142.

"I think we can call the witness now."

THE CHAIRMAN: "All right; would you call Mr. Frazier, please." (35)

At this point, perhaps I should identify more fully the three Commission Exhibits which have been introduced and which were in front of Frazier during his examination. The following descriptions are directly from the Contents page of Vol. 16 of the 26 Volumes.

CE 139: "Mannlicher-Carcano rifle, serial No. C2766 (this rifle will subsequently be referred to 'the C2766' rifle)."

CE 142: "Bag made out of wrapping paper, found on the sixth floor of the Texas School Book Depository Building after the assassination."

CE 364: "Replica of the paper bag found on the sixth floor of the Texas School Book Depository Building shortly after the assassination." (36)

What we had there were *two* paper bags. Firstly the actual bag that was allegedly carried from Irving to Dallas in Frazier's car and then found on the sixth floor of the TSBD; and secondly, a replica of that bag into which had been placed the rifle which was found on the sixth floor. That rifle had been disassembled before being placed into the replica bag. The riddle of the replica bag will be discussed later. At this stage it is vital to bear in mind that throughout the testimony or both Buell Wesley Frazier and Mrs. Linnie Mae Randle, the paper bag which they each claimed to have seen in Oswald's possession was there in plain view in front of them.

Mr Ball led most of Frazier's interview. After considerable introductory preamble, he got around to asking Frazier about his ride home from work on the afternoon of Thursday 21st November 1963. Frazier stated that he had agreed to give Oswald a lift home to the Paine house in Irving that day and he had asked Oswald: "Why are you going home today?" Oswald's reply, as remembered and quoted by Frazier, represents one of the major cornerstones in what would have become the prosecution case: "I am going home to get some curtain rods. You know, put in an apartment." [37]

It is vital to note that Buell Wesley Frazier is the one and only person ever to attribute the words "curtain rods" to Lee Harvey Oswald.

Less than half a dozen other people used those words—Linnie Mae Randle, when quoting her brother Buell, Oswald himself when he denied that he ever made that remark to Frazier, plus of course, some of those questioning him. [38] We have only Frazier's word that Oswald gave that as his reason for wanting a lift that afternoon and the following morning. Both Ruth Paine [39] and Marina Oswald [40] denied emphatically that Oswald had mentioned anything to them about curtain rods.

As agreed, Frazier drove Oswald back to Irving that afternoon, leaving the book depository at 4.40pm and arriving at Irving (as far as can be determined) sometime between 5.20pm and 5.25pm. Mr Ball asked Frazier if any conversation had passed between them during the journey and Frazier could not remember anything being said. It is important to note here that on the only occasion that Frazier was asked if he had ever seen Oswald "taking home anything from the Texas Book Depository Building" he replied in the negative. He also denied ever seeing Oswald "taking a package home with him." [41] As we shall see later, if it were Oswald's intention to bring a rifle to work in a large paper bag on the 22nd November, his lift to Irving the evening before would be his only opportunity to take the empty bag to the Paine house.

In reply to a question from Mr Ball, Frazier stated that his sister, Linnie Mae Randle, who lived in the same house, had asked him that evening why he had brought Oswald back to Irving on that particular day. Frazier said: "I told her that he had rode home with me and told her he said he was going to come home and pick up some curtain rods or something." [42]

The following morning, the 22nd, according to Frazier's testimony, he and Oswald walked to Frazier's car, [43] which was parked just outside Frazier's carport, at a minute or so after 7.21am. [44] I find it odd that Frazier's very precise recollection of the time—literally to the exact minute after an interim period of three and a half months—was never queried.

Mr Ball asked what happened when they got into the car, and the dialogue continued:

FRAZIER: "Let's see, when I got in the car I have a kind of habit of glancing over my shoulder and so at that time I noticed there was a package laying on the back seat, I didn't pay too much attention and I said,'What's the package Lee?' And he said, 'Curtain rods' and I said, 'Oh, yes, you told me you was going to bring some today.' That is the reason, the main reason he was going over there that Thursday afternoon when he was to bring back some curtain rods, so I didn't think any more about it when he told me that."

BALL: "What did the package look like?"

FRAZIER: "Well, I will be frank with you, I would just, it is right as you get out of the grocery store, just more or less out of a package, you have seen some of those brown paper sacks you can obtain from any, most of the stores, some varieties, but it was a package just roughly about two feet long."

BALL: "It was, what part of the back seat was it in?"

FRAZIER: "It was in his side over on his side in the far back."

BALL: "How much of that back seat, how much space did it take up?"

FRAZIER: "I would say roughly around 2 feet of the seat." [45]

Buell Frazier's nervous state of mind can be judged by those answers. Note, however that without any prompting, he twice volunteered his impression of the length of the package as being about two feet. Unfortunately, of course, that was not the estimate that Mr Ball was seeking. There is no way of knowing whether Frazier had noticed the two bags (one containing the disassembled rifle) which were present in the room. There is no record that they had been pointed out to him. However, on being questioned about the length of the bag in the back of his car, he did not refer specifically to either of them or point to them.

At this point Mr Ball did not press Frazier to reconsider his estimate of the length of the package. Instead, he led him through an account of the drive into Dallas that morning, only once returning to questions about the mysterious back seat cargo.

BALL: "Anything else said about curtain rods?"

FRAZIER: "No, sir; there wasn't"

BALL: "Anything else said about the package?"

FRAZIER: "No, sir; there wasn't." [46]

In response to Mr Ball's questioning, Frazier said that Oswald did not take his lunch in with him that day.

Frazier described his exact route, street by street and turn by turn, to the TSBD employees' parking lot where he parked his car as normal. Mr Ball referred to a diagrammatic map of the book depository and its immediate area, including its three authorised employees' parking lots. [47] Frazier stated that he parked in Parking Lot No. 1 at the junction of Munger and Broadway and said that he sat there with his car engine running "letting my engine run and getting to charge up my battery, because when you stop and start you have to charge up your battery." [48]

Oswald alighted from the car and Frazier followed as he walked towards the book depository building carrying the brown paper package:

FRAZIER: "He got out of the car ... and he put the package that he had, you know, that he told me was curtain rods up under his arm, you know, and ... he started walking off and so I followed him in."

BALL: "Did you usually walk up there together?"
FRAZIER: "Yes, sir; we did."

BALL: "Is this the first time that he had ever walked ahead of you?"
FRAZIER: "Yes, sir; he did."

BALL: "You say he had the package under his arm when you saw him?"
FRAZIER: "Yes, sir."

BALL: "You mean one end of it under the armpit?
FRAZIER: "Yes, sir; he had it up just like you stick it right under your arm like that."

BALL: "And he had the lower part—"
FRAZIER: "The other part with his right hand."

BALL: "Right hand?"
FRAZIER: "Right."

BALL: "He carried it then parallel to his body?"
FRAZIER: "Right, straight up and down."

Rep. FORD: "Under his right arm?"
FRAZIER: "Yes, sir."

At later points in Frazier's testimony, Joseph Ball returned to the question of the length of the paper bag again and again. Frazier, however, refused to be browbeaten and even when the replica bag (CE 364) was specifically shown to him, he stated "No, sir" when asked if it appeared to be the same length as the package on the back seat of his car. He was also a little more explicit concerning the way that Oswald had held the package, saying that "he had it cupped in his hand." [49]

A few minutes later, in respect of what was claimed to be the 'original' bag (CE 142), Frazier repeated what he had said earlier: "I told them (the FBI) that as far as the length there, I told them that it was entirely too long." [50]

A minute or so later, Mr Ball handed Frazier CE 142, the bag allegedly found on the sixth floor, and asked him to "show about how he carried the bag." This turned into a complete pantomime which culminated in the following:

BALL: "How tall are you?"
FRAZIER: "I am 6-foot, a little bit over 6-foot."

BALL: "Do you know what your arm length is?"
FRAZIER: "No, sir; I don't."

BALL: "We can probably measure you before you leave." [51]

I have been unable to ascertain whether or not Frazier's arm was measured before he returned to his home in Irving.

This detailed and positive description of the way Oswald carried the package, with one end under his armpit and the other with his right hand, was given on 11th March 1964. It was, however, neither the first nor the last time he gave this positive account—and always totally without variation.

FRAZIER'S AFFIDAVIT ON 22ND NOVEMBER 1963

Frazier's account of the drive from Irving, parking his car, and his and Oswald's walk to the book depository had already been recorded in a Dallas Sheriff's Department affidavit on the day of the assassination. [52] Part of this document reads as follows:

"Before I got in the car, I glanced in the back seat, and saw a big sack. It must have been about 2' long, and the top of the sack was sort of folded up, and the rest of the sack had been kind of folded under ... I parked the car and sat there awhile and run the motor to charge the battery, and while I was doing that, Lee got out and opened the back door and got the package out of the back seat and walked behind the car, then I got out of the car and started walking toward the building where I work. I noticed that Lee had the package in his right hand under his arm, and the package was straight up and down, and he had his arm down, and you could not see much of the package ... I saw him go in the back door at the Loading Dock of the building that we work in, and he still had the package under his arm."

FRAZIER'S TELEVISED INTERVIEW (SHOWN IN NOVEMBER 1986)

In the Channel Four (London) production *The Trial of Lee Harvey Oswald*, [53] Frazier repeated his description of the way Oswald carried that package. He did, in fact, indicate to both Vincent Bugliosi (prosecuting) and Gerry Spence (defending) that Oswald carried it with one end cupped in his right hand and the other end under his armpit:

> BUGLIOSI: "As I understand it, when the two of you got out of the car he started walking ahead of you to the entrance to the building. Is this correct?"
> FRAZIER: "That is correct."

> BUGLIOSI: "As he was walking ahead of you, was he carrying the bag that had been on the back seat?"
> FRAZIER: "Yes, sir."

> BUGLIOSI: "Did you recall how he was carrying the bag?"
> FRAZIER: "Yes, sir. He was carrying it parallel to his body."

> BUGLIOSI: "Okay, so he carried the bag right next to his body. On the right side?"
> FRAZIER: "Yes, sir, on the right side."

> BUGLIOSI: "Was it cupped in his hand and under his armpit? I think you said that in the past."
> FRAZIER: "Yes, sir."

> BUGLIOSI: "Mr. Frazier, is it true that you paid hardly any attention to this bag?"
> FRAZIER: "That is true."

> BUGLIOSI: "So the bag could have been protruding out in front of his body and you wouldn't have been able to see it. Is that correct?"
> FRAZIER: "That is true."

I cannot help but suspect that Mr Bugliosi's last two questions in that dialogue were an attempt at what we now describe as "damage limitation".

Later, cross-examination by Gerry Spence (defending) produced the following exchange:

> SPENCE: "And you believed that the bag that you saw, that he was carrying, was one that he could put under his arm and carry in his

palm, isn't that true?"
FRAZIER: "Yes, sir, that is true."

SPENCE: "And that's longer than the rifle would be if it was broken
down, isn't that right?"
FRAZIER: "That's correct."

Another televised interview (shown 1991)

Some five years later (1991) Frazier was interviewed in Part 2 ('The
Patsy') of Nigel Turner's *The Men Who Killed Kennedy* [54] and was again
asked about the manner in which Oswald carried the package. Frazier said:
"Lee got out of the car, took the package that he said contained curtain rods,
and he put one end of the package in the cup of his hand and the other up under
his armpit—and put the package under his arm that way and he walked off
towards the Texas School Book Depository up on Elm Street." As he speaks,
Frazier demonstrates the way he says Oswald held and carried the package.

I feel it significant that in an affidavit (22nd November 1963), sworn testimony before the Warren Commission (11th March 1964), a televised interview (1986) and another television production (1991), Buell Wesley Frazier
was unswerving in describing how Oswald had carried that package. It was
cupped in his right hand—and it was up into his armpit. There is absolutely no
disputing this. Mr Frazier says so, he was the only witness to it, and his account has remained constant and unchanged over the years.

To carry a package about two feet long in this fashion would present no
problem. The shortest length which can be achieved with a disassembled
Mannlicher-Carcano identical to CE 139 (the alleged assassination rifle), however, is 34.8 inches. [55] To carry something that long in the manner consis-
tently described by Frazier (over a period of 28 years) would require a body
height in excess of seven feet and arms like an orang-utan. That is hardly an
accurate description of the 5'9" Lee Harvey Oswald. [56]

I am pleased to have had researcher Don Roberdeau prepare a special
version of his graphic representation showing the relative dimensions of
Oswald's arm, the paper bag and the disassembled rifle. [57]

I think that like Helen Louise Markham and Howard Leslie Brennan,
much would have been expected of Frazier in the quest to confirm the guilt of
the deceased Oswald. Each of them, however, in their own way, would have
proved a severe embarrassment to the prosecution had the case ever gone to
court.

FRAZIER TESTIFIES AGAIN

As mentioned earlier, Buell Wesley Frazier was called to testify a second time. This took place on 23rd July 1964 and on this occasion he was spared the long journey to Washington, D.C. He attended at the US Attorney's Office, 301 Post Office Building, Bryan and Ervay Streets, Dallas. Only Assistant Counsel Wesley J. Liebeler was present. His sole object was to confirm that Frazier had seen Oswald "carrying a large brown package from the car into the Texas School Book Depository Building and that also you saw that package in the car." Frazier agreed.

Frazier also confirmed that there had been no other occasion on which he had seen Oswald with a similar package. [58]

I remain at a loss as to why this brief question-and-answer session was felt necessary. I can only suggest that it could have been another 'damage limitation' exercise. Perhaps it was significant that the question of the bag's length was never raised.

Mr Ball and his Commission colleagues were undoubtedly disappointed at Frazier's lack of agreement with their hoped-for estimates of the paper bag's length. Imagine how they must have felt, then, when he had stated in his Washington testimony that it had been his impression at the time, from the front entrance steps of the book depository, that the shots had been fired from "down there, you know, where that underpass is. There is a series, quite a few number, of them railroad tracks running together and from where I was standing it sounded like it was coming from down the railroad tracks there. " [59]

CORROBORATION OF FRAZIER'S TESTIMONY?

Perhaps we should now seek some sort of corroboration of this part of Frazier's testimony. Was there anyone who could confirm that Oswald left Frazier's car and walked into the book depository carrying a package that morning? That walk, from TSBD Parking Lot No. 1, was a distance of about 350 yards. [60] The lot was located on the northeast corner of the Broadway and Munger Street intersection but has since disappeared beneath the West End development scheme.

JACK EDWIN DOUGHERTY

Dougherty was a fellow book depository worker (a shipping clerk) and he testified before the Warren Commission in Dallas on 8th April 1964. He stated that he had seen Oswald arrive for work on the morning of the assassination. As his testimony indicates, however, he was unable to confirm that

Oswald was carrying anything. After telling Assistant Counsel Ball that he (Dougherty) was inside the building by 7.00am, his testimony on this point went thus:

> BALL: "Did you see Oswald come to work that morning?"
> DOUGHERTY: "Yes—when he first come into the door."
>
> BALL: "When he came in the door?"
> DOUGHERTY: "Yes."
>
> BALL: "Did you see him come in that door?"
> DOUGHERTY: "Yes; I saw him when he first come in the door—yes."
>
> BALL: "Did he have anything in his hands or arms?"
> DOUGHERTY: "Well, not that I could see of."
>
> BALL: "About what time of day was that?"
> DOUGHERTY: "That was eight o'clock." [61]

At this point, it should have been obvious to Mr Ball that this line of questioning was unlikely to elicit the replies he was seeking. After a brief diversion to confirm exactly where Dougherty had been at the time, he returned to it in a very unsubtle way. In my opinion, the following brief exchange represents one of the very worst examples of witness harassment in this investigation:

> BALL: "Do you recall him having anything in his hand?"
> DOUGHERTY: "Well, I didn't see anything, if he did."
>
> BALL: "Did you pay enough attention to him you think, that you would remember whether he did or didn't?"
> DOUGHERTY: "Well, I believe I can—yes, sir—I'll put it this way; I didn't see anything in his hands at the time."
>
> BALL: "In other words, your memory is definite on that, is it?"
> DOUGHERTY: "Yes, sir."
>
> BALL: "In other words, you would say positively he had nothing in his hands?"
> DOUGHERTY: "I would say that—yes, sir."
>
> BALL: "Or are you guessing?"
> DOUGHERTY: "I don't think so." [62]

Aware at last that Dougherty was either unable or unwilling to confirm that Oswald had carried a package into the building, Mr. Ball moved on to other matters before unexpectedly returning to the subject perhaps hoping to catch Dougherty unawares. Dougherty, however, was not only ready for this—he was also becoming increasingly unhappy with the way he was being harassed. Now he sought an escape route.

BALL: "Did you ever see Lee Oswald carry any sort of package?"
DOUGHERTY: "Well, I didn't, but some of the fellows said they did."

BALL: "Who said that?"
DOUGHERTY: "Well, Bill Shelley, he told me that he thought he saw him carrying a fairly good-sized package."

BALL: "When did Shelley tell you that?"
DOUGHERTY: "Well, it was—the day after it happened." [63]

It is surely obvious to anyone reading that passage that Dougherty had grown tired of his treatment and was anxious to remove the pressure being exerted upon him. We must ask why he did not mention Shelley earlier. As becomes plain when we study Shelley's version of events, Dougherty probably just blurted out the first suitable name which came to mind.

William Hoyt Shelley

Shelley, the Manager of the Miscellaneous Department, had been examined by Mr Ball on 7th April 1964—the day immediately before the Dougherty testimony. Part of that testimony concerning Lee Harvey Oswald was as follows:

BALL: "On the 22d of November 1963, did you see him come to work that morning?"

SHELLEY: "No, he was at work when I got there already filling orders."
[64]

Other TSBD employees

You will search in vain for any employee of the Texas School Book Depository (other than Buell Wesley Frazier of course) who said that Oswald had been in possession of any sort of package when he arrived at work that morning. Furthermore, nobody ever stated that they had seen him with a package inside the building at any time that day.

Mrs Linnie Mae Randle

Frazier's married sister, Mrs Linnie Mae Randle, testified immediately after him—and before the same powerful gathering of Warren Commission heavyweights. There does not even appear to have been a break in the proceedings between Frazier's examination and the start of Mrs Randle's. It is also apparent that the paper bags (CE 142/626 and CE 364) were still on display. Like her brother, Mrs Randle was questioned by Assistant Counsel Joseph A. Ball.

After the usual preamble and a few questions about Lee Harvey Oswald and how he had obtained employment at the TSBD, Mr Ball reached the point when Buell Wesley Frazier had brought Oswald back to Irving on the Thursday evening. Mr Ball went straight on to the attack in a very positive way with a classic leading question:

BALL: "Do you remember anything about curtain rods?"
RANDLE: "Yes."

BALL: "What do you remember about that?"
RANDLE: "He had told Wesley — "

BALL: "Tell me what Wesley told you."
RANDLE: "What Wesley told me. That Lee had rode home with him to get some curtain rods from Mrs. Paine to fix up his apartment."

Mr Ball quickly switched to the following morning as Frazier was preparing to leave for work. He asked Mrs Randle if she had seen Lee:

BALL: "Where did you see him?"
RANDLE: "I saw him as he crossed the street and come across my drive-way to where Wesley had his car parked by the carport."

BALL: "Was he carrying any package?"
RANDLE: "Yes; he was."

BALL: "What was he carrying?"
RANDLE: "He was carrying a package in a sort of heavy brown bag, heavier than a grocery bag it looked to me. It was about, if I might measure, about this long, I suppose, and he carried it in his right hand, had the top sort of folded down and had a grip like this, and the bottom, he carried it this way, you know, and it almost touched the ground as

he carried it."

BALL: "And where was his hand gripping the middle of the package?"
RANDLE: "No, sir; the top with just a little bit sticking up. You know, just like you grab something like that."

BALL: "And he was grabbing it with his right hand at the top of the package and the package almost touched the ground?"
RANDLE: "Yes, sir." [65]

Possibly unaware of whether or not he had received the answer he was seeking, Mr Ball went on to another minor matter before suddenly returning to the package. He showed the replica bag to Mrs Randle and, according to the record, asked a strange question:

BALL: "Now, was the length of it any similar, anywhere near similar?"
RANDLE: "Well, it wasn't that long. I mean it was folded down at the top as I told you. It definitely wasn't that long."

BALL: "I see. You figure about two feet long, is that right?"
RANDLE: "A little bit more."

BALL: "Is that about right? That is 28 and a half inches."
RANDLE: "It measured 27 last time."

BALL: "You measured 27 once before?"
RANDLE: "Yes, sir." [66]

At this point, perhaps satisfied that he had got Mrs Randle to increase her original estimate of the bag's length from two feet to 27 inches, Mr Ball asked a few inconsequential questions before the witness was dismissed.

SOME FACTS ABOUT THE DISASSEMBLED MANNLICHER-CARCANO

The 6.5mm Mannlicher-Carcano Model 1938 (91/38) rifle found half-hidden on the sixth floor of the Texas School Book Depository (CE 139) has a reported overall length of 40.2 inches. As already explained, its longest component when disassembled, the wooden stock, is 34.8 inches long. [67] It follows that any paper bag in which it is carried must be longer than that. The disassembled rifle consists of 13 components including the sling, one end of which remains fixed to the wooden stock. An ammunition clip and ammunition are additional items.

It is not a simple matter to take the rifle apart and slide the parts into a paper bag. My own practical experiments in this field, using a Mannlicher identical to CE 139 plus a reconstructed paper bag, are very revealing [68] The second longest individual component consists of the barrel, the trigger mechanism, the chamber, the scope, etc. All these are predominantly metal and they do not make a smooth, easily-handled item. Several parts, particularly the trigger itself, the foresight, the rear sight, the scope, the safety catch and the rear mounting screw of the tang all protrude at different angles. The total length of this assembly is 29.5 inches.

The most practical way to place a disassembled Mannlicher-Carcano into a suitable paper bag is to place the metal barrel assembly on top of the wooden stock and then slide them into the bag together. This is best done with the barrel pointing rearwards towards the butt plate. The smaller components (wooden top stock, metal collars, sling swivel, trigger guard and five screws) are best dealt with by placing them into a large envelope or something similar and putting that into the paper bag last. I have carried out this procedure many times.

Something very important results from this treatment—something that I have never seen mentioned in any published work I have read on the Kennedy assassination. When the components of the rifle are removed from the bag, it is found that the first seven or eight inches of the stock show obvious signs of severe scoring and scratching. This is caused by the protruding parts of the barrel assembly—principally the trigger—rubbing against it as the bag is moved or carried. It does not require very much imagination to work out the result if the bag has been carried a total of something like 400 yards and has undergone a journey of 15 miles on the back seat of a car.

So what is the significance of these facts? Quite simply, no such scratches have ever been reported on the CE 139 rifle. Furthermore, they are not evident in any photographs taken of that rifle. To me, this provides irrefutable physical proof that the rifle was never transported in a disassembled state in a long paper bag as has been claimed by the investigative agencies and the Warren Commission.

WOULD OSWALD HAVE HAD THE OPPORTUNITY TO MAKE THE BAG?

The answer to this vital question is simple. No, he would not. Let us examine the facts.

Commission Exhibit 142 (or, if you prefer, CE 626—for some unexplained reason the 'original' bag was assigned two exhibit numbers) purports to be the paper bag found in the south eastern corner of the sixth floor. As we shall see, there is no dispute that CE 142/626 had been constructed using wrapping paper and tape available at the Texas School Book Depository. [69] For Lee Harvey Oswald to have brought a rifle into the building inside that paper bag it would have been necessary for him to have constructed the bag *there inside the building*. As we can learn from the Warren Commission testimony of FBI Special Agent James C. Cadigan and TSBD employee Troy Eugene West, however, he had neither the time nor the opportunity to do this.

FBI Special Agent James C. Cadigan

SA Cadigan was based at the Washington, D.C. FBI Laboratory as an examiner of questioned documents. As such, a major part of his expertise was in the field of paper. He testified before the Warren Commission as an expert witness on 3rd and 30th April 1964. On the first occasion, it was in connection with the long paper bag.

He told Assistant Counsel Melvin Aron Eisenberg that he had examined CE 142/626 (the paper bag) in the FBI Laboratory on 23rd November 1963, together with samples of paper and tape obtained from the Texas School Book Depository on the day of the Kennedy assassination. [70] An FBI report sent by J. Edgar Hoover to DPD Chief Curry on 23rd November 1963 includes the paragraph: "The paper of the wrapping and the tape, Q10, were found to have the same observable physical characteristics as the known brown wrapping paper and tape, K2, from the Texas School Book Depository." [71] That statement obviously pertains to SA Cadigan's examination, FBI exhibit Q10 being the paper bag. Although we have the professional opinion of an accepted expert witness here, the actual significance of his conclusion is worthless if, as I maintain, the paper bag was manufactured from material in the book depository by someone other than Oswald.

SA Cadigan also commented on a series of marks running down the centre of the tape: "I might explain that these are made by a wheel in the paper-tape dispenser ... as you pull the operating handle that pulls the paper tape from the roll through the machine and over the wetting brush, the wheel, in the process leaves these markings on the tape." [72] As we shall see shortly, these marks are significant.

SA Cadigan went on to throw some valuable light on why it had been felt necessary to construct the replica bag. In fact he did not wait to be asked about it, as the following exchange shows:

CADIGAN: "Do you want me to discuss this replica sack yet?"
EISENBERG: "You mentioned a replica bag?"
CADIGAN: "Yes."

EISENBERG: "Could you explain what that is?"

CADIGAN: "Yes; this is Commission Exhibit 364. It is a paper sack similar to Commission Exhibit 142. It was made at the Texas School Book Depository on December 1, 1963, by special agents of the FBI in Dallas to show to prospective witnesses, because Commission's Exhibit 142 was dark and stained from the latent fingerprint treatment and they thought that this would—it wouldn't be fair to the witness to ask 'Did you see a bag like that?' So they went to the Texas School Book Depository and constructed from paper and tape a similar bag."

EISENBERG: "This was made December 1?"

CADIGAN: "December 1, of 1963." [73]

I am astounded at this action on the part of the FBI—and by the fact that one of their agents should openly (and almost eagerly) admit what happened. In my eyes, this is a classic example of attempting to pervert the course of justice. Just what is the point of showing a 'replica' or 'copy' exhibit to a witness? How many similar occurrences were there during this investigation? How can we now be certain that *any* of the exhibits are really what they purport to be? A very dangerous precedent had been set.

SA Cadigan's explanation that the replica bag was needed because the original had been stained during its fingerprint examination does not say much for the forensic skills of those who examined it. His account of the visit to the book depository to construct the bag omits one important fact. 1st December 1963 was a Sunday—a non-working day—so they very conveniently had the place to themselves.

Another part of SA Cadigan's expert testimony concerned his opinions regarding any contents the paper bag may have ever had. This important exchange was as follows:

EISENBERG: "Mr. Cadigan, did you notice when you looked at the bag whether there were—that is the bag found on the sixth floor, Exhibit 142—whether it had any bulges or unusual creases?"

CADIGAN: "I was also requested at that time to examine the bag to determine if there were any significant markings or scratches or abrasions or anything by which it could be associated with the rifle, Commission Exhibit 139, that is, could I find any markings that I could tie to that rifle."

EISENBERG: "Yes?"

CADIGAN: "And I couldn't find any such markings." [74]

SA Cadigan was not alone in failing to associate the rifle forensically with the paper bag. There is no testimony or hard evidence to suggest that anybody else could. The aforementioned FBI report (Hoover/Curry, 23rd November 1963) even contained the sentence: "The inside surface of specimen Q10 did not disclose markings identifiable with the rifle, K1" (Q10 was described as 'Wrapping paper in shape of a large bag') [75]

An official letter from FBI Director Hoover to J. Lee Rankin (General Counsel to the Warren Commission) on 20th August 1964 states, among other things, that the rifle was in a "well-oiled condition". [76] Marina Oswald testified that when they were living at 214 Neely Street, Dallas, she had seen her husband clean his rifle "about four times—about four or five times, I think." [77] Nowhere, however, was it ever reported that any oil-stains were found on the paper bag—the same paper bag that had been so badly stained by the application of fingerprint powder as to render it useless as an exhibit to show to witnesses! The inference here is too obvious for me to mention.

TROY EUGENE WEST

One of the most important (and indisputable) facts about the paper bag is that it could *only* have been made inside the book depository. Furthermore, it could *only* have been made at the first floor work bench where the relevant materials were kept. It was not possible for Lee Harvey Oswald (or anybody else) to smuggle the materials out of the building and make the bag elsewhere. The reason for this becomes obvious with the testimony of Troy Eugene West, the sole full-time mail wrapper employed at the Texas School Book Depository.

West gave his Warren Commission testimony before Assistant Counsel David W. Belin in Dallas on 8th April 1964. West explained that he was the only full-time mail wrapper employed in the building and that his permanent place of work was at what he described as a "mail wrapping table" on the first floor. All the materials he required—wrapping paper, tape and string—were kept at this table and he never had occasion to leave it. It seems that he even made his coffee and ate his lunch at this table. As he said to Mr Belin: "I never did hardly ever leave the first floor. That is just I stayed there where my work was, and I just stayed there." [78]

Not even a presidential motorcade passing within a few feet of the building could tempt him away from his wrapping table. When that happened, at 12.30pm on Friday 22nd November 1963, West was sitting at his work table, halfway through his lunch. He did not hear any shots and the first he knew of anything untoward was when "the police and things was coming in, and I was just spellbound. I just didn't know what was the matter" [79]

West explained to Mr Belin that the gummed tape used to secure the packages of books was dispensed through a special machine. The tape was automatically moistened as it was pulled through. There was only one way to obtain unmoistened tape—as would have been necessary for the paper bag to have been made elsewhere.

> BELIN: "If I wanted to pull the tape, pull off a piece without getting water on it, would I just lift it up without going over the wet roller and get the tape without getting it wet?"
> WEST: "You would have to take it out. You would have to take it out of the machine. See, it's put in there and then run through a little clamp that holds it down, and you pull it, well, then the water, it gets water on it."

> BELIN: "Is this an electrical machine or is it just kind of a little apparatus for pulling it through by hand?"
> WEST: "Well, it is not electric, no, sir." [80]

We know from SA Cadigan's testimony that the tape on the original paper bag showed unique markings indicating that it has passed through *that* tape dispenser and no other. It follows, therefore, that the bag was manufactured at West's wrapping table and nowhere else. It was not a case of the materials being removed from the building and the bag being assembled somewhere else.

West's replies to Mr Belin's questions established several vital facts: he knew Oswald by sight; Oswald had never helped him to wrap mail; he was unaware that Oswald had ever borrowed or used any wrapping paper for himself; he had never seen Oswald around the wrapper rolls or the wrapper roll machines. [81] He also stated that on 22nd November, he had arrived at work at 7.50am—earlier than was normal for Oswald. [82]

It would be extremely difficult to suggest an opportunity which Lee Harvey Oswald would have had to put together a long paper bag at Troy Eugene West's table—and that task *cannot* have been performed elsewhere.

Oswald's rooming house—1026 North Beckley Avenue

Before closing, perhaps we should cast a glance in the direction of 1026 North Beckley Avenue, Oak Cliff—the rooming house at which Oswald was renting a room at this time. Is there any evidence to suggest that his room there required curtain rods? No. Is it even feasible that a tenant would be required to supply the curtain rods for his rented room? Again, no.

The co-owners of the property (Mr and Mrs Arthur Johnson) and the housekeeper (Mrs Earlene Roberts) testified before the Warren Commission. A study of the testimony given by Mr and Mrs Johnson clearly tells us all we need to know regarding the question of curtain rods in Oswald's room.

MRS ARTHUR CARL (GLADYS J.) JOHNSON

Mrs Johnson was 61 years old at the time of the assassination and she had owned and occupied 1026 North Beckley for 21 years. Her testimony, taken by Assistant Counsel Joseph A. Ball in Dallas on the afternoon of 1st April 1964, revealed that the house had 22 rooms and that when Oswald began his tenancy there on 14th October 1963, there were "about 10 or 12" tenants in residence. [83]

The subject of curtain rods was covered in a straightforward way and left no doubt that there was no need for Oswald, or anybody else, to provide curtain rods for his room. The relevant questions and answers concerning the room and its windows were as follows:

JOHNSON: "Yes, sir; it had curtains and venetian blinds."

BALL: "What kind of curtains did it have?"
JOHNSON: "Well, it just had side drapes and panels."

BALL: "Were the curtains on curtain rods?"
JOHNSON: "Yes, sir."

BALL: "They were in the room when he rented it?"
JOHNSON: "Yes, sir."

BALL: "Did Oswald ever talk to you about redecorating the room?"
JOHNSON: "No, sir; he never mentioned it."

BALL: "Did he ever talk to you about putting up new curtains in his room?"
JOHNSON: "No, sir."

BALL: "Did he ever tell you he was going to get some curtain rods?"
JOHNSON: "No; he didn't."

BALL: "The room had curtain rods on the window when he came in there?"
JOHNSON: "Yes, sir; sure did."

BALL: "Also curtains?"

JOHNSON: "Yes, sir." [84]

Arthur Carl Johnson

Arthur Johnson testified immediately after his wife and he confirmed to Assistant Counsel David W. Belin what she had told Mr Ball about the room rented to Oswald. The relevant exchange was as follows:

BELIN: "Could you describe that little room for us?"
JOHNSON: "Well, it's just a—a small room. I believe it's about 8 by 12, or something like that. It was a library room."

BELIN: "Did it have any windows in it?"
JOHNSON: "It has—uh—three—four windows, I believe."

BELIN: "On one side, two sides, three sides?"
JOHNSON: "One side."

BELIN: "They are all on one side?"
JOHNSON: "All on one side."

BELIN: "Do you have any curtains on the windows?"
JOHNSON: "Yes."

BELIN: "How were the curtains put up—by curtain rods, or by what?"
JOHNSON: "Yes. Curtain rods. Yes. They were just regular curtain rods."

BELIN: "There were already curtain rods in the room, then, when this O.H. Lee came there—is that correct?"
JOHNSON: "Yes, uh-huh." [85]

In addition to confirming the existence of curtain rods prior to 22nd November 1963, Mr Johnson's testimony is also useful in determining the dimensions of the room, the fact that there were four separate windows and that they were all along one wall.

Freelance photographer Gene Daniels

Gene Daniels (possibly Daniel) was a local freelancer who took somewhere around 24 black-and-white still photographs in the area of Dealey Plaza and City Hall on the day of the assassination. The following morning, 23rd November 1963, he took a further 11 photographs of both the interior and exterior of 1026 North Beckley. Nine of these show Mrs Johnson and/or her husband making up or standing on Oswald's bed and adjusting the curtains. As indicated by Mr Johnson, the curtains stretch the entire length of the room.[86]

I originally understood that these photographs had been taken covertly by Daniels but an interesting passage in Howard Roffman's book *Presumed Guilty* suggests otherwise. [87] Roffman quotes directly from a letter he received from Daniels on 19th March 1970:

> "I went to the rooming house the following morning (Saturday 23rd November 1963) and requested permission to make a photograph from the landlady. I'm not sure of her name but I don't think she was the owner. We went into the room and she told me she preferred not to have me take any pictures until she put 'the curtains back up.' She said that newsmen the evening before had disturbed the room and she didn't want anyone to see it all messed up. I agreed and stood in the room as she and her husband stood on the bed and hammered the curtain rods back into position. While she did this, I photographed them or possibly just her I forget right now, up on the bed with the curtain rods, etc."

Obviously, the lady in question *was* the owner, Mrs Johnson. I feel that it is important that Daniels stated in his letter that the Johnsons had hammered the curtain rods *back* into position. This indicates that they had been installed already. One is left to wonder exactly what activities the newsmen had been practising the previous evening.

It is also important to note that all four curtains appear to have been hung from one continuous curtain rod—which must be approximately 12 feet long. [88]

Daniels, like many freelance photographers of the period, used the Black Star Photographic Agency, New York City, for the marketing and distribution of his work. [89] I have been given to understand that Daniels' nine photographs taken inside Oswald's room at 1026 North Beckley have been suppressed, possibly by Black Star, and remain unpublished. [90]

WAS OSWALD ANTICIPATING MOVING OUT OF HIS ROOM AT 1026 NORTH BECKLEY?

This question should be considered in light of Oswald's alleged remark to Frazier that he needed the curtain rods to "put in an apartment." [91]

There is nothing in the testimony or evidence of any person—Oswald, his wife, Mrs Paine, the Johnsons, Mrs Roberts, Frazier, Mrs Randle or any of the employees of the book depository – to suggest that Oswald was either seeking alternative accommodation or had found some. His weekly rent at 1026 North Beckley ($8.00 weekly, payable in advance) had been paid on Monday 18th November 1963. [92]

Unfortunately, there is no record of this question ever being put to Lee Harvey Oswald during his lengthy but allegedly unrecorded interrogation at the hands of the Dallas Police.

CONCLUSION

My conclusion is short. It consists of just ten individual findings—each of which I have sought to prove in the foregoing—plus one overall conclusion.

1. The long paper bag was not photographed at the scene because at that time it did not exist.

2. The long paper bag was 'made up' (in both the mental and physical senses) by members of the investigative agencies—whether by the Dallas Police Department, the Dallas County Sheriff's Department, or somebody else, I do not claim to know.

3. The long paper bag was assigned two separate exhibit numbers (142 and 626) in a deliberate attempt to confuse the issue.

4. A replica of the long paper bag was manufactured to cause further confusion and was given exhibit number 364. The official reason for its manufacture—to show to witnesses instead of the original which had been damaged during forensic examination—is just too ridiculous to consider seriously.

5. The long paper bag (CE 142/626) exhibited no physical signs of ever having contained a 'well-oiled' rifle or anything else with jagged edges.

6. The wooden stock of the Mannlicher-Carcano rifle (CE 139) did not carry any marks to suggest that it had ever been carried in a disassembled state inside the long paper bag.

7. Lee Harvey Oswald did *not* manufacture a long paper bag for the purpose of carrying a concealed rifle into the Texas School Book Depository.

8. Lee Harvey Oswald did *not* carry a long paper bag from the Paine house to

the Randle/Frazier house, place it into Buell Wesley Frazier's car and then carry it from a parking lot to the book depository, with one end under his right armpit and the other cupped in his hand.

9. Lee Harvey Oswald did *not* utter the words 'curtain rods' in any conversation he had with Frazier.

10. Lee Harvey Oswald did not have any requirement to install curtain rods in his room since an adequate curtain rod system was already in place.

   Overall conclusion: Lee Harvey Oswald did not fire a rifle at anybody that day.

NOTES

1. Warren Report, page 19.
2. 2H 210-245 and 7H 531 (Testimony of Buell Wesley Frazier).
3. 2H 245-251 (Testimony of Mrs Linnie Mae Randle).
4. Warren Report, page 135.
5. 4H 249-278 (Testimony of Lieutenant John Carl Day).
6. 4H 266 (Testimony of Lieutenant John Carl Day).
7. CE 729 (Photograph taken in the sixth floor of the Texas School Book Depository Building, showing location of Commission Exhibit No. 142, when discovered).
8. 7H 144 (Testimony of Detective Robert Lee Studebaker).
9. 7H 145 (Testimony of Detective Robert Lee Studebaker).
10. Warren Report, page 79.
11. 6H 268 (Testimony of Deputy Sheriff Roger Dean Craig).
12. 7H 46 (Testimony of Sergeant Gerald Lynn Hill).
13. 7H 65 (Testimony of Sergeant Gerald Lynn Hill).
14. 7H 289 (Testimony of Detective John B. Hicks).
15. 7H 161 (Testimony of Detective Richard M. Sims).
16. 7H 162 (Testimony of Detective Richard M. Sims).
17. Sylvia Meagher: *Accessories after the Fact*, published by Vintage Books, New York, 1976; page 59.
18. 7H 103 (Testimony of Detective Marvin Johnson).
19. Studebaker Exhibit G (21H 647).
20. 7H 104 (Testimony of Detective Marvin Johnson).
21. 7H 98 (Testimony of Detective L. D. Montgomery). See also Studebaker J (Nos. 1, 3 and 4 are plainly visible but No. 2 cannot be seen. Its location must be in the dark area immediately to the right of the dark-shaded box at top left.)

22. Richard B. Trask: *Pictures of the Pain*, published by Yeoman Press, USA, 1994; page 552. See also 13H 105 (Testimony of Ira Jefferson "Jack" Beers, Jr., *Dallas Morning News* photographer).
23. Batchelor Exhibit No. 5002 *(DPD* Personnel Assignments, November 1963), page 29 of exhibit (19H 146).
24. 7H 138 (Testimony of Detective Robert Lee Studebaker).
25. ibid.
26. Studebaker C (21H 645).
27. 7H 140 (Testimony of Detective Robert Lee Studebaker).
28. 7H 143 (Testimony of Detective Robert Lee Studebaker).
29. Studebaker F (21H 647).
30. 7H 144 (Testimony of Detective Robert Lee Studebaker).
31. ibid.
32. 7H 145 (Testimony of Detective Robert Lee Studebaker).
33. 7H 149 (Testimony of Detective Robert Lee Studebaker).
34. 2H 210 (Introduction to the testimony of Buell Wesley Frazier).
35. 2H 210-211 (Preamble to the testimony of Buell Wesley Frazier).
36. Index to Vol. 16 of the 26 Volumes.
37. 2H 222 (Testimony of Buell Wesley Frazier).
38. Warren Report, page 604 *(Report of Captain J.W. Fritz, Dallas Police Department)*, page 621 (FBI report of SA James W. Bookhout, 23rd November 1963) and page 626 (Report of Inspector Thomas J. Kelley, U.S. Secret Service). These apparently relate to the same interrogation/interview of Oswald at 10.25am on 23rd November 1963.
39. 3H 75-76 (Testimony of Mrs Ruth Hyde Paine). Relevant extract as follows:
    Assistant Counsel Albert E. Jenner, Jr.: "Had there been any conversation between you and Lee Oswald, or between you and Marina, or any conversation taking place in your presence prior to this occasion, in which the subject of curtain rods was mentioned?"
    Mrs Paine: "There was no such conversation."

    Mr Jenner: "Was the subject of curtain rods—had that ever been mentioned during all of these weekends that Lee Oswald had come to your home, commencing, I think you said, with his first return on October 4, 1963?"
    Mrs Paine: "It had not been mentioned."

    Mr Jenner: "Never by anybody?"
    Mrs Paine: "By anybody."

    Mr Jenner: "Had the subject of curtain rods been mentioned even inadvertently, let us say, by some neighbor talking about the subject,

as to whether you had some certain rods you weren't using?"
Mrs Paine: "No."

For some light relief, it is worth reading 3H 72-78 in which Mrs Paine is faced with questions relating to curtain rods and venetian blinds from five members of the Warren Commission (Jenner, Cooper, Liebeler, McCoy and Ford).

40. 1H 68-69 (Testimony of Mrs Marina Oswald). Relevant extract as follows:

General Counsel J. Lee Rankin: "On the evening of the 21st, was anything said about curtain rods or his taking curtain rods to town the following day?"
Mrs Oswald: "No, he didn't have any."

Mr Jenner: "He didn't say anything like that?"
Mrs Oswald: "No."

See also CE 1401 (page 272 of exhibit) at 22H 751, an FBI report of an interview of Mrs Marina Oswald on 2nd December 1963, which contains the following:
"MARINA stated that when OSWALD visited the PAINE house on Thursday evening, November 21, 1963, he did not bring anything with him when he arrived at the house . She said he had departed from his work at the Texas School Book Depository and had been driven to the PAINE house by the young neighbor of the PAINE's who also worked at the Texas School Book Depository.
She further advised that she does not know of anything that OSWALD took with him from the PAINE house to work the next morning, November 22, 1963."
41. 2H 241 (Testimony of Buell Wesley Frazier). See also CE 1401 (page 272 of exhibit) at 22H 751 as detailed at footnote 40 above.
42. 2H 224 (Testimony of Buell Wesley Frazier).
43. The car arrowed in CE 447 (Photograph of west side of Randle home showing carport and location of Buell Wesley Frazier's car on the morning of November 22, 1963) has been identified as a 1961 Plymouth Belvedere. That, however, was not Frazier's car. Despite it never being positively identified (make, model, year) in the Warren Report or the 26 Volumes, I am satisfied that Frazier's car was a 1953 Chevrolet sedan. See the 1964 film *Four Days in November* in which Frazier re-enacts the journey to work on the day of the assassination. (I am obliged to US researchers Stephen Stocker and Steve Thomas and Australian James Richards for their assistance in this connection.).
In an FBI Memorandum from C. D. DeLoach to Mr. Mohr, dated 6th December 1963 (copy in author's possession), it is stated that Frazier "has a black

Chevrolet." This is the only time I have seen any colour attributed to that car.

44. 2H 226 (Testimony of Buell Wesley Frazier).

45. ibid.

46. 2H 227 (Testimony of Buell Wesley Frazier).

47. CE 361 (Diagram showing the Texas School Book Depository Building and the immediate area with relation to the parking lot used by employees).

48. 2H 227-228 (Testimony of Buell Wesley Frazier). I am grateful to researcher Joel Gruhn (Barrington, Rhode Island), the former owner of two 1953 Chevrolets, who explained to me that it was necessary to run the engine for a few minutes as the charging system used a generator rather than an alternator. The electrical system was 6 volts.

49. 2H 239 (Testimony of Buell Wesley Frazier).

50. 2H 240 (Testimony of Buell Wesley Frazier).

51. 2H 241 (Testimony of Buell Wesley Frazier).

52. CE 2003 (Dallas Police Department file on investigation of the assassination of the President), page 26 of exhibit (24H 209).

53. *The Trial of Lee Harvey Oswald*: Channel Four (London). Shown in the United States (Showtime Cable Television) on 21st/22nd November 1986, and in the UK the following evening. There have been several TV productions of Oswald trials. This is the one in which Vincent Bugliosi is the Prosecuting Attorney and Gerry Spence the Defense Attorney.

54. *The Men Who Killed Kennedy*: Thames Television (London). Shown in the UK on 20th/21st/22nd November 1991.

55. Physical measurements made by the author. See also my article "The Mannlicher-Carcano—a practical experiment in its reassembly", originally published in *The Fourth Decade*, Volume 2, No. 1, November 1994.

56. CE 1981 (Autopsy report dated November 24, 1963, at Dallas, Tex., on Lee Harvey Oswald). See opening page of exhibit (24H 7).

57. Don Roberdeau, a researcher from Dry Ridge, Kentucky, has produced computerized graphics illustrating many aspects of the Kennedy assassination. The graphic included here is developed from one which he prepared specifically for *The Dealey Plaza Echo*, vol. 6, no. 3 (November 2002). A former member of the U.S. Navy, Don Roberdeau served on the aircraft-carrier *USS John F. Kennedy*. See Photo Section Two.

58. 7H 531 (Testimony of Buell Wesley Frazier).

59. 2H 234 (Testimony of Buell Wesley Frazier).

60. As (47) above.

61. 6H 376 (Testimony of Jack Edwin Dougherty).

62. 6H 377 (Testimony of Jack Edwin Dougherty).

63. 6H 381 (Testimony of Jack Edwin Dougherty).

64. 6H 328 (Testimony of William Hoyt Shelley).

65. 2H 247-248 (Testimony of Mrs Linnie Mae Randle).

66. 2H 249-250 (Testimony of Mrs Linnie Mae Randle).

67. 3H 395 (Testimony of SA Robert A. Frazier, FBI Laboratory, Washington, D.C.).

68. Carried out using a 6.5mm Mannlicher-Carcano rifle (serial no. S 1003) identical to CE 139, and a large paper bag made as closely as possible to CE 142/626. Practical demonstrations given at the meeting of the national British research group Dealey Plaza UK at Sutton Coldfield, UK, on 11th February 1996 and several subsequent research meetings, seminars, etc.

69. FBI report from J. Edgar Hoover to DPD Chief Curry, dated 23rd November 1963, page 4. This document is reprinted on pages 90—94 of Jesse Curry's *JFK Assassination File*, published by American Poster and Printing Company, Dallas, Texas, 1969.

70. 4H 89 (Testimony of James C. Cadigan).

71. As footnote 69 above.

72. 4H 91 (Testimony of James C. Cadigan).

73. 4H 93 (Testimony of James C. Cadigan). See also CE 2009 (FBI report dated December 2, 1963, of interview of Buell Wesley Frazier at Irving, Tex.) page 3 of exhibit (24H 409).

74. 4H 97 (Testimony of James C. Cadigan).

75. As footnote 69 above.

76. CE 2974 (Letter dated August 20, 1964, from FBI to Commission, concerning certain information regarding assassination rifle).

77. 1H 14, also 1H 93-94 (Testimony of Mrs Marina Oswald).

78. 6H 362 (Testimony of Troy Eugene West).

79. 6H 361 (Testimony of Troy Eugene West).

80. *ibid.*

81. 6H 360 (Troy Eugene West).

82. 6H 357 (Troy Eugene West).

83. 10H 292-293 (Testimony of Mrs Arthur Carl (Gladys J.) Johnson).

84. 10H 297 (Testimony of Mrs. Arthur Carl (Gladys J.) Johnson).

85. 10H 302 (Testimony of Arthur Carl Johnson). See also Robert S, Groden: *The Search for Lee Harvey Oswald*, published by Penguin Studio Books, NY, USA, 1995; page 97, on which the photograph at top left shows the four adjacent windows from the outside.

86. *John R. Woods II: J.F.K. Assassination Photographs: A Comprehensive Listing*, self-published (limited edition of 50), 1993; page 109. See also Daniel photographs 1-34 and 1-36 which show Mrs Johnson making up the bed in Oswald's room and also show a major part of the wall in which the windows were located, and the curtains hung from what appears to be a single long curtain rod.

87. Howard Roffman: *Presumed Guilty*, published by A.S. Barnes and Co., Inc., Cranbury, NJ, USA, 1976; page 160.

88. Gene Daniel photographs as footnote 86 above.
89. Woods (footnote 86 above), page 10.
90. Information from The Collector's Archive, Beaconsfield, Quebec, Canada.
91. See footnote 37 above.
92. Johnson (Gladys J.) Exhibit A (Copy of a roominghouse register, dated October 14, 1963, through November 25, 1963, bearing the signature O.H. Lee).

Written 1995.
First published July and November 1996 in *The Dealey Plaza Echo, vol. 1, nos. 1 , 2.*
Later published March/April 1997 on internet website *Fair Play*, no. 15.
Presented as a research paper at the *Fourth Decade Conference*, Fredonia, New York, July 1996.
Appears in the Articles Section of the Dealey Plaza UK website

The Author accompanied by a DPD Public Relations official and two Vice Squad detectives on the exact spot where the Oswald line-ups were held. Can you guess who is playing the part of Oswald? (Photograph by Mark Rowe)

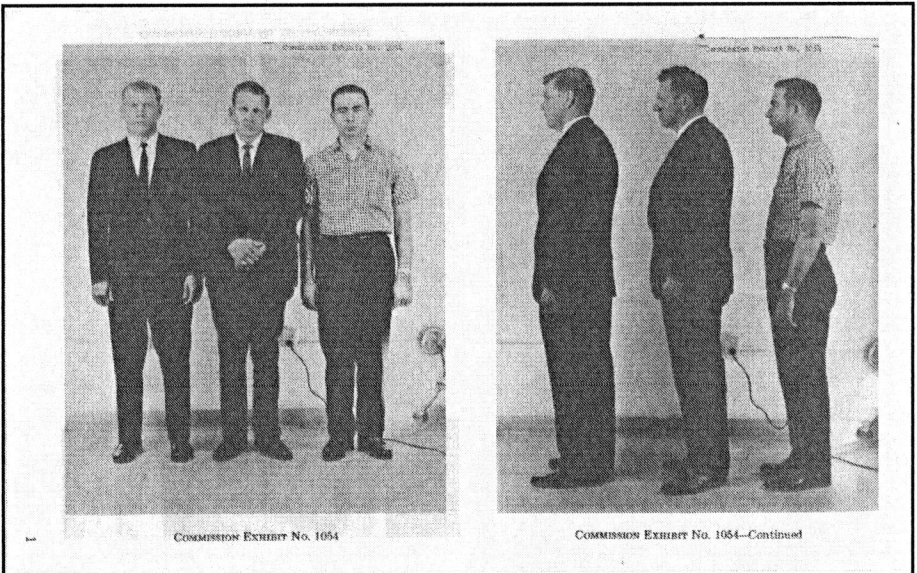

Left to right: Detective William Perry, Detective Richard Clark, and Jail Clerk Don Ables.

SHOWUPS ON OSWALD

#1.

11-22-63, 4:35 pm

To: Helen Markham, positive identification.

Officers with Oswald: R. M. Sims, M. G. Hall, E. L. Boyd

Officers with witness: L. G. Graves, J. R. Leavelle, Chief Curry, C. W. Brown
                       Captain Fritz.

In the showup: #1, Bill Perry, #2 Lee Harvey Oswald, #3 R. L. Clark #4 Dan Ables
#2.
11-22-63, 6:30 pm

To: Cecil J. McWatters, positive identification
    Sam Guinyard, positive identification
    Ted Calloway, positive identification

ifficers with Oswald: R. M. Sims, E. L. Boyd, M. G. Hall

ifficers with witnesses: J. R. Leavelle, C. . Brown, C. N. Dhority
i Showup: #1Billy Perry, #2 Lee Harvey Oswald, #3 R. L. Calrk, #4 Dan Ables

3.

1-22-63, 7:55 pm

o: Barbara Jeanette Davis, positive identification
   Virginia Davis, positive identification

ifficers with Oswald: M. G. Hall, R. M. Sims, E. L. Boyd, H. M. Moore

ifficers with witnesses: C. W. Brown, C. N. Dhority
i showup: Richard Walter Borchardt, #2 Lee Harvey Oswald, #3 Ellis Carl
          Braswell, #4 Dan Ables

lovember 23, 1963, 2.15 pm

o: W. W. Scoggins, positive identification
   William Wayne Whaley, positive identification

ifficers with Oswald: B. L. Senkel, W. E. Potts, M. G. Hall, C. W. Brown

ifficers with witnesses: J. R. Leavelle

i showup:#1 John Thurman Horn, #2 David Knapp, #3 Lee Oswald, #4 David Lujan

Commission Exhibit No. 2003, page 293 of exhibit, at 24H 347
Exact and complete copy of the original, including spelling and other errors.

#1 120

11-22-63 4:35 PM
To: Helen Markham – Positive Ident.
with Oswald: Sims, Hall, (———) Boyd
with witness: Graves, Leavelle, Fritz, Curry,
Brown
In Show up: #1 Bell, Perry #2 Lee Harvey
Oswald. #3 R.L. Clark,
#4 Don Ables

#2
11-22-63 6:35 PM.
TO: Cecil J McWatters Positive "
Sam Guinyard "
Ted Callaway "
Officers with Oswald: Sims Boyd Hall
" witnesses J R Leavelle, C W Brown
C N Dhority
In Show up: #1 Billy Bury #2 J.H. Banks
#3 R L Clark #4 Don Ables

#3 1-22-63 7:55 PM
TO: Barbara Jeanette Davis Police
Virginia Davis Positive
Officers with Oswald Hall Sim Boyd, Moore.
" witnesses Brown Dhority
L Show up. #1 Richard Walter Borchgardt
#2. L Lee Harvey Oswald
#3 Ellis Carl Braswell
#4 Don Ables

Original handwritten notes (author unknown) with full details of the line-ups. (City of Dalla Municipal Archives, John F. Kennedy Collection, box 7, file 7, item 17)

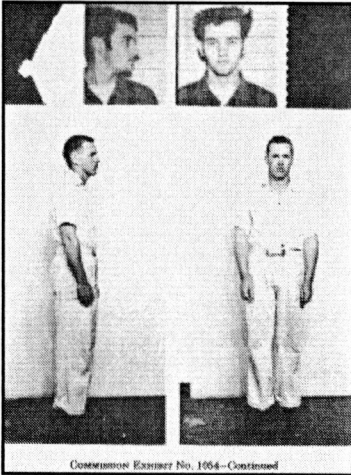

Commission Exhibit No. 1054—Continued

Two unidentified remand prisoners who lined up with Oswald. The lower pictures may be Richard Borchgardt.

Dallas cab driver William Whaley. "But you could have picked him out without identifying him by just listening to him..." (John R. Woods, II collection)

NAME	AGE	HEIGHT	WEIGHT (LBS)	HAIR	EYES	COMPLEXION	LINE-UPS ATTENDED		AND POSITION IN THE LINE
Lee Harvey Oswald (Suspect)	24	5'9"	131	Brown	Grey	Medium	2	2	2	3
William E. Perry (A/Det, Vice Squad, DPD)	Late 20's	5'11"	150	Brown	Blue	Medium Fair	1	1		
Richard L. Clark (Det, Vice Squad, DPD)	Late 20's	5'11"	177	Blond	Blue	Fair	3	3		
Don R. Ables (Jail Clerk, DPD)	Mid 20's	5'9"	165	Dark	Brown	Ruddy	4	4	4	
Richard W. Borchgardt (Remand Prisoner)	23	5'9"	161	Brown	Blue	Fair			1	
Ellis C. Brazel (Remand Prisoner)	21	5'10"	169	Blond	Green	Ruddy			3	
John T. Horne (Remand Prisoner)	18	n/k	n/k	n/k	n/k	n/k				1
David E. Knapp (Remand Prisoner)	18	n/k	n/k	n/k	n/k	n/k				2
Daniel G. Lujan (Remand Prisoner)	26	5'8"	170	Brown	Brown	Olive				4

Comparison chart demonstrating any similarities in age and appearance Oswald and his line-up companions. (Graphic by Steve Griggs)

Left: *The Hotel Torni today.*
Right: *The Hotel Torni on its 1930 postcard.*

I believe this is the total extent of the CIA's investigation into Oswald's sojourn in Helsinki. At least I visited the city and hotels.

CENTRAL INTELLIGENCE AGENCY
WASHINGTON, D.C. 20505

MEMORANDUM FOR: Mr. J. Lee Rankin
General Counsel
President's Commission on the
Assassination of President Kennedy

SUBJECT: Lee Harvey OSWALD

In response to your request, I forward information regarding Lee Harvey OSWALD's stay in Helsinki.

According to a reliable source, OSWALD stayed at the Torni Hotel in Helsinki from 10 to 11 October 1959 and then moved to the Klaus Kurki Hotel where he stayed until 15 October, apparently waiting for a visa to be issued him by the Soviet Consulate in Helsinki. He traveled to the USSR by train, crossing at Vainikkala on 15 October.

Richard Helms
Deputy Director for Plans

COMMISSION EXHIBIT No. 2676

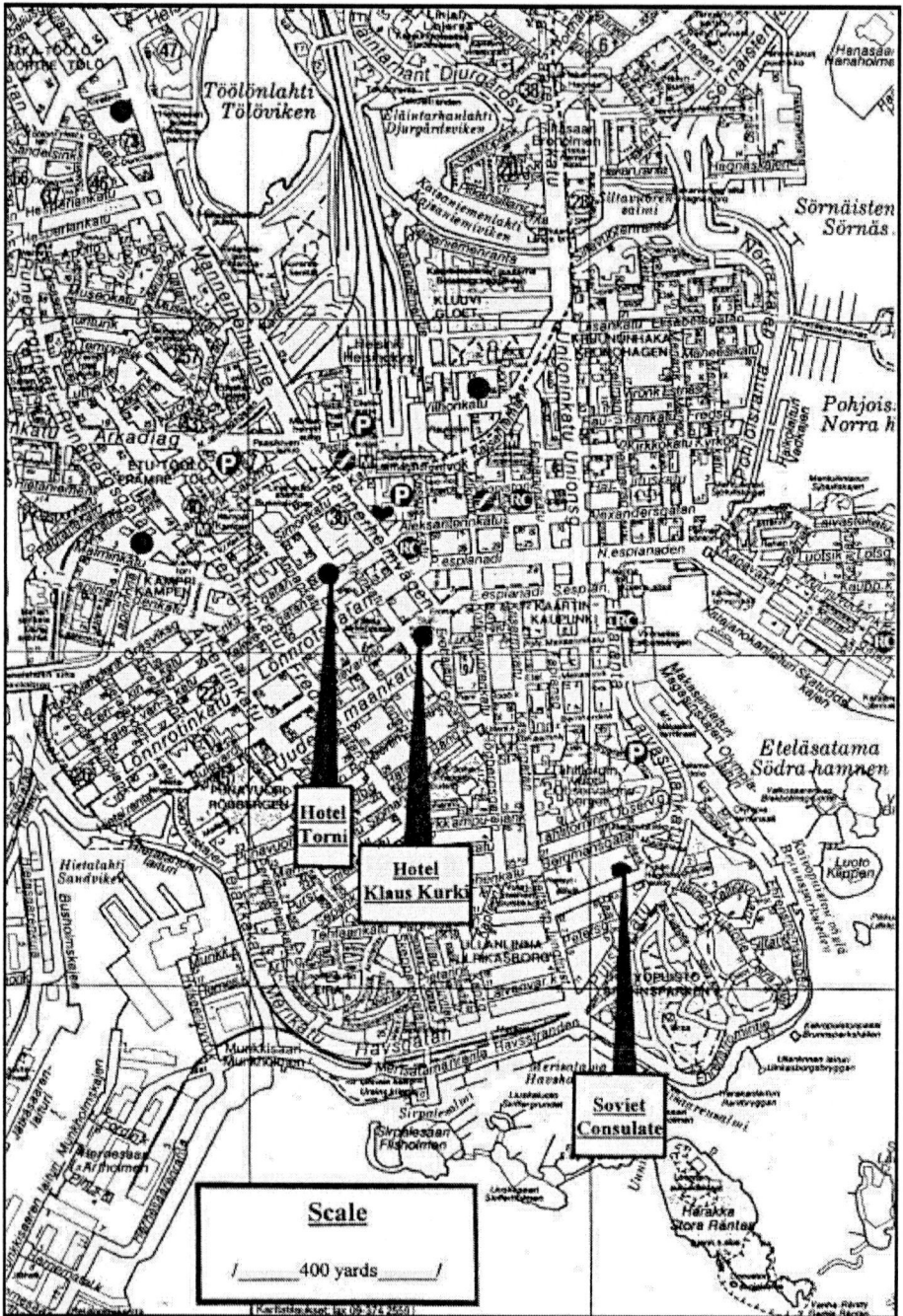

Helsinki street map identifying locations of the Hotel Torni, the Hotel
Klaus Kurki and the Soviet Consulate.

Oswald's Jacket

Approximately 15 minutes before the shooting of Tippit, Oswald was seen leaving his roominghouse.[595] He was wearing a zipper jacket which he had not been wearing moments before when he had arrived home.[596] When Oswald was arrested, he did not have a jacket.[597] Shortly after Tippit was slain, policemen found a light-colored zipper jacket along the route taken by the killer as he attempted to escape.[598] (See Commission Exhibit No. 1968, p. 164.)

At 1:22 p.m. the Dallas police radio described the man wanted for the murder of Tippit as "a white male about thirty, five foot eight inches, black hair, slender, wearing a white jacket, white shirt and dark slacks." [599] According to Patrolman Poe this description came from Mrs. Markham and Mrs. Barbara Jeanette Davis.[600] Mrs. Markham told Poe that the man was a "white male, about 25, about five feet eight, brown hair, medium," and wearing a "white jacket." Mrs. Davis gave Poe the same general description: a "white male in his early twenties, around five foot seven inches or eight inches, about 145 pounds," and wearing a white jacket.

As has been discussed previously, two witnesses, Warren Reynolds and B. M. Patterson, saw the gunman run toward the rear of a gasoline service station on Jefferson Boulevard. Mrs. Mary Brock, the wife of a mechanic who worked at the station, was there at the time and she saw a white male, "5 feet, 10 inches * * * wearing light clothing * * * a light-colored jacket" walk past her at a fast pace with his hands in his pocket. She last saw him in the parking lot directly behind the service station. When interviewed by FBI agents on January 21, 1964, she identified a picture of Oswald as being the same person she saw on November 22. She confirmed this interview by a sworn affidavit.[601]

At 1:24 p.m., the police radio reported, "The suspect last seen running west on Jefferson from 400 East Jefferson." [602] Police Capt. W. R. Westbrook and several other officers concentrated their search along Jefferson Boulevard.[603] Westbrook walked through the parking lot behind the service station [604] and found a light-colored jacket lying under the rear of one of the cars.[605] Westbrook identified Commission Exhibit No. 162 as the light-colored jacket which he discovered underneath the automobile.[606]

This jacket belonged to Lee Harvey Oswald. Marina Oswald stated that her husband owned only two jackets, one blue and the other gray.[607] The blue jacket was found in the Texas School Book Depository [608] and was identified by Marina Oswald as her husband's.[609] Marina Oswald also identified Commission Exhibit No. 162, the jacket found by Captain Westbrook, as her husband's second jacket.[610]

The eyewitnesses vary in their identification of the jacket. Mrs. Earlene Roberts, the housekeeper at Oswald's roominghouse and the last person known to have seen him before he reached 10th Street and Patton Avenue, said that she may have seen the gray zipper jacket but

175

Warren Commission Report page 175 contains the only mention of Captain Westbrook. In his testimony, Westbrook denied being the one responsible for finding the jacket.

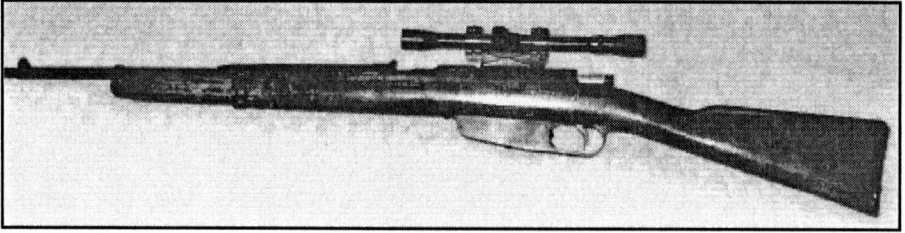

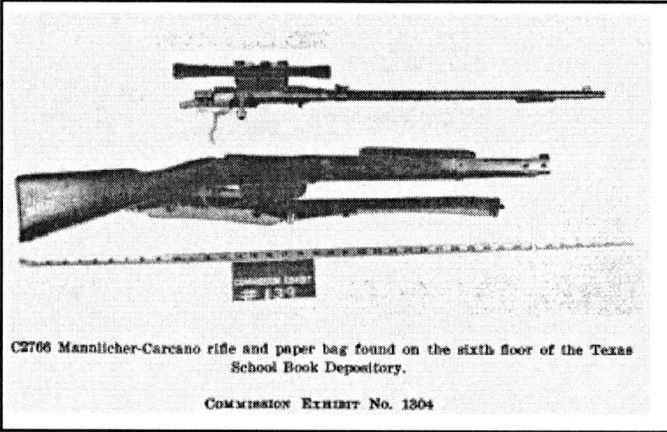

C2766 Mannlicher-Carcano rifle and paper bag found on the sixth floor of the Texas School Book Depository.

COMMISSION EXHIBIT No. 1304

Top: The author's Mannlicher-Carcano—identical to the alleged assassination weapon.

Center: A totally misleading official photograph of the Oswald rifle deliberately attempting to show how simple it was to disassemble.

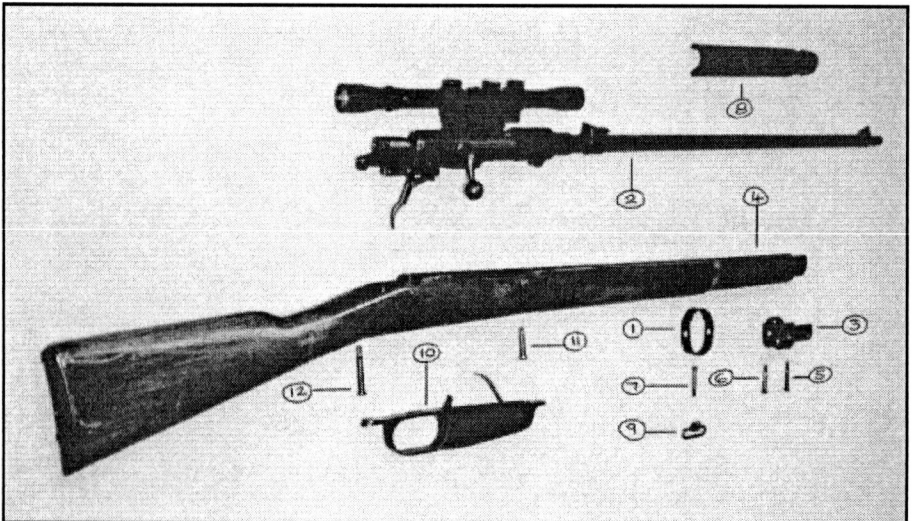

The author's MC showing the 12 components and the order in which they have to be reassembled.

COMMISSION EXHIBIT 729

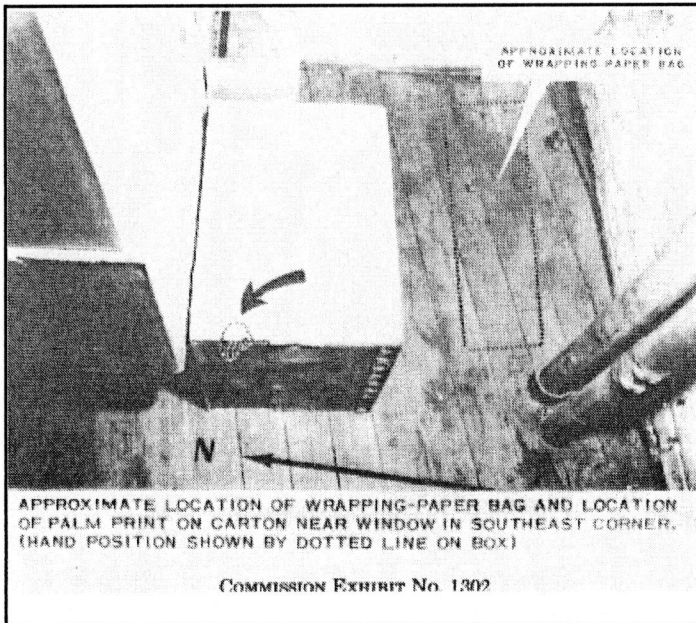

APPROXIMATE LOCATION OF WRAPPING-PAPER BAG AND LOCATION
OF PALM PRINT ON CARTON NEAR WINDOW IN SOUTHEAST CORNER.
(HAND POSITION SHOWN BY DOTTED LINE ON BOX)

COMMISSION EXHIBIT No. 1302

Top: Where is the paper bag?
Bottom: CE729 purports to show location of CE 142 (the paper bag) when discovered.

Dallas Detective L. D. Montgomery holds a paper bag (balanced in an upright position) outside the Texas School Book Depository. See pp 182/183 for comments. (Photograph from the "Fort Worth Star-Telegram", NARA, John Hunt collection)

The FBI Crime Lab technicians do not appear to have exercised much care in preventing cross-contamination between the blanket and the bag. Here, the bag appears to have been placed directly on top of the blanket. (Photograph from NARA, John Hunt collection)

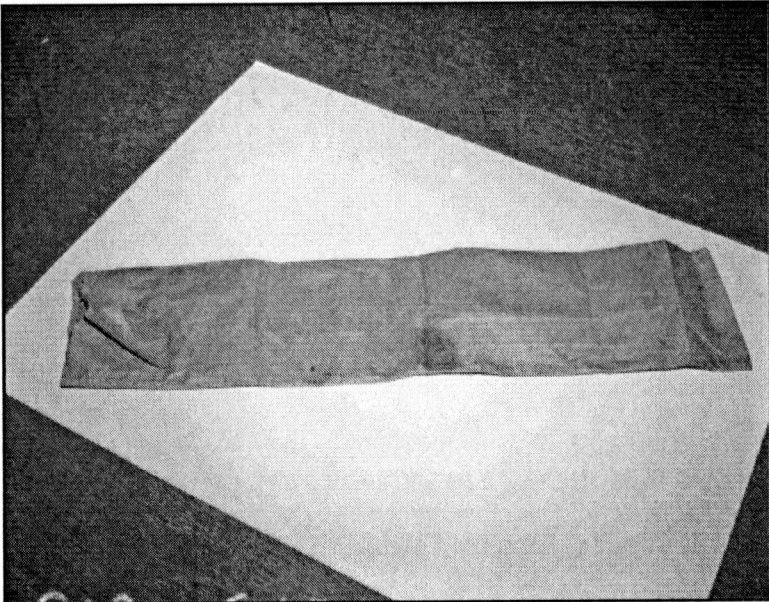

Here, the bag has been isolated - but has the damage already been done? (Photograph from NARA, John Hunt collection)

The paper bag currently held at the National Archives clearly shows how it was discoloured and contaminated by silver nitrate when being examined for latent fingerprints at the FBI Laboratory. The original colour of the bag can be seen at the right end. A two-feet rule has been placed in front of the bag to indicate its scale. Are we seriously expected to believe this is the bag about which Buell Wesley Frazier said, at 2H 226:

"... was a package just roughly about two feet long." (it took up) "I would say roughly around 2 feet of the seat." "... that would be around two feet, give and take a few inches." "... around 5 inches (wide), something like that. 5, 6 inches or there."

When shown CE 364 (a bag manufactured by the FBI and allegedly identical to CE 142 shown above) by Mr. Ball and asked "Does it appear to be about the same length?" he replied "No, sir." (2H 239)

"I told them that as far as the length there, I told them that was entirely too long." (2H 240)

"It must have been about 2' long" (affidavit 22nd Nov. '63)

He also described in detail that Oswald carried it with one end in his right armpit and the other cupped in his right hand (2H 239). At one point, Mr. Ball even had Frazier try to physiclly re-enact how Oswald had held the bag in that fashion. This developed into an embarrassing scene almost as laughable as that of O.J. Simpson and the infamous black glove.

Rather than present the means by which Oswald conveyed his rifle into work that morning, this National Archives exhibit serves to prove that he did no such thing and the paper bag story is just that—a story!"

Above: Buell Wesley Frazier (John R. Woods, II collection)

Next Page: Oswald scaled to the rifle and paperbag in evidence, and a theorized disassembled rifle. (Chart by Don Roberdeau)

Notes for Chart: Cadigan testified that the bag in evidence showed no marks, holes, oil, impressions, nor scatches that matched the "Oswald" rifle. He also said the bag never contained any rifle.

The FBI analyzed the paper from the bag, supposedly found on the 6th Floor, CE142, with a sample that Lt. Day got from the TSBD (CE677), and found they had the same composition. A sample the FBI got from the TSBD (CE364) did not match either CE142 or CE677.

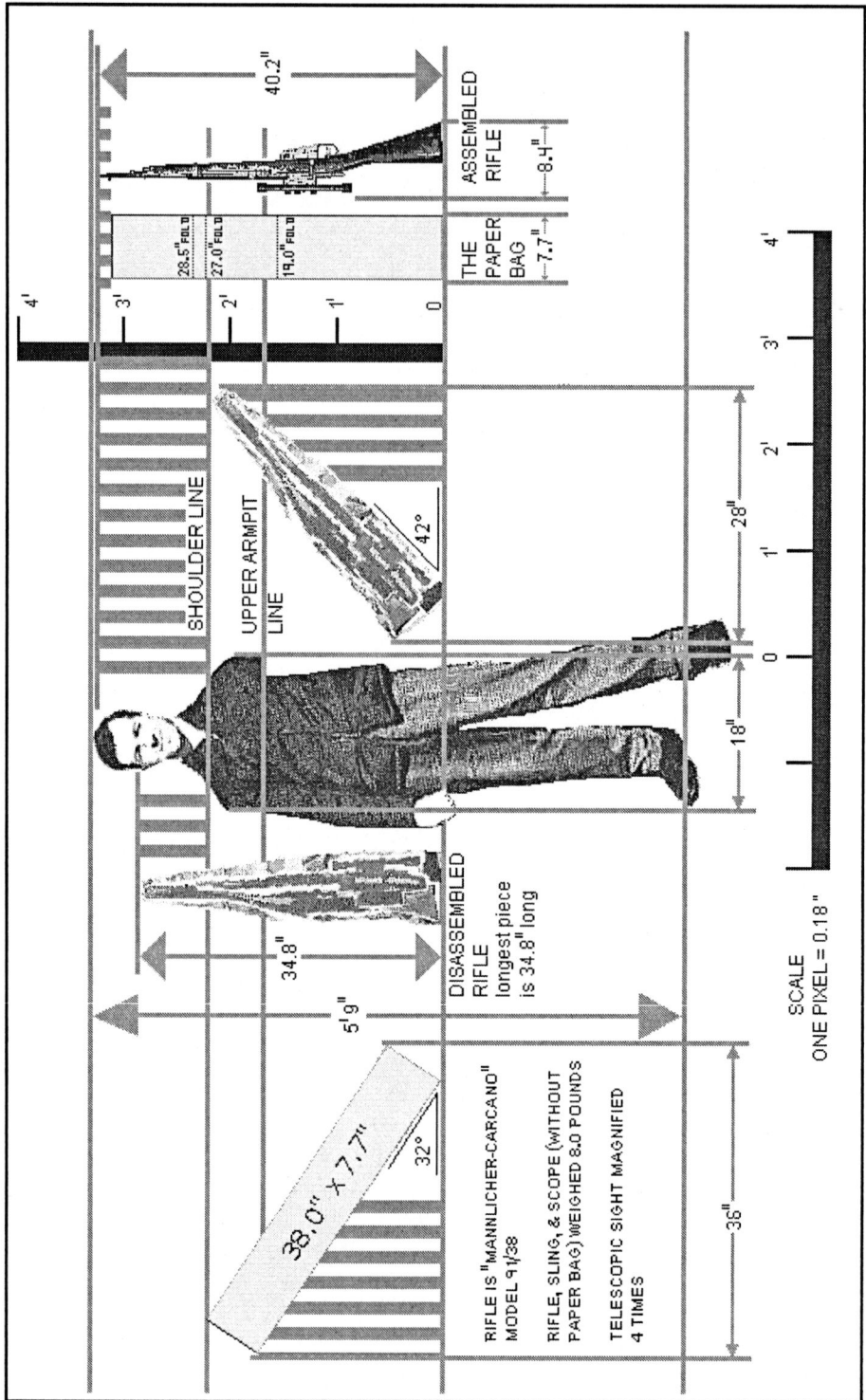

ASSEMBLED RIFLE

40.2"

8.4"

THE PAPER BAG

7.7"

28.5" FOLD

27.0" FOLD

19.0" FOLD

4'

3'

2'

1'

0

SHOULDER LINE

UPPER ARMPIT LINE

42°

28"

18"

4'

3'

2'

1'

0

DISASSEMBLED RIFLE
longest piece is 34.8" long

34.8"

5'9"

38.0" X 7.7"

32°

36"

RIFLE IS "MANNLICHER-CARCANO" MODEL 91/38

RIFLE, SLING, & SCOPE (WITHOUT PAPER BAG) WEIGHED 8.0 POUNDS

TELESCOPIC SIGHT MAGNIFIED 4 TIMES

SCALE
ONE PIXEL = 0.18"

Part V: Jack Ruby, his club and his girls

19. Jack Ruby's Carousel Club

In 1999, after successfully identifying several of Jack Ruby's strippers on an internet website, I gained the title "the world's top expert on 60s era Dallas booby bouncers." [1] Whether that honour is something of which I should be proud or ashamed remains to be seen.

Introduction

Back in June 1995, in volume 1, number 2 of *The Assassination Chronicles*, I published a full-page listing of 58 of Jack Ruby's Carousel Club dancers. With the majority of them, I had succeeded in matching up stage names to real names. I am sure that many of the stage names are familiar to researchers. Several, such as Kathy Kay, Little Lynn and Rose Cheramie, featured in the Kennedy assassination investigation, whilst Shari Angel is well known to those people who have attended the annual *November in Dallas* conferences in recent years. Others, of course are less well known, despite having remarkable stage names like Robin S. Hood, Alice from Dallas and Diana the Huntress. One of my favourite names is Friday Knight ("Everyone loves Friday night!").

The main part of this paper will take the form of "Frequently Asked Questions" about the Carousel Club which I will endeavour to answer. I will conclude with an updated list of some of the strippers who worked there.

"Where was it?"

This is a question which continues to be raised with some regularity.

Unfortunately, neither the Carousel Club nor the building which housed it is still in existence. It was located at 1312¹/2 Commerce Street and in the words of Jack Ruby's newspaper advertisements it was at the "Corner of Field and Commerce" and "Across from the Adolphus Hotel."

The ^{1}/2 suffix to the street number indicates that the club was located on the second floor (in the UK, that would be called the first floor). The entrance to the club was up a narrow, single-flight stairway from street level.

One of the club's rival establishments, the Colony Club, was located next door. This was owned and operated by Ruby's bitter competitors, the Weinstein brothers, Abe and Barney.

Today's visitors to Dallas will search in vain for Jack Ruby's Carousel Club or the Weinstein brothers' Colony Club. They will doubtless be disappointed to learn that they were originally somewhere on the site now occupied by a bus stop and a huge slab of featureless concrete known as the Southwestern Bell building.

WHEN DID IT CLOSE?

The Carousel Club functioned for the last time under Jack Ruby's control on the evening of Thursday 21st November 1963. The following evening, out of respect for the slain President, Ruby did not open the club. It remained closed again on the Saturday evening and on Sunday morning, Ruby shot and killed Lee Harvey Oswald. He had lived his last day as a free man and would never set foot in the place again.

There was a half-hearted attempt by a few of the employees including Andy Armstrong, Diana Hunter and Alice Anderson to keep the Carousel Cub going [2] but it never attracted any of its previous talent and after a few days, it folded for good.

WHAT BECAME OF IT THEN?

Ironically the building was converted into a police gymnasium, a function it maintained for several years, before its eventual demolition.

HOW DID RUBY RUN IT?

Surprisingly, it seems that Jack Ruby ran the Carousel Club in a reasonably legal and proper manner. Despite his constant mood swings and alleged short temper, he treated his employees well and very few of them ever had any complaints about him. He operated the club strictly within union rules and his employees were all required to be members of the American Guild of Variety Artists (AGVA), otherwise known as 'the strippers' union'. All club acts, whether strippers, musicians or comedians, were booked within the provisions of AGVA rules and were paid above the normal union rate. There was little doubt that AGVA was Mob-connected, almost certainly having links with the notorious Teamsters Union. Perhaps that was a factor to be considered here. [3]

Possibly stemming from his lowly beginnings on the streets of his native Chicago, Jack Ruby strove continuously for "class". On 28th October 1963, when the notorious stripper Jada went beyond what Jack considered were the normal bounds of decency ('popping her G-string'), he turned the lights off on her. He would not allow his comedians to tell Jewish or racist jokes. He did not employ burly bouncers. If a customer was out of line, Jack dealt with the situation personally—even if it meant throwing the troublemaker out *via* the stairs. This was by no means a rare occurrence [4] but Jack was determined to run a decent place and unruly customers were not welcome.

Jack Ruby was present whenever the club was open in the evenings. He acted as the principal Master of Ceremonies and would mingle with the customers. He was also present to deal with any problems—and to provide personal attention to any special guests or visitors such as Mob associates or members of the Dallas Police Department or other law enforcement agencies who might drop in for any one of a variety of reasons. He was always neatly dressed, liked to be recognized as the proprietor of the club and had the habit of introducing himself as "Your host, Jack Ruby."

WAS THE CAROUSEL CLUB A SLEAZY CLIP JOINT OR A SOPHISTICATED NIGHTCLUB?

You could probably place the Carousel Club midway between those two extremes. In the sense that customers were charged exorbitant prices for drinks, it qualified as a clip joint. It appears, however, that many of the patrons were aware of this and did not seem to complain.

As former Carousel Club feature stripper Shari Angel told me: "Back in 1962, you could sell a bottle (of champagne) for 25 dollars. Cheap bottles that you could buy for 5-99. But then guys was so—back then there wasn't all this TV, movies, all this stuff. All they wanted to come and see was this downtown live ... and they knew they was being suckered in." [5]

Against that, of course, was Jack Ruby's unrelenting search for "class". The performers at the club, be they strippers, musicians or variety acts, were always top professionals being paid top money. The club was situated on a major street opposite the prestigious Adolphus Hotel in the heart of the thriving city of Dallas—it was not a back street dive. A check of its members' list is very revealing and includes several city officials. That is dealt with later.

The club's normal evening opening hours were from 8.00pm to 1.00am (2.00am on Saturday night) but it must not be overlooked that it also opened its doors in the afternoon. This is when it took on a Jekyll and Hyde character and the *clientele* was very different. In a conversation in 1994, Madeleine Duncan Brown told me that she was a regular at some of the afternoon cards and dominoes sessions. [6] There was no social stigma in being known as a Carousel Club regular.

The *decor* inside the club was tasteful, but in a tacky sort of way. The main stage had three runways extending out into the audience, the latter feature being very unusual and one which Ruby stressed in his press advertisements. Customers would be seated at well-spaced tables and served by waitresses. These 'waitresses' were mainly champagne girls whose job was to ensure that the patrons spent as much as possible on drinks. Maybe this was the part of the operation which resembled a clip joint.

WHAT WAS JACK RUBY'S BACKGROUND AND HISTORY IN CLUB MANAGEMENT?

Jacob Leon Rubenstein was born in Chicago on 25th March 1911. He spent much of his youth in that city mixing with the gangs and allegedly running numbers for Al Capone. He served in the US Army Air Force from May 1943 to February 1946 and moved to Dallas in 1947. On 3rd November 1955, he changed his name to Jack Ruby. [7]

Together with a partner, Joe Slatin, (some sources call him Slayton), Ruby established the Sovereign Club in late 1959. He had previously owned or been connected with several other Dallas clubs, notably the Singapore Supper Club (which became the far better known Silver Spur), Bob Wills' Ranch House, the Vegas Club and Hernando's Hideaway. The Sovereign was a private club which held a permit to serve mixed drinks at the tables. [8] An ex-waiter who had worked there, however, claimed that this concession, which was unique in Dallas, existed only because the District Attorney and other city officials were regular visitors. [9]

Following a succession of financial and personal problems, Slatin withdrew in early 1960 and Ralph Paul took over as Ruby's business partner. The Sovereign then became the Carousel Club, changing not only its name but also its image.

The Carousel Club now became one of the three downtown burlesque clubs, the others being the Theatre Lounge and the Colony Club. Although Ralph Paul had a considerable financial interest in the Carousel, Ruby was the front man, the organizer and the man who liked to be known as the proprietor.

WHAT SORT OF ACTS PLAYED THE CAROUSEL CLUB?

Following Oswald's murder, the press and general media described his killer in such terms as "the owner of a sleazy night club" and "a strip club owner." There was far more to the place than that, however. The club had a full-time band which included a trumpeter, Johnny Anderson, who had previously played in the Stan Kenton Orchestra. The drummer, Bill Willis, was a former successful wrestler from the 50s ('Mr. Texas'). [10] Willis and William Simmons (pianist) lived at 2530 West Fifth Street, Irving, just across the street from the Paine house. [11] As well as strippers, the club's customers could also enjoy stand up comedians, ventriloquists, vocalists and other general variety acts

Bill DeMar was a regular attraction. He was billed as a 'versatile ventriloquist and comic—master in the art of extra-sensory perception.' DeMar (real name William D. Crowe, Jr.) claimed that Lee Harvey Oswald may have been a member of the Carousel Club audience he had used to assist in his 'memory act' one evening in the week before the assassination. [12] It is understood that Bill DeMar is still active on the entertainment circuit (2001).

Harry Blackstone, Jr. seemed to perform just the odd casual date at the Carousel rather than week or two week bookings. He performed a magic act, and like his father before him, went on to become one of the leading stage illusionists in the country. He was best-known for an illusion called 'the floating lightbulb' but it is doubtful that he ever performed anything as sophisticated as that at the Carousel. He died in 1997, aged 62.

I understand (from her own website and other sources)—but never had confirmed for certain—that the exotic half-Cherokee, half-Japanese film actress Tura Satana had a brief spell as a Carousel Club dancer in her early days. Her original name had been Tura Luna Pascual Yamaguchi but she used her married name Satana for the stage. Whether she used that name or something different at the Carousel Club I have been unable to ascertain. She later went on to star in Russ Meyer's 1965 film *Faster Pussycat! Kill! Kill!*

It was normal for four (sometimes five) strippers to perform each night. During November 1963, Kathy Kay, Little Lynn, Joy Dale and Tammi True were regulars.

WERE THERE ANY OTHER EMPLOYEES?

Other regular employees included waitresses, a porter and an emcee (MC/ Master of Ceremonies). There was also the versatile Andrew Armstrong. Andy seemed to be just about everything from odd-job-man and part-time barman to assistant cashier. Although I doubt that Jack Ruby completely trusted anyone, he certainly seemed to put his trust in Andy more than in any other employee.

DID BEVERLY OLIVER EVER APPEAR AT THE CAROUSEL CLUB?

No, she did not. Beverly Oliver was a top-class vocalist who performed next door at the Colony Club. She did, however, visit the Carousel Club regularly as she was friends with Jack Ruby and with several of his performers, including Shari Angel and Kathy Kay.

Another famous name who *never* worked for Jack Ruby was the notorious Candy Barr. Candy (real name Juanita Slusher Dale Phillips Sahakian) was sentenced to 15 years imprisonment for possession of less than half an ounce of marijuana in 1958. She was released on parole after serving less than three years. One of the conditions of her parole was that she was not allowed to continue her normal profession as a stripper. Jack Ruby tried repeatedly to persuade her to work for him at the Carousel Club but she could not afford to violate her parole conditions as that would have taken her straight back to jail.

Another big star who was never employed at the Carousel Club was Chris Colt ("and her 45s"). She was starring at the Colony Club at the time of the assassination. Precious Diamond, (real name Helen Vines), had worked briefly for Ruby as a waitress at the Silver Spur but although she then became a stripper, she never worked at the Carousel Club. [13]

WHAT SORT OF ACTS DID THE STRIPPERS PERFORM?

It seems that each stripper had her own gimmick. This could involve balloons, a snake ("Toni Turner"), playing the part of a Roman goddess, ("Diana the Huntress"), or talking to the audience during her act, (the London-born "Kathy Kay"). Tura Satana was a celebrated tassel spinner.

Shari Angel performed what she called a Gypsy Rose Lee act. In the Carousel Club newspaper advertisements, she was described as "Dallas' Own Gypsy". She was married to the Carousel Club's principal comedian Wally Weston, a man who had won many local awards for his act. He also brought massive free publicity to the club when he completed the local JFK 50-mile hike for charity. [14]

Ruby was adamant that his girls would perform on stage in a "decent" manner. He never had two strippers on stage together and he was always ready to step in and put the lights down if, in his opinion, a girl took her act to extremes (like Jada). Like the other Dallas clubs, he held an amateur night on which non-professional strippers would perform, until this practice was banned in early-1963. I believe that the only full-time stripper to be produced by this method was 'Jeanine' (Martha Churchman).

WHAT WAS JACK RUBY LIKE AS A PERSON?

Although she worked for Ruby for only three years, feature stripper Shari Angel had known him since she was in her mid-teens. In an interview with the author in Dallas in November 1994 she spoke about Ruby at some length. She said: "He was a very kind, sweet person. Treated people. Went out to the Veterans' Hospital. Took care of them when nobody cared about them. I mean this is stuff that nobody ever gives Jack credit for." She also mentioned some of the not-so-good times: "I seen the Mafia in there so often—maybe once a month—so-and-so he knew from Chicago ..."

On Ruby's private life she said: "He had a girlfriend he'd had for years but he never brought her around any of us. She was an older woman. I can't think of her name. He had her for years and years" (This is probably a lady called Alice Reaves Nicholls, a secretary at a local insurance company—ILG.) and "Jack did not drink liquor, he did not smoke, he did not take dope." Shari also stressed that Jack Ruby was not homosexual. She said: "He wasn't no molester, he wasn't no queer. Excuse me but that's what they tried to say." [15]

WAS THERE EVER ANY TROUBLE IN THE CAROUSEL CLUB?

In an establishment of this type, it was inevitable that there would be the occasional unruly customer or drunk. Such people were normally dealt with swiftly and effectively by Ruby himself—sometimes by the simple method of literally throwing them out *via* the stairs. This violent side to Ruby's nature came about through his short temper and his old Chicago upbringing which had taught him always to be first to the punch. It was not unknown for Ruby to offer a warm welcome to a customer whom he had ejected violently 24 hours earlier

Two *Dallas Morning News* employees, Robert Landers and Charles Miller, reported that they were in the Carousel Club on the night of Thursday 21st November 1963 and Ruby ejected a customer who was drunk and unruly. On this occasion, Ruby "did not have to use any force to get the man to leave." [16] That date, of course, was the last on which Ruby was present when the club was open.

Were members of the Dallas Police Department regular patrons of the Carousel Club?

The easy answer to this one is yes—and in far greater numbers than the Warren Commission ever disclosed.

Certain Dallas police officers such as the Vice Squad had occasion to visit the club on official business (licensing, etc.) at regular intervals. They were always looked after well by Ruby, and if they returned in their off duty time, they were again treated favourably.

Nancy Perrin Rich, who worked as a bartender at the Carousel Club, stated in her Warren Commission testimony that Ruby ordered her to serve hard liquor to "special customers." When asked what this particular group was, she replied simply: "The police department." She was then asked whether they paid and she replied: "Oh no; of course not" almost as if the answer was so obvious that the question was unnecessary. [17]

There have been various estimates of the number of Dallas policemen who were familiar with Jack Ruby. I would guess it was somewhere between 200 and 400 out of the total strength of just over a thousand sworn officers.

One of the best-known Dallas police officers to frequent the Carousel Club was Patrolman Harry Neal Olsen. He met, dated and later married stripper Kathy Kay. He socialized with Jack Ruby and some of his strippers and sustained a serious knee injury when Ruby ran over his leg during an ice skating session at Fair Park. [18] This injury caused Olsen to be off duty on the day of the President's assassination.

Ironically, the estranged husband of one of Ruby's strippers, Toni Turner, was the nephew of Dallas Police Homicide Detective Jim Leavelle. [19]

When I asked Shari Angel about the presence of DPD officers in the club she told me that they also visited the other clubs and that they "all got payola ... to look over—a lot of stuff. ... You could see 'em right up to the office getting their little pay." She added: "Patrolmen didn't usually do it. It was detectives, vice squad and all that." [20]

Ruby cultivated not only police officers but other citizens he thought could possibly assist him in one way or the other. Amongst items found in Ruby's possession when he was arrested were Carousel Club permanent passes prepared in the names of Andy Anderson (the Manager of the Adolphus Hotel), Dallas District Attorney Bill Alexander and numerous local media people and businessmen. [21]

Did Lee Harvey Oswald ever visit the Carousel Club?

This is one of the most frequently asked questions about both Oswald and the club. There have been claims and counter-claims for many years. For example, in two FBI interviews in 1976 the former Kathy Kay initially stated that she had "danced with the man who shot President Kennedy" but later she testified that she had *not* done so and had never seen him in the club.

Shari Angel confirmed that her husband, comedian Wally Weston, had hit Oswald in the Carousel Club after he had called Weston a communist. Colony Club *chanteuse* Beverly Oliver claimed that Ruby had introduced Oswald to her (as a CIA man) in the Carousel Club. Others, however have denied that he ever set foot in the place. My opinion? I simply don't know.

CONCLUSION

There are as many unanswered questions about Jack Ruby and the Carousel Club as any other aspect of the case. I have tried to address the most frequently asked but I know that there will always be more.

NOTES

1. Post from researcher Mike Sheppard on Rich DellaRosa's *jfkforum* website, 28th September 1999.
2. Author's interview with Shari Angel, Adolphus Hotel, Dallas, 19th November 1994.
3. Peter Dale Scott: *Deep Politics and the Death of JFK*, University of California Press, Berkeley and Los Angeles, 1993, pp.232-233.
4. ibid.
5. ibid.
6. Meeting at the Top o'the Cliff Club, Oak Cliff, 21st June 1995.
7. CE 1318 (Extract of information in the Social Security Administration files concerning Jack Ruby reported January 24, 1964), first page of exhibit (22H 193).
8. CE 1675 (FBI report dated January 14, 1964, of interview of Robert Daigneault at Farmers Branch, Tex.)
9. CE 1656 (FBI report dated January 2, 1964, of interview of Bill Gus Komodore at New York City, N.Y.), page numbered 178 (23H 128).
10. Garry Wills and Ovid Demaris: *Jack Ruby*, Da Capo Press, New York, 1994, page 10
11. Whether or not they were acquainted with Ruth Paine and/or Marina Oswald is not known.
12. CE 2831 (FBI report dated November 25, 1963, of interview of William F. Simmons at Irving Tex.)
13. CE 1685, first page of exhibit (23H 15).

14. Shari Angel interview as (2) above.

15. ibid.

16. CE 2434 and 2435 (FBI reports dated December 21, 1963, of interviews of Robert G. Landers and Charles Miller at Dallas, Tex.)

17. 14H 341 (Testimony of Nancy Perrin Rich)

18. As (2) above.

19. CE 1684 (FBI report dated January 22, 1964 of interview of Joan Leavelle at West Palm Beach, Fla.)

20. As (2) above.

21. CE 1322 (FBI report dated November 25, 1963, concerning inventory of items taken by Dallas Police Department from Jack Ruby's person, automobile, and residence), page 735 of exhibit (22H 502).

Written 2001.

First published July 2001 in The Dealey Plaza Echo, vol. 5, no. 2.

N.B. See updated list of Ruby's strippers, which follows.

Addendum to *Jack Ruby's Carousel Club*: Brief notes on some of "Jack Ruby's Girls"

Alice from Dallas (Alice Anderson) ….. Alice co-wrote the 1970 book *Jack Ruby's Girls* with Diana the Huntress *(qv)* and appears in the photographs taken outside the club with Jack Ruby and Kathy Kay (Armstrong Exhibit nos. 5300-A to 5300-F).

Anita Adams (Real name not known) ….. She is listed in Jack Ruby's telephone record cards as an 'Exotic' and lived in Oak Cliff.

April Flowers (Real name not known) ….. Listed in Ruby's telephone record cards. Lived in Houston. Uncertain whether she actually performed at the Carousel.

Betty McDonald (Nancy Jane Mooney) ….. This former Ruby stripper, who often appears to be confused with others of similar name, provided an alibi for Darrell Wayne Gardner when he was accused of shooting Warren Reynolds, a witness close to the murder of Officer J.D. Tippit. This occurred on 5th February 1964. Just eight days later, she was arrested in Dallas and charged with a minor public order offence. She was locked up in the City Jail and later found dead in her cell, apparently having committed suicide by hanging herself with her toreador pants. Her name inevitably appears on the list of suspicious deaths. Whether or not that is justified, I am unable to say.

Burny Lane (Real name not known) ….. Mentioned in Carousel Club advert in *Dallas Times Herald*, date not known. This is the advert which has the pictures of Wally Weston after his 50-mile hike for charity and Shari Angel as Gypsy Rose Lee. Also mentioned in CE 1322 at 22H 510.

Chelo (Chelo Castillo) ….. Listed in Ruby's telephone record cards as an 'Exotic'. Uncertain whether she ever performed at the Carousel Club as she had a Miami address.

Cherie Delamour (*aka* Cherie Lamour, Jeannie Skelton, Cherie Waring) ….. Listed in Ruby's telephone record cards as an 'Exotic', she lived at various addresses in west and south Dallas.

Cindy Ember(s) (Real name not known) ….. In his WC testimony (13H 360), Carousel Club employee Andrew Armstrong explained that hers should have been one of the featured names displayed outside the club but some of the letters had fallen off and left only 'EMBER' (Armstrong Exhibit nos. 5300-A and B).

Colette Collins (Real name not known) ….. Listed in Ruby's telephone record cards as an 'Exotic'. She had a Denver telephone no. but a Dallas AGVA (union) no.

Darling Star (Mary Ann Cook) ….. Mentioned in a Denver FBI report, 25th November 1963.

Delilah/Miranda (Marilyn Moore Walle aka Marilyn Magyar Moon and Marilyn April Walle) ….. According to *The Dead Witnesses* by Craig Roberts and John Armstrong, she was working at the Carousel Club at the time of the assassination. She was allegedly planning a book on the assassination and was shot and killed on 1st September 1966. Her husband was convicted of her murder.

Diana the Huntress (used the name Diana Hunter but her legal name was actually Marilyn Owens) ….. Co-author with Alice from Dallas *(qv)* of the 1970 book *Jack Ruby's Girls*. Part of her normal act involved her playing the part of a Roman goddess. A passage in *Jack Ruby's Girls* described how the club band would take cover whenever they saw her fit an arrow into her bow. She married Grand Prairie resident Harry Edward Wysong in February 1964.

She also said that two of Ruby's strippers, Lisa Land and Toni Turner were lesbians. (Source: Dallas FBI report, 19th June 1964.)

Diane Durette (Real name not known) ….. Described as an 'Exotic' in Ruby's telephone record cards. Dallas telephone no. and AGVA no.

Dior Angel (Delores Silva) ….. CE 1481 is a San Antonio FBI report of an interview with her on 21st December 1963 in which she said that her only engagement at the Carousel Club was for three or four weeks in April 1963.

Felissa Prell (Karen Green Williams) ….. She was one of 'Five Exotics' billed to perform on 22nd November 1963 (the others were Kathy Kay, Little Lynn, Joy Dale and Marilyn Moone). See advert on page A25 in *Dallas Times Herald* of that date. CE 2990 is a Dallas FBI report of an interview with her at the club on 26th November 1963 in which she said that she had only been hired by Ruby on 19th November. She appears almost certain to have been the newest of the Carousel Club dancers.

Francine (Mrs. Fannie Birch) ….. She was the mother of Carousel Club stripper Penny Dollar (Patricia Ann Birch Kohs) *(qv)* and was interviewed by the Dallas FBI on 8th December 1963. She stated that she (Francine) had worked as a stripper at both the Carousel Club and the Vegas Club for around two months (Friday evenings only) in late 1960. She said "it was common practice for police officers in uniform to visit the club (Carousel), talk with Jack Ruby and the girls and to come back later in the evening dressed in civilian clothes and apparently accompanied by girl friends." See CE 1495.

Friday Knight (Real name not known) ….. She appears in Ruby's telephone record cards as an 'Exotic' but no details other than an Oklahoma City telephone number. Her stage name was said to have come from the expression "Everyone loves Friday night."

Gail Raven (Barbara Murphy) ….. In an FBI interview on 25th November 1963, Nancy Monnell Powell (*aka* Tammi True) described Gail Raven as being about 19 years old and said that she was attending a beauty school at Woodsboro, Texas. Gail was also mentioned by stripper Precious Diamond (Helen Vines) in a Dallas FBI interview on 22nd January 1964. Gail was one of the dancers whose photograph was displayed outside the Carousel Club.

Geneva Foster (Believed her real name) ….. Mentioned in *San Diego Union* newspaper, 25th November 1963.

Gloria Jerome (Real name not known) ….. Mentioned in Ruby's telephone record cards. Lived in Oak Cliff.

Jada (Janet Mole Adams Bonney Cuffari Smallwood Conforto Washington) ….. When his star performer, Shari Angel, was obviously going to be absent for some time through sickness, Jack Ruby went to New Orleans where he signed up Jada from the Sho-Bar. Jada was one of the best-known club strippers on the scene in the early 60s and she commanded higher wages than any other Carousel Club performer. She began work at the Carousel Club on 17th July 1963 and extensions to her contract would have kept her there until 1st January 1964. She caused Ruby several problems. In particular, she had a habit of going too far with her act and on occasion Ruby would turn the lights out on her. Local journalist Seth Kantor described her as being "supercharged with animalism" in his 1978 book *Who was Jack Ruby?* Following arguments and disagreements with Ruby, she quit the Carousel Club during the first week of November 1963. She was killed in Albuquerque, New Mexico, on 9th May 1980 when the motor cycle she was riding was in a collision with a school bus. She was 44 years old. Jada was one of the stars of the 1960s burlesque film *Naughty Dallas* (available on video).

Jan Tabor (Jan Humphrey) ….. Mentioned in a Denver FBI report, dated 25th November 1963.

Janice O'Brien (Janice Aniger) ….. Mentioned in Ruby's telephone record cards as an 'Exotic'. She lived in south-east Dallas.

Jeanine (Martha Churchman) ….. To my knowledge, she is the only full-time Carousel Club stripper who was 'discovered' during the club's amateur nights. In his possession when arrested, Ruby had her AGVA contract for seven days work (dated 2nd November 1963). She lived in central Dallas.

Joy Dale (Joyce Lee Witherspoon McDonald, now Joyce Gordon) ….. One of the 'Five Exotics' who were due to perform on 22nd November 1963, she had worked for Ruby since August 1963. She is the girl on the left in a series of five photographs taken in Ruby's office (Armstrong Exhibit Nos. 5301-A to E). She was interviewed extensively in the video *Jack Ruby on Trial*.

Julie Taylor (Julie Case) ….. CE 1541 is a Syracuse, New York, FBI report of an interview with her in which she described working at the Carousel Club and her opinions of Jack Ruby. She was booked there for five weeks, July/ August 1962.

Kathy Kay (born Lilian Helen Harvey in England, 1936) ….. she is dealt with at length in Chapter 20 "Search for a Stripper" herein.

Kim Athas (Laveda Greer) ….. Described as an 'Exotic' in Jack Ruby's telephone record cards. She was also in the film *Naughty Dallas*. Kim has been studied by Dallas researcher Rachel Rendish, who has interviewed her live on video.

Lee Sharon (Real name not known) ….. Mentioned in the Warren Commission testimony of Norman Earl Wright (15H 250)

Libby Chase (Gail Summers) ….. Described as an 'Exotic' in Jack Ruby's telephone record cards. This also gives her legal name.

Little Lynn (Karen Lynn Bennett Carlin, later *aka* Teresa Norton) ….. Possibly the best known of Ruby's girls, mainly through her plea to him to send her some money urgently. This resulted in him visiting the Western Union office in Dallas and wiring $25 to her in Fort Worth – just a matter of three minutes before he entered the City Hall basement and shot Oswald to death. She was only 19 years old (born 20th July 1944) and had only worked at the Carousel Club for about two months. I have a copy of her AGVA contract at the Carousel Club for seven days from 6th November 1963. Her salary, for three shows daily, was $110 per week. It has been suggested, though not confirmed, that whilst living in Houston, Texas under the name Teresa Norton in 1964, she was shot to death in a hotel room.

Lisa Land   (Real name not known) ….. A Dallas FBI report dated 19th June 1964 stated that stripper Diana the Huntress *(qv)* described her as one of Ruby's strippers and as a lesbian

Liza Sommers (Real name not known) ….. Mentioned in the Warren Commission testimony of Little Lynn at 13H 213-214. She described Liza Sommers as 'a hose act'.

Lori Adams (Laurie Adams) ….. Described in Ruby's telephone record cards as an 'Exotic.' Lived in Live Oak, Dallas.

Margo (Norma Jean Bostick) ….. A Dallas FBI report dated 15th December 1963 indicated that Norma Bostick and her husband Harvey Davis Bostick had worked at the Carousel Club at various times between May 1961 and March 1963. She had been a cashier and part-time dancer. He was a bartender and doorman. See CE 2380.

Marilyn Moone (Real name not known – but perhaps identical to Delilah/ Miranda above) …..

Mili Perele (Real name?) ….. Interviewed by the El Paso, Texas, FBI on 29th November 1963, when it was revealed that she worked as a stripper at the Carousel Club for eight months in 1961 and a further two months in 1962. She mentioned that Ruby "operated a very strict burlesque show" and that "many police officers, both in and out of uniform, patronized Ruby's clubs but were not known to have any dealings with them." She also mentioned that she had worked at the Carousel Club with Kathy Kay, Sherry Lynn and Najada. See CE 1540.

Miranda/Delilah – see Delilah/Miranda above.

Mona Lu (Elvira Bertha Scott) ….. She was interviewed by the Fort Worth FBI on 21st January 1964 and stated that she worked at the Carousel Club as a stripper for around two weeks during the summer of 1961. See CE 1682.

Naja (Naja Karamuru) ….. Described in Ruby's telephone record cards as a 'Feature Exotic.' However, she had a New York City address and AGVA membership and I cannot confirm that she ever appeared at the Carousel Club.

Najada (Beatrice Calgrove) ….. Interviewed by the Houston, Texas, FBI on 25th November 1963. She stated that she worked as a featured exotic dancer at the Carousel Club for about six months from the winter of 1961. She had a violent argument with Ruby at the bar of the club around New Year's Eve 1961. This resulted in Ruby slapping her. She complained to a DPD Vice Squad Lieutenant or Captain who was in the club at the time but he told her she was crazy. Najada and Ruby obviously resolved their differences and her contract was later extended to 25th February 1962. See CE 1513.

Nikki Joy (Maxine Joy Williams) ….. Included in Ruby's telephone record cards, she had a Dallas telephone number. Mentioned in a Dallas FBI report of 5th August 1976.

Peggy Steele (Real name not known) ….. In his WC testimony, former Carousel Club employee Larry Crafard said of her: "She had been a stripper, she was a stripper who had worked there at the Carousel Club." (14H 61). This was confirmed in the testimony of George Senator at 14H 286.

Penny DiMone (Betty Dawson) ….. Described as an 'Exotic' in Ruby's telephone record cards. She had a Lubbock, Texas, address.

Penny Dollar (Patricia Ann Birch Kohs) ….. The youngest daughter of Mrs. Fannie Birch (Francine – *qv*). She was interviewed by the Irving, Texas, FBI on 14th December 1963 and stated that she had known Ruby for 15 years, since she was six years old. She worked as a "dancer" at the Carousel Club for one week and three days around the middle of 1962 but had quit after disagreements with Ruby. She had to go to AGVA to get her salary. See CE 1499.

Pepper Payne (Sue Pepper) ….. According to a Cincinnati FBI report of 3rd December 1963, she worked as a Carousel Club stripper from late February to late August 1963.

Pixie Lynn (Helen Kay Smith) ….. Was a stripper at the Carousel Club during December 1961 and also a friend of Candy Barr (Juanita Slusher). On 6th December 1963, she was interviewed in Houston, Texas by Lt. Jack Revill (DPD) and flatly denied ever being at a party which had allegedly been attended by Jack Ruby and Lee Harvey Oswald. See CE 2795. The reason for the interview was an informant's telephone call to the DPD stating that she had information that Ruby and Oswald "attended the same homosexual parties in Dallas." See CE 2794.

Ramona Wagner (Tuesday Regan, Tuesday Ryan, Mrs. Mickey Ryan) ….. Wife of Mickey Ryan, Ruby's bookkeeper. Dates of her employment at the Carousel Club not known.

Reba (Reba Jane Lance) ….. Reba and her husband, Philip Lance, were each interviewed by the Dallas FBI on 5th December 1963. From those interviews we know that Reba worked for Ruby at both the Carousel and the Vegas Club as a stripper for around a year, quitting in January 1963. She was severely embarrassed by Ruby and she said that she "hates Jack Ruby more than any person she has ever met." See CE 1532 and CE 1533.

Robin S. Hood (Shirley Ann Marie Mauldin) ….. Interviewed by the Omaha, Nebraska, FBI on 8th December 1963. She revealed that she had worked for Jack Ruby as a dancer at the Carousel Club for one week in 1962. See CE 2821 at 26H 259. She was allegedly present at the Carousel Club with a Dallas attorney called Carroll Erskine Jarnagin on 4th October 1963. According to information furnished by Jarnagin to the Dallas FBI on 6th December 1963, Jack Ruby and Lee Harvey Oswald were together at an adjacent table and he (Jarnagin) overheard them discussing a plot to assassinate the Governor of Texas. See CE 2821 at 26H 257. Shirley Mauldin, who was there with Jarnagin on a date, was unable to recall this incident when interviewed at Omaha, Nebraska.

Rose Cheramie (Melba Christine Marcades *aka* Roselle Renee Cheramie, Melba Christine Youngblood) ….. Born on 14th October 1923 and died on 6th September 1965. She is best known through her alleged claim, made on the evening of 20th November 1963, that JFK would be killed when he came to Dallas. At the time, Rose, who was a former Ruby employee, an alcoholic and a heavy drug user, who had just been the victim of a road accident, was not believed. After the assassination, however, she was interviewed by Lieutenant Francis Fruge (Louisiana State Police) and claimed knowledge of connections between Ruby, Oswald, and a major drugs deal. Despite lengthy police enquiries, these allegations were never substantiated. Rose Cheramie again came to prominence when she was the victim of an alleged hit-and-run road accident on 4th September 1965. She was found lying on a lonely road near Big Sandy, Texas in the middle of the night. She was declared DOA (dead on arrival) at the local Gladewater Hospital. At her autopsy, it was concluded that the cause of death was "traumatic head wound with subdural and subarachnoid and petechial hemorrhage to the brain caused by being struck by an auto." The hospital is now unable to locate these records. I am grateful to English researcher Chris Mills for his exhaustive research into this woman, which forms the basis of my comments above. The reader is directed to Chris' article "Rambling Rose" in the May 1994 issue of the now defunct journal *Dallas '63*.

Shari Angel (Bobbie Louise Stone Dempsey Weston Messerole, Mrs. Wally Weston) ….. Shari, who has been of great help in my research over the past 12 years, is the subject of an earlier piece here and is also mentioned in the body of this article on the Carousel Club. She died in Dallas on 21st June 2005, aged 71.

Sherry Lynn (Kay Garcia) ….. In her Warren Commission testimony, Tammi True *(qv)* claimed to be a *protégé* of Shari (Sherry) Lynn. I have copies of two AGVA contracts in the name of Sherry Lynn in which she is named as an 'Exotic' . These are for one night only, 1st February 1962 and for four nights commencing 14th March 1962, both at the Carousel Club. She was married to Joe Garcia, a member of the Carousel Club band. She and her husband were each interviewed by the Dallas FBI on 30th November 1963. Joe recalled Ruby being friendly with numerous Dallas police officers and detectives over a long period of time. Sherry Lynn had very dark hair and a distinctive kiss-curl over her forehead. She can be recognized in several well-known photographs with Jack Ruby, Tammi True and a very tall, unidentified Carousel Club dancer.

Sue Emmons (Real name) ….. Information from a meeting with her sister in Dallas in November 1993. She is now believed to be living in Alaska.

Tammi True (Nancy Monnell Bowlen Powell) ….. She had worked for Ruby on and off since around late 1961 and claimed to be *protégé* of Sherry Lynn (Kay Garcia). She quit her Carousel Club job on 20th November 1963. During her Warren Commission testimony, Tammi responded to Burt Grffin's question about the difference between an exotic dancer and a striptease dancer as follows: "Now you have goofed me up. The difference between them is, an exotic is like a belly dancer, comes out on stage with veils and panels and things, like the dancer of the seven veils. And a stripper comes out fully clothed and takes it off. But an exotic dancer doesn't take anything off. It is like, I don't know, Egyptian or something." Mr Griffin asked: "What kind of dancing do you do, striptease or exotic?" to which she replied: "A lot of girls would prefer to be exotic, but as far as I am concerned, it is a dirty old stripper." (15H 407-408).

Tawney Angel (Mary Hopkins) ….. Copies of AGVA contracts in my possession indicate that Tawney Angel worked at the Carousel Club as an 'exotic' dancer for seven days from 6th April 1962 and a further nine days from 7th December 1962.

Tikki Time (Peggy Lee Stone) ….. Sister of Shari Angel – who supplied this information to me.

Toi Rebel/Toni Rebel (Sue Bailey) ….. Mentioned in the Warren Commission testimony of Larry Crafard at 14H 60 and of George Senator at 14H 285.

Toni Turner (Joan Leavelle) ….. Interviewed by the West Palm Beach, Florida, FBI on 20th January 1964 when she stated that she had worked at the Carousel Club as a dancer for about four weeks in 1962 (CE 1684). I have a copy of one of her AGVA contracts for that period. She is described as an 'Exotic Snake Act.' DPD Homicide Detective James R. Leavelle was the uncle of her estranged husband Bill.

Torri Shane (Evelyn Webster) ….. Mentioned by Pixie Lynn *(qv)* in her statement to the Houston Secret Service on 6th December 1963: "I went to the Carousel with Torri Shane, also known as Evelyn Webster, another dancer." See CE 2249 at 25H 161.

Tura Satana (Tura Luna Pascual Yamaguchi) ….. Dealt with in the body of this piece.

Vanita/Venita (Real name not known) ….. Information from Dallas researcher Rachel Rendish but not yet confirmed.

Wanda Joyce (Mrs. Thomas Henry 'Hank' Killam) ..... The death of Wanda's husband was one of the most mysterious and bizarre of the so-called 'suspicious' deaths of assassination witnesses. It occurred on 17th March 1964 in Pensacola, Florida. It appeared that his throat had been cut and he had then been thrown through the plate glass window of a department store. Cause of death was given as "suicide." Thomas Killam was a friend of John Carter, one of Oswald's fellow roomers at 1026 North Beckley. Exact dates of Wanda's Carousel Club engagements not known.

(Mrs. Billy Don Williams) ..... Stage name not known. Her husband was interviewed by the Dallas FBI at the Carousel Club on 27th November 1963 and stated that his wife worked there as an exotic dancer. He said that she had got the job after answering a newspaper advertisement.

Yum Yum (Stella Bray, *nee* Kalifa) ..... Interviewed by the Cleveland, Ohio, FBI on 30th December 1963 and stated that she had worked at the Carousel Club for three months during the summer of 1956. She also commented that it was her first engagement as a stripper. See CE 1670.

This listing originally written 1993
Regularly updated
This version expanded and compiled 2005

20. Search for a stripper — the Kathy Kay story

I am about to introduce you to one of the most mysterious and charismatic ladies in this entire case. Many researchers know her by her Carousel Club stage name KATHY KAY or perhaps by her supposed real name KAY COLEMAN or maybe as KAY HELEN OLSEN, the name under which she testified before the Warren Commission in 1964. I doubt, however, that many know that she began life in London, England in 1936 with the unremarkable name LILIAN HELEN HARVEY.

(Author's note: I have spent several years studying this important character in the case. What follows is a longer and more comprehensive version of my current research in this area than has previously been published or presented at conference. I have tried to cover the subject's life and background as well as the period of over two years that she worked for Jack Ruby and her subsequent and permanent disappearance from Dallas.

I have deliberately omitted details of several of my original sources since some of them involve people occupying sensitive positions of authority on both sides of the Atlantic. Those of you familiar with my previous published research know that I make a point of acknowledging my sources. However, discretion and certain assurances I have given dictate that this cannot be done in every case here.)

INTRODUCTION

When I first undertook to study, and hopefully trace, Kathy Kay, I did so purely because she was another 'British connection' in this case. At that point, (1993), I did not even know her full real name. Having already carried out a comprehensive study of the Carousel Club entertainers, I was well aware that a stripper's real name seldom bore any similarity to her stage name. In those early days I was assured by several people that Kathy Kay was dead. Although I have proved that belief wrong, I am satisfied that those opinions were genuinely and honestly held—if erroneous. I do not think there was anything sinister here.

The knowledge that Kathy Kay had been born in England proved the very stimulus I needed. Just who was this mysterious lady? How had she become one of the most popular strippers in Jack Ruby's Carousel Club? Was it true that she had danced with Lee Harvey Oswald there a few weeks before the assassination? What had happened to her after Friday 22nd November 1963? Was she still alive? I was determined to find out.

TRUE IDENTITY

Although it takes just a few lines here to identify Kathy Kay correctly and provide her early background the process of obtaining even the most basic information occupied several months. I have neither the time nor the space here to explain my methods in depth, so the following paragraphs provide only a rough framework.

Working purely from some very sketchy descriptive information I found in an Oklahoma City FBI report dated 11th December 1963 [1] I conducted intensive research at the Office of Population Census & Surveys (OPCS) at St Catherine's House in London. This is a repository for the records of all births, marriages and deaths in England and Wales since 1837, these records having previously been lodged at the nearby Somerset House. Following much hard work and effort, I eventually succeeded in locating and obtaining certified copies of the lady's Birth Certificate and her first Marriage Certificate. [2]

These documents showed that the lady we have come to know as Kathy Kay had been born at 85 Dryfield Road, Edgware, Middlesex on 13th April 1936. Her mother was Jane Frances Harvey, *nee* Knott, and her father was Herbert Maxwell Harvey, a photographic works storekeeper. She was named Lilian Helen Harvey. I later visited Dryfield Road and found no. 85 to be a small terraced house in what had obviously been a pleasant, well-to-do district of north-west London back then, but now rather run down.

MARRIAGE TO THE USAF STAFF SERGEANT

On 5th June 1954, less than two months after her 18th birthday, Lilian married Kennerd Joseph Coleman (formerly known as Davis), official service number A.F. 18379450, a Staff Sergeant serving with the 20th Fighter Bomber Wing of the United States Air Force, based at Wethersfield, Essex. [3] I subsequently learned that Coleman was a specialist technician working mainly on F-100 *Super Sabres* (jet fighters).

Coleman was six years Lilian's senior, having been born on 3rd March 1930 in Nashville, Tennessee. [4] At the time of her marriage, Lilian was living with her parents at a house at 19 Chelsea Avenue, Thorpe Bay, on the outskirts of the better known town of Southend-on-Sea, Essex. From local records held at the Southend-on-Sea main public library, [5] I established that the Harveys had moved there from Edgware in 1952.

At the time of her marriage, Lilian was three months pregnant.

Lilian's Marriage Certifiate gave her occupation as 'Buncher, Artificial Flowers Factory' but despite many hours poring over local directories and almanacs, my efforts to trace her former employers proved fruitless. Back in the early 1950s, there had been nearly a dozen local firms engaged in this sort of work, but 40 years later, they had all ceased trading. I was, however, able to find out what the work entailed. The raw materials used were not flowers in the usual sense, but different coloured seaweeds, gathered locally, dried and tied in small bunches ready to be sold as household decorations. It was hardly a job requiring any special skills or qualifications and was not a suitable occupation for someone with the good education which Lilian had enjoyed. [6]

Initially, I was perplexed how a teenage girl in Thorpe Bay would have come to meet a member of the USAF based at Wethersfield, some 50 miles away in rural Essex. With local help, however, I established with 99% certainty that young Lilian Harvey had met Staff Sergeant Coleman at one of the regular weekend dances at the base where girls from the surrounding towns and villages were bussed in to provide dance partners. [7]

I visited and photographed the Edgware house, the Thorpe Bay house and the Roman Catholic Church of Our Blessed Lady and St. Helen Empress, Southend, where the marriage ceremony had been performed. The incumbent, Father Tom Lavin, was very helpful and was able to show me the original documents pertaining to the marriage. These contained many personal details of both parties to the marriage.

As a married man, Staff Sergeant Coleman was allowed to live off-base. The newly-married couple lived at a house called Talma in Braintree Road in the Essex village of Felsted about 12 miles from the Wethersfield USAF base. [8] I have been unable to establish whether this was privately rented by the couple or provided as a married quarter for American personnel by the USAF. Local enquiries on my behalf, including a tour of the area, a visit to the local post office and a search of local records, have failed to locate any house of this name. [9] If it still stands, it is no longer called Talma.

The Colemans' first child, a daughter they called Susan Helen, was born at St John's Maternity Hospital, 48 Wood Street, Chelmsford, Essex on 12th December 1954. [10]

Going to America

On 14th May 1956, just under two years after their marriage, Kennerd and Lilian Coleman left England for the United States. They lived initially at Victoria, Texas. Coleman was still serving in the USAF at this time [11] so it is reasonable to assume that this transatlantic move was in connection with his job. I also know that he had family connections in Texas, having been confirmed in Houston in 1941. [12]

The Colemans had a second daughter, Sheri (born in the US around August 1957) but in 1958 the couple separated. Lilian retained custody of the children and moved to Riverside, California. Kennerd, still serving in the USAF, went to Illinois, possibly transferring into Scott AFB where I believe there was an F-100 squadron. The couple reunited briefly later that year when Lilian and the children joined Kennerd in Illinois and they then moved to Kansas, living initially in Salina (Schilling AFB?) and then in Wichita (McConnell AFB?). During this period, Kennerd was in very poor health and this may have been the main reason for their brief reconciliation. This situation was not to last, however, and they divorced, Lilian citing Kennerd for "extreme cruelty and gross neglect of duty" towards her. [13]

Lilian was given custody of their two daughters and Kennerd was ordered to pay "a reasonable sum per month for the support of said parties' minor children." The divorce case was filed in the District Court of Saline County, Kansas on 1st December 1959. The divorce was finalized with effect from 11th December 1961 by which time Lilian had moved back to Texas. [14]

Kansas researcher Mark K. Colgan has located records indicating that Kennerd Coleman died in Harris County, Texas on 1st May 1969. He had never remarried and was just 39 years old. Cause of death not known.

And so to Dallas

Together with her two daughters, Lilian had moved to Dallas, Texas in June 1961. [15] The reason she came to this particular city is not clear. Initially, she found employment as a waitress at Barney Weinstein's Theatre Lounge. The following month she went to work as a stripper at the Carousel Club—and Lilian Helen Coleman became Kathy Kay. According to her Warren Commission testimony she was introduced to Jack Ruby when she "just went up to his club to see some girlfriends." Whether these girlfriends were on Ruby's payroll or were other acquaintances I do not know. Lilian's activities between divorcing Coleman and moving to Dallas are unclear.

In his Warren Commission testimony, Norman Earl Wright (stage name

Earl Norman) explained that he had worked at the Carousel Club from June 1961. He said: "I am a comic, MC, and I sing and do comedy, and run the show." When asked if Kathy Kay was working for Jack Ruby when he (Wright) worked for him, he replied: "Yes; in fact we started her off as a professional entertainer when I was there ... she did a couple of amateur shows and then he put her to work as a regular dancer." [16] Wright also said that he believed that at the time of the assassination, Kathy Kay had worked for Ruby longer than any of the other girls.

Apart from a brief spell in 1962 when she worked at the Colony Club, [17] Kathy (as I shall now call her) continued to work for Ruby right up until the eve of the assassination. The Carousel Club advertisement in the *Dallas Times Herald* of 22nd November 1963 names Kathy Kay as one of 'Five Exotics' due on stage that evening. Ironically, Bill DeMar, the ventriloquist and memory man who later claimed to have used Oswald in his act a few days earlier, was top of the bill. Kathy's name was also 'up in lights' above the club entrance on Commerce Street. [18] That performance, of course, was never to take place as Ruby closed the club reportedly out of respect for the slain President.

KATHY KAY—ONE OF THE STARS OF THE CAROUSEL CLUB

Kathy Kay was one of the most popular of Jack Ruby's girls. She was tall, she was slim, she was blonde and she was very pretty. She also had something which stood her apart from every other Carousel Club performer—an English accent. [19] Several former patrons of the Carousel Club have mentioned to me that Kathy would often talk to the audience when she was on stage. That was to become an accepted part of her act. It was almost a trademark. Kathy Kay had no need to incorporate balloons or a snake into her act. Her natural speaking voice became her gimmick.

In a tape-recorded interview in November 1994, the former Carousel Club feature stripper Shari Angel told me: "She was English. She was my pal. She spoke a lot of cockney." [20] Shari was unaware that true cockneys do not originate from that part of London where Lilian Helen Harvey/Kathy Kay was born, but her remark was nevertheless a very interesting one.

A San Jose FBI Report of 8th September 1975 [21] describes an interview seven days earlier when "Mrs. Coleman said that during her act on the stage, the twist was in style at this time and she would call a customer to come up on the stage and she would show this customer how to do the twist." In September 1999, a photograph circulated on Rich DellaRosa's JFK Research website which showed Kathy Kay on the main Carousel Club runway doing just this. An intriguing aspect of this picture is that the customer in question is a very young looking Jim Marrs. At this time, the future author of *Crossfire* was a student at North Texas State University at Denton and was obviously enjoying a night out in Dallas, away from his studies. [22] I have since shown the photograph to Jim Marrs and he has confirmed that he is indeed the man shown. [23]

ENTER PATROLMAN HARRY OLSEN

Despite the protestations of the Warren Commission investigators to the contrary, it is now plain that the Carousel Club and similar clubs in Dallas were indeed regular haunts for many off-duty police officers. [24] One such officer was Patrolman 1523 Harry Neal Olsen, a member of the Headquarters Station staff within the Patrol Division of the Dallas Police Department. [25] He became a regular visitor to the Carousel Club throughout 1963. DPD records show that Olsen had been born on 16th February 1934 at Wichita Falls, Texas. [26]

I have seen only two photographs of Olsen but according to DPD records he was 6' 2" tall and weighed 195 pounds. Margaret Ruth Richey, a Carousel Club waitress, said that he was "a real tall guy, nice built ..." [27]

Olsen claimed that he had first met Jack Ruby during a routine police check of the Carousel Club in 1961 and he became a regular patron. [28] During his Warren Commission testimony, he agreed with Arlen Specter that he was "going with or steadily dating Kay, then, from the early fall of 1963 on up until the time that you married her ..." [29] During an FBI interview on 10th December 1963 however, Kathy said that she had dated Olsen "on a regular basis for over a year ... and that she and Olsen had discussed marriage but due to her occupation no wedding plans had been made." [30]

At this time, Kathy was a divorcee and Olsen was separated from his wife and waiting for his divorce to become final, which it did in October 1963. Perhaps this latter factor was influential in Olsen claiming that his close liaison with Kathy was much shorter than it really was.

Jack Ruby had no objection to one of his star performers dating a policeman; in fact he welcomed it. Kathy would usually dance seven nights a week and Olsen would be there to watch her on at least one of those nights, usually Saturday. It appears to me that Ruby and Olsen did not particularly like one another. However, Ruby came to trust Olsen's judgment and would sometimes consult him when he had personnel problems. In her Warren Commission testimony, Kathy mentioned that she sometimes had disagreements with Ruby over her getting time off (to see Olsen). [31] It seems that the club owner and the cop got to know one another without becoming close friends. As I will explain later, there was at least one occasion when they went ice-skating together—with grave consequences.

KATHY'S HOME LIFE IN DALLAS

During this period, Kathy was living at Apartment 111 at 325 North Ewing Street, Oak Cliff. [32] I have been told by one of her ex-neighbours that she and her two daughters were well-liked in the immediate apartment complex and they would join in the usual activities at the pool, barbeque area, etc. Kathy's employment at the Carousel Club was no secret and it did not carry any social stigma.

One interesting but unsubstantiated rumour I picked up here is that Kathy was visited at her apartment by Lee Harvey Oswald at least twice. Unfortunately, this came to me *via* a third party and I have to treat it with a great deal of care and suspicion. Having been unable to find any corroboration, I prefer to treat it with disbelief.

Harry Olsen was sharing a home with DPD motorcycle officer Bobby Joe Dale at 3615 Theatre Lane at this time. [33] This was close to the Lemmon Avenue/Turtle Creek Boulevard intersection in the Oak Lawn district of Dallas, some two miles north of the downtown area. At least some of the time, however, I understand that Harry stayed with Kathy at her apartment. I believe this was the situation at the time of the assassination, although Kathy herself denied it. In the preamble to an FBI Report of an interview of Harry Olsen on 16th December 1963, his address is shown as 325 North Ewing Street, Dallas. [34] This was Kathy's apartment.

From her Warren Commission testimony it becomes obvious that Kathy Kay got on well with Jack Ruby. He visited her several times at her apartment but these visits were strictly in connection with club business. She also pointed out that he entertained "all the employees" at his own apartment on 4th July each year.

THE DAY OF THE ASSASSINATION

Kathy Kay worked at the Carousel Club on the evening of Thursday 21st November 1963 as usual. Later, she could not remember what she did the following morning but surmised that after getting up in mid-morning, she had been by the pool with her children. She then visited Harry Olsen at "an estate just a ways from where I lived." The odd claim that Olsen had been 'guarding' an estate for a DPD motorcycle officer who was engaged in the motorcade has never been satisfactorily explained. Neither the motorcycle officer not the exact location of the 'estate' has ever been identified. It is not clear whether he had this job just on the 22nd or whether it had been an ongoing task. Neither is it clear whether it was a 24-hours-a-day job.

Patrolman Olsen was off duty at this time having broken his kneecap on 4th November. He was forced to wear a cast on his injured leg and he walked with the aid of crutches. When asked by the Warren Commission's Arlen Specter: "What sort of an accident did you have to injure your leg?" Olsen simply replied: "I fell and broke my kneecap." Had Assistant Counsel Specter pursued that line of enquiry he may have learnt the exact circumstances of that fall. It had occurred when Jack Ruby, Kathy Kay, Shari Angel and Olsen had been ice-skating together at Fair Park. Ruby had accidentally crashed into Olsen on the ice and had run over his leg, seriously injuring his kneecap. [35]

Both Harry Olsen and Kathy Kay remained strangely reticent about their actions on the afternoon of the assassination. The location of the estate which Olsen claimed to have been guarding has never been positively identified. He claimed to remember only that it was "on 8th Street in Dallas." At about 1.15pm Kathy telephoned the Carousel Club and was told by Andy Armstrong that the club would not open that evening. She then sat with Mrs Hall, her landlady, presumably following the unbroken coverage of the assassination on television. On completion of his 'guarding job' Harry arrived at just after 6.00pm (according to Kathy) or about 8.00pm (according to him). They then watched TV together.

Later that evening, Kathy Kay and Harry Olsen drove in his car to Dealey Plaza "to see where the President was shot." At around midnight they were sitting in the parked car outside Simon's Garage, a parking garage on the corner of Jackson and Field, in downtown Dallas, where they met Jack Ruby. Whether this was a chance meeting or a pre-arranged rendezvous has never been established. According to Olsen's testimony, he then spoke with Ruby for "two or three hours" in the presence of Kathy Kay. In her version, the conversation went on for "an hour or so at least." A Dallas FBI Report of an interview with Olsen whilst he was in hospital on 12th December, however, stated that he claimed the conversation had lasted "for about ten minutes." [36]

In his Warren Commission testimony, Jack Ruby stated: "I left the KLIF (local radio station) at 2a.m., and I spent an hour with the officer and his girlfriend ..." [37] A discrepancy in time of this magnitude, between ten minutes and three hours, demands close examination but it appears to have gone unchecked.

Accepting the accuracy of Ruby's estimate that this conversation continued for an hour, we have to ask what the two men could have discussed in that time. The Warren Commission does not appear to have made any efforts to find out.

During this conversation Kathy Kay was alleged to have passed the remark about the alleged assassin: "Well, if he was in England, they would drag him through the streets and would have hung him." [38] In their Warren Commission testimony, however, both she and Olsen denied that she had ever used those or similar words. I am inclined to accept these denials as this expression does not appear to be one which would come naturally from a Londoner – even one who has been living in the United States for seven years.

Nothing remarkable appears to have happened to Kathy Kay the following day (Saturday 23rd). However in his Warren Commission testimony, Olsen stated that he and Kathy spent the day together and that they "watched some television and listened to the radio a little bit." In the evening, they "drove by where the President was shot, we drove by there several times, and drove around town a little bit." He then took Kathy to her apartment around 2 or 3 in the morning and claimed that he could not recall where he spent that night. "I could have slept on her couch. Either that or I went back to my apartment."

RUBY SHOOTS OSWALD

At about 11.30am on the morning of Sunday 24th Kathy was awoken by one of her daughters who told her: "Jack shot Oswald." [39]

According to Kathy's Warren Commission testimony, at about 4 o'clock that afternoon, she and Harry Olsen drove to Henrietta, Texas (near Wichita Falls) to visit Harry's parents. [40] It would be interesting to learn the reason for this visit. Since Kathy worked seven nights a week at the Carousel Club, and would normally have expected to work this night as usual, this had to be a spur-of-the-moment visit. It has been suggested to me that Harry may have been trying to obtain money from his parents to help to finance his and Kathy's forthcoming marriage. Perhaps it could have been an attempt to get money to help them skip town. Olsen's father was a religious man and he was unaware of his future daughter-in-law's occupation. Leaving Henrietta at around 10 o'clock that night, Kathy and Harry drove back to Dallas. Kathy had a driver's license at this time and in view of Harry's incapacity, it is almost certain that she drove the car on the 320-mile round trip.

For some unexplained reason, Harry Olsen failed to mention anything about the Henrietta trip in his own testimony. He stated that he stayed at Kathy's house with her and her children for "several hours" and left at "say 9 or 10 o'clock" when they both drove around Dallas before returning to Kathy's apartment. This testimony had been taken at the same *venue* in Los Angeles and by the same Warren Commission Assistant Counsel, (Arlen Specter), just under two hours *before* Kathy's. Specter apparently failed to notice this glaring discrepancy, either then or later, and the point was never pursued.

FAREWELL TO THE CAROUSEL CLUB

Two days later, on Tuesday 26th November, after obtaining clearance from the union (the American Guild of Variety Artists - AGVA), Kathy Kay collected her costumes, back- pay and personal effects from the Carousel Club. Tom Palmer, the AGVA branch manager in Dallas, told the Warren Commission that Kathy had indicated to him that she was frightened and wanted to get out of town as quickly as possible. He claimed that he did not know the reason for this. [41] Strangely enough, Palmer also performed at the Carousel Club as an occasional magician and comedian. In an FBI interview in August 1978, Olsen claimed that Kathy, by now his ex-wife, had been scared by something Ruby told her. Although he claimed to know what it was, Olsen refused to expand on it. [42]

On 2nd December Kathy went to work at the King's Club in Oklahoma City because she "wanted to make some money for Christmas." [43] Another of Ruby's ex-strippers, Nancy Monnell Powell (stage name Tammi True), was living in Room 6 at the Siesta Motel there [44] and Kathy stayed with her for three weeks. This seems a strange arrangement since Shari Angel had told me that " ... she and Tammi True fought like cats and dogs. They loathed each other. If you'd go to the bathroom, they'd be socking it out." [45]

Harry Olsen, who remained in Dallas at this time, suffered multiple injuries when he was involved in a mysterious car crash on 7th December. His car was a total wreck after a collision with a telegraph pole. No other vehicle was involved and he was alone in the car. It has been suggested that this could have been an attempt on his life. Maybe it was a warning not to talk. On the other hand, I feel it can just as easily be dismissed as the result of him simply losing control of the vehicle. He still had his leg in plaster at this time.

Harry spent two weeks in Methodist Hospital, Oak Cliff. He stated in his Warren Commission testimony that he was visited there by Jack Ruby's ex-Carousel Club employee Wally Weston. No reason for this odd visit is volunteered. Since Olsen was still unfit for normal police duties and had used up all his allowable sick time, he was discharged from the Dallas Police Department on 29th December. [46]

That, however, was not the complete story. Olsen had joined the DPD on 21st July 1958 when aged 22. He completed his recruit's training on 31st October 1958 and was appointed full Patrolman on 21st October 1959. His career was notable for a series of disciplinary lapses including allegations of a love affair with a Mrs. Clarice Carroll in May 1960. As a result of this incident, he resigned from the department on 27th May 1960. He was reinstated in September 1960 but continued to commit minor indiscretions and abuse his official position in a series of incidents. Patrolman Olsen, it seems, had two weaknesses—women and money. Chief Curry was looking for an excuse to kick Harry out of the department and his extended sick leave, although legitimate, provided just that excuse.

This period of Kathy's life presents a few problems. There is a record of an interview of the Carousel Club emcee/comedian Wally Weston (a former husband of Shari Angel) by FBI Special Agents Jesus Homero and John M. Erwin at Casselberry, Florida on 3rd September 1976. [47] This suggests that

Kathy was present at a meeting (venue unspecified) "approximately three weeks after the shooting of President Kennedy." In the course of this interview Weston said that during the meeting "he was talking with Kathy Kay in the presence of Billy Willis, a drummer about Jack Ruby killing Lee Harvey Oswald. Kay told him that she had danced with the man who shot President Kennedy about one month before the shooting, which was about a week before Weston slugged the customer who called him a Communist (claimed by Weston to have been Oswald, but now believed more likely to have been local gun dealer, John Thomas Masen). [48] Kay remarked that it was the same man that shot President Kennedy that she had danced with earlier and that Weston had slugged." Could this possible encounter with Oswald be what Olsen knew had scared her?

The next definite event I have established is Kathy's marriage to Harry Olsen. After obtaining Marriage License no. 06960 on 10th January 1964, they were married at the Rosemont Christian Church, Dallas on 18th January 1964. [49] Since Olsen no longer had his DPD job, there was nothing to keep them in Dallas, and they fulfilled an ambition to move to California, using the financial settlement from Olsen's car insurance claim and some money which Kathy had managed to save. When asked by Arlen Specter: "Was there any special reason why you went to California?" Olsen produced the flippant reply: "We heard the climate was nice out here." [50]

The newly-wed Olsens, together with Kathy's two daughters by her previous marriage, moved from Dallas to Apartment 2 at 1260 Second Avenue, Long Beach, California on 1st February 1964. [51] Later in the year they moved to Apartment 12 at 315 Obispo Avenue, still in Long Beach and were reported to be running a business called the Doctor's Business Bureau from Room 1006, Hartwell Building, 19 Pine Avenue, Long Beach. [52]

Lilian Helen Harvey/Kay Helen Coleman/Kathy Kay had now become Mrs Kay Helen Olsen, the name under which she testified before Assistant Counsel Arlen Specter of the Warren Commission on 6th August 1964 in Los Angeles, California. [53] Although she has lived in a succession of different addresses in and around the coast of California since then, I do not believe the former Kathy Kay has ever left the state.

As well as the two Long Beach addresses, I have located records showing that she has lived in San Jose, (where she worked in real estate), Campbell, Riverside, Santa Cruz and Sunnyvale, in addition to her current address in northern California.

DIVORCE AND RE-MARRIAGE

The marriage between former stripper Kathy Kay and ex-cop Harry Olsen was not to last, but I have been unable to establish either when it ended or the circumstances. I am unaware that they had any children together. In 1995, however, I managed to trace the name of her third (and current) husband, together with their current address but I am sworn to divulge neither. As I have mentioned above, like all this lady's addresses since she left Dallas in 1964, it is in California.

AN UNSATISFACTORY ENDING

Naturally, there was only one way that I hoped all this research would finish; conducting a video or audio interview face to face with the former Kathy Kay.

On 13th June 1995, I flew to San Francisco (*via* Dallas, Texas and Albuquerque, New Mexico) to take part in a live TV show, *Assassination Update*, being hosted by my good friend and first-generation researcher Hal Verb. This would be the obvious opportunity to get out and visit the lady. I had kept her home address and telephone number very much to myself. The only researchers who know them are a close contact in Kansas (who was instrumental in finding them), a colleague in California, another in Dallas and my friend and collaborator Melanie Swift in the UK.

A few months prior to this California visit I had spoken with Beverly Oliver in Dallas. During her time as a singer in the Colony Club, Beverly had got to know Kathy Kay and they had become friends. Beverly very kindly gave me a copy of her recently-published autobiography *Nightmare in Dallas* in which she wrote a personal note to Kathy. It closed with the sentence: "You can trust Mr. Griggs with everything." It was hoped that this would help to put Kathy at her ease when we met.

When I arrived in San Francisco I stayed in a very pleasant motel close to the marina, just a mile from the Golden Gate Bridge. I had still not attempted to make contact with the former Kathy Kay so I was quickly on the telephone, hoping to reach her. I must have telephoned a dozen or more times within a four-day period but I never got further than an answering machine. This provided a very strange message spoken by her current husband Stephen but it did confirm to me that I had the correct number. Her current married name was mentioned and part of the recorded message referred to her as *"Kay."* Furthermore, the message concluded with her laughing in the background.

Despite leaving the telephone number and address of my motel, I did not receive any return call from either Kathy or her husband. I even sent her a letter, explaining who I was and my reason for being in San Francisco. I enclosed a few photographs I had taken of the Edgware house where she had been born, the church where she married for the first time etc. Maybe she watched my television appearance. I don't know.

One evening, a couple of days before I was due to fly back to Dallas and then home, I received a telephone call at my motel. The caller was an unidentified male person (not Kathy's husband) who told me simply that "the lady does not want to meet you and it will be best if you pack your bag and return to England as soon as you can" (or words to that affect). Despite having met some fairly shady characters during my assassination research, not to mention my police career, I had never experienced anything like this. I knew exactly what it meant, however and I took it seriously. I immediately cancelled my plans to drive out into the desert to try to meet the former Kathy Kay. Instead, I spent my last two days in San Francisco playing the innocent tourist. I wandered the city's many attractions, visited Haight-Ashbury (to pay homage to Janis Joplin and Jefferson Airplane), walked the bridge, took the Bay Tour, ate at the Hard Rock Cafe and rode those incredible cable cars. I even spent a few hours at City Hall trying (unsuccessfully) to trace records of my great grandfather who had perished in the 1906 earthquake. Then I flew home.

I certainly made no further attempt to contact the lady who had begun her life as Lilian Helen Harvey in Edgware, London back in 1936.

That was it. Maybe I'll try again some day. Maybe I won't.

RUMOURS

Rumours abound about the lady who is the subject of this paper. As is so often the case, however, most of them are just that. Rumours.

Apart from Wally Weston's uncorroborated claim made to the FBI in 1976, there is no proof or confirmation that Kathy Kay ever danced with Lee Harvey Oswald in the Carousel Club. She later denied that she ever saw him in there. [54]

There is *nothing* to substantiate stories that Lee Oswald saw her dance at the Carousel, became infatuated with her and visited her apartment.

There is *nothing* to give credence to a story which circulated a few years ago to the effect that she may have been the blonde lady in her mid-20s who was seen to drop a paper bag, later found to contain a pistol, somewhere in the "immediate vicinity of the assassination." This was alleged to have occurred within minutes of the Dealey Plaza shots. [55]

There is *nothing* to suggest that she was in any way implicated in the assassination of President Kennedy or the murders of either Officer J.D. Tippit or Lee Harvey Oswald.

As I have proved, there is no truth in the rumour that she is dead. The lady in question is alive and well and living the good life in relative luxury in northern California. She is now 69 years old (2005) and has absolutely no wish to be 'found' and interviewed by researchers like you and I. Her husband Stephen, who I understand is a millionaire, has an Italian-sounding surname, but an American voice which seems to have a touch of Welsh about it. Perhaps in her mature years, the lady who captivated the Dallas nightlife of the early 1960s with her English accent has reverted to her European roots.

A FINAL THOUGHT

I have not totally rejected the following bizarre theory:

Is it possible that Lilian/Kathy/Kay, who has obviously married well (at last), became alarmed at my attempts to contact her. Perhaps the scary telephone call I received was at her instigation. Perhaps she is concerned that her millionaire husband would learn of her life as a stripper at the notorious Carousel Club. As fellow stripper Tammi True told the Warren Commission: " ... she had this boy friend that she had been going with that was a policeman, and they were going to get married, and his parents didn't know she was an exotic, and her parents didn't know she was an exotic ... and she didn't want her parents in England to know she is an exotic dancer." [56]

Perhaps *he* doesn't know .....

NOTES

1. CE 1480 (FBI report dated December 11, 1963, of interview of Kay Helen Coleman at Oklahoma City, Okla.), page 2 of exhibit (22H 901).
2. The OPCS has since changed both its title and its location. It is now the Family Records Centre and is at 1 Myddelton Street, London EC1.
3. (a) This unexpected Wethersfield connection proved to be another of those strange coincidences which seem to occur with great regularity in this case. I was already very familiar with the base as it now houses the Headquarters & Training Centre of the Ministry of Defence Police. I spent nearly 23 happy years as a member of this force and have visited and stayed at Wethersfield many times on duty.
(b) Whilst checking this piece prior to its publication in this form, US researcher Larry Hancock expressed surprise and almost disbelief that Coleman was a Staff Sergeant at just 24 years of age, Larry, a former member of the US Air Force, told me that it was exceptional for somebody to attain that rank

below the age of 30.

4. Personal details of Kennerd Coleman provided by Fr Tom Lavin. See (12) below.

5. Kelly's Directories, telephone directories, electoral rolls etc. consulted on 3rd March 1995 with the assistance of researcher Melanie Swift.

6. In her Warren Commission testimony, when asked about her education, Lilian said: "Oh, I went to an all girls school, I won a scholarship to an all girls school ..." (14H 641). She is referring here to what was the forerunner of 'the eleven-plus.' It was known simply as 'the scholarship' and passing it (at age 10 or 11) invited entry to the local grammar school. I have established that the 'all girls school' she mentioned was Orange Hill School for Girls, Edgware (best-known former pupil—film actress Jean Simmons, some seven years earlier). In 1971, following educational reforms, Orange Hill was swallowed up by the much larger co-educational Mill Hill County High School. (I am obliged to the secretary and senior staff at Mill Hill County High School for assistance here.) Examples of Lilian's handwriting which I have seen also appear to indicate a well-educated person.

7. Information supplied by Barbara Carlyon, Dealey Plaza UK member living at Shoeburyness, Essex. Barbara also revealed that the transport which collected the young ladies from her own district was known, rather unflatteringly, as 'the pig bus'.

8. From Birth Certificate of Susan Helen Coleman, born 12th December 1954.

9. I am much obliged to my long-time friend and former colleague, retired (Woman) Police Sergeant 'Misty' Culpin, MBE, formerly based at MOD Police Headquarters, Wethersfield, for carrying out these enquiries on my behalf.

10. As (8) above.

11. The Colemans' later divorce documents included a Petition for Separation Maintenance dated 1st December 1959 which mentioned that Kennerd Coleman was still serving in the USAF at that date.

12. Information from documents produced by Fr Tom Lavin of the Roman Catholic Church of Our Blessed Lady and St. Helen Empress, Southend, where Lilian and Kennerd were married.

13. Copies of District Court of Saline County, Kansas documents in my possession (dated between 1st December 1959 and 11th December 1961). These all pertain to the divorce of Lilian H. Coleman (Plaintiff) and Kennerd Coleman (Defendant), case no. 22561.

14. Like much of the personal information contained in this paper, these details come from the Warren Commission testimony of Kay Helen Olsen (14H 640-655).

15. 14H 642 (Testimony of Kay Helen Olsen).

16. 15H 245, 250 (Testimony of Norman Earl Wright).

17. As (1) above, but page 1 of exhibit.

18. See Armstrong Exhibit Nos. 5300-A and 5300-B at 19H 24-25. Kathy Kay is on the left. The other lady is Alice Anderson ('Alice from Dallas').

19. As (1) above.

20. Author's interview of Shari Angel at the Adolphus Hotel, Dallas, 19th November 1994.

21. FBI report dated 8th September 1976 describing an interview of Kay Helen Coleman by Special Agents Joseph Chiaramonte and Ervin Thibault, Jr. in San Jose, California. Copy of document in author's possession.

22. Exchange of email posts on the JFK Research website forum involving Jack White, Mike Sheppard, Karl Lessman, Thomas Fohne, Rich DellaRosa and the author (September 1999).

23. Photograph shown to Jim Marrs (he signed it!) in Dallas on 20th November 1999.

24. As (20) above. See also 14H 626 (Testimony of Harry N. Olsen).

25. Batchelor Exhibit No. 5002 (DPD Personnel Assignments: November 1963), page 10 of exhibit (19H 127) and Olsen's official DPD Personnel File.

26. CE 2433 at 25H 538 (FBI reports dated July 31 and August 11, 13, 22 and 27, 1964 of checkout examination of telephone company records for Harry Olsen and Kathie (sic) Kay Coleman subsequent to November 14 1963).

27. 15H 199 (Testimony of Marjorie Ruth Richey).

28. 14H 626 (Testimony of Harry N. Olsen).

29. 14H 627 (Testimony of Harry N. Olsen).

30. As (1) above but page 1 of exhibit. See also 14H 643 in which Kathy is reported as telling Arlen Specter: "But we couldn't (marry) because of me working, and, you know, the police department, the wives couldn't work in a place like that, you know."

31. 14H 642-643 (Testimony of Kay Helen Olsen).

32. 14H 643 (Testimony of Kay Helen Olsen).

33. Information supplied by the late Mary Ferrell. To complicate things even further, I learnt from Indiana researcher Martha Moyer that Dale's wife, a stewardess with American Airlines, was living in the next apartment to Jack Ruby under her maiden name. This was undoubtedly to get around the American Airlines ruling that their stewardesses remain unmarried. Whether there was a connection between Bobby Joe Dale and Jack Ruby is open to conjecture.

34. CE 2318 (FBI report dated December 16, 1963 of interview of Patrolman Harry Olsen at Dallas Tex.)

35. As (20) above.

36. As (34) above.

37. 5H 193 (Testimony of Jack Ruby).

38. 5H 191 (Testimony of Jack Ruby).

39. 14H 650 (Testimony of Kay Helen Olsen).

40. 14H 650-651 (Testimony of Kay Helen Olsen). She describes the

mysterious Henrietta trip in some detail. As well as Harry's parents she and Harry visited "another friend of the family" also called Harry. She did not say who he was or why they met him and Mr. Specter never bothered to ask.

41. 15H 214 (Testimony of Thomas Stewart Palmer).
42. FBI Outside Contact report dated 14th August 1978, describing interview of Harry Olsen in San Jose, California. Copy in author's possession.
43. 14H 653 (Testimony of Kay Helen Olsen).
44. According to CD 4, page 442, this establishment was owned by Jake Samara, an associate of Jack Ruby.
45. As (20) above.
46. 14H 637 (Testimony of Harry N. Olsen) and CE 2433 (FBI reports dated July 31 and August 11, 13, 22 and 27, 1964, of checkout examination of telephone company records for Harry Olsen and Kathie (sic) Kay Coleman subsequent to November 14, 1963), page 5 of exhibit, (25H 538).
47. Copy of this document in author's possession.
48. George Michel Evica: *And We Are All Mortal*, University of Hartford, USA, 1978, pp. 97, 110-111.
49. DPD Criminal Intelligence Section internal memorandum dated 28th January 1964, Detective Westphal to Captain Gannaway. Copy in author's possession. I visited the church, which is situated at 1304 South Hampton, Dallas, on 18th November 1999. The Pastor, Dr Frank E. Mace, was very obliging but was unable to add anything of significance other than to inform me that the relevant official records are now housed at the Courts Building in Dallas.
50. 14H 637 (Testimony of Harry N. Olsen.
51. DPD Criminal Intelligence Section internal memorandum dated 5th March 1964, Detective Westphal to Captain Gannaway. Copy in author's possession.
52. As (26) above but page 6 of exhibit at 25H 539.
53. Warren Commission testimony given before Assistant Counsel Arlen Specter in Room 644 (Grand Jury Room) of the US Post Office Building, 312 North Spring Street, Los Angeles commencing at 4.30pm on 6th August 1964. (Harry Olsen had testified at this *venue* at 2.50pm the same day.) This building, which also incorporates the Hall of Justice, was to become the venue for the Charles Manson 'Family' murder trial (1970-71) and the O.J. Simpson murder trial (1994-95).
54. San Francisco FBI communication to Director, FBI, dated 10th September 1976. Copy in author's possession.
55. This strange incident is described fully in J. Gary Shaw's comprehensive article "A 'Smoking Gun" for the Grassy Knoll' published in *Dateline Dallas*, vol. 1, no. 4 dated 30th December 1994.
56. 15H 428 (Testimony of Nancy Monnell Powell)

ACKNOWLEDGEMENTS

As I explained in the preamble to this paper, I am not at liberty to divulge all of the primary sources which I have used here. Several people who have assisted my research must, at their own request, remain anonymous.

Much information was gleaned from the Warren Commission testimony of both Harry Neal Olsen (14H 624-640) and Kay Helen Olsen (14H 640-655). I have also referred occasionally to the testimony of some of the 18 other people who mentioned Kathy Kay when they appeared before the Commission.

I would acknowledge with gratitude the generous assistance I have received from fellow researchers Malcolm Blunt, Barbara Carlyon and Melanie Swift (in the UK) and from Brian Edwards,George Michael Evica, the late Mary Ferrell, Larry Hancock, Martha Moyer, Rachel Rendish, Gary Shaw, Russ Shearer, Hal Verb, Betty Windsor and the late Mike Blackwell (in the USA), together with others (who know who they are!).

Several acquaintances of Kathy Kay, notably Beverly Oliver, the late Shari Angel and ex-Oak Cliff neighbour Johnny Calvin Brewer, have been particularly helpful.

Some excellent photographs of Kathy Kay can be found in the Warren Commission 26 Volumes. See Armstrong Exhibit No. 5300, a series of six photographs showing Kathy Kay with Alice Anderson ('Alice from Dallas') and Jack Ruby. Armstrong Exhibit No. 5303-I is a photograph, believed to have been taken by freelance photographer Eddie Rocco about two weeks before the assassination. It shows Kathy Kay on the Carousel Club main runway during her act. A note on the Contents page of Volume 19 states that the photographs Nos. 5303 A - H "are not reproduced because of their questionable taste and negligible relevance." I have acquired copies of them and they all appear to show Kathy Kay. By today's standards they are perfectly acceptable.

Written between 1994 and 1996.
Originally published July 1998 in *The Dealey Plaza Echo*, vol. 2, no. 2.
Revised and expanded 1999.
Further expanded 2000.
Abridged version published 22nd March 2003 in *The East Anglian Daily Times*.
Presented as an exhibit at the JFK-Lancer November in Dallas conference, 2000.

Updated 2005.

Presented as a research paper at the DPUK Seminar, Canterbury, Kent, June 2005. Incorporated into a longer piece entitled "Kathy Kay, Jack Ruby and Harry Olsen" and presented as a research paper at the JFK-Lancer November in Dallas conference, 2005.

21. An interview with Shari Angel

INTRODUCTION

On Saturday 19th November 1994, at the Adolphus Hotel, Dallas, I conducted a tape-recorded interview with former Carousel Club dancer Shari Angel. She had no idea in advance what I would ask her. I think the results are fascinating as Shari talks freely about Jack Ruby, the Carousel Club, some of her fellow strippers, the Dallas Police and her thoughts on the assassination and the murder of Lee Harvey Oswald. Finally, at the end of the interview, she drops a bombshell concerning a meeting involving Jack Ruby and Lyndon B. Johnson.

Some of the things Shari told me will, I know, raise a few eyebrows. However, having spoken with her at length many times both before and after this interview, I am satisfied that she was telling me the truth as she sees it. Shari has a peculiar habit of lowering her voice at the end of a sentence when she says something that she believes to be true but which she knows will perhaps surprise or even shock the listener. Shari did that on several occasions during this interview.

You may believe or disbelieve Shari Angel's answers to my questions. I have no reason to query anything she told me.

THE INTERVIEW

(What follows is a transcription of the tape I had running, with Shari's knowledge and approval, during the interview. It has been edited only for the sake of clarity and continuity. None of the questions or answers have been materially changed.)

ILG: First of all, Shari, would you just tell me how you started at the Carousel Club and how you first met Jack Ruby.

SA: I met Jack when I was 15 years old at the Silver Spur Inn, here in Dallas. The Silver Spur, you know. The Roundup. We used to go in there and dance a lot when we were kids and that's how we met. Me and Candy and those others, to do the be-bop.

ILG: That's Candy Barr?

SA: Uh huh. And I met Jack there. I've known him since I was a kid. My father was a racketeer here in Dallas and they knew me through that. That's why Jack cried when I got sick and he always treated me like I was a little kid.

ILG: You obviously liked Jack. That comes through in what you're saying.

SA: Oh yeah, yeah.

ILG: He treated you well?

SA: Very well.

ILG: And you were 15 when you began?

SA: Yeah—when I was a kid. Me and Jack went to other clubs and other places, and then, you see, I started working for Barney at the Theatre Lounge. He was my manager.

ILG: That's Barney Weinstein?

SA: Yes, that's right.

ILG: Right.

SA: And he was my manager. Barney. And Abe Weinstein, we worked for him, he was Barney's brother. And he was kind of a manager-type thing. They was brothers. And then one night, um, Wally—that's Wally Weston, my husband—got mad at Abe. It was something after we'd been there nine years— at the Theatre Lounge. He got my wardrobe, and his, and we went over to Jack's and we started there. I was Jack's feature and Wally was his comedian for three years.

WORKING FOR JACK RUBY

ILG: So you worked for Jack Ruby for three years? With Wally, with your husband?

SA: That's right.

ILG: And he was the emcee comedian. And you worked there at the same time. What about some of the other girls at the Carousel at that time, Shari? I'm interested in people like Kathy Kay.

SA: Kathy?

ILG: Kathy Kay. She was English.

SA: She was my pal. She spoke a lot of cockney.

ILG: Good!

SA: Yes, she was my pal. And she was from England. And she had two children by a soldier, when they moved down here. She divorced her soldier, her husband, and she and her two children stayed here.

ILG: Her soldier husband. Was that a man called Kennerd?

SA: Uh huh.

ILG: And then she married .....

SA: Harry Living .....

(laughter)

ILG: Oh no!

SA: Now the laugh's on me. It was Harry Olsen.

ILG: This is good stuff! Now he was a Dallas police officer, wasn't he?

SA: Yes.

ILG: Now, I'm interested in Harry Olsen.

SA: Well he was married and she was married and they went together and was in love for a long time and everything. And when the assassination happened, they left and got married.

ILG: How did they meet? Did they meet at the Carousel Club?

SA: Uh huh.

ILG: They did?

SA: Yeah.

ILG: So Harry Olsen was a serving police officer and he visited the Carousel Club?

SA: Yeah that's right.

ILG: Was that usual?

SA: He stayed there. He went everywhere we went.

ILG: Really?

SA: Like we'd go ice-skating or to the Veterans' Hospital. Jack did all that good work. We'd do shows that Jack put on for the Veterans' Hospital. Uh, Jack Kennedy had a JFK 50 mile hike for all the colleges and schools and Wally was the first one to walk that in Dallas, even passing the newspaper reporters and everything, and Jack would drive along beside him and feed him sandwiches and drinks and everything. But Wally couldn't stop, he said, because his feet would swell up. He had to keep trotting. He couldn't quit trotting. But he made it and we had to get an ambulance for him, but he made it.

ILG: Fifty miles for charity?

SA: Fifty miles. He beat the newspapers, radio, all of them.

ILG: I remember seeing a photograph—I think it was taken inside the Carousel Club—of a poster which was boasting about it. Wally Weston, our emcee, our comedian, has done this hike.

SA: It was a photograph of his feet.

ILG: Really. Were you married to him then or was this before?

SA: Oh yeah, I was married to Wally. I was at the Colony Club. I was just a young kid.

ILG: That's Weinstein's club? Abe Weinstein's club?

SA: Yeah. And he worked for Abe for nine years and Dallas was his. Like

Sinatra. Dallas was his home town. And he sang songs like 'You're nobody till someone loves you'—he sang that to me all the time. But anyway, Wally was a great guy and the best comedian. He won all the awards here in Dallas. Everything. Until this nightmare happened.

HARRY OLSEN'S LEG INJURY

ILG: I'd like to go back to Harry Olsen briefly, Shari. Earlier on today, at a presentation here at the ASK conference, you mentioned how Harry Olsen got the injury to his leg that prevented him being on duty the day that President Kennedy was killed. Would you tell me again how he sustained that injury.

SA: Err—Jack Ruby ran over him with a pair of hockey skates on out at Fair Park ice arena. We were all out there ice-skating and he broke Harry's leg. Kathy and Harry and Jack and me.

ILG: This was an accident? This wasn't deliberate?

SA: Oh no. Jack didn't mean it.

ILG: How long before the assassination was this?

SA: Right soon.

ILG: Okay. And it was because of that, obviously, that Harry was off duty on the 22nd of November?

SA: With a broken leg.

ILG: Now you told me that Harry Olsen was seeing Kathy Kay. How did that go down with Jack Ruby? Did he approve of this or not?

SA: Oh yeah, he loved Harry—we all loved each other.

ILG: How about a policeman dating one of his girls? Was that okay with Jack?

SA: Yeah, Jack did nothing.

POLICE PAYOLA

ILG: It's a point in question with a lot of researchers how many police officers used to use the Carousel Club. How many do you think there were?

SA: Oh they were also in the Theatre Lounge, the Colony Club .....

ILG: All the clubs?

SA: Yeah. Because they all got payola, okay? They got paid to look over—a lot of stuff. Like champagne after hours in coffee cups. And it was just normal. You could see 'em right up to the office, getting their little pay.

ILG: Are we talking about detectives as well as patrolmen?

SA: Oh yes, detectives. Patrolmen didn't usually do it. It was detectives, vice squad and all that. That's when they had all this big-name stuff. They said the vice squad and this and that and whoever, wouldn't lock you up.

ILG: What was Harry Olsen? He was a patrolman, wasn't he?

SA: He was a patrolman, yes.

ILG: There are stories about his whereabouts when the President was assassinated. Have you any views on that? Did he have any connection with it at all?

SA: Not that I know of.

ILG: Not that you know of?

SA: Err, Kathy and I were very close. We were best of friends. And we'd run around together, and she'd come to my house, I'd go to her house and we always went together. We were just like a family. But she and Tammi True fought like cats and dogs.

ILG: Really? Kathy Kay and Tammi True?

SA: They loathed each other. If you'd go to the bathroom, they'd be socking it out.

ILG: Yeah?

SA: Yeah. She wouldn't take much off her, that English girl.

ILG: What about the two girls who wrote the book *Ruby's Girls*? That's Alice Anderson and Diana Hunter. Did you know them?

SA: Yeah, they were champagne girls.

ILG: I'm English, you'll have to help me here. What exactly does that mean, Shari? What did a champagne girl actually do?

SA: It means like you sell bottles of champagne. Back in 1962 you could sell a bottle for 25 dollars. Cheap bottles that you could buy for 5-99. But then guys was so—back then there wasn't all this TV, movies, all this stuff. All they wanted to come and see was this downtown live.

ILG: Right.

SA: And they knew they was being suckered in. That the girl would get five dollars on a bottle and two-fifty on a cocktail. And—err—that's what a champagne girl is. They'd get played with, and all this dancing, you know. I never was one 'cos I was married to Wally and he wouldn't allow it and Barney wouldn't ask me to work the place like that.

ILG: Diana Hunter—didn't she strip sometimes? Wasn't she a part-time stripper?

SA: No. After Jack killed Oswald, she and Andrew and 'Alice from Dallas' got into a little conflict. Andrew says he was the manager. He wasn't.

ILG: This is Andy Armstrong?

SA: Yeah. Jack had no managers, no bouncers. He did all that himself.

ILG: When you say he had no bouncers, this is where if someone was causing trouble he would take them out and they're down the stairs?

SA: Oh yeah!

ILG: Did that happen very often, Shari?

SA: Oh gosh, every night. (laughter) Then he had to take more people and I had to cook more on Sunday.

ILG: What sort of things would someone have to do in the Carousel Club to have Jack Ruby throw them down the stairs like that?

SA: Lots of stuff. But he was a very kind, sweet person. Treated people. Went out to the Veterans' Hospital. Took care of them on Sundays when nobody cared about them. I mean this is stuff that nobody ever gives Jack credit for. I loved Jack. He never one time embarrassed me or abused me. One time I got so sick at the club and the man downstairs come and picked me up and an ambulance took me to the thing. But anyway, Jack cried. He says he remembers Jack crying about me going to hospital. And Jack was right out there. So—I loved Jack. I knew only good things.

The bad things was—I seen the Mafia in there so often—maybe once a month—so-and-so he knew from Chicago. But I got to know them too much and my husband did too, so I shut up and he disappeared.

ILG: Where were you when Jack shot Oswald? Do you remember that?

SA: I was laying in my bed at home, in Maryland Apartments, watching—looking at it on TV.

ILG: You actually saw it happen on TV?

SA: I knew when I saw the back of his head that it was Jack. It happened right fast but I mean I knew it was Jack.

LEE HARVEY OSWALD IN THE CAROUSEL CLUB

ILG: Now, the man that Jack Ruby killed that day—the man we believe was Lee Harvey Oswald .....

SA: Lee Harvey Oswald.

ILG: Now, had you ever seen that man in the club at all?

SA: Oh yeah.

ILG: You'd seen Lee Oswald in the Carousel Club?

SA: My husband hit him for calling him a Communist. He served in World

War Two. He didn't like that very much.

ILG: Oswald called Wally a Communist?

SA: Yeah.

ILG: Then what did Wally do?

SA: He hit him. Knocked him out.

(laughter)

ILG: And then what? Did Jack intervene and take over?

SA: Yeah. He got rid of Oswald. I don't know what he did with him but he disappeared.

ILG: He threw him out?

SA: I don't know if he threw him out or told him to go home or what.

ILG: And what was Jack's reaction then to Wally? After Wally had done that.

SA: Oh, he loved Wally. Didn't hit him or anything. Wally was Jack's whole life. Wally was such a great, great comedian. Getting Wally Weston in his club was the greatest thing he ever did. And me too, because I was Barney and Abe's little darling.

ILG: Right. Now you were known as—you did a Gypsy Rose Lee act, didn't you?

SA: Yeah. Dallas's answer to Gypsy Rose Lee.

ILG: I read, I think it was in *Ruby's Girls*, in the book, that Diana the Huntress once fired an arrow from the stage .....

SA: And she hit the big gold sign—and Jack fired her. (laughter) It was his pride, that big gold horse.

ILG: It was a big horse on the wall, wasn't it?

SA: Yeah, it was gold. And she reached that. I wasn't there because she never got to dance when I was there. Anyway, she pulled back and hit that and put a hole in there. Jack couldn't stand her.

ILG: Really?

SA: Oh he threatened to kill her worse than he did most drunks who came up there.

ILG: So he fired her for that but then he re-hired her, didn't he?

SA: Yeah.

ILG: And she came back?

SA: Yeah.

ILG: Did you ever know Geneva White?

SA: No. I knew of her. I knew her husband. I went off sick just a little bit before … err … so they brought Jada in to take my place. I had peritonitis. And … err … while I was off, Geneva's supposed to come to work. But I don't remember her because I wasn't there.

ILG: I see. But you knew her husband?

SA: Oh yeah.

ILG: He used to come to the club, did he?

SA: Yeah.

ILG: What, regularly?

SA: Oh yeah.

ILG: Did he know Jack Ruby?

SA: Oh yeah.

ILG: Now what about Oswald? How often did you see Lee Oswald in the club?

SA: I've only seen him about three or four times in the club. 'Cos I took off sick.

ILG: But you saw him with Jack?

SA: Oh, I saw my husband drop him on his behind. But Wally was a featherweight or a lightweight or something. A fighter growing up in Wisconsin.

ILG: So he could handle himself. He knew what to do.

SA: He was getting on but he sure did. He was tall and thin but he could bounce 'em.

ILG: Shari, the other girls. We've spoken about Kathy Kay and Tammi True. What about Little Lynn?

SA: Little Lynn I didn't know too well because that was when I was getting sick. I thought she was pregnant when she first started. I may be wrong. But the way I'm thinking is that real young little girl was pregnant. And, err, I was so sick but Wally would take me up there some nights. And, um, I heard that she was assassinated. So I don't know. I heard that vibe from everything that was done. Jack sent her 25 dollars and all that and that's what I heard. Whether she is alive or not I do not know.

KATHY KAY

ILG: What about Kathy Kay? I've heard reports she's dead. I've also heard reports she's alive.

SA: No, she's alive.

ILG: I've had people tell me she may be living in California. Do you think that's true?

SA: I think she's in California. She's not dead.

ILG: What about Olsen?

SA: They're divorced.

ILG: Oh I see. Any idea where he may be?

SA: No.

ILG: After the assassination and after Jack Ruby killed Oswald, Shari, what happened to the club then? I mean Ruby was obviously out of the scene then. Did the club carry on under somebody else?

SA: No. It carried on a few days but nobody important worked there.

ILG: And what happened to it then? Did it ever reopen?

SA: It became a police gymnasium.

ILG: So it didn't operate again as a club?

SA: It did for a few days but Andrew, 'Diana the Huntress' and 'Alice from Dallas' tried to keep it open but they couldn't.

ILG: So then it became a police gymnasium and that was that. Where did you go to work when the Carousel had closed?

SA: Over at the Theatre Lounge with Wally. He come in town 'cos he'd been out of town. People knew this move was coming, but not against Kennedy. We knew that something was going real big so Jack got Wally to go to Oklahoma for the weekend to work. And when Wally came back in town he took my wardrobe back to the Theatre Lounge for me, and my manager stood there by me all the way through the questions and everything. He was there on the Sunday night. He never came to town on Sunday nights unless something was wrong. And FBI Joe Brown—which I considered a good friend of mine—but he died.

ILG: Was there anything in Jack Ruby's behaviour that, you know, between Kennedy being killed and .....

SA: I tell you, Jack cried, because he loved Jack Kennedy. He and Wally and us campaigned for Jack Kennedy. We voted for Jack Kennedy.

JACK RUBY AFTER THE ASSASSINATION

ILG: So after Kennedy was shot, Ruby was obviously affected by that?

SA: He loved the Kennedys. But, um we don't know. Wally talked—I was with him on his dying day but Wally talked to him right after it happened 'cos he was—only two of us could usually visit him.

ILG: Did you visit Ruby when he was dying of cancer?

SA: I visited him all the time in jail. They called me to come down there and calm him down and stuff. But anyway, I loved Jack. I'm sorry but that's how I feel.

ILG: I know. That shows.

SA: I mean if somebody mistreats me, it shows in my eyes. Like he wasn't no molester, he wasn't no queer. Excuse me but that's what they tried to say.

ILG: I've read the Warren Commission questions and that was asked of a lot of people. But he was a straight guy?

SA: Far as I knew.

ILG: Did he ever date any of the girls?

SA: No. He had a girlfriend he's had for years but he never brought her around any of us. She was an older woman. I can't think of her name. He had her for years and years. (*I believe this was a lady called Alice Reaves Nicholls - see Gary Wills and Ovid Demaris: "Jack Ruby", DaCapo Press New York, 1994, page 40 - ILG.*)

ILG: So he was natural as far as sex goes? He wasn't gay.

SA: He never did around me. Now I remember one time—Tawny Angel, this girl named Tawny Angel, went to his door, she told me he dropped his pants and she was at the door, and he reached—you know, pardon me—all that. Whether that was true or not, I do not know. That is the only thing I've ever heard bad about Jack himself. But I don't believe her, she's an alcoholic. (laughter) Jack didn't even drink. We never knew Jack going out and having a drink. Jack did not drink liquor, he did not smoke, he did not take dope.

Jack Ruby and Lyndon Johnson

ILG: Shari, just one more question. This is probably the most difficult of all. Why did Jack Ruby shoot Lee Harvey Oswald?

SA: (Lowering her voice almost to a whisper) 'Cos he was told to.

ILG: You honestly believe that? It was a Mafia hit? It wasn't this thing about saving Jackie?

SA: Lyndon Johnson had it done.

ILG: Johnson?

SA: I'll always believe that with all my heart and soul. Did you notice the motorcade? Jack Kennedy did not have one security guard riding on his car. Johnson's was filled with 'em. I'll never believe anything else and I have seen Jack Ruby and President Lyndon Baines Johnson together in this same hotel where we are right now.

ILG: In the Adolphus Hotel, here on Commerce Street?

SA: Yeah—me and Madeleine Brown saw them.

ILG: When was that, Shari?

SA: Err, that was before the assassination.

ILG: So you're telling me that before the assassination, here in the Adolphus Hotel in Dallas, you saw Jack Ruby with the Vice President .....

SA: And H. L. Hunt, W. O. Bankston, all these people. A lawyer, I forgot his name. And Lyndon—and Madeleine was with me.

ILG: Madeleine Brown.

SA: She was still in love with him, with Lyndon. She told me to come over here. I didn't know what was going on over here.

ILG: About when was this, Shari? How long before the assassination?

SA: Probably about three or four months before the assassination.

ILG: So the story that was put out that Jack Ruby shot Oswald to save Jackie the pain of a court job—that's nonsense. Is that what you believe?

SA: Yes, but he loved Jackie, he really did.

ILG: Shari, it's been a delight talking to you. I'm grateful for your time and all I can say is thanks.

SA: You're quite welcome.

Written 1995
First published March 1999 on the Australian internet website *JFK Link*, no. 1.
Later published November 1999 in *The Dealey Plaza Echo,* vol. 3, no. 3.

22. A brief examination of Jack Ruby's possessions at the time of his arrest

"Jack Ruby's pockets and the trunk of his car served as his bank."
(Warren Report, page 797)

INTRODUCTION

What follows are a few comments on items of personal property belonging to Jack Ruby. I begin with a brief account of his arrest. I then discuss those items found on his person when he was searched after that arrest and continue with the contents of his car. [1] I have not dealt with the contents of his residence at this point.

The searches of Jack Ruby's person and his car revealed a large variety of items. Some were personal possessions and others were connected with his business at the Carousel Club. Some, such as aluminium knuckles, may well have come within either category. I will save the reader the trouble of continuing to look here if he hopes to find some reference to the oft-claimed Oswald/Ruby connection. I will confess that I hoped to stumble across something to substantiate that, but I have to admit that there was absolutely nothing to suggest or support any such link.

THE ARREST OF JACK RUBY

This was undoubtedly one of the fastest, most widely witnessed and best-publicised arrests in the history of crime. It occurred about a second after the commission of the offence and was seen simultaneously by millions of TV watchers throughout the United States. The Dallas police may have arrested the wrong man two days earlier but there can be no question that they got the right man on this occasion.

The murder for which Ruby was arrested was simplicity itself. He stepped forward from the cover of a group of pressmen, thrust his snub-nosed .38 Colt Cobra under the left side of his victim's rib cage and fired a single shot before being immediately overpowered and disarmed. That bullet struck just about every vital organ in his victim's body except his brain—truly a magic bullet! Ruby's target, of course, was Lee Harvey Oswald, the alleged assassin of President John F. Kennedy. Jack Ruby's single shot, which was to bring about the formation of the Warren Commission a few days later, was fired at 11.21am CST on Sunday 24th November 1963. [(2)]

In his Warren Commission testimony, Detective Don Ray Archer, one of several police officers involved in the arrest, claimed that Ruby said to him: "Well, I intended to shoot him three times." [(3)]

Oswald had been brought from the third floor (Room 317) of the Dallas Police Department Headquarters at City Hall to the police garage in the basement of the building. The object was to transport him swiftly, securely and safely to the Dallas County Jail on Houston Street, overlooking Dealey Plaza. Ruby, however, had other ideas and the result was what the Warren Commission rather quaintly referred to as the abortive transfer. [(4)] The only thing to be aborted was Oswald's life. He was rushed to Parkland Hospital, and was brought to the emergency operating room there at 11.32am. This was a mere 11 minutes after Ruby's shot. He was treated immediately but never regained consciousness and was declared dead at 1.07pm the same day. [(5)]

THE SEARCH OF RUBY'S PERSON

Within seconds of shooting Oswald, Jack Ruby had been hustled away to the jail office and searched. The search of a newly-arrested prisoner is standard police procedure and fulfils four basic purposes. Firstly to take possession of anything which may be of evidential value; secondly, to seize anything with which the prisoner may cause injury or damage; thirdly, to remove anything which may aid the prisoner's escape, and finally to take from him anything with which he may attempt to harm himself.

As with several other aspects of this case, there is some confusion as to exactly who did what. According to a record produced by Assistant Jailer Billy G. King: "Ruby had been searched by Kenneth Hoake, Jailer, Dallas City Police Department on November 24, 1963 on the fourth floor of the Dallas City Police Headquarters, which houses the jail" [(6)]

In his own Warren Commission testimony, however, Detective Don Ray Archer, a member of the Auto Theft Bureau, described how he and between two and four other police officers took Ruby up to the fifth floor (where the cellblock was situated). There they carried out a thorough search of his person. Archer's comment about this is one of the oddest I can recall in any testimony given in this case. He said: "We stripped him and stripped him of his clothing, and I wasn't too interested in personal property, but mainly searching for weapons or bombs, or anything else he might have concealed on him." [(7)]

Yes, you did read that correctly—bombs.

In response to a question as to whether any personal property had been found on the prisoner, Detective Archer replied: "Yes, sir, I searched him. I did remove some personal property. I recall a large roll of money and perhaps some change. I'm not sure about that. The main thing I remember was the large roll of money."

Detective Archer went on to state that "one of the other jailers, uniformed jail officers, Haake, (sic) came up and what personal property I took out of his pockets, I handed right to him. I didn't bother to itemize it or anything else, because it is their job, not ours ..." [8]

The testimony of Detective Leslie Dell Montgomery (Homicide & Robbery Bureau) appears to be more explicit in identifying the officers involved in this personal search. He names Acting Detective William J. ('Blackie') Harrison and Detectives Roy Lee Lowery, Thomas Donald McMillon, Wilber J. Cutchshaw and Archer as being the officers who took Ruby upstairs. [9] It is not confirmed, however, that all of them actually participated in the search.

All of Ruby's possessions seized during that initial search of his person were listed, presumably by Patrolman/Jailer Kenneth H. Haake [10] and they now make very strange reading. Some of them are exactly what you would expect to find in any man's possession; others are very revealing, and some are strange. I will also mention later two items which one would expect to find but which were conspicuous by their absence.

PROPERTY FOUND ON RUBY'S PERSON

When the property found on Ruby was listed, it consisted of 34 items. Many of these listed 'items', however, consisted of more than one single object. [11]

The "large roll of money" mentioned by Detective Archer was an accurate description. It was exactly that. It amounted to $2,014, comprising nine $100 bills, forty $20 bills, thirty $10 bills, two $5 bills and four $1 bills. That sort of money was no small sum back in November 1963 and $100 bills must have been particularly unusual. Ruby had a further $1.33 in change. As will be mentioned later, a further substantial amount of cash was found in Ruby's car.

Several of Ruby's items of personal jewellery confirmed his determination to maintain a 'class' image. There was a ring with three diamonds, a 14 carat gold and diamond Le Coultre wrist watch, a necktie which was described as '100 percent silk' and two tie clasps, one silver and one gold-plated. It is not clear from the DPD documentation which, if either, he was actually wearing at the time of his arrest.

Together with all the 'normal' items such as a comb, several pens, keys and a pair of spectacles, Jack Ruby's pockets appear to have been crammed with a great variety of business cards, receipts, photographs, letters and assorted papers. One of the most important individual items was listed by the DPD as follows:

> "A Western Union Telegram, date stamped 11:16 AM, November 24, 1963, Addressed to KAREN BENNETT, Western Union, Ft. Wprth, *(sic)* for $25 from JACK RUBY, 1313½ Commerce Street." [12]

That is exactly how the note was written in the DPD listing, including the time error (the telegram had actually been dispatched at 11.17am), the misspelling of 'Worth' and the error in the street number of the Carousel Club (it should have been 1312½).

This particular document was later to prove of great importance in establishing Ruby's whereabouts and movements immediately before the Oswald shooting.

The vast majority of the paperwork scattered about Ruby's person appears to have been connected with the Carousel Club, including business cards for the club and the names, addresses and telephone numbers of many past, present and potential performers there.

As I have already mentioned briefly, two items which one would expect him to carry were not found. It would appear that Jack Ruby had the need for neither a handkerchief nor a wallet on this particular morning.

When the search of Ruby's person had been completed, he was locked in cell F2 in the City Hall cellblock on the fifth floor. Either by accident or design, this was the same cell that had been occupied by Lee Harvey Oswald prior to his murder at Ruby's hand.

THE SEARCH OF RUBY'S CAR

At the time of this incident, Jack Ruby owned and drove a "1960 Oldsmobile, two door, white in color, bearing 1963 Texas License PD-678." [13]

According to the Dallas FBI Office, the search of Ruby's Oldsmobile, which he had left on a parking lot on the north-east corner of Main and Pearl Streets, was carried out by "Detective Richard E. Swain, Jr." and "other detectives." [14] The problem here is that there was no such person on the strength of the Dallas Police Department. The only Richard E. Swain (there was no Jr. suffix) was a Lieutenant in the Burglary & Theft Bureau. [15] His duties on 24th

November 1963 are clearly described in his official report to Chief Curry (dated 4th December 1963) but they did not include the searching of Ruby's car. [16] In the testimony of Lieutenant Vernon S. Smart of the Auto Theft Bureau, however, he (Lieutenant Swain) is mentioned as being present at that search. [17]

It is almost certain that the names of these officers have been confused or misread or both. Lieutenant Smart was the man specifically instructed by Assistant Chief Stevenson to carry out the search of Ruby's car. The initial stages of the attempted search did not proceed smoothly and the Warren Commission testimony of two car park attendants, John L. Daniels and Theodore Jackson, makes amusing reading as they describe how they watched the actions of the police during the search of the car. [18]

Ruby had parked his car on the All State Parking Lot, situated on the north-eastern corner of the Main Street/Pearl Street intersection, directly across the street from the Western Union office. [19] There was no parking attendant there when he parked at a few minutes past 11.00am. As we shall see shortly, he removed the keys from the ignition but did not lock the car. For some unexplained reason in view of what he was about to do, he left Sheba, his favourite dachshund, on the front seat of the car. He did, however, retrieve his revolver from its usual place in the trunk (boot) of the car and take it with him. According to Larry Craford, one of Ruby's Carousel Club employees, Ruby kept his revolver "in a money sack in the trunk of the car." [20]

In the light of much conflicting information, I have decided to rely on the evidence of Lieutenant Smart in trying to establish the truth about the car search. [21]

His instructions from Assistant Chief Stevenson were to go to the parking lot, search the car, remove a sum of money from it (amount unspecified), take the car to the pound and then return to the police station with the money. In addition, he was ordered to take a dog from the car and have it placed in an animal shelter. Accompanied by Lieutenant Swain, he found the car to be unlocked and "the dog had crawled under a newspaper in the front seat." In his own words: "We had the squad come by and get it and take it to the animal shelter."

PROPERTY FOUND IN RUBY'S CAR

Lieutenant Smart began his search of Jack Ruby's Oldsmobile by opening up the glove compartment. No explanation of this is offered but I think it likely that Ruby had mentioned to the police that he kept the key to the trunk in there. The glove compartment was found to contain Ruby's wallet, some business cards and the trunk key. The wallet, described as a billfold, contained Ruby's driver's license and several cards of identification, but no cash.

Underneath the wallet, Lieutenant Smart found a single General Motors key. After trying it in the ignition switch and finding that it did not fit, he rightfully assumed that it would fit the trunk and he then proceeded to search the trunk before continuing with the interior of the car.

All the property found in Ruby's car, with the exception of Sheba, was carefully listed and described in as much detail as necessary. Like the items removed from Ruby's person, this list of property makes fascinating reading.
(22)

Assistant Counsel Burt W. Griffin, questioning Lieutenant Smart during his Warren Commission testimony, asked him: "What did you see when you opened that trunk?" He replied: "Well, some paper bags and some bank sacks, maybe one bank sack, and just full of junk, except there was a set of keys laying right down in the open." Our Mr. Ruby does not appear to have been the world's tidiest man.

One of the keys did indeed fit the car's ignition. Lieutenant Smart also found "the money" and he took possession of it as instructed. Leaving the vehicle where it was, he returned to City Hall where he handed over the wallet, the keys and the money (which had been inside a large grocery bag) to "these two homicide officers. All I did was count the money and initial it." The money amounted to $873.50, including approximately $73.50 in silver and about $400 in $5 bills. It would be expected that Lieutenant Smart would have written and submitted a report of his actions in respect of that car search—but he did not. This was queried quite strenuously by Assistant Counsel Griffin.
(23)

Later the same day, detectives from the Homicide & Robbery Bureau completed the search of the vehicle and Detective Guy Rose compiled a comprehensive list. (24) Some of the more noteworthy items found were as follows:

- 59 numbered Permanent Passes to the Carousel Club in respect of a variety of people, including Dallas District Attorney Bill Alexander, Andy Anderson (the manager of the Adolphus Hotel), Dallas Police Patrolman Ray Hawkins, several local media people (press and radio) and some local businessmen.
- An item described as "Pistol holster, musty and moldy, for snub-nose"
- A "set of aluminium knuckles"
- A "Wynnewood State Bank zipper bag containing a new set of aluminium knuckles" (I am tempted to ask how they could be recognized as "new" as opposed to the preceding pair, described as "used".)
- One Victor Adding Machine, serial number 1743-377.
- Several crutch or chair leg rubber tips (huh?)

The following assortment of strange and apparently unrelated objects was also found:

- A dog muzzle
- An umbrella
- A radio
- A partially filled can of varnish stain
- A pair of long white ladies gloves
- A black plastic raincoat
- A paper For Sale sign
- A white bathing cap
- A pair of brown golf shoes (size 10½)
- A phonograph record entitled *Figure Control for Women*
- A carton containing several hundred 8 x 10 glossy photographs of exotic dancer "Jada"
- A "Twist Waist Exerciser"

There were also assorted items of gentleman's clothing, including slacks, a sports jacket and a grey two-piece suit.

In keeping with Ruby's use of the trunk as an office, there were numerous bills, papers, documents, stationery, business cards, accounts, receipts, slips of paper bearing telephone numbers, bank drafts, telephone bills, newspaper clippings, stamps, envelopes, AGVA contracts, parking tickets, etc. He even had the Carousel Club Certificate of Occupancy and his Texas Liquor Control Board Permit in there. Should they not have been kept, perhaps even displayed, in his office?

The final part of the car to be searched appears to have been the ashtray. This was found to contain "twelve cigarette butts, some filter tip, others not filter tip, some bearing lipstick traces. Only brand name readable was Winston." Jack Ruby was a non-smoker but I would like to know who was responsible for the butts with the lipstick traces.

CONCLUSION

As mentioned earlier, the searches of Jack Ruby's person and his car revealed absolutely nothing to suggest an association between him and Lee Harvey Oswald. Jack Ruby appears to have been a very untidy and somewhat disorganized person and security does not seem to have been one of his priorities. I find this strange in view of the amounts of cash he seemed to carry around and the fact that some of the people with whom he was associated would undoubtedly have been less than tolerant if things went wrong through his sloppiness or lack of organization.

I am particularly curious about the large bankroll found on his person. The Carousel Club had been closed the previous two evenings so it was hardly the weekend's takings ... and where did Ruby get all those $100 bills? The total cash found on Ruby's person and in his car came to $2,888.83—more than enough in 1963 to buy a brand new car.

The swimming cap can be explained as his own. He used to swim each morning in the open-air pool outside his apartment block. The golf shoes are interesting for two reasons. Firstly, Jack Ruby is not the sort of person I can visualize striding round 18 holes with a bag full of niblicks and mashies, and secondly, they were size 10^1/2 (UK equivalent size 10). Surely someone of Ruby's physical stature would not have feet as big as that. [25]

This study is intended to whet the reader's curiosity rather than impart enormous amounts of new information. Even after over 40 years, the enigma that was Jack Ruby has never been fully explained. I wonder who he really was? In some ways, he is still as much a mystery figure as the unfortunate young man he was allowed to gun down in cold blood in the basement of the police station.

Notes

1. CE 1322 (FBI report dated November 25, 1963, concerning inventory of items taken by Dallas Police Department from Jack Ruby's person, automobile, and residence).
2. Warren Report, page 21.
3. 12H 401 (Testimony of Don Ray Archer).
4. This rather odd expression was coined by the Warren Commission and is really nothing more than a euphemism for "The Murder of Lee Harvey Oswald'. That section of the final Warren report dealing with Ruby's shooting of Oswald is entitled "The Abortive Transfer" (see pages 208-216).
5. CE 2024 (FBI report dated November 25, 1963, of interview of C. J. Price, administrator, Parkland Hospital, at Dallas, Tex.)
6. CE 1322, as footnote 1 above, page numbered 725 of exhibit (22H 497). It should be noted that the Jailer mentioned was Kenneth H. Haake (not Hoake, which is a misspelling).
7. 12H 400 (Testimony of Detective Don Ray Archer).
8. 12H 401 (Testimony of Detective Don Ray Archer).
9. 13H 30 (Testimony of Detective Leslie Dell Montgomery).
10. Batchelor Exhibit No. 5002 (Dallas Police Personnel Assignments,

November 1963), page 20 of exhibit (19H 137) gave this officer's name as Kenneth H. Haake. He was described as 'Patrolman (Relief) and was on jail duty (7.00am to 3.00pm).

11. CE 1322, as footnote 1 above.

12. CE 1322, as footnote 1 above, page numbered 726 on exhibit (22H 498). The Western Union telegram is numbered (22) on the listing.

13. Smart Exhibit No. 5021 (Copy of an FBI report of an interview with Lieutenant Vernon S. Smart, dated November 25, 1963)

14. CE 1322, as footnote 1 above, page numbered 732 on exhibit (22H 501).

15. Batchelor Exhibit No. 5002, as footnote 10 above, page 29 of exhibit (19H 146).

16. CE 2002 (Dallas Police Department file on investigation of operational security involving the transfer of Lee Harvey Oswald, November 24, 1963), page 96 of exhibit (24H 171).

17. 13H 271-276 (Testimony of Lieutenant Vernon S. Smart).

18. 13H 296-299 (Testimony of John L. Daniels); 13H 299-302 (Testimony of Theodore Jackson).

19. See Smart Exhibit No. 5023 (Sketch drawn by Vernon S. Smart of the corner of Pearl and Main Streets in Dallas).

20. 14H 85 (Testimony of Curtis LaVerne Crafard).

21. Smart Exhibit Nos. 5021 and 5023 (described in footnotes 12 and 20 above) and Lieutenant Smart's Warren Commission testimony at 13H 271-276.

22. CE 1322, as footnote 1 above, pages of exhibit numbered from 732-761 (22H 501-515).

23. 13H 275 (Testimony of Lieutenant Vernon S. Smart).

24. CE 1322, as footnote 1 above, pages of exhibit numbered from 733 – 751 at 22H 501-510).

25. Details on Jack Ruby's Fingerprint Card, completed following his arrest, indicate him to be 5' 8¹/2" tall and weigh 179 lbs.

Written 1995.
First published Summer 1997 in *The Kennedy Assassination Chronicles*, vol. 3, no. 2.
Published March 2005 in *The Dealey Plaza Echo*, Vol. 9, No. 1.

PART VI: HOW THE WORLD REACTED

23. Kill that myth!

INTRODUCTION

In a case as complex and baffling as the Kennedy assassination, it is inevitable that some facts will become obscured, altered, misinterpreted or just lost over the years. As I have stressed on many occasions, it is essential for the serious researcher to go back to primary sources whenever possible. It is all too easy to blandly accept something as fact simply because it appears in an eminent author's book.

Even researchers and authors as reliable and thorough as Anthony Summers or Joachim Joesten are not immune, and it is possible that they could make an honest error just as easily as Joe Soap or Dolly Golightly. The problem comes when one such lauded researcher/author *does* commit an unintentional and unnoticed inexactitude and it appears in print. In later years, researchers referring to their work will have that unconscious faith that "if *he* or *she* says that, then it *must* be right!" In reality, however, that is not necessarily true.

Having mentioned the names of two of the most prominent and respected authors in this field, perhaps it is appropriate to use one of them as my first example.

THE MYTH OF THE ROMAN NUMERALS

In Anthony Summers' book *Conspiracy*, he discussed the handwritten inscriptions on the back of the 'backyard photograph' found by George de Mohrenschildt on his return from abroad (Haiti) in early 1967. [1] The inscription is dated "5/IV/63" - the style and order used by some Europeans to write a date. The first Arabic numeral indicates the 5th day of the month, the Roman IV indicates April (the fourth month) and 63 is obviously the year. Summers stated: "A researcher's check of the dozens of letters and documents written by Oswald has produced not one example of a date written like the one on the back of the photograph."

In a footnote, [2] Summers repeated that statement and wrote: "As stated, no similar trace of Roman-numeral usage can be found in Oswald's writings."

Note that in neither case did he qualify the statement by saying something like "in my opinion" or "as far as can be ascertained". No; the inference is clearly that no such example exists anywhere. That is the myth; written and published by Anthony Summers in 1980 and accepted without question by researchers ever since.

Now I would ask you to go to Warren Commission Exhibit 321. [3] This is a postcard written by Lee Harvey Oswald (in Minsk) to his brother Robert (in Fort Worth) on which the date is written as "10/V/62". In it, the message referred to Lee's daughter June being "almost 3 months old now" and since she was born on 15th February 1962, we can tell that the date on the postcard (10/V/62) is 10th May 1962.

By the same token, we can interpret the date on the back of the de Mohrenschildt 'backyard photograph' (5/IV/63) as 5th April 1963.

It is obvious that the 'researcher's check' mentioned by Summers was either incomplete or undertaken with such haste as to be worthless. Furthermore, since the alleged results of that 'researcher's check' had been described as negative by somebody of Summers' stature and status, subsequent researchers never bothered to examine its accuracy. We had to wait until that task was undertaken by my friend and fellow British researcher Melanie Swift in 1995. She found the CE 321 postcard exactly where it had been since the publication of the Warren Commission 26 Volumes, less than a year after the assassination.

In 2001, whilst researching something totally different, I stumbled across another fine example of Oswald writing the date in the European style.

CE 1314 is a single-page note written by Lee Oswald to the Director of the Minsk Radio Factory. In it, Oswald tendered his resignation. Twice, he wrote the date "18/V/62". It also appears a third time, but in another hand.

The exhibit includes an English translation which confirms the date as being 5-18-62. We can therefore accept that Oswald's notice of resignation was dated 18th May 1962. [4]

When an updated and enlarged version of *Conspiracy* was published in 1998 under the title *Not in your Lifetime* the references to the 'researcher's check' remained unaltered. [5] It seems that this is one myth which will be allowed to persist.

THE MYTH OF OSWALD AND THE DRY CLEANERS

At around 1.25pm - 1.30pm on 22nd November, a zipper jacket was found under a parked car on the parking lot behind the Texaco Service Station at the junction of West Jefferson Boulevard and Crawford, Oak Cliff. Although it was claimed in the Warren Report [6] that DPD Captain W.R. Westbrook was responsible for this find, he denied it. He stated that he had been present when it was found by somebody he believed to be a DPD officer (unnamed). Its importance lay in the fact that it was found on the route supposedly used by the killer of Officer J.D. Tippit as he fled the scene.

This is not the place to discuss the vexed question of whether or not that jacket had ever been owned by Lee Harvey Oswald. That question, however, did become the origin of another myth in the case.

A DPD Identification Bureau document listed certain items released to the FBI for examination on 28th November 1963.[7] The zipper jacket was included and described in detail as follows:

"1 - Gray mans jacket with 'M' size in collar, laundry mark 30, and 030 in collar. Zipper opening, name tag (created in California by Maurice Holman) on lining of jacket. Bearing initials WEB and GMD placed by officers. Laundry tag B-9738 on bottom of jacket."

Obviously, if investigators could trace the source(s) of those laundry marks and tie them to Oswald, their case against him would be considerably strengthened. The initials WEB and GMD obviously belonged to Detective Willie E. Barnes and Captain George M. Doughty of the DPD Crime Scene Search Section /Identification Bureau.

Canadian researcher Gary Murr, in his unpublished manuscript on the Tippit killing [8] quotes Archives CD 868, CD 1066 I and Archives CD 993, CD 1245. Here it is stated that by 21st April 1964, the FBI had contacted all 424 dry-cleaning establishments in the Dallas-Fort Worth area but had been unable to trace either laundry mark. The FBI had then extended their search to include 293 laundry and dry-cleaning establishments in the Greater New Orleans area, again with negative results. They also ascertained that none of Oswald's clothes bore similar marks.

When questioned by Warren Commission Assistant Counsel Albert Jenner, Mrs Ruth Paine agreed that neither she nor Marina Oswald "ever sent any laundry out for cleaning or washing."[9]

In an FBI report of an interview of Marina Oswald on 1st April 1964, we read the following: "She said she cannot recall that Oswald ever sent either of these jackets to any laundry or cleaners anywhere. She said she can recall washing them herself."[10]

The inference here is very clear. Lee Harvey Oswald never used a laundry or dry cleaning facility. It was left at that.

The testimony of Arthur Carl Johnson, husband of Oswald's landlady at 1026 North Beckley, should have put investigators on the right trail. In supplying background information on Oswald's activities and lifestyle, he told Assistant Counsel David Belin: "I suppose he'd go out and eat or maybe to the washateria or somewhere like that."[11] This was never followed up by Mr Belin.

Perhaps the decisive piece of information, however, has been staring us in the face for years. For this I am again indebted to researcher Melanie Swift for bringing it to my attention.

The vital document is an FBI report of an interview with Leslie Lawson, the owner and manager of Gray's Cleaners, 1209 Eldorado, Oak Cliff on 5th December 1963. [12] Although not mentioned in the interview notes, this location is only a hundred yards from Oswald's rooming house. Lawson stated that "he had seen Lee Harvey Oswald on one particular occasion that he can recall and possibly on other occasions which he could not specifically recall." Mr Lawson then said that "approximately one month ago" Lee Harvey Oswald had entered his cleaning establishment and handed in a tie, white shirt and black pair of trousers for cleaning. Two days later, when Oswald called to collect these items, he had been charged $1.25. Lawson said that Oswald was "somewhat disturbed over the fact that he was charged 25 cents for cleaning his tie."

Lawson also stated that he had seen Oswald on several occasions at Sleight's Speed Wash, 1101 North Beckley. This establishment had, in fact, changed its name to Reno's Speed Wash in August 1963. A former Reno's employee, Joseph Johnson, was interviewed by the FBI on 28th July 1964 and stated that on the evening of 20th or 21st November 1963, Lee Harvey Oswald was "washing laundry at Reno's Speed Wash." Oswald, he said, had remained there, reading magazines, until midnight. [13]

Those examples, I contend, are sufficient to show that the myth of Oswald never using any kind of laundry or dry-cleaning establishment is disproved.

THE MYTH OF THE J. D. TIPPIT PHOTOGRAPH

In his 1968 book *How Kennedy Was Killed*, the early Warren Commission critic Joachim Joesten stated that J.D. Tippit "bore a remarkable facial resemblance to Oswald." Joesten then went on to explain that the Dallas Police, being aware of this, "did not promptly make available to the press any pictures of Tippit and that his widow also kept the family album under lock and key." [14]

Joesten did not stop there. He continued: *"Indeed, there is nothing in the annals of the contemporary press to match this unique pictorial anonymity of a world celebrity"* and then stated that there is *"no picture of the great man!"* Remember, he was referring not to JFK here, but to Dallas Police Department Patrolman J. D. Tippit. Powerful stuff – but complete nonsense.

Joesten eventually divulged that "the first, and only, Tippit picture was released in connection with the Warren Report ... " [15] I presume that he was referring here to the well-known Tippit portrait that appears in the Warren Commission 26 Volumes as Carlin (Bruce Ray) Exhibit No. 1. This was, in fact, the photograph which appeared on Tippit's DPD Identity Card—despite the fact that Tippit is wearing a highly-patterned open-necked shirt and looks more like an extra from Hawaii Five-O than a Dallas cop. Furthermore, it is hardly "the first, and only" such picture as there is another photograph of Tippit immediately below it, on the same page. [16] (*Author's note: Personally, I cannot see any such likeness between the two men.*)

It is unfortunate that Joachim Joesten did not go to the trouble of checking the facts before he went into print so positively and vehemently on this point. Had he done so, he would very probably have come across the Hugh Aynesworth story on page 5 of Section 4 in the *Dallas Morning News* of Saturday 23rd November 1963.

That same photograph appears alongside the Aynesworth story above the caption "J. D. Tippit ... He always gave everything he had."

Far from being deliberately suppressed by the authorities for a year, the likeness of the slain J.D. Tippit was published in the *Dallas Morning News* less than 24 hours after his death. Furthermore, since that was Tippit's official DPD photograph, it does not need a genius to work out where the newspaper obtained it.

There is obviously a double-edge at work here. Not only had Joachim Joesten fallen into the trap of not checking his material, but any subsequent researcher, relying solely on Joesten's very positive statement, also got it completely wrong.

THE MYTH OF THE LEFT-HANDED GUN

The 6.5mm Italian Mannlicher-Carcano rifle (CE 139) allegedly found half-concealed by the stairs of the TSBD sixth floor has been the source of much controversy almost from the moment of its discovery. Doubts concerning even such basic details as its nationality, make and calibre have caused discussion, dissent and disagreement amongst researchers. The one thing which has never been in dispute is the fact that the weapon found was a bolt-action rifle.

On a rifle of that type, the bolt is physically activated by the shooter and he has to remove his finger from the trigger in order to do so. The working of the bolt throws out the just fired empty cartridge case and replaces it with the next unexpended round in the clip. Obviously it is necessary for this to be done between each shot and the next. Since the majority of people are right-handed, the bolt is situated in such a position as to be easily and quickly accessible to a right-handed shooter and is thus on the right side of the weapon.

Bolt-action rifles, like golf clubs, tin openers and guitars, are normally designed and manufactured for right-handed people. There are versions specially made for left-handed people but these are not common.

As far as I am aware, it has never been suggested that the rifle found on the sixth floor had its bolt anywhere other than on the right side. Photographs of it bear this out and I understand that the Mannlicher-Carcano which presently sits in the US National Archives and is known as CE 139 is a normally manufactured 'right-handed' rifle.

Confusion arose as the result of a telephone message received by the Warren Commission from the Ballistics Research Laboratory of the Aberdeen Proving Ground, Maryland on 6th April 1964. After explaining that the rifle had been examined by the BRL gunsmith and that the scope was pointed "leftward with respect to the gun" it was stated that "the gunsmith observed that the scope as we received it was installed as if for a left-handed man." [17] Three shims had been installed between the scope base plate and the rifle to achieve this.

Now with all due respect to the expert gunsmith who came up with this opinion, that statement is nonsense. Furthermore, he would have known that it was nonsense. It was said that Oswald would have been hard-pressed to fire that rifle three times in six seconds. Here, we have a picture being painted of him pulling the trigger and then working the bolt with his *left* hand. This scenario would probably have increased the required time from six seconds to something like half a minute. Exactly what did he really mean by "installed for a left-handed man"? It just makes no sense at all.

I know of no researcher who has seriously addressed this odd situation. I can do so, however, since I have a certain physical advantage (or rather, disadvantage) over most people. I have suffered from extremely weak eyesight in my right eye since birth. This condition is so marked that if I close my left eye, I am barely able to read this page. Vision in my left eye is perfect. During my period of two years National Service in the British Army (1960-1962), this visual disability caused me considerable problems in using the iron sights of a rifle. I am right-handed and it would have been normal for me to use my right eye. Due to my vision problem, however, I had to use my *left* eye. This necessitated me stretching my head across the top of my rifle from left to right to line up my left eye with the sights. I never used any weapon fitted with a telescopic sight.

Through my experience, it is obvious to me that the BRL gunsmith was not describing a scope installed for a left-handed man, but one installed for a left-*eyed* man. A photograph of Lee Harvey Oswald taken during USMC firearms training clearly shows that in the process of firing a rifle, he was strictly right-handed and right-eyed. [18]

A 'left-handed' gun? I think not. The left-handed Jimi Hendrix could restring a right-handed guitar or play it upside down—but he was a genius. Neither the unfortunate Oswald nor the people who crudely but effectively framed him come into that category.

THE MYTH OF THE CHANGED MOTORCADE ROUTE

It remains a mystery to me that there are still people who believe that there was a late change to the motorcade route to divert it from Main Street to Elm Street as it passed through Dealey Plaza. This is one of the most lasting myths connected with the event but perhaps the easiest to debunk.

The truth of the matter is that the final motorcade route was published in both Dallas newspapers, the *Dallas Morning News* and the *Dallas Times Herald*, in their editions for Tuesday 19th November—three days prior to the presidential visit. Perhaps the fact that it was published only as part of a news item and not as a map has not helped. The three paragraphs, which came at the end of a front-page item in the *Dallas Morning News*, also included details of the route back to Love Field after the Trade Mart luncheon:

> "The News learned Monday evening that the presidential motorcade will travel 10 miles to the Trade Mart using this route:
>
> From Love Field to Mockingbird Lane, along Mockingbird Lane to Lemmon, then Lemmon to Turtle Creek, Turtle Creek to Cedar Springs, Cedar Springs to Harwood, Harwood to Main, Main to Houston, Houston to Elm, Elm under the Triple Underpass to Stemmons Expressway and on to the Trade Mart.
>
> The return trip will be more direct: Stemmons to Harry Hines, Harry Hines to Mockingbird and on to Love Field—a distance of 4.2 miles."

The complete cutting, under the headline "KENNEDY LUNCHEON: Yarborough Seating Pondered" is included in the 26 Volumes. [19]

Conclusion

I have cited only five examples of myths which have been perpetuated in just over a third of a century since the Kennedy and Tippit murders. I know of some others and there are undoubtedly many more still undiscovered. There is, therefore, only one conclusion to this piece. If you consider yourself to be a competent and honest researcher, act like one and go back to primary sources at every opportunity.

Notes

1. Anthony Summers: *Conspiracy*, published by McGraw-Hill Book Company, USA, and Victor Gollancz Ltd., UK, 1980, page 241.
2. ibid, note 68 on page 564.
3. CE 321 is described as follows on the Contents page to Volume 16 of the 26 Volumes: "Post card from Lee Harvey Oswald to Robert Oswald, dated April 4, 1962". I remain completely baffled how anyone could interpret "10/V/62" as being 4ᵗʰ April 1962.
4. CE 1314 is described as follows on the Contents page to Volume 22 of the 26 Volumes: "One-page note dated May 16, 1962, from Lee H. Oswald to Director of Minsk Radio Factory; apparently a rough draft; with translation". As with the written date in foot note 3 above, an elementary error has been made with the date.
5. Anthony Summers: *Not in your Lifetime*, published by Marlowe & Company, NY, USA, 1998, page 166 and footnote 66 on page 422.
6. Warren Report, page 175.
7. CE 2003 (Dallas Police Department file on investigation of the assassination of the President), page 117 of exhibit (24H 253).
8. Gary Murr: *The Murder of Dallas Police Officer J. D. Tippit*, unpublished manuscript, 1971—copy in author's possession.
9. 9H 343 (Testimony of Mrs Ruth Paine)
10. CE 1843 (FBI report dated April 3 1964, of interview of Marina Oswald at Richardson, Tex.).
11. 10H 306 (Testimony of A. C. Johnson).
12. CE 3000 (FBI report dated December 7, 1963, of interview of Leslie Lawson at Dallas, Tex. and FBI report dated December 17, 1963, of interview of Jack Hammond at Dallas, Tex.).
13. CE 3001 (FBI report dated July 31, 1964, of investigation of possible acquaintance between Oswald and Ruby) at 26H 518.
14. Joachim Joesten: *How Kennedy Was Killed*, published by Peter Dawnay, Ltd., UK, 1968, page 131.

15. Joesten, page 132.
16. Carlin (Bruce Ray) Exhibits 1 and 2 appear in the 26 Volumes at 19H 304.
17. CE 2560 (Commission memorandum for record concerning accuracy tests performed with the assassination rifle).
18. Robert Groden: *The Killing of a President*, published by Viking Studio Books, New York, 1993, page 165.
19. CE 1363 *("Yarborough Seating Pondered," Dallas Morning News,* November 19, 1963), page 1.

Written 1997.
First published November/December 1998 on internet website *Fair Play*, no. 25.
First published (hard copy) November 2001 in *The Dealey Plaza Echo*, vol. 5, no. 3.

24. "The most carefully planned stamp in postal history" The USA 5 cents Kennedy Memorial postage stamp (1964)

INTRODUCTION

The quotation which gives this paper its title is a description of the 1964 Kennedy Memorial postage stamp from the lips of the US Postmaster General of the time, John A. Gronouski. The stamp owes its existence initially to the assassination of a President, then to the express approval of his widow and to the actions of his successor in office. It went on to involve a major design team, a New York firm with no previous experience in the field whatsoever and a set of rotary printing presses. After reading the following, I am sure that you will agree that Mr Gronouski's opinion of this stamp is an accurate one.

As somebody who is not only a dedicated assassination researcher but who has long had a great interest in philatelic matters, it is natural that I should be particularly attracted towards the single stamp issued by the United States Post Office Department to commemorate President John Fitzgerald Kennedy.

The 5 cents memorial stamp was issued simultaneously at all US post offices on 29th May 1964, the date that would have marked the late President's 47th birthday. Not surprisingly, many other countries also produced special postage stamps in memory of JFK and there were also examples of commemorative overprints being applied to existing issues of postage stamps and carriage labels.

Since the total issue of the 5 cents Kennedy stamp ran to over 500 million individual stamps, it is not surprising that it is anything but scarce. It is of little or no monetary or rarity value to collectors. It proved to be one of the most popular stamps ever issued in the United States. Official Post Office Department records reveal that 2,003,096 envelopes bearing the stamp were postmarked (all at Boston) on the official first day of issue. That figure easily surpassed the previous record of 1,656,346 which had been gained by the New York World's Fair stamp on 22nd April 1960. In the early '60s new US stamps normally averaged about a half million for first day cancellations.

BACKGROUND TO THE ISSUE

The initial proposal for a special stamp to honour the late President came from the recently-appointed US Postmaster General John A. Gronouski when he met President Lyndon Johnson during a brief Cabinet meeting on the day following the assassination. Presidents Warren G. Harding (1921 - 1923) and Franklin D. Roosevelt (1933 - 1945) were the only previous Presidents to have been honoured by the issue of a commemorative postage stamp following their deaths.

The US Bureau of Engraving and Printing was authorized to supervise the preparation of suitable designs and three Bureau artists began work at once. They were Robert J. Jones, Robert L. Miller and Victor S. McCloskey Jr. By Tuesday 26th November eight design sketches had been completed. Mr Gronouski, however, felt that it was more important to produce a design of real quality than to rush the issue out too quickly and he asked the Bureau to prepare more design sketches. It was envisaged from the start that the commemorative issue would be a single 5 cents stamp rather than a set.

Eventually 135 small preliminary sketches were developed into a portfolio of 16 finished designs. Several of these completed designs were similar in basic format. All of them naturally included a Kennedy portrait and two of them also incorporated the eternal flame and a poignant quotation from the late President's inaugural address: " ... and the glow from that fire can truly light the world."

THE CHOSEN DESIGN

The task of selecting the design to be used was appropriately given to Mrs Jacqueline Kennedy and in mid-February 1964 she was shown the portfolio of the final 16 designs. Together with members of the Kennedy family, the former First Lady studied the designs carefully before expressing her preference for what would become the final stamp. On 13th March 1964, the feasibility of that design from a printing production point of view was passed and Mr Gronouski gave his final approval on 17th March 1964.

Mrs Kennedy also saw many unsolicited designs which independent artists, both amateur and professional, had submitted to the Post Office Department. Incredibly, one of these, sent in by a 15-year-old San Francisco high school student, Richard Burkley, was almost identical to the chosen design. It featured not only the Kennedy portrait and the eternal flame in the same places as on the final stamp, but also the same quotation positioned around the main design.

Mrs Kennedy's choice was one of the designs submitted by Robert L. Miller, a member of the original three-man US Bureau of Engraving and Printing team. Two minor amendments were made to it. The words *"U.S. POSTAGE"* were added to the left of the eternal flame and the *"5c"* was moved from the bottom left corner of the portrait section to a position low on the extreme left of the stamp. The need for space to include this latter change also necessitated the exclusion of quotation marks at each end of the quoted words. These final design changes were made by another of the original Bureau artists, Victor S. McCloskey, Jr.

The task of developing the basic design was awarded to the large New York industrial design firm of Raymond Loewy/William Snaith, Inc. This company had no experience in the field of postage stamp design but was an acknowledged leader in package design and graphic identification work. Loewy/Snaith had been heavily involved in the exterior graphics and interior design of Air Force One and it had been reported that President Kennedy himself had been very impressed with their work.

THE KENNEDY PORTRAIT USED

There has been considerable speculation regarding the origin of the Kennedy portrait used in the final design. I have learnt from the US Post Office Department Information Service that the photograph had been taken by William S. Murphy, a *Los Angeles Times* photographer, at the Malibu home of actor Peter Lawford, brother-in-law of the late President, on 13th November 1958. It appeared in the newspaper the following day. The *Los Angeles Times* still retains ownership of the original negative.

PRODUCTION OF THE STAMP

Postmaster General Gronouski submitted the order for an initial print run of 250 million stamps on 29th April 1964. This was twice the number of stamps normally printed for a new issue. With the swift realization that even this number would be inadequate for the anticipated demand however, an order for another 250 million stamps was submitted on 21st May—eight days before the date on which the stamps were to be issued.

Six printing plates, numbered 27791-96, were made and two of them, 27792-93, were sent to press on 1st May. There proved to be technical problems, however, mainly concerning the portrait and it was necessary to halt production and destroy the entire printing.

Re-engraving was necessary and ten replacement plates, 27600-09, were made. Due to this enforced delay, the actual printing production was not begun until 14th May—just two weeks and a day prior to the date on which the stamp *had* to be available for sale.

A single rotary Cottrell press began production and two days later, two more were added to the job. Because of the urgency of the task, a three-shift, seven-day week schedule was adopted. The presses continued to operate at full capacity, even through lunch and changeover periods. Eight further plates, 27818-25, were manufactured but only two were needed (27818-19). These went to press on 25th May, as the run was nearing completion.

The first shipment of printed stamps from the Bureau, two million in total, went to San Francisco on 15th May 1964 and the normal automatic distribution to post offices was completed six days later. A second shipment was made on 25th May. The press run was completed on 28th May 1964—with just one day to spare before the official launch of the stamp.

The total number of stamps printed was an incredible 554,732,400. They were produced in 2,773,662 sheets of 200.

First Day of Issue ceremonies

The day of issue of any new postage stamp is always an important event both for the Post Office and for its millions of customers be they philatelists or just ordinary people who want to post a letter.

Because of the additional interest in this particular stamp, it was decided to put it on sale simultaneously at every United States post office on 29th May 1964. It was normal practice for a town or city closely associated with a new stamp's subject to be chosen for a first day ceremony. The stamp would then be available *only* in that town or city on its day of issue before being put on national sale from the following day. On this occasion, Mr Gronouski announced:

> "The major factor dictating simultaneous issuance of the John Fitzgerald
> Kennedy memorial postage stamp is the unusually widespread interest
> already expressed in the stamp."

The US Post Office decided to retain its practice of allowing only one city to use the 'First Day of Issue' cancellation. Washington, D.C. and Boston were the obvious contenders and the Kennedy family expressed its preference for Boston. As mentioned in the Introduction to this paper, first day cancellations at Boston totalled just over two million—four times the normal first day figure for a commemorative issue. The first day sales of the stamp in the Boston postal district totalled 4,795,030. A temporary postal station set up at the Statler-Hilton Hotel, Boston sold 47,182 alone.

THE SPECIAL "DALLAS" CANCELLATION OF 22ND NOVEMBER 1963

In the strictest sense, the *"DALLAS NOV 22"* postmark is probably the most widely spread 'forgery' in philatelic history. Many thousands of commemorative envelopes have been produced purely for collectors and others anxious to have a permanent philatelic reminder of the Dallas tragedy. What appears at first glance to be a normal machine-struck, wavy line cancellation is nothing of the sort. It is *printed* on to the envelope *over* the stamp. These covers were produced, perfectly legally, for many months following the issue of the stamp but obviously it was never suggested that the postmark was genuine.

The printed impression shows the exact date, time and place of the assassination. Envelopes bearing the stamp together with its printed 'postmark' have continued to be marketed worldwide over the years.

TECHNICAL DATA

Five cents blue-grey on white wove paper, horizontal format, 1.44 x 0.84 inches, printed from 200-subject plates on three of the US Bureau of Engraving and Printing's rotary Cottrell presses, electric eye perforated 11 x 10.5 and divided into 50-subject panes for post offices.

Because of the serious nature of the stamp's subject, the Mr Zip cartoon, printed in the selvedge of recent issues, was omitted.

The stamp is numbered 1228 in the current Stanley Gibbons stamp catalogue (UK) and is no. 1246 in the Scott catalogue (USA).

SPECIAL THANKS

I must acknowledge the help afforded me by Secretary Ernest Malinow and Tom Brown of the American Stamp Cub of Great Britain, particularly during the early stages of my research into this subject. I was also able to use the facilities of the reference library at The British Philatelic Centre, London to advantage.

The American Philatelic Research Library, State College, Pennsylvania (run by the American Philatelic Society) has also been a valuable source of information. Ms Susan Dixon, Secretary to the Librarian, provided me with copies of many relevant US Post Office documents plus copies of articles which had appeared in *The Washington Star* (24th May 1964) and *The Society of Philatelic Americans Journal* (November 1964).

Written 1997.
First published March 1999 in *The Dealey Plaza Echo*, vol. 3, no. 1.
Reprinted March 2000 in *The Mayflower*, the Journal of the American Stamp Club of Great Britain, no. 171.

25. Forty years of press coverage of the Kennedy assassination

INTRODUCTION

This chapter is an amalgamation and development of two articles which have been previously published.[1] Basically, they dealt with the manner in which the print media in the United States, the United Kingdom and the rest of the world handled the assassination of President Kennedy and its immediate aftermath. Over 40 years on, we find that the subject has neither gone away nor been forgotten. I will include here not only what was published in the two Dallas local newspapers within a few hours of the assassination but bring the story up to date with items which have appeared in various United Kingdom newspapers, even up to late 2003.

I will also venture across the Pacific Ocean for an in-depth examination of that apparently and allegedly 'too early' account of the assassination and Oswald's arrest which appeared in the New Zealand newspaper, *The Christchurch Star.*

Some of my adverse comments and observations concerning the nature of the press coverage, including some glaring inaccuracies, may appear a little strong. In my defence, however, I would mention that I have been involved in magazine journalism at various levels throughout much of my life. This included a seven-year unbroken period when I edited a nationally-distributed monthly police journal in the United Kingdom, so I am fully aware of the necessity for speed in getting the story out as early as possible. I think it safe to say that the Kennedy assassination was immediately recognized as 99% certain to be the biggest story the Dallas journalists of the day were ever likely to cover. Errors were inevitable. Some of them can be seen to have occurred through mishearing reports coming in by telephone. Others were due to the lack of corroboration of witness accounts as the frantic activity to get the news in and the papers out created more pressure and stories were rushed into print without being fully checked out.

For convenience, I have split what follows into six separate compartments:

- Firstly, a critical examination of some of the newspaper headlines describing the various aspects of the case and the investigation.

- Secondly, I have concentrated on one particular event—the reported discovery of a rifle on the sixth floor of the Texas School Book Depository. I will show how what should have been a simple and straightforward reporting task has caused problems which have still not been satisfactorily resolved over 40 years on.

- Thirdly, press coverage of the JFK assassination around the world. In many cases, treatment of the assassination was greatly influenced by the relevant country's relationship with the U.S. Some countries used the tragedy to push their own particular political views.

- In the fourth section, I have dealt with the supposed problems of *The Christchurch Star* in New Zealand.

- Fifthly, I have attempted to lower the temperature a little and present a few examples of unintentional humour. Gallows humour? Maybe. So be it.

- Finally, I have described and commented on one of the first published press interviews, brought assassination coverage right up to date with the UK items I mentioned earlier and have ended with some items that do not fit in anywhere else.

HEADLINES

Normally, the purpose of a front page main headline is to sell a story and thus, the newspaper. This was not necessary on 22nd and 23rd November 1963 since the story was so immense. However, a complete list of front page main headlines would make interesting reading.

In the United Kingdom, where we tend to have 'national' rather than city newspapers, most headlines were identical or very similar on 23rd November 1963.

Four major national newspapers, *The Daily Mirror*, *The Daily Express*, *The Daily Mail* and *The Daily Herald*, gave us KENNEDY ASSASSINATED whilst three others, *The Times*, *The Guardian* and *The Scotsman*, led with PRESIDENT KENNEDY ASSASSINATED.

The Daily Telegraph's headline was slightly longer and included an extra and, in my opinion, totally unnecessary word: PRESIDENT KENNEDY IS ASSASSINATED.

As a point of interest, every one of those papers carried the same front page photograph—the Associated Press wirephoto taken by James Altgens,

showing the presidential limo picking up speed as it approaches the triple underpass, with Clint Hill struggling to maintain his grip and his balance on the
rear of the vehicle.

In the United States, the 23rd November 1963 *Knoxville Journal* (Tennessee) headline had only six words but it was one of many to include the
names of both the assassinated President and his successor in office:

JOHNSON ASSUMES PRESIDENCY AFTER KENNEDY
ASSASSINATION.

American newspapers occasionally tend to use very long headlines. I am
personally very unhappy with the *New York Times* 23rd November headline:

KENNEDY KILLED BY SNIPER AS HE RIDES IN CAR IN
DALLAS: JOHNSON SWORN IN ON PLANE.

In my humble opinion, those 16 words do not constitute a headline—
more an opening paragraph. We find an even worse example of this in *The
Washington Post* of Monday 25th November 1963:

300,000 JOIN IN TRIBUTES TO KENNEDY AS NOTABLES
ARRIVE FOR FUNERAL TODAY; OSWALD IS SHOT TO DEATH
AT DALLAS JAIL.

Perhaps the editor could not decide which was the more important lead
story—the tributes to JFK or the death of Oswald. Either way, that is hardly a
true headline in the accepted journalistic sense.

The Chicago Tribune was another big city newspaper to mention both
Presidents by name in its headline of Saturday 23rd:

ASSASSIN KILLS KENNEDY: LYNDON JOHNSON SWORN IN.

For some reason, many newspapers away from the major American cities tended to concentrate more on the global significance of the assassination
than their bigger brothers. For example, the main headline of the *Panama City
News* (Florida) on Saturday 23rd:

WHOLE WORLD ENGULFED IN SORROW OVER BRUTAL
SLAYING OF PRESIDENT

And the *Mishawaka Times* (Indiana), same date:

WORLD MOURNS JFK.

Of the two, I think the latter has by far the greater impact.

We cannot discuss the headlines spawned by this event without casting an eye in the direction of the city in which it happened. Paradoxically, the two Dallas newspapers each had both an advantage and a disadvantage with regard to the other. *The Dallas Times Herald* was published each afternoon and so was first with the news of the assassination. *The Dallas Morning News*, however, with its far later deadline, was able to locate and interview eyewitnesses, attend the police press conference and take far more time to consider and express its views on what had happened.

In the words of former *Dallas Times Herald* journalist Connie Kritzberg in an article in *The Dealey Plaza Echo* in 1997: "The scenario for the day was an editing challenge ... one that made the *Dallas Morning News* situation a stroll in the park. They had all afternoon to work before their first presidential edition—we had a half hour." [2]

Another *Dallas Times Herald* journalist, Bill Sloan, told me that they normally produced just one afternoon edition, occasionally two. [3] On 22nd November 1963, however, the presses just kept rolling and updates were made continually as the picture changed. He also mentioned that demand for the *Herald* was so great, that the paper, with a cover price of five cents, was being snapped up at ten dollars a time. There was not even enough time to get the paper out to the normal distribution and sales locations. The public gathered outside the building, scrambling to get the latest edition with the latest news. [4]

The *Dallas Times Herald* main headline remained constant throughout its several editions, just four words—PRESIDENT DEAD, CONNALLY SHOT—in block capitals $2^5/16$ inches high. In technical terms, that's 166 point. In any terms, that's enormous!

Of the American newspaper headlines I have seen, the *Dallas Morning News* of 23rd November 1963 had by far the best. It summed it all up—the event, the location, the pathos—in just five words: KENNEDY SLAIN ON DALLAS STREET. I cannot see any way in which that could be improved.

This was in smaller letters than the *Herald*—$1^1/2$ inches high, 108 point. I cannot recall a poll for 'Headline of the Millennium' when we entered the 21st century, but had there been one, this would have got my vote. Every word is perfect:

KENNEDY—the subject of the headline and a name which instantly provokes interest, respect and newsworthiness.

SLAIN—a slightly archaic word but one which is so much more powerful and sinister than KILLED and more positive and final than SHOT.

ON DALLAS STREET—we immediately have a specific location— both a named city (*this* city!) and 'on the street', a phrase which suggests a somewhat sordid and undignified place for anyone to breathe their last.

These five short and unambiguous words tell the complete story and at the same time convey feelings of both horror and disgust.

Back in Britain, another of my favourite headlines appeared in *The Evening News* (London) on 23rd November. By that time, well over 24 hours after the assassination, reporters had been given the time and the opportunity to gather their facts and shed the more sensational 'shock-horror' style of the previous day. The *Evening News* headline was dramatic in the extreme but at this stage it was obvious that a little doubt about Oswald's guilt was becoming evident—in Britain at least—with the words:

I MEET THE MAN THEY CALL ASSASSIN.

Other elements of the British press, however, were not totally blameless when it came to the more sensational headlines which appeared. The headline in *The People* on Sunday 24th:

IS THE KILLER A MADMAN?

was followed by a sub-head

KHRUSHCHEV DISOWNS THE FANATIC WHO CALLS HIMSELF A COMMUNIST

THE RIFLE

Although I have grave doubts about things like the alleged paper bag, I am happy to accept the claim that a rifle was found inside the Texas School Book Depository on the early afternoon of Friday 22nd November 1963. That, however, is just the start of a mystery which has rumbled on from that day to this. The rifle which Lee Harvey Oswald is alleged to have purchased by mail order was an Italian 6.5mm Mannlicher-Carcano. The rifle which the Warren Commission later designated Commission Exhibit 139 was an Italian 6.5mm

Mannlicher-Carcano. It all seems so simple and straightforward—but somehow, that rifle, assuming it is the *same* rifle, has assumed a cloak of mystery more akin to Earle Stanley Gardner than Earl Warren!

It is not my intention here to identify CE 139 positively as a Mannlicher, a Mauser, a blowpipe, a crossbow or a catapult. All I will do is quote a few of the descriptions and claimed identities of that weapon as they appeared in the press on both sides of the Atlantic:

> "The murder weapon reportedly was a 30-30 rifle" *(Orlando Evening Star*, 22nd November 1963)

> "A rifle slug (believed of high-power 30-30 caliber) hit the President in the head" *(New York Herald-Tribune*, 23rd November 1963)

> "An immediate investigation was begun on the gun's origin. It looked to me like a Mauser, one they sell surplus for deer rifles"(Patrolman Bobby Hargis—quoted in the *Dallas Times Herald*, 22nd November 1963)

> "In the building, a depository for school books, overlooking the underpass, officers found an old 30-caliber Enfield with telescopic sights" *(Mishawaka Times* and *Panama City News*, 23rd November 1963. AP syndicated)

> "The rifle believed to have fired the fatal shots was made in Japan" *(The Times*, UK, 23rd November 1963)

> "At the crucial moment, he raised a 7.65 Mauser rifle, and a split second later the short triumphant life of John Kennedy had run its course" *(London Evening News*, 23rd November 1963)

> "Lieutenant Erich Kaminski, of the Secret Service Bureau, said the assassin's weapon appeared not to have been a Lee-Enfied as at first thought, but a high-powered army or Japanese rifle of about 25-calibre" *(Dundee Courier & Advertiser*, 23rd November 1963)

That final quote is actually a correction of a previous inaccuracy—but the correction itself also appears to be inaccurate. There is a further error there regarding Lt Kaminski's unit. He was with the DPD Special Service Bureau, rather than the Secret Service.

These are just a few of the misidentifications of the rifle. I am sure there were others.

INTERNATIONAL PRESS COVERAGE OF THE ASSASSINATION

During visits to the UK National Archives (formerly the Public Record Office). I have studied the Kennedy Assassination files held there. One of the largest such files is entitled *International reaction to the death of President Kennedy, 1963*. It comprises three smaller individual files and there is much reference to press coverage of the event in various countries. Please allow me to quote directly from a few of them:

> The Czechoslovakian newspaper *Rude Pravo* (24ᵗʰ November 1963) referred to *"contrary rumours as to the forces behind the assassination. Some rumours indicated that the FBI and the CIA are at back of it."*

> In Red China, an unattributed quote from the press stated: "The obvious, in fact the only line to take, I should think, is that the United States ruling classes (reactionary, imperialist, etc.) decided that Kennedy was betraying their interests in some way and had to be liquidated."

> The Jugoslav newspaper *Borba* stated, on 25ᵗʰ November 1963: "Oswald's murder took place with police connivance." No comment from me on that one!

> In East Germany, the official daily *Neues Deutschland* (25ᵗʰ November) used the significant headline DEAD MEN TELL NO TALES over one of those infamous pictures of Jack Ruby shooting Oswald and a story which included: "the horror of the international public at the new crime is mixed at the same time with disgust at conditions in the land that is praised as 'the freest in the world' and is in reality ruled by the revolutionary mob with the Colt."

> Egypt adopted an Orwellian approach and took the opportunity to blame the entire affair on an old enemy! We have the following from the daily newspaper *Al Jumhuriyah* on 23ʳᵈ November: "President Kennedy had a desire for real peace and for sparing the world the afflictions of a new war. We have no doubt that he was the victim of this moderation at the hands of extremist elements, warmongers, supporters of Israel, and defenders of the policy of racial segregation."

> In India, the nationalist newspaper *The Indian Express* of 23ʳᵈ November linked the assassination with America's racial troubles: "With every new martyr, the cause leaps forward to victory. This is bound to be so with the great civil rights battle in America,"

Nigeria's *Lagos Morning Post*, also on the 23rd, took a similar line with: "President Kennedy's murder was organized and executed according to plan. The assassination is the result of the active machinations of racial bigots."

The Soviet Union, like Cuba, expressed immediate fear that the blame for President Kennedy's assassination would be laid at its door and was quick to present its denials. The following comes from *Tass*, the Soviet official news agency, the day following the assassination: "All the circumstances of President Kennedy's tragic death give grounds for considering that the murder was conceived and carried out by ultra-right, Fascist and racialist circles."

Still in the Soviet Union, the newspaper *Pravda*, above a photograph of the Oswald killing, had the headline ULTRAS COVER UP THEIR TRACES (Yes, the translation gives TRACES, not TRACKS.)

Another Soviet newspaper, *Izvestia*, in considering the shooting of Oswald by Ruby, asked a question which remains unanswered today: "One of the most important questions is: were these two men linked in one plot?"

The Danish newspaper *Politiken*, in its front page story on 23rd November, mentioned that "a member of the Security Police was killed"—presumably a reference to the rumour about the death of a Secret Serviceman. The newspaper's headline was simple and straightforward: KENNEDY KILLED. [5]

On 27th November, *The Dallas Morning News*, under the headline EURO-PEAN PRESS DOUBTS THAT ENTIRE TRUTH REVEALED ran the following: "The European press, both Communist and non-Communist, voiced dark suspicions on Tuesday that the entire truth had not been told in the assassination of President Kennedy and the slaying of Lee Harvey Oswald. There was widespread condemnation of the Dallas Police Department for allowing television coverage of Oswald, and expressions of indignation at what the *London Daily Telegraph* called the monumental absurdity of Dallas Police Chief Jesse Curry's declaration that the Kennedy case was closed."

The mystery of *The Christchurch Star*

It seems to me that researchers are unaware that New Zealand has more than just one newspaper. I wonder how many researchers can name any New Zealand newspaper other than *The Christchurch Star*. How many realize that *The Christchurch Star* was not a morning newspaper but was published in the early afternoon? Researchers in general are familiar with *The Christchurch Star* and the problems it is supposed to have caused, but why does no other New Zealand paper get a mention? Perhaps the research community believes that New Zealand had only *The Christchurch Star*—an afternoon newspaper— back in November 1963. [6]

I regret to point out that much of the confusion and suspicion surrounding the news and pictures published in *The Christchurch Star* on the afternoon of Saturday 23rd November 1963 have been unwittingly caused and developed by L. Fletcher Prouty and Oliver Stone.

In his 1992 book, *JFK: The CIA, Vietnam and the Plot to Assassinate John F. Kennedy*, L. Fletcher Prouty spoke of the speed of modern communications. [7] However, he threw in a short assassination-related paragraph in which he questioned whether "the information that traveled around the world (was) the truth of legitimate news, or was it more like a mixture of real news items and orchestrated propaganda that had been prepared and written even before the crime took place?"

Now however you read that, Prouty is asking if it were possible that there was some degree of pre-knowledge of the Kennedy assassination, and that advance information of it had somehow reached a section of the print media on the other side of the world.

Prouty goes on to state that for people like him "who just happened to be in far-off Christchurch, New Zealand" the assassination took place at 7.30am on Saturday 23rd November 1963. That, however, is not so.

I have gone to great lengths to ascertain the time difference between Dallas, Texas (Central Standard Time) and New Zealand (just one time zone— New Zealand Standard Time). [8]

It was 18 hours. That puts the assassination at 6.30am on Saturday morning in New Zealand—a significant error on Prouty's part.

I even explored a suggestion that as it was early Summer in New Zealand, Daylight Saving Time may have been in operation to add another hour. I established, however, that this was not the case in 1963.

Incidentally, at least one other leading researcher, Harrison Edward Livingstone, confused the time difference. In his 1992 book, *High Treason 2*, he claimed that *The Christchurch Star* informed him that the time difference was 16 hours. [9] Perhaps, as another researcher suggested to me, someone was violating the International Date Line rules and was counting the time zones westwards. The difference was *not* 16 hours. It was 18 hours. Fact.

Back to Fletcher Prouty. In his book he claims that "The Christchurch Star hit the streets with an 'Extra' edition." That is not so. No 'Extra' edition was published that day. The newspaper appeared in its usual format and at roughly its normal time, around 2.00pm NZST Saturday (equivalent to 8.00pm CST Friday in Dallas). This was another major Prouty error. The newspaper consisted of 36 pages, of which the front page and page 3 were devoted to the news of the assassination (including pictures) and those infamous Oswald biographical notes. Page 5 consisted solely of a collage of photographs outlining the Kennedy presidency.

In the Oliver Stone film *JFK*, 'Mr X', played by Donald Sutherland, was a composite character, based to a large extent on L. Fletcher Prouty. We do, in fact see 'Mr X' at a New Zealand airport, holding a copy of *The Christchurch Star* with the headline "KENNEDY SHOT DEAD" plainly visible. Whilst that headline and the rest of the newspaper's front page appear accurate, there are at least two glaring errors. Firstly, the newspaper is shown as a wide tabloid whereas the real *Christchurch Star* was a broadsheet. With all his money and resources, could Oliver Stone not have obtained either an original or an accurate facsimile of the *real* newspaper? Secondly, some parts of the newspaper (*not* the front page) shown in the film, were not identical with the original.

With errors such as those I have briefly outlined, is it any wonder that there is so much confusion about this issue?

The fact that *The Christchurch Star* of 23rd November 1963 also carried much accurate biographical data on Lee Harvey Oswald, together with what is known as the 'Moscow Hotel studio portrait' of him, has also raised a few suspicions. Once again, however, the situation is nowhere near as sinister as has sometimes been suggested. The international news agencies such as Reuter, Associated Press, *Agence France Presse*, British United Press, etc. all circulated the story. Whilst the internet was still a thing of the future, newsflashes and wirephotos (*aka* radiopictures in New Zealand) routinely carried news stories and pictures around the globe almost instantaneously.

I have seen it suggested that since Oswald was not arraigned for the assassination of the President until 1.30am in the morning of Saturday 23rd, his name could not have been known early enough for it to appear in the New Zealand press. However, both Associated Press and *Agence France Presse* newsflashes mentioned him by name at 2.40pm CST and 2.45pm CST respectively, just an hour or so after his arrest. [10]

The Christchurch Star, like other New Zealand newspapers, got its news stories *via* the Australian Associated Press. They were routed through Australia and Auckland to Christchurch. The other New Zealand newspapers like the *Wellington Evening Post* carried similar assassination coverage, including the Oswald portrait. Although it seems to be the only New Zealand newspaper mentioned in this controversy, *The Christchurch Star* was by no means unique in carrying this story. It was one of many papers doing so.

The biographical data and portrait photograph of Lee Harvey Oswald which appeared on page 3 of *The Christchurch Star* were nowhere near as unusual as has been claimed by some researchers. As the newspaper's Chief Reporter Bob Cotton has stressed, all newspapers carry a reservoir of biographical material in respect of various people in the public eye. Oswald had attracted considerable media coverage in the American mainstream press when he defected to Russia in 1959 and again when he returned home in 1962. It was hardly surprising that the international news agencies were able to locate and circulate this material very quickly after the Dallas tragedy.

I fear that I may have dwelt overlong on the perceived problems raised by the 23rd November 1963 edition of *The Christchurch Star* and I apologise for that. However, in dealing with the subject of media coverage of the assassination, I cannot fail to address this issue. I just hope that I have shown that the fears raised by L. Fletcher Prouty and perpetuated in the Oliver Stone film have been seriously exaggerated. I believe that this resulted from faulty calculations of the Dallas/New Zealand time difference, plus a seeming reluctance to refer to primary sources in Christchurch.

The bottom line is this. There was no advance warning of the assassination given in New Zealand and the coverage afforded by *The Christchurch Star* was no more suspicious than that anywhere else on the planet.

WHICH IS THE MORE CREDIBLE—THE 'HOT NEWS' AT THE TIME, OR THE LATER VERSION?

The journalists of the day found themselves thrust into a situation which none of them could have foreseen. Together with events like Pearl Harbour, Hiroshima and the first Moon landing, the events of the weekend of 22nd to 24th November 1963 produced news stories like no other, before or since. Errors were made, witnesses were misquoted, hurried opinions later proved inaccurate and conclusions were clouded. Fortunately, many of these inaccuracies were obviously absurd and very easily disproved by later events.

By way of a short humour break, please let me share a few of them with you. This is from *The New York Herald-Tribune* of 23rd November 1963. I have been told that a virtually identical story appeared elsewhere so I presume that it originally came *via* the press agencies. I like to call this one "Gunfight at the Texas Theatre Corral."

"Police got a call that a man answering the description of the suspect had entered the Texas Theater. Patrolmen J. D. Tippit and M. N.

MacDonald followed. An usher told them the shabbily-dressed man had run into the theater a short time before.

They spotted the slim, balding 5 foot, nine inch man crouched by a red-lighted exit door.

They yelled. Patrolman Tippit fired once. Oswald fired once and Patrolman Tippit fell dead. Patrolman MacDonald then rushed Oswald and they struggled.

Oswald was subdued. Patrolman McDonald was slashed several times across the face with a gun butt in the struggle, he said."

So that's how it happened. I have always been curious about the shooting of Tippit. It seems it was a shoot-out in a cinema. Perhaps this explains why there was never any photograph of Tippit's body beside his patrol car. (*My transcription above is exactly as it appeared in the paper—including the different spellings of McDonald's surname.*)

Another outstanding example of misreporting can be found in the *Dallas Times Herald* which was rushed out on the afternoon of the assassination. I can only surmise that the extreme differences in age and hair colour in three descriptions of the same man came about through human error on the part of the eyewitnesses themselves. In particular, note how the suspect goes from being *"about 30"* to *"about 25 years old"* and ends up as *"the youth"*. As for the suspect being armed with a rifle—well your guess is as good as mine. Here is the full and unedited account, with nothing excluded:

"The police radio reported the officer, identified as J. D. Tippitt [*note the misspelling*] was slain by a white man, about 30, about 5-foot 8, and slender with dark hair.

The suspect was caught about an hour later, at 2:10pm at the Texas Theater on West Jefferson.

'There may be a tie-in,' investigators said. "On a thing like this we have to check everything. We have a report the fellow who did the shooting of the policeman had a rifle with him.'

'His description fits what we've heard from some witnesses' one officer declared.'

The suspect in the shooting of the officer was about 25 years old with his blond hair cut short. He was slightly built with a ruddy complexion.

Wearing dark pants and a brownish sportshirt, the youth put up a fight when police went into the theater to arrest him.

Another Dallas police detective said the general description of the suspect captured in Oak Cliff matched that of the man who eyewitnesses say shot the President.

But detectives gave no details on how the descriptions matched."

Naturally I have saved the best until last. *The Chicago Tribune* describes itself as 'The World's Greatest Newspaper' and this is exactly what it came up with on 23rd November 1963:

> "It is now believed that Oswald, having left the book depository building, entered an automobile and drove three-quarters of a mile into the Oak Cliff residential area of Dallas which is southwest of the main business district.
>
> Somewhere during that drive he was intercepted by Dallas Policeman J. D. Tippitt *(sic)* on Kent street, one of the main streets of Oak Cliff.
>
> One witness, as yet unidentified, has told Dallas Police that Tippitt approached Oswald in the latter's car. As the policeman stood talking to Oswald the latter drew a revolver and fired two shots at point blank range into the officer's face.
>
> As Tippitt fell dead, Oswald jumped from the car and ran along 10th street dodging into doorways and areaways of apartment buildings and a few business shops."

Note that in this description, we have Oswald in a car and Tippit approaching him. Whether Tippit was on foot or also in a car is not mentioned—but there is no indication that a police car was found empty at 10th and Patton. The mention of 'Kent street' is almost certainly the result of someone mishearing 'Tenth Street' on the telephone. There are so many errors in this passage that it could almost be deliberate! After all, it does come from the self-styled 'World's Greatest Newspaper' the day following the shooting it describes. Why could they not get the story more accurate than this? Surely, they had enough time?

SOME THINGS THAT DON'T FIT IN ABOVE

The Dallas Morning News, in its edition for 23rd November, included both Kennedy and Tippit in its daily DEATHS AND FUNERALS announcements. It was normal for such notices to conclude with details of the internment if they were known. Consider, however, how the Kennedy notice closed: *"Remains forwarded to Washington, D.C. Friday."*

Many of the United States Sunday newspapers quoted the Dallas Police as saying in very positive terms that Oswald was undoubtedly guilty of the assassination of the President. Please bear in mind that these claims were being made less than 48 hours after the commission of the crime.

Chicago's Sunday American, with strong local interest in the knowledge that the alleged assassination rifle had been ordered from a mail-order firm in its own city, led simply with: "OSWALD DID IT—POLICE". The *Sunday World-Herald*, published in Omaha, Nebraska, went even further and announced Oswald's inevitable punishment: "OSWALD CERTAIN TO GET DEATH PENALTY". Ironically, that is exactly what happened, at the hand of Jack Ruby, a few hours after the paper appeared.

The situation was little different in small-town America. In Indiana, *The South Bend Tribune* carried a very positive front page headline on that Sunday: "OSWALD CASE IS WATERTIGHT".

I maintain that *The Dallas Times Herald* secured one of the scoops of the century on the day of the assassination. This came in the form of its published interview with DPD motorcyclist Bobby Hargis which appeared on page A-19 under the headline "DALLAS POLICEMAN RECOUNTS INSTANT ASSASSIN STRUCK". In it, Hargis described his part in the motorcade and what he saw, heard and did when Kennedy was shot.

Significantly, he did *not* claim that he was hit so hard by blood, brain matter, etc. that he thought that he himself had been hit. To find, isolate and interview Hargis and then print that account in the second edition of the paper at around 3.30pm represents an incredible feat on the part of the *Herald*. Why has it never received the credit it deserves?

COMING RIGHT UP TO DATE IN THE UK

Approaching the present day, we cross the Atlantic to England and come to the *Grimsby Telegraph* of Saturday 25th January 2003. On page 3 it carries a piece under the incredible headline "WAS FORMER GRIMSBY MAN PART OF PLOT TO KILL JFK?" Obviously very much a local story, this was brought about by a BBC-TV *Inside Out* programme earlier in the week in which it was claimed that Grimsby-born Albert Osborne (*aka* John Howard Bowen) had been a major suspect in the assassination. [11] He was, indeed, a shady character who was apparently familiar with the Dallas area, but I disagree that he was actively involved in any nefarious activity there.

Also in 2003, my own research into the life and times of the English-born Carousel Club stripper Kathy Kay was the subject of a double-page centre spread in the *East Anglian Daily Times* of Saturday 22nd March. Once again, this is very much a local interest story. It produced another remarkable headline: "STRANGE TALE OF THE ESSEX GIRL AND THE KILLING OF JFK". A former United States Air Force base within the circulation area of the newspaper—Wethersfield—was where the future Carousel Club stripper Kathy Kay met her first husband, a USAF Staff Sergeant, at one of the weekend dances on base. They fell in love, married, later moved to the USA together, divorced, she moved to Dallas, she met Jack Ruby ..... and the rest is history.

In May 2003, for some reason I cannot explain, *The Grimsby Evening Telegraph* issued a complete reprint of its issue of Saturday 23rd November 1963. As that original issue included the English football results as LATE NEWS, we know that it was printed and distributed at around 5.30pm—that was around 11.30pm (Saturday 22nd) Dallas time. It bore the front page headline "EX-MARINE HELD FOR MURDER". This indicates to me that at this time, just 23 hours after the assassination, Oswald had become so well-known as an 'ex-Marine' that there was no need to use his actual name. The alleged murder weapon, furthermore, was still being described as "the 7.65 Mauser— the German rifle". [12]

On 17th September 2003, *The Asian Age*, a London-based local newspaper carried an account of Barr McClellan's book *Blood, Money and Power: How LBJ killed JFK*. This was printed on page 13 beneath a prominent headline "JOHNSON-JFK CONSPIRACY THEORY REVIVED". [13]

THE BOTTOM LINE .....

To close, I offer two significant quotes from *The New York Times*:

"One way to heal some of the scars afflicted on the United States ... is for the evidence against Oswald to be brought out fully."

That appeared on 26th November 1963—just four days after the assassination. Forty years on, we are still waiting.

"The year 2000 will see men still arguing about the President's death."

That appeared on 22nd November 1964, the first anniversary of the assassination. During this piece, I have levelled come criticism at the press. On that occasion, they got it right!

AND FINALLY .....

In July 1998, a clear and visually-enhanced version of the Zapruder Film became available to all in the United States. Here is how that story was covered by two vastly different British newspapers:

The Daily Telegraph is a quality broadsheet which wrote as follows: "Abraham Zapruder's home movies of President Kennedy's assassination went on sale in America yesterday in a digitally-enhanced video format. Distributors hope to sell 100,000 copies at £12 each."

The Sun is a popular tabloid which used the headline "JFK VIDEO NASTY" and said: *"Ghouls in America are flocking to buy a film of President Kennedy's brains being blown out."*

To slightly misquote the words of the popular song: *"It ain't what you say, it's the way that you say it!"*

NOTES

1. "The President, the Press and the Patsy" published in *The Kennedy Assassination Chronicles*, vol. 1, no. 3, September 1995; "How the Rest of the World viewed the Kennedy Assassination" presented as a research paper at the JFK-Lancer Conference, Dallas, 1997.

2. "A Personal Story: Reporting the Death of a President": *The Dealey Plaza Echo*, vol. 1, no. 3, July 1997.

3. Meeting and discussion with Bill Sloan in Dallas, 20th November 1993.

4. In a letter to UK researcher Chris Mills in mid-1955, Mary Ferrell described how she began her collection of JFK assassination memorabilia, artefacts and documentation on Friday 22nd November 1963: "That afternoon, I put one of my teen-aged sons at the loading dock of the Dallas Morning News and one at the loading dock of the Dallas Times Herald. I used the third son to relieve first one and then the other. I had them buy every issue of every paper that came out during the next four days."
(This letter was reprinted in full in the *Dallas '63* journal, vol. 2, no, 2, December 1995.)

5. Information from Danish researcher Kim Reinholt.

6. In November 1963, the four principal New Zealand cities each had both a morning and an afternoon/evening newspaper. The capital city of Wellington had *The Dominion* (morning) and *The Evening Post*. Christchurch (the country's second city) had *The Press* (morning) and *The Christchurch Star* (afternoon/ evening). Auckland had *The New Zealand Herald* (morning) and *The Auckland Star* (evening). Finally, Dunedin (a larger city then than now) had *The Otago Daily Times* (morning) and also an evening newspaper (title not recalled).

I am appreciative of the great assistance I have received here from Mike Lee, a New Zealand researcher I met in Dallas several years ago. He still has a copy of the *Wellington Evening Post* of 23rd November 1963 and confirms that it carries the same Oswald studio portrait under the heading PRIME SUS-PECT. The accompanying piece mentions "Dallas police say Oswald shot a policeman shortly after the shooting of the President."

DPUK stalwart Dr Mike Dworetsky, Director of the University of London Observatory, also provided valuable information on time zones.

The specialist knowledge and patience of these two gentlemen in the face of my continued questions is greatly appreciated. The files and archives of *The Christchurch Star* have also provided much useful information.

7.   L. Fletcher Prouty: *JFK, The CIA, Vietnam and the Plot to assassinate John F. Kennedy*, published by Birch Lane Press/Carol Publishing Group, New York, 1992, page 306.

8.   See para 3 of footnote 6 above.

9.   Harrison Edward Livingstone: *High Treason 2*, published by Carroll & Graf, New York, 1992, page 532.

10.   Ian Griggs: *Kennedy Assassinated! Oswald Murdered!* published jointly by the author and the JFK Resource Group, Dallas, 1994, pages 52 and 55.

11.   UK researcher David Watford (a Grimsby resident) brought this to my attention and supplied a copy of the story.

12.   ibid.

13.   UK researcher Francesca Akhtar kindly presented me with this cutting.

Written in this form 1998
Presented as a research paper 30th March 2003 at the DPUK Inaugural Weekend Seminar, Canterbury, Kent.
Also presented as a research paper 22nd November 2003 at the JFK-Lancer Conference, Dallas, Texas.
First published under this title July 2003 in *The Dealey Plaza Echo*, vol. 7, no. 2.

26. World reaction to the Kennedy Assassination

A brief examination of World opinion of the events of 22nd/24th November 1963, using British Government documents released by the UK Public Record Office in 1994 and 1995.

(Author's note: Since the completion and original publication of this piece, the official title of the Public Record Office has changed to the National Archives. All other details remain as before.)

INTRODUCTION

In the United Kingdom, the Public Record Office (PRO) is the equivalent of the United States National Archives. It is the national repository for all UK governmental and other official records which are to be permanently preserved. Such documents are available for public examination at the PRO and range from the Domesday Book (1086) to the Magna Carta (1215), the will of William Shakespeare (1616) and even the Deed Poll document legalizing a certain musician's official change of name from Reginald Kenneth Dwight to Elton Hercules John (1970).

The PRO was established by Act of Parliament in 1838 and its records currently occupy four different locations in London. Its main building, and by far the largest, is situated at Kew, on the western outskirts of London. It is here that the British Foreign Office records, which include the Kennedy-related files referred to herein, are stored. Records held are normally available for study by members of the public after 30 years.

This paper describes the eight Kennedy Assassination-related files which I located and examined at the PRO in the course of my visits on 12th September 1995 and on 30th November 2001. As far as I am aware, there are no further British Government files on the subject, either open or closed. As noted later, however, a section of one of these files does, for some undisclosed reason, remain closed to public scrutiny.

THE KENNEDY ASSASSINATION FILES

On my first visit to the PRO (September 1995), I studied seven files. All had been closed and sealed until 1ˢᵗ January 1994 under the general 30-years rule. Another remained closed for an extended period and was to be the subject of my second visit in November 2001. Prior to my first visit, I communicated with the PRO by telephone and was very fortunate to make contact with Ms Abi Husainy of the PRO Reader Services Department. This lady was not only very helpful in advising me the location of the relevant files but she also takes an interest in the Assassination and has more than passing knowledge of its significance and complexities. She took the trouble to meet me and proved of great assistance during my visit.

FILE: FO 371/168406-8

The main file I studied (numbered above) consists of three smaller related files linked together under the common title *International reaction to the death of President Kennedy, 1963*. Within each of them there are individual files dealing with reaction in specific countries. Much of the material within consists of communications and reports sent to Her Majesty's Foreign Office in London from British Embassies and Consulates around the world. Most of these had been sent within a week of the assassination—some within just two or three days. Presumably the Foreign Office had requested this information urgently following the assassination of President Kennedy and the murder of Lee Harvey Oswald.

When you study documents like these in some depth, you inevitably get an overall feeling about the situation. As is to be expected, the main feeling is one of shock. Whether you are reading about the reaction of the public in Russia, the Government in France, or British ex-patriots in Australia, that feeling is the same. These papers do not only deal with those countries, however. Also included—and given equal prominence—are countries from the emerging third world in Africa, Asia and South America.

Every individual country was obviously concerned about its own future and situation following Kennedy's death and the unexpected emergence of Lyndon Johnson as President. Some countries feared a sudden change in American policy towards them. Would existing trade agreements continue as before? Would US aid be cut off? Would there be a change in attitude towards the Eastern Bloc? What would happen in Vietnam?

I learnt that only two countries in the entire world did not treat Kennedy's death with the reverence and respect it deserved. One was Red China and the other, somewhat surprisingly to me, was Portugal. In Communist China, there

2222222222222222222

was nothing in the way of a public tribute and one major newspaper carried a front-page cartoon showing JFK face down in a pool of blood with the caption *Kennedy bites the dust*. I subsequently learnt that Portugal's cold attitude was due to something of a breakdown in relations with the US as the result of serious ongoing trade disputes.

SOME DIRECT QUOTES

Allow me to quote directly from some of these files. I think you will, like me, find several of these remarks somewhat prophetic.

1. This is from a file dealing with reactions to the assassination in Czechoslovakia. President Antonin Novotny sent a message of sympathy to the new President in which he said that Kennedy was *"the victim of a criminal plot."* This comment was made as early as 23rd November.

2. Remaining with the Oswald murder, here are the comments of an official at the British Embassy in Tokyo, Japan in a report to the Foreign Office on 26th November: "The shooting of Oswald, the alleged assassin, aroused unfavourable comment in the Japanese press. The impression has been given in some headlines that the United States is a country where lynch law prevails and the whole episode has, in the opinion of the Japanese press, tarnished the American image abroad."

3. The British Embassy in Buenos Aires, Argentina, sent a lengthy *communique* to the Foreign Office on 29th November. It included the following rather odd statement: "The quantity of material published, broadcast and televised was staggering; the American Embassy must be far better equipped with obituary material than we are."

4. Now for a brief visit to Africa. This is from an official communication sent from the British Embassy in Khartoum, Sudan to the Foreign Office. It is dated 6th December—obviously well after the event and at a time when it was possible to judge the situation more objectively. I find this statement strangely prophetic in view of subsequent views and opinions. "Later speculation on the assassin's motives has laid stress on the influence of Zionism and the extreme right in the United States." Well, I don't know about the Zionist angle but as far as the right wing goes .....

5. The final extract I quote here comes from an internal British Government document prepared by the Foreign Office itself on 23rd December—a month and a day after the assassination. It is unclear whether this was intended to

be presented to the Prime Minister, the Foreign Secretary, or whoever. It is taken from a lengthy report in which the world is divided into convenient geographical and political boxes for individual comment. Under the heading *Eastern Europe*, we read the following: "Most eastern bloc countries stuck to the story that President Kennedy had been killed by a right wing racist and denounced the killing of Oswald by Ruby as a fascist plot to cover up the truth."

WHAT DOES IT ALL MEAN?

The above represents just a small cross-section of the material contained in this file. I have obviously been somewhat selective in my quotes but it seems that many of the initial opinions have changed very little over the years. I am intrigued by the regularity with which words like *"racist"* and *"fascist"* are used to describe the plot.

Not surprisingly, two particular countries were anxious to allay any suspicions that they had been connected with the assassination in any way. Both the Soviet Union and Cuba strenuously denied any involvement. Cuba especially seemed gripped with fear that the blame would be laid at its door. Russia was not quite as paranoid but nevertheless stressed from an early date that it was innocent.

I find it interesting—and perhaps significant—that very few countries seemed to accept that the assassination was the act of one deranged lone-nut. That feeling was strengthened when that "deranged lone-nut" was dispatched quickly and efficiently by a second "deranged lone-nut" called Jack Ruby less than 48 hours later.

THE OTHER FILE

Amongst other assassination-related files I examined during that first PRO visit were some dealing with attendance at the late President's funeral.

Much diplomacy was exercised regarding who would attend the funeral. One of the problems was the lack of time available to plan exactly who would represent each country. In the UK, it was decided almost at once that Prince Philip would represent The Queen. Prime Minister Alec Douglas-Hume and Opposition Leader Harold Wilson were obvious attendees but the name of Liberal Party leader Jo Grimond was only added to the official party as an afterthought. He perhaps took this as something of a snub and travelled to Washington on a normal commercial flight rather than with the official party.

There was some concern when the official list of those in the British party included "three young ladies" who were not named. It later transpired, however, that they were members of the Prime Minister's staff.

Several countries appeared confused as to whether they should send their head of state, their prime minister, their ambassador or whoever. In most cases, they contacted the US State Department for guidance.

A Policy File—FO 953/2109

A Policy File, usually referred to as a P-File, is one prepared by or connected with the British Government's Information Policy Department. In view of its subject matter, this one carries the familiar Foreign Office prefix FO.

This file was released in 1994—or rather, most of it was. There is a notice inside the file cover advising that certain parts of it remain closed. No reason is given. It appears that the British Broadcasting Corporation (BBC) was in unofficial contact with the Foreign Office around 27th November. The BBC was finding it difficult to deal with certain Russian propaganda concerning the assassination. The story had been circulated by the Soviets that the assassination had a right-wing origin and that the murder of Oswald was part of a cover-up, also by the right-wing. The BBC requested that if the Foreign Office gained any information disproving such allegations, or even something to suggest that there could be some truth in some in them, they hoped that they (the BBC) would be given the earliest possible guidance.

It remains to be seen what is contained in the closed section of this file. Normally the reason a file (or part of a file) remains closed after the usual 30 years period is because it is deemed to contain material sensitive to the security of the nation. Did the BBC perhaps know something about the assassination which the Government was anxious to cover up?

The Kennedy files held at the Public Record Office

The seven files I consulted during my first visit to the PRO were as follows:
• FO 371/168406-8 - International reaction to the death of President Kennedy, 1963

• FO 371/168487-9 - Death of President Kennedy

• FO 372/7792-3 - Death of President Kennedy; Memorial Service; Funeral arrangements for Sir Winston Churchill, 1963

• FO 372/7794 - Death of President Kennedy; Official Mourning

• FO 953/2109 - British Government's approach to Europe; Guidance for the BBC over Soviet Propaganda on President Kennedy's Assassination (Part of file remains closed for indeterminate period)

• PREM 11/4408 - Death of President Kennedy, Nov 1963; arrangements for attendance of Prime Minister at funeral

• PREM 11/4582 - Assassination of President Kennedy, 22 Nov 1963

A SECOND VISIT TO THE PRO

On 30th November 2001, having learnt that the eighth and final Kennedy Assassination file had been opened and released for public scrutiny, I returned to the Public Record Office. In the five years since my previous visit, the PRO had undergone an immense modernization programme. Although the records and information are still physically contained in cardboard boxes and file covers, the methods of search and retrieval now demand considerable computer knowledge and a virtually compulsory half-hour computer induction course for first-time visitors has been introduced.

FILE: FO 371/171941

I found that this Foreign Office file which had still been closed on my previous visit was now open in its entirety. No reason was available to explain why, like its fellow Kennedy files, it had not been opened and available for public scrutiny as usual after 30 years. I noted that parts of it had been marked CONFIDENTIAL. That, however, is a very low security classification and would surely not have been the cause of it remaining closed for a year longer than normal. [1]

This file was by far the largest of any I studied. It consisted of three separate sub-files, each individually numbered and titled. I will deal with each of them in turn here.

SUB-FILE: NS 103145/29

Marked CONFIDENTIAL, there are two separate parts to this file. The first bears the title Soviet Foreign Policy in the light of President Kennedy's Death and is a lengthy internal Foreign Office Report dated 27th November

1963. It is a very general and non-committal overview which comes to the conclusion that "President Johnson's assumption of office does not suggest that any sudden change in Soviet policy is planned" and that "the Soviet leaders will probably adopt a wait-and-see policy." It was stressed that the Soviets remained embarrassed at Oswald's alleged Communist and Cuban connections and that they continued to deny that he was ever a member of the American Communist Party or was connected with any pro-Cuban movement.

Mentioning Kennedy's strong handling of the Berlin situation within six months of taking office, however, it is stated that "we cannot exclude the possibility that Khrushchev will again be tempted to see whether the new President has the strength and determination to withstand a crisis."

Of historical as well as political interest, it is mentioned that Soviet television made use of Telstar (the world's first low-altitude active communications satellite) to transmit pictures directly from Washington. (I am tempted to ask if the shooting of Oswald was also shown live in Moscow, and if so, what reaction it caused.)

The second part of this sub-file is a report prepared by the Foreign Office Research Department. It is entitled Likely Effects of President Kennedy's Assassination on Soviet Foreign Policy. It pre-dates the previous document by one day and deals with virtually the same matters. It appears to be the basis upon which the main report is based.

It does contain more comment on the Soviets' embarrassment at Oswald's alleged links:

> "The first announcements attributed the deed to 'ultra right-wing organisations'. Thereafter, reports assumed a more defensive tone, denying that Oswald had ever been a member of the American Communist Party or connected with a pro-Cuban movement, and asserting instead that 'madmen' had prepared the crime. Pravda also insinuated that Oswald had Trotskyist connections and had unexplained meetings with the F.B.I."

Sub-file: NS 103145/30

Under the general title Soviet Coverage of the Assassination of President Kennedy, this lengthy file comprises five sections. The first four cover specific dates (22nd-24th, 25th, 26th and 27th-28th November 1963) whilst the fifth is an overall report specifically entitled Soviet Treatment of the Assassination of President Kennedy. This report is undated but as it is based upon the four dated files, it was probably compiled on 29th November 1963.

The file is concerned with the assassination's daily media coverage in the Soviet Union. It explains that the first news was of an attempt on Kennedy's life and was given on the Moscow Home Service (radio) at 19.28 GMT (1.28pm CST). [2] It then quotes the principal Soviet newspapers. *Pravda* stressed that Kennedy had insisted that Congress should ratify the Nuclear Test Ban Treaty despite sharp attacks from the American 'wild men'. On Sunday 24th November, *Nedelya*, the *Izvestiya* weekly supplement, published a large photograph of President Kennedy on its front page under the headline

"TRAGIC NEWS FROM TEXAS: VILLAINOUS ASSASSINATION OF PRESIDENT KENNEDY". [3]

Moscow Radio continued major coverage of the assassination as the news came in and a *Tass* dispatch from Washington blamed the Birchites and the Ku Klux Klan.

It appears that during the period between the 22nd and the 24th, the Soviet media was at great pains to indicate that the assassination was a *"carefully planned political plan"* and that "the police authorities ... were striving to implicate the 'left-wing forces' apparently in an effort to channel the anger and indignation of the American people away from the real culprits."

The daily report of Soviet media coverage on 25th November opens in sensational style. I feel compelled to quote the first sentence of the opening paragraph *verbatim*:

"The Soviet coverage of events related to the assassination of President Kennedy came to a climax on November 25 when television viewers saw a thirty-minute direct transmission from Washington on the funeral, a documentary film on the events leading up to the President's death, including the speech he made at Houston, and then the actual shooting, and also a film of the shooting of the suspect Oswald."

When I initially read this, I was both baffled and excited by the words *"the actual shooting"*. Since the shooting of Oswald was mentioned separately, this was obviously a reference to the assassination itself. I circulated a plea for more information *via* two internet forums and was delighted when Sixth Floor Museum Curator Gary Mack promptly responded with information that the Muchmore Film had been shown on a New York TV station, and probably others, on the 25th. He added that since the film was owned by UPI, it was likely to have been distributed to other news outlets and so it was very probable that the film shown on Soviet TV was Marie Muchmore's footage. [4]

Not surprisingly, the Soviet media, particularly the press, used Jack Ruby's successful attack upon Oswald to further distance their country from the assassination. A direct connection between the two men was mentioned on the

25th and it was claimed that they had been seen together at Ruby's club the day before the assassination. Once again, there were strenuous denials that Oswald had ever been a member of the Communist Party.

The newspapers *Pravda* and *Izvestiya* each intimated 'an inside job' and likened the assassination of President Kennedy to the Reichstag fire. On the 26th, *Izvestiya* spoke of "dark deeds in Dallas" and emphasised the suspicious behaviour of the Dallas police particularly in regard to Oswald's transfer.

On 27th and 28th November, Soviet communications media were devoting more space to the suspicious circumstances of Oswald's death than to the assassination itself. At the same time, however, President Johnson was being given a generally favourable press.

Pravda (28th) carried several reports from foreign sources to support claims that right-wing extremists were responsible for the murders of both Kennedy and Oswald. These included pieces under headlines such as "WHO ARMED THE MURDERER?" (from Rio de Janeiro), "REVEALING DETAILS" (Rome), "TOO MANY MISSING PIECES" (Paris) and "WERE THERE TOO MANY SNIPERS?" (Vienna). There was also a report from Paris that one of Ruby's former dancers had stated that she had been hired to kill Oswald and had been paid for it. I would be intrigued to learn just which dancer that was alleged to be!

As mentioned above, the fifth section of this file is in the form of a report in which the foregoing daily notes and extracts are briefly outlined and evaluated. Again it was stated that the Soviet media had continued to stress the Soviet Union's total innocence throughout this period. *Pravda* had printed the CPUSA statement that Oswald was "completely unknown to them" and went on to mention that "Trotskyist literature had been found in his room."

Sub-file: NS 103145/32

This sub-file contains just one document, this being the CONFIDENTIAL report sent direct to the British Foreign Office by the British Ambassador in Moscow. It is dated 6th December 1963. The title of the report is Soviet Reactions to the Assassination of President Kennedy and it opens with the following Summary:

"The news of President Kennedy's assassination provoked immediate expressions of genuine regret and sympathy on the part of the Soviet authorities and the Soviet people (paragraphs 1-3).
The Soviet Press, radio and television gave the event widespread coverage and soon adopted the line that the assassination was the work of right wing extremists (paragraphs 4-7).
The Soviet Government has good reason to regret President Kennedy's

death. We are unlikely to see any change in Soviet policy in the near future as a result of President Kennedy's disappearance from the scene (paragraph 8)."

This official report, carefully prepared two weeks after the assassination of President Kennedy, is couched in straightforward, non-sensational terms. As can be seen from the Summary, it indicates that the Soviet media in general had continued to maintain that "the assassination was the work of right wing extremists." Whether this was a genuinely held view or just intended to deflect possible blame from the Soviet Union is unclear. It was also repeated that Soviet policy was unlikely to change following President Kennedy's "disappearance from the scene." (What a classic euphemism those four words produce!).

Once again, it was pointed out that the Soviet press had continued to intimate that the Dallas Police "of whom they had nothing good to say ... were not merely inefficient but were implicated either in the assassination itself or in attempts to hush it up."

CONCLUSION

The overall impression I gained from my two visits to the PRO, particularly the first, was that in the days and weeks following the assassination, the world was in complete confusion. I can recall my own thoughts at the time. It quickly became a period of intense insecurity, uncertainty and fear. Looking back on it now, I personally feel that we could well have been closer to nuclear war in the two or three weeks after 22nd November 1963 than we had been even at the height of the Cuban Missile Crisis the year before.

Fortunately, the Soviet Union felt it more important to sit back and concentrate on vociferously maintaining its own innocence than to take any more positive action. One can only speculate on the outcome had the Soviets decided that this time of confusion could provide the ideal opportunity to launch a pre-emptive physical attack upon the United States and her allies. From the files quoted above, it seems they were far too busy implicating the Dallas Police Department and the right wing in the Kennedy and Oswald murders than in pressing the red nuclear button.

Notes

1. The five basic document security levels in use at this time were TOP SECRET, SECRET, CONFIDENTIAL, RESTRICTED and OPEN. Even something as boring and uninspiring as a minor UK Government Department internal telephone directory was allocated a CONFIDENTIAL *caveat*.

2. Ian Griggs: *Kennedy Assassinated! Oswald Murdered!* published jointly by the author and the JFK Resource Group, Dallas, Texas, 1994, page 31. This illustrates a BBC Monitoring Service newsflash timed at 1938 GMT (1.38pm CST), 22nd November 1963, which stated (verbatim):

> "MOSCOW RADIO, HOME SERVICE, BROADCAST THE FOLLOWING, BREAKING INTO ITS NEWS BULLETIN AT 19.28 GMT: +IT HAS JUST BEEN REPORTED FROM NEW YORK: ACCORDING TO AMERICAN PRESS AGENCIES. DURING THE STAY OF U.S. PRESIDENT IN DALLAS, AN ATTEMPT WAS MADE ON HIS LIFE. KENNEDY HAS BEEN SEVERELY WOUNDED BY A FIREARM.+"

3. "The Photographic Record: No. 5 - The Soviet Press", *The Dealey Plaza Echo*, vol. 3, no. 2 (July 1999), p. 35.

The Vegas Club, an early Ruby venture into the club world. (John R. Woods, II collection)

Jack Ruby with stripper Sherry Lynn. She was the wife of Joe Garcia, the Carousel Club band drummer.

Infamous Entertainers
Top: Stripper Jada
Center: Stripper Little Lynn
Bottom: Stripper Tammi True

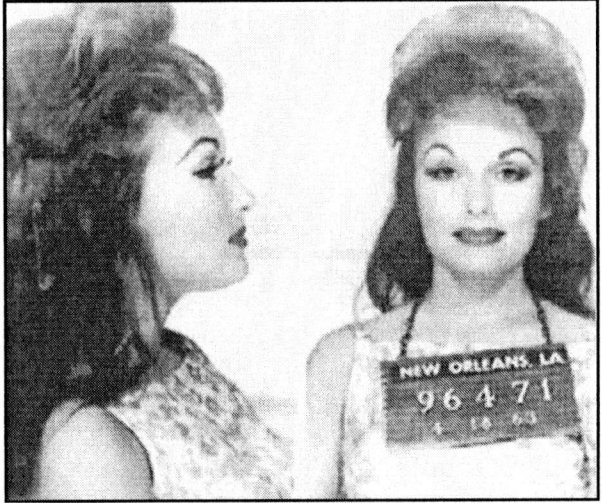

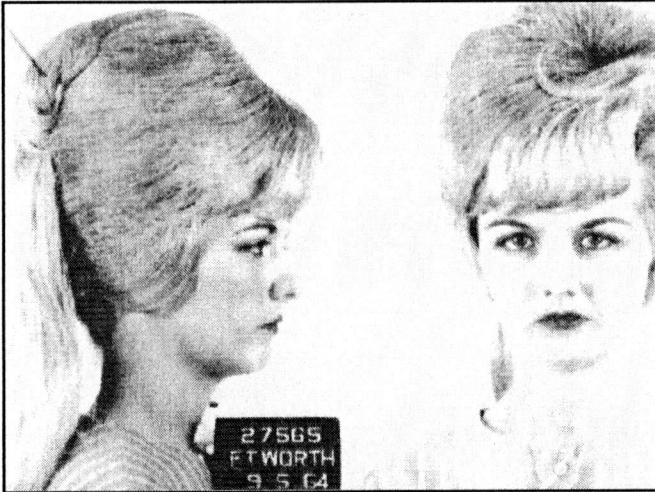

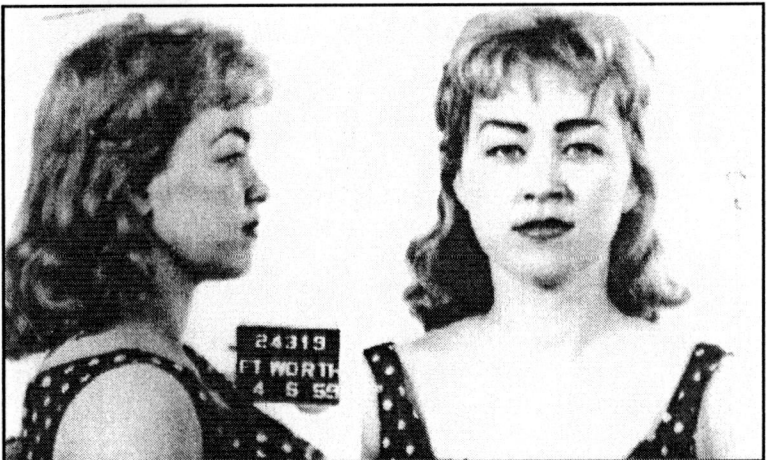

The Carousel Club advertisement in the "Dallas Times Herald" of Friday, 22nd November 1963. Following the assassination, Ruby closed the club and the show never took place.

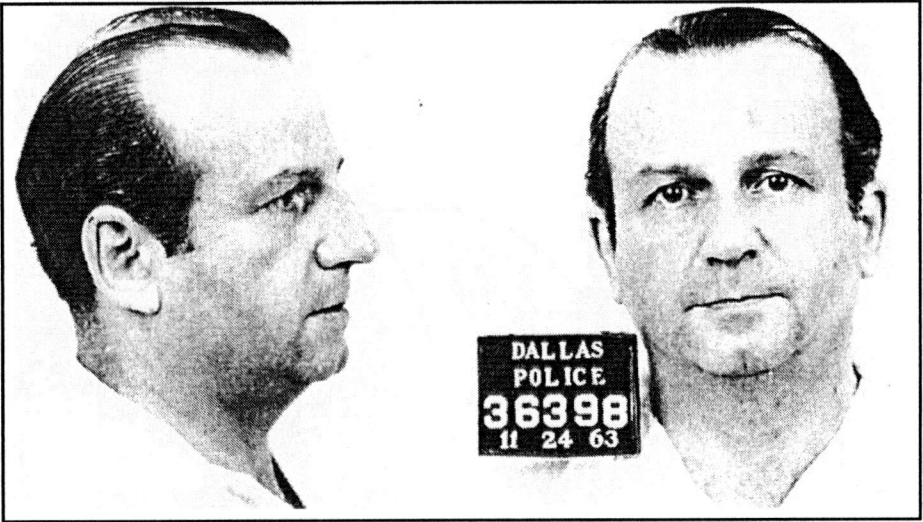

Jack Ruby's mugshot after killing Oswald.

The "CLOSED" sign outside the Carousel Club on the evening of 22nd November (John R. Woods, II collection)

Top: The author with former stripper Shari Angel, June 1995

Bottom: Kathy Kay at work on the Carousel Club runway. (WC Armstrong Exhibit No. 5300-A)

Kathy Kay teaches teenage university student Jim Marrs how to do the twist. (Photo courtesy Rich DellaRosa Forum)

The European-style date on the back of the backyard photograph.

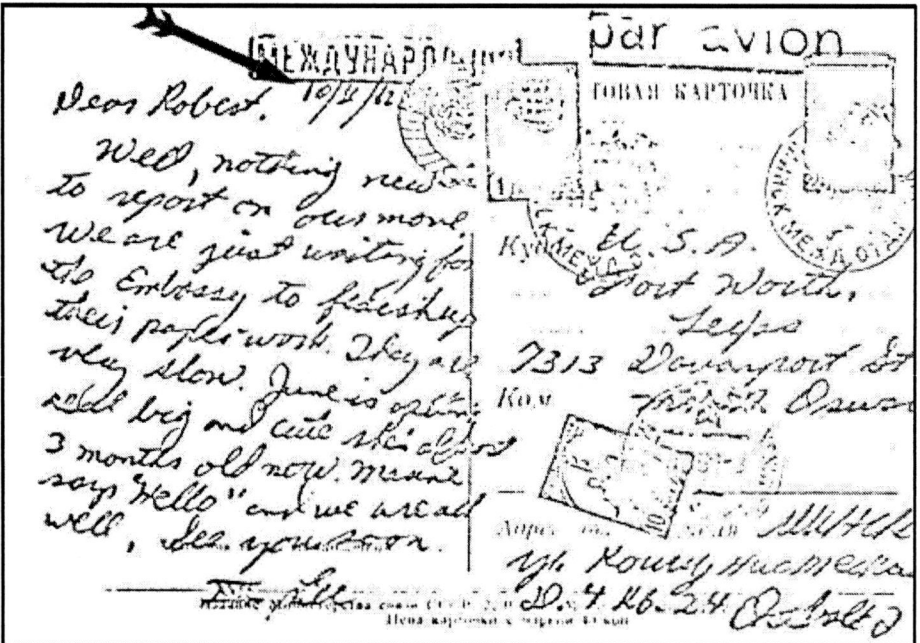

CE 321 Postcard from Lee Oswald to to Robert Oswald dated erroneously in the INDEX to Volume XVI as "April 4, 1962" -- now shown to have been written on 10th May 1962.

FD-302 (Rev. 3-3-39)   FEDERAL BUREAU OF INVESTIGATION

1   Date _____12/7/63_____

       Mr. LESLIE LAWSON, 7300 Second Avenue, Dallas, Texas, was interviewed at which time he advised that he is the owner and manager of the Grays Cleaners which is located at 1209 Eldorado, Dallas, and has owned this business for approximately 12 years.

       In regards to any information concerning LEE HARVEY OSWALD or JACK RUBY, Mr. LAWSON stated that he is not acquainted with nor has he ever seen RUBY other than in the local newspapers and television; however, he has seen LEE HARVEY OSWALD on one particular occasion that he can recall and possibly on other occasions which he could not specifically recall. Mr. LAWSON went on to say that approximately one month ago, exact date he could not recall, an individual who he identified as LEE HARVEY OSWALD entered his cleaning establishment and gave one of his employees a tie, white shirt and a black pair of pants for cleaning. Mr. LAWSON identified this employee who accepted the clothing as being Mrs. ROSALEE WILLIAMS. Approximately two days later LEE HARVEY OSWALD returned to LAWSON's place of business and requested his cleaning. Mr. LAWSON advised that he obtained OSWALD's items from the hanger and told OSWALD that the bill was $1.25. He noticed that OSWALD became somewhat disturbed over the fact that he was charged 25 cents for cleaning his tie and could recall that OSWALD was a little belligerent when he paid the bill. LAWSON advised that he could not recall the exact text of OSWALD's conversation on this particular occasion, but that he was under the impression that OSWALD was pretty much disturbed over the entire cleaning bill.

       Mr. LAWSON went on to say that he could recall seeing OSWALD on a few other occasions at the Sleight's Speed Wash which is located next to his establishment, but that to the best of his knowledge OSWALD never patronized his place of business after the first time.

       A photograph of LEE HARVEY OSWALD was shown to Mr. LAWSON at which time he identified this photo as being that of LEE HARVEY OSWALD.

       The photograph of JACK RUBY was exhibited to Mr. LAWSON at which time he advised that he has never personally

on __12/5/63__ at __Dallas, Texas__   File # DL 89-43
                                                   DL 44-1639
         ALTON E. BRAMBLETT and
by Special Agent a __LANSING P. LOGAN - gi__   Date dictated __12/7/63__

This document contains neither recommendations nor conclusions of the FBI. It is the property of the FBI and is loaned to your agency; it and its contents are not to be distributed outside your agency.

594

COMMISSION EXHIBIT No. 3000

CE 3000, which indicated that Oswald was no stranger to dry cleaning establishments.

J. D. Tippit portrait which appeared in the "Dallas Morning News"
less than 24 hours after his murder. (Carlin [Bruce Ray] Exhibit)

1.

2.

3.

4.

1. *Enlargement of the issued stamp showing the facsimile postmark with the date, time and place of the assassination.*

2. *One of the officially submitted, but rejected, designs.*

3. *Another rejected design.*

4. *Design submitted by San Francisco student Richard Burkley. It was remarkably similar to the eventual design chosen.*

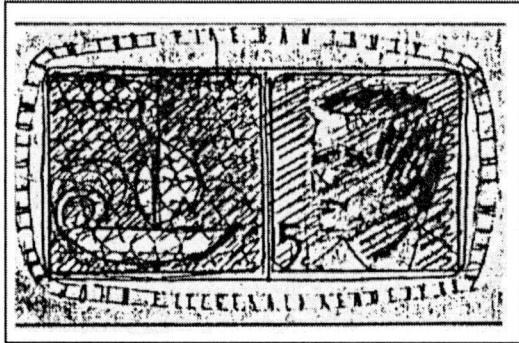

5.

6.

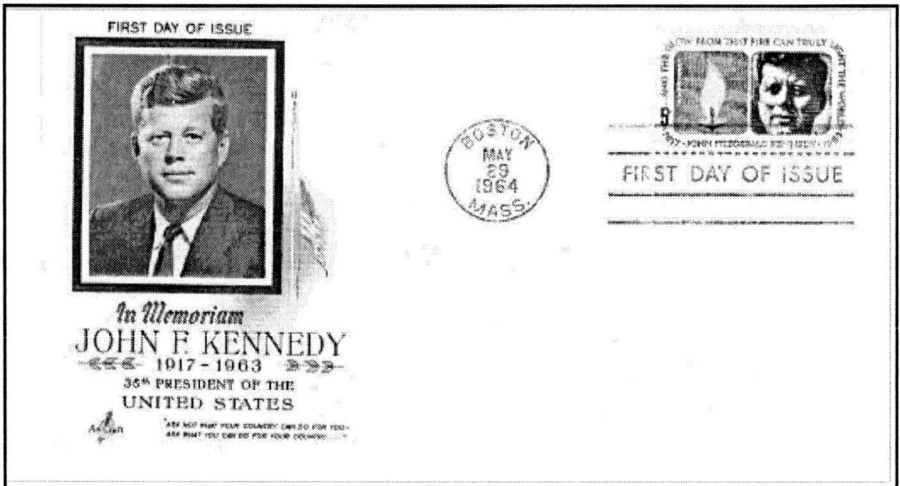

7.

5. *One of the rough sketches of what was to become the chosen design.*
6. *Stamp from lower right corner of the sheet, showing the printing plate no. (which was always in this position). Stamp is mounted on black card to show perforations. (Author's collection)*
7. *The BOSTON machine cancellation on first-day cover.*

The "Dallas Times Herald" of 22nd November 1963.

Johnson Takes Nation's Helm, Pages 4 and 5

The Dallas Morning News

John F. Kennedy Life History, Pages 16 and 17

VOL. 115—NO. 54 · DALLAS, TEXAS, SATURDAY, NOVEMBER 23, 1963—50 PAGES IN 4 SECTIONS · ★★★★ · PRICE 5 CENTS

KENNEDY SLAIN ON DALLAS STREET

★ ★ ★ ★ ★ ★ ★ ★ ★ ★ ★ ★ ★ ★

JOHNSON BECOMES PRESIDENT

Receives Oath on Aircraft

By ROBERT E. BASKIN
Washington Bureau of The News

In a solemn and powerful hour, with a nation mourning its dead President, Lyndon B. Johnson Friday took the oath of office as the 36th chief executive of the United States.

Lyndon B. Johnson

Gov. Connally Resting Well

By MIKE QUINN

Impact Shattering To World Capitals

By the Associated Press

Pro-Communist Charged With Act

A sniper shot and killed President John F. Kennedy on the streets of Dallas Friday. A 24-year-old pro-Communist who once tried to defect to Russia was charged with the murder shortly before midnight.

Four Hours in Surgery

Friendly Crowd Cheered Kennedy

John F. Kennedy

GRAY CLOUDS WENT AWAY

Day Began as Auspiciously As Any in Kennedy's Career

(Robert E. Baskin, chief of the Washington Bureau of The News, this one of four newsmen representing the wire services in the pool ...

FUNERAL FOR PRESIDENT WILL BE HELD ON MONDAY

WASHINGTON (AP)—President Kennedy's funeral will be held Monday at St. Matthews Roman Catholic Cathedral, the White House announced Friday night.

"The Dallas Morning News" of 23rd November 1963.

THE CHRISTCHURCH STAR

KENNEDY SHOT DEAD

Gunned Down During Drive Through Dallas

DALLAS (Texas), November 22.

RESIDENT KENNEDY was assassinated to-day. The President was hot as he drove through this Texas city in an open car. The overnor of Texas (Mr John Connally) was seriously wounded. he President died at 7 a.m. Saturday, New Zealand time. After he burst of gun-fire cut down the President, he was rushed to arkland Hospital, where blood transfusions were given.

ENLIGHTENED AND FIRM ACTION WAS HIS MARK

Arrested Man Lived in Russia

"The Christchurch Star" front page of 23rd November 1963.

ASSASSINATION, FROM PAGE 1

Battle by Doctors to Save President's Life

THE MAN THEY ARRESTED

WORLD MOURNS DEAD PRESIDENT

55-year-old Texan Sworn In as U.S. 35th President

MEMORIAL SERVICE ARRANGED

To Lie in State

FOURTH PRESIDENT TO DIE BY BULLET

Wife Tells of Events in Car

Another Blow for Kennedys

"The Christchurch Star" page 3, 23rd November 1963

11 a.m. Saturday. Rev. L. G. Haggard officiating. Interment Laurel Land.
CAMPBELL. 300 W. Davis

GUINN

Mrs. Myrtle. Passed away in Greenville. Survived by sister. Mrs. Pearl Clifton Fort Worth; number of nieces and nephews including Miss Hazel D. Morrow and Mrs. Madaline Rollwage, both of Dallas, Mrs. Louise Lummes. Ennis. Mrs Francis Parter. Eclar, Texas. Mis Kahma T. Long. Hempstead. Texas; a great niece. Mrs. Peggy Long, Houston a great nephew. Fred Lummes. Greenville. Chapel services 2 p.m. Saturday Rev. Norman Taylor officiating. Interment Greenview.
COKER-MATHEWS-PETERS
FUNERAL HOME
Greenville. Texas

HOOE

Park, Melrose Hotel. Survived by wife Mrs. Lois Hooe Dallas, sister. Miss Katherine Hooe, Louisville. Ky.; several nieces and nephews. Services Saturday. 2:30 p.m. East Chapel. Hillcrest Mausoleum. Dr. Fred R. Edgar officiating. Interment Hillcrest Mausoleum. Pallbearers: J. G. Balle, J. W. Crosland. Joe T. Lee. Bragdon Manning. Raymond M Myers. L. A. Armstrong.
SPARKMAN S ROSS AVENUE
2115 Ross Ave. R18-2137

JANOSKY

Mrs. Anna. 619 E. Colorado. Survived by daughter. Mrs. W. J. Leonard; sisters. Mrs. B. F. Goebel. Mrs. R. C. Morris Jr. all of Dallas: Mrs. Frank Pastorek: brother. John J. Kauba. both of Ennis; Frank Kauba of Arkansas; one grandson. Requiem Mass. 9 a.m Saturday. Blessed Sacrament Catholic Church. Rt. Rev. Msgr. Paul Charcut, celebrant Interment Calvary Hill.
LAMAR & SMITH W16-2146

KENNEDY

President John F. Beloved husband of Jacqueline Kennedy; dear father of John and Caroline Kennedy; parents. Mr. and Mrs Joseph Kennedy; brothers Robert and Ted Kennedy; sisters, Mrs. Peter Lawford. Mrs. Robert Shriber. Remains forwarded to Washington, D.C. Friday.
ONEAL INC
3206 Oak Lawn LA6-5271

LACKEY

Harry Tucker 926 Dale St. Arrangements pending.

DUDLEY M. HUGHES FUNERAL HOME
400 E. Jefferson WH6-5133

TIPPIT

J. D., 238 Glencairn. Survived by wife. Mrs. Marie Tippit: sons, Allen and Curtis Tippit: daughter, Miss Brenda Tippit: parents. Edgar Tippit and Mrs. Mae Peterson: brothers, Donald Ray, Wayne, Edward, Ronnie Tippit: sisters, Mrs. Christine Christopher. Mrs. Joyce Debord. Arrangements pending.
DUDLEY M. HUGHES FUNERAL HOME
400 E. Jefferson WH6-5133

WATSON

James Fillmore. 3435 Sharon Survived by wife. Mrs. Cora Watson: brothers. Dewey Terry, Louie and Harold Watson: four sisters. Chapel services Saturday. 11:30 a.m., Rev. Floyd Baker and Rev Elwynn Wray officiating. Interment Oakland Cemetery. Terrell, Texas.
DUDLEY M. HUGHES FUNERAL HOME
400 E. Jefferson WH6-5133

WHITE

Conner C. (Cap) Sr., 14061 Janwood Lane Farmers Branch. Survived by daughters. Mrs. Dorothy Sangster. Mrs. Louise Mason. Mrs. Ruby Kessner: sons, Clarence. William, Johnny, Edwin. Edward, Tuey. Conner White Jr : ninetten grandchildren: great-grandchild. Arrangements pending.
DUDLEY M. HUGHES FUNERAL HOME
400 E. Jefferson WH6-5133

WHITTLE

Travis Alton. Survived by wife. Katherine Rose: daughters. Jerry Ann. Susan Kay: son. Travis Lynn: brothers. Edgar Whittle. Hobbs. N.M.: Buck Whittle. Mesquite: sisters. Hazel Shankles. Ida Belle. Okla.: Mozel Shute. Longview: Mira McClough. Las Vegas. Nev. Chapel services 3:30 p.m. Saturday. Rev. Preston Stuart officiating. Interment Laurel Oak Cemetery.
ANDERSON-CLAYTON BROS
Mesquite AT5-5489

WINKLE

Mrs. Linda. 1208 Cockrell Hill Road. Survived by husband. Jesse Winkle; son Wallace R. Winkle: daughter. Mrs Richard Young; sister. Mrs. Sue Jordon: three grandchildren. Rhonda Jean, Linda Rae and Richard Young Jr. Chapel services Saturday 2 p.m. Rev. Jeff Pritchard officiating. Interment Mesquite Cemetery.
DUDLEY M. HUGHES FUNERAL HOME
400 E. Jefferson WH6-5133

From the Deaths and Funerals column of "The Dallas Morning New"s of 23rd November 1963.

EPILOGUE:

27. Kennedy and Caesar

A brief examination of the similarities between the two most important and significant assassinations in history

INTRODUCTION

The assassination of John Fitzgerald Kennedy, 35th President of the United States of America, on Friday 22nd November 1963 was the most significant political crime since the assassination of Julius Caesar. Caesar, correct name Gaius Julius Caesar, was slain in Rome some 2,007 years earlier. An examination of the parallels between these two world leaders reveals that they shared many common characteristics—similar to those *contrived* links between Kennedy and Abraham Lincoln.

It is not my intention here to magnify such frivolities as the fact that the names Julius Caesar and John F. Kennedy each contains 12 letters. I think that the similarities shared by these two men—in life and in death—surpass such superficialities.

THEIR LIVES ...

(1) Caesar and Kennedy are acknowledged as the most powerful leaders of the known world at the time of their deaths. Each was the leader of the strongest and most influential nation on earth. Furthermore, each had distinguished himself in the world of literature as well as in the fields of diplomacy, political leadership and war.

(2) As undisputed leader, (one may even say dictator), of the Roman Empire, Caesar had destroyed the power of the corrupt Roman nobility. It is not difficult to find parallels in Kennedy's actions and attitude towards increasingly influential groups such as the Mafia and the CIA.

(3) Both men were social reformers of considerable stature. Caesar had introduced the Julian calendar and planned further major reforms. Kennedy had shown great support for the civil rights movement, sought to increase his country's sphere of influence through the space programme, and was engaged in a major change in his country's fiscal system.

... AND THEIR DEATHS

(4) It is likely, though by no means certain, that each man's increasing sovereign power led to his assassination.

(5) Both John Kennedy and Julius Caesar were, in my humble opinion, killed (directly or indirectly) by elements from within their own administration.

(6) Caesar was forewarned of his impending doom. Recall the warning "Beware the Ides of March" (Act I, Scene 2, *Julius Caesar* by William Shakespeare). Kennedy's death was also anticipated by such diverse characters as Rose Cheramie and Joseph Milteer.

(7) In Act II, Scene 2 of *Julius Caesar*, Caesar remarks to his wife Calpurnia: "Death, a necessary end, will come when it will come". I cannot be alone in likening this to John Kennedy's observation to Jackie, on the morning of this death, that it would be a simple task for someone to assassinate him. He even went as far as to say that all it needed was a tall building and a high-powered rifle. Both men were perhaps resigned to an untimely end.

CONCLUSION

I find some obviously marked similarities between the two men, their lives and their deaths. There is, however, one important and ironic contrast. Caesar's death was subject of the famous and stirring "Friends, Romans, countrymen" speech by Mark Antony, but all Kennedy got was the Warren Commission's dishonest and inadequate report!

I do not claim to be the first researcher to notice similarities between the Kennedy and Caesar assassinations. Go to the final sentence of Jim Marrs' all-encompassing book *Crossfire - The Plot that killed Kennedy*. It consists of just three little words: "Et tu, Lyndon?"

Written 1997.
First published October 1997 in *JFK/Deep Politics Quarterly*, vol. 3, no. 1.
Also published March 1998 in *The Dealey Plaza Echo*, vol. 2, no. 1.

Name Index

Subject Index

Printed in the United Kingdom
by Lightning Source UK Ltd.
120595UK00001B/324